The Information Environment: A Reader

The Information Environment: A Reader

SELECTED AND INTRODUCED BY

GERALDENE WALKER

G.K. HALL & CO.
NEW YORK

Maxwell Macmillan Canada
TORONTO

Maxwell Macmillan International
NEW YORK   OXFORD   SINGAPORE   SYDNEY

Copyright © 1992 by G.K. Hall & Co.
An Imprint of Macmillan Publishing Company

G.K. Hall & Co.   Maxwell Macmillan Canada, Inc.
Macmillan Publishing Company   1200 Eglinton Avenue East
866 Third Avenue   Suite 200
New York, NY 10022   Don Mills, Ontario M3C 3N1

Macmillan Publishing Company is part of the Maxwell Communication Group
or Companies.

LIBRARY OF CONGRESS CATALOG CARD NUMBER: 91-39347

Printed in the United States of America

printing number
1 2 3 4 5 6 7 8 9 10

LIBRARY OF CONGRESS CATALOGING-IN-PUBLICATION DATA

The information environment : a reader / selected and introduced by
  Geraldene Walker.
      p.   cm. — (Professional librarian series)
    Includes bibliographical references and index.
    ISBN 0–8161–1946–5 (hard : alk. paper). — ISBN 0–8161–1947–3
  (pbk. : alk. paper)
    1. Information science.   2. Information technology.   I. Walker,
  Geraldene.   II. Series.
  Z665.I579   1992
  020—dc20   91–39347
                                                              CIP

The paper used in this publication meets the minimum requirements of American
National Standard for Information Sciences—Permanence of Paper for Printed Library
Materials. ANSI Z39.48-1984.   ∞™

FOR CAREY
daughter and friend
who shares my enthusiasm
for
the challenges of the
Information Age

Contents

Introduction

The goal of this book is to define a framework of concepts and outline a set of issues within which to discuss the changes in forms of social organization and contemporary lifestyles resulting from developments in information processing technologies during the last thirty years. Many writers have discussed aspects of the information society as it affects their own field—social, technological, political, or legal. This selection from their work provides a broad overview of the information environment and is intended as an interdisciplinary introduction to this topic. That is, it introduces the idea of information, not only as an agent for social change, but also as a resource that is basic to every area of professional and service employment in modern society. The success of all human organizations depends on this intangible resource known as "information." Different societies have different information needs, but in general, the more complex a society, the more dependent it is on the availability and accuracy of information in order to function effectively.

Various trends in contemporary society have led a number of writers to suggest that an information "revolution" has been taking place over the last thirty years. The exponential growth in scientific research and technical innovation, the use of computers for information handling, and the resultant explosion in publishing have all emphasized the importance of information as an economic and strategic resource. This revolution has changed almost every aspect of our lives—production processes and communications equipment, transportation and work patterns, the nature and content of education, the character of both work and leisure, and the ways in which social values are formed and political decisions are made. Information has become a significant economic commodity and the information industry has become the largest segment of the national economy in most developed countries. Every individual, both at work and as a private citizen, now needs more information in order to function effectively, and society in general needs a more highly educated workforce.

The fact that different writers have chosen a variety of names to describe this new way of life—global village, postindustrial, electronic, technological or information societies—and have expressed different views of its likely effects, has produced a number of misconceptions. These include the equation of information with knowledge, the belief that more is necessarily better, the assumption that computers are infallible, and the expectation that greater access to information will inevitably lead to a more equitable distribution of wealth and opportunity within society. The tendency to regard technology as a panacea for a variety of social problems and to endow it with mythical egalitarian powers is particularly attractive to contemporary American culture. The rhetoric of the technological dream needs to be rationalized by practical realities for, like Pandora's box, it can provide either the answer to our problems or a threat to our democratic way of life. It is a major paradox that the growth of leisure and affluence and the increasing availability of information in our society have not improved the overall quality of life for all our citizens.

Despite the differences in terminology used to describe these changes and a variety of opinions regarding their likely effects, it is clear that we have entered a period of accelerated and significant change based largely on the new technologies. American society is continuing its transformation from an industrial to an information-based economy, in which immediate access to accurate information is the key resource in areas as diverse as medicine, law, education, and government.

The overwhelming expansion of information in recent years has necessitated the use of computers in order to facilitate the organization and transmission of increased amounts of data. Information in all its manifestations—verbal, printed, or machine-readable—is the lifeblood of modern society. It has become a negotiable commodity, a basis of power, and the cornerstone of every nation's intellectual and competitive viability. The ultimate impact of the information revolution and the changes it will produce are difficult to predict, but its impact to date has changed the entire social system by

1. speeding the transfer of information

2. enhancing the ability to process and organize greater amounts of information, and
3. facilitating the retrieval of a specific item of information.

As long ago as 1976 Futures researcher John McHale suggested that changes would be world-wide in scope, affecting every aspect of our social, economic, and political lives. Other writers since then have predicted that the longterm effects would be even more far-reaching than those resulting from the invention of the printing press that facilitated the transfer of information through the printed word, or the Industrial Revolution that harnessed machinery to expand human strength. Although, traditionally, all workers have needed some kind of knowledge in order to perform their work, in the information age the creation, processing, and distribution of information *is* the complete job for many workers.

As publication rates and the information needs of an increasingly educated user population have grown, the proportion of professional and clerical workers in the American workforce has increased, as has the range of organizations involved in the task of collecting, organizing, and disseminating information. It is unfortunate that many libraries in their role as the traditional providers of information have been slow in recognizing the necessity of refocusing their services. Commercial providers of information, particularly in electronic form, have emerged to fill this gap created by the growth in information requirements and the limitations of the established information providers. Technology has become the agent of these new information agencies in their race to produce the simplest, most current, and best value-for-money information products and to provide ready access for the expanded enduser market. Speed and presentation have become the essence of information provision and libraries are having to learn to compete in this new entrepreneurial environment. Nevertheless, despite the increase in new information formats (CD-ROM, videotext, and the like), it seems that early forecasts that predicted the demise of the book and the rise of a paperless society were premature.

Against the background of a society that is generating and transmitting information on an unprecedented scale and at electronic speeds, Chapter 1 attempts to clarify what exactly we mean by "information" and why the conception has become so important. Confusion arises because the term has developed different meanings in different situations for different writers. How information is generated, used, and how it is communicated between sources and recipients are topics of interest to information scientists. The practice of information science is a highly interdisciplinary field that draws on theories from a wide range of other fields including linguistics, computer science, communications, and cognitive science. It has evolved in order to study the laws and principles that govern information systems and their operation.

In order to gain an overall perspective on these societal changes, it is necessary to integrate the idea of information as a phenomenon with the technologies that are used for its most efficient processing, and with the endproduct of such processing—information access and use. Chapter 2 discusses the rise of the information society and looks at how information has affected almost every organizational and behavioral aspect of our lives. Chapter 3 examines how the widespread availability of computing power—especially through the use of personal computers—and the increasing reliance on data networks for the transfer of information has streamlined business operations and enhanced and personalized methods of scholarly research.

Chapter 4 presents a view of the organizations and the individuals involved in the provision of information products and services—many in new and more efficient formats. Chapter 5 discusses the variety of information needs among different user groups and the cognitive aspects of information-seeking behavior. Chapter 6 addresses the often conflicting claims of different individuals and of the individual versus society at large. Information can be viewed as a means either to enhance the democratic integration of society or to foster the development of new cliques of power and privilege.

Chapter 7 expands similar ideas into the international arena. It offers an explanation of how national interests may vary depending on the stage of technological development within an individual country. Finally, Chapter 8 takes a broad-based look at the ramifications of regarding information as a commodity. That is, how such a view affects the rights and the responsibilities of those who provide information.

Any selection from a wide-ranging and often fragmented field such as information science must, through necessity, be subjective. The variety of topics that might legitimately be included is so vast that any choice is open to criticism on one ground or another. The author has attempted to select areas of major interest that are capable of providing a variety of different interpretations conducive to discussion. The emphasis is on an attempt to identify principles through the provision of alternative viewpoints. Overall the readings are intended to provide an introduction to the interdisciplinary field of information science in its human (rather than theoretical) dimensions and also to suggest a framework for wider investigation of the field based on the list of additional readings concluding each chapter.

The intended audience for this collection includes the undergraduate student in a range of social science disciplines, the inquiring lay person, and in particular, the beginning student of library and information science. In fact, the idea for the book arose from the author's lack of a basic text for an introductory course on the information environment for graduate students at the School of Information Science and Policy at the State University of New York at Albany. As courses in this area have broadened to encompass information as a major ingredient for almost all social interactions, they have had to rely on the collection of appropriate readings from widely scattered sources. This volume is intended to bring together a selection of this material, and to fill the gap between the now dated library-oriented texts and the newer information science texts that tend to concentrate on the theoretical aspects of the field. There are no simple correct answers where information is concerned. This volume is intended to provoke thought and provide a basis for wide-ranging discussion.

1

Information and the Nature of Information Science

Information is everywhere, forming the basis for all human interaction. It is the foundation of all works of scholarship, a necessity for the practice of all professions, and its organization and processing are the essence of their work for a range of new information professionals. Yet, despite its pervasive presence and essential role in an information society, our understanding of its basic nature and processes tends to be imprecise, inconsistent, and frequently ambiguous.

The term "information" has been used in such a variety of contexts that one suspects that it is almost impossible to formulate any definition encompassing all of its aspects. The term has been used in different situations to describe a commodity of commerce, an indicator of wealth and power, a basis for decision making, and a source of entertainment. Even dictionaries do not provide one standard definition. The entry in Webster's, for example, includes three options.

1. the communication or reception of knowledge or intelligence
2. knowledge obtained from investigation, study, or instruction
3. knowledge of a particular event or situation

Webster's lists "news," "fact," and "data" as synonymous terms and implies that "knowledge" and "information" are interchangeable. A similar lack of focus exists among professionals working in the information field—with quantity, accuracy, meaning, utility, value, timeliness, precision, organization, and impact being some of the desirable characteristics of information that are listed in the literature. Although such a recitation of essential characteristics is an appropriate first step in any attempt at identification, Alvin Schrader has quite rightly pointed out that such a definition requires that "ambiguity, imprecision, overlap, circularity, and contradiction must be ruled out."[1]

However, grouping the ideas behind these definitions together provides a starting point for the clarification of the term and the identification of some of its essential features.

• something that is communicated (transmission)
• something previously unknown (novelty)
• something that changes what one already knows (effectiveness)
• something needed by the receiver (usefulness)
• an interpretation and synthesis of factual data (transformation)

This last criterion implies some kind of assimilation or integration beyond the mere communication of information and suggests a basis for differentiation between "information" and "knowledge." The well-known economist Peter Drucker makes an interesting distinction suggesting a sequence of increasing complexity and value when he defines information as "organized data refined into knowledge and combined into wisdom."[2]

Information is also frequently considered to be synonymous with communication, though, more accurately speaking, one becomes "informed" through the transfer of information from a source to a receiver (user). Frequently the transfer of information occurs through the means of a document. The formal version of this process is what is known as an "information retrieval system," and frequently involves the intervention of a third party such as a librarian. In practice such a system involves not only a series of processes—writing, publication, distribution, analysis, storage, retrieval, and use—but also a whole range of individuals from author to reader. It is clear that when such an extended chain of information transfer is involved, the opportunities for pollution by "noise" are numerous and a large percentage of information in any system is likely to be garbled, misinterpreted, or even downright wrong.

Perhaps the most attractive approach to a definition of "information" for the general reader is that provided by the famous university scholar and political scientist Harland Cleveland, who suggests it should be regarded as a crucial new resource that necessitates a whole new way of looking at the organization of society. Cleveland's list of the characteristics that make information so important and different from other, more traditional resources includes the following: it is expandable, not resource-hungry, substitutable, transportable, diffusive, and shareable. Such terms highlight the increasing importance of information at all levels within society and also help to explain its recent emergence as a distinct subject of academic study.

The foundations of information science as a discipline lie in library science and documentation but its independent emergence was prompted by accelerating publication rates and the increased funding available for research in the United States during the 1960s. The search for a theoretical framework has been hampered by the lack of a consensus on the nature of information itself, coupled with the different approaches that have been taken by the fields of information theory, librarianship, linguistics and semantics, management, communication, and computer science. Theories of information transfer and pragmatic "laws" for the management of information have been based on interdisciplinary principles and a degree of agreement is gradually emerging. Although definitions are still (understandably) imprecise, it is agreed that the focus should now be on the way in which people create, use, and communicate information. Those who call themselves "information scientists" have tended to concentrate on the processes and systems of information storage and retrieval, devoting less attention to the communication and use of information or to its value as an economic commodity. This range of interests and participants makes it difficult to call information science a "discipline" in the accepted sense, though its multidisciplinary base provides a great range of models and research tools and its development has been fueled by the growing interest in information products and services.

Although a definition broad enough to be agreed upon by all involved in the academic study of information science might be an impossibility, the following areas are suggested as a personal selection:

- the patterns of messages transmitted and the channels of their transmission
- the problems involved in the analysis, storage, and retrieval of information
- the behavior of people as generators, transmitters, and receivers of information
- the social environment within which information transfer occurs.

The readings in this chapter attempt to provide a flavor of the range of different areas of interest to the information scientist and to give an indication of the variety of current approaches to their study. It should be clear that information science as an academic discipline is still in its infancy, concerned largely with the development of basic theories and research methodologies. Future growth will be influenced, not only by the expected increase in demands for information worldwide, but also by a wider recognition of its intellectual and economic value and the social and political implications of access to information.

Notes

1. Schrader, Alvin M. "In Search of a Name: Information Science and its Conceptual Antecedents." *Library & Information Science Research* 6(3) (July-September 1984):203.
2. Cleveland, Harland. "Education for Citizenship in the Information Society." *EDUCOM Bulletin* 2(3) (Fall 1985):12.

The Nature of Information

JASON FARRADANE

Definitions and Concepts of Information

In a paper[1] presented to the Annual Conference of the Institute of Information Scientists in June, 1976, I suggested that "information" should be defined as any physical form of representation, or surrogate, of knowledge, or of a particular thought, used for communication. As Belkin[2] correctly notes, I advanced this definition because such "information" is the only external element available as a physical object in the communication chain, but that, as I had also remarked, it does not, by itself, relate to the originator or to the effect of such information on the recipient. In my previous paper, specifically prepared for reading to a conference, I also did not explore the problems of the content or meaning of such information, and it is now proposed to consider these wider implications. In doing so, the limiting conditions for a useful concept noted by Belkin will be borne in mind.

A statement by an originator, or a request made to an information re-

Reprinted from *Journal of Information Science* 1(1) (April 1979): 13–17.

trieval system, is thus, by definition, "information." The "translated" (indexed) versions of the information, and the output from a system, are also physical objects of the same *type*, but must be considered separately. The indexed material results from a secondary communication chain to and from an indexer, whose reactions are specialized and different from those of an ultimate recipient. The indexer's "output" is a stylized form of "information" whose relationship to the original document needs more study than it usually receives. Although the output from a retrieval system may be only a reprinting of original "information," it has acquired a special status of having been *selected* by the system, and also still has to be communicated to (read by, and understood by) a recipient.

All other stages of communication are mental in nature and cannot be directly examined. Only the ultimate effects of communication, the actions of recipients, will be identifiable as directly observable processes. None of these other stages can clearly be identified or defined as "information." Nevertheless, many other attempted definitions of information[3] have been based on some assumed mental state of a recipient, to which properties have been ascribed such as "novelty," "an increment of knowledge," "usefulness," "interpretation of external stimuli," "a fundamental property of matter and consciousness," "increasing the state of knowledge of a recipient," "resolving uncertainty," "value in decision making," "a structure or organization," "transforming the structure of the recipient's image," or "the generator's perceptual structure underlying the text." Such definitions seem to be only expressions of ignorance of the nature of thought.

Alternatively, information is considered by many writers as some holistic "system" concept involving people, their attitudes and needs, and the effects of information transfer on decision making, social behaviour, etc., or on even a wider environment. Such concepts make it almost impossible to study any isolated part of the system, and lead to philosophic speculations which provide no reliable explanations, especially since there are many different points of view.

If information science is to be at all an experimental science, one must have some observable elements or phenomena which can be isolated for initial study, and proceed from these to the more complex and difficult phenomena related to them. My *definition* of information as the written or spoken surrogate of knowledge is more explicit than treating information as a concept; one can deal with the permanent written record as an invariant starting point, and can hope to derive, as far as possible experimentally, evidence of its conversion from thought in the originator, or to thought and its consequences in the percipient and others. Some of these consequences may hopefully be found to be physical objects or reproducible behavioural patterns which can be isolated for study. All aspects must at first be considered at a very elementary level. The following discussion is not intended as a predictive model; it can be only a description of the phenomena concerned.

Content and Meaning

Since information, as defined, is sterile until it is related to people who produce it or are affected by it, we must immediately consider how the mental phenomena in people are connected with information. The content of information, as defined, comprises individual words, each of which has its own meaning (or possibly several meanings), but these are not necessarily any guide to the meaning of the whole, which also depends upon the interconnected structure of the words, i.e., the grammar; but the grammar is only rules for dealing with the words: it is not the meaning of the information. Many writers concentrate on meaning as perceived by the recipient of information. As is well known, however, the meaning of a communication can be perceived differently by different recipients, according to their initial states of knowledge and ability to understand the communication, and even by the same recipient at different times, since his state of knowledge will change with time and experience. We cannot therefore look for any fixed meaning in the orbit of the recipient. The *only valid meaning* must be sought in the *originator's thought;* it is certainly not independent of the originator. Even so, the originator's processes of converting his thought into information may have distorted the meaning unintentionally, for example by inadequate command of language. Thought does not necessarily exist, in the first place, in linguistic terms, and the conversion to language involves finding suitable words and then connecting them grammatically, and then speaking or writing them accurately. It is well known that people making impromptu remarks at a meeting are often surprised at what they hear on a taped recording, which is not what they thought they said, or even meant to say. In some cases there may be deliberate distortion of an initial thought in order to present limited, generalized, or even misleading information (possibly, in social contexts, with the best of motives). One might consider such changes as second-stage thoughts, but they are also possibly the result of interaction of thought with unconscious controls just before utterance. In all cases, however, the information is a purposeful communication by the originator.

There is no direct method of finding out what the original thought was. Mental states cannot be observed directly. One cannot go back from the information to the thought in the originator, and the thought produced in the mind of the reader or investigator is that of a recipient. Investigation of the originator by asking questions which will elicit further versions of the thought, or explanations, cannot be reliable even if confined to "yes" or "no" answers. The originator's knowledge structure will change in reaction to questioning. People are not accustomed to analysing their own stages of thinking, and do not respond well to questioning on the subject. Moreover, the investigator is himself being a recipient of information (original or in replies) and must interpret it according to *his* state of knowledge, which is different from that of the originator. The method of investigation thus inevitably disturbs and possibly distorts the phenomena investigated. However, the investigator's interpretation of the meaning of a piece of information is probably the most reliable that is available (especially if the originator can not be examined), since he is aiming at objectivity.

Information and the Recipient

It is also necessary to take into account the probable ordering of ideas in the mind. It is generally accepted that the thoughts of which one is aware exist in an active conscious level of the mind, but that there is also an unconscious level at which much experience is stored, and at which individual characteristics are dominant. Furthermore, there is a short-term memory for casual observations, from which only some experience is transferred to a long-term memory which seems to be distributed over the whole brain. Incidentally, there is evidence that long-term memory is redistributed and reorganized ("classified?") during sleep. There must exist a sort of quick-reference language store by which observations can be very rapidly interpreted. Language is not essential for the acquirement of meaning, but it is a very important aid to understanding. After the first assessment, or signal interpretation, there can be a check of what has been interpreted against long-term memory, which will chiefly determine the response made to information. "Meaning" still remains elusive, and is probably a secondary phenomenon, the result of the reaction of the interpreted information with associated experience. Other factors are the relation between the recipient and the originator, such as whether the recipient trusts the originator or has a bias or prejudice against him. Meaning is still very much an unsolved concept in psychology.

Let us first consider the situation of a recipient receiving *unrequested* information, which may be random information on any topic, or possibly information within a field which is currently being experienced. There are at least four consequences of receiving such information. It must first be noted that such information does not have to be *new* to the recipient; it is still information, as defined. It is only the reaction of the percipient that will differ according to the novelty to *him*. If the information has previously been received and is remembered, the percipient may (1) reject it at the interpretative stage; on the other hand, it may be found acceptable as useful reinforcement of previous experience. As noted above, it may also be rejected because of associations with bias against the originator. It may be accepted, but not passed on to long-term memory because it is treated as transitory, trivial, or not related to the general interests of the recipient. All such negative responses need to be studied as much as positive responses in considering the phenomena related to information.

If the information has not already been received and stored in memory, it may be considered as being dealt with in three ways, in addition to the first case of rejection. It may (2) be just added on to existing knowledge without changing it. It may be pictured as an isolated element of knowledge, or as just *added* on to some point in a chain of interconnected concepts forming a field of knowledge. It may (3) complete a gap in the percipient's existing knowledge structure; this is the idea of 'resolving uncertainty', although not requested. The information may be pictured as connecting two previously isolated elements of knowledge, or as forming a bridge between two points of an existing structure. Finally, it may (4) transform an existing knowledge structure, such as when the information contradicts existing knowledge.

The purpose of such speculations is to suggest methods by which research might provide answers, such as studying responses to the communication of information. Thus simple rejection responses might be "I know," or even "I don't want to know that." The response to (2) might be just "yes," or "I see." The answer to (3) might be "that explains things," and the answer to (4) might be "that alters the position." Such investigations, simple at first, will need much refinement. Personally, I am hopeful that relational indexing may find application by picturing knowledge structures to which information is being presented; a definite "knowledge structure" could first be "learned" by the recipient, so that the effect of an additional item of information could be compared with prediction.

Wider effects of the information may be seen in the recipient's *actions;* the thought produced in a recipient can not be examined directly, but one might make inferences from his behaviour. Investigation of this will need isolation of the recipient from many local conditions which might influence his actions at the time of communication, for instance by setting him in a relaxed state in a sound-proof room.

If the information is being given *in response to a question*, the position is partly more restricted in scope than in the random information situation, but is also complicated by several additional factors. A question indicates an enquirer's realization of a missing element in his knowledge; the question is however itself a type of information, which must be interpreted by some recipient who will answer directly, or perhaps act as intermediary in putting the question to a retrieval system; the enquirer may be his own intermediary, but this does not alter the necessary intermediate steps. The conditions for response to the information are now probably restricted to types (3) or (4).

Information Retrieval Systems

An information retrieval system introduces many other factors. The available information exists in the form of documents (or their indexed representations) stored in the system. The originator of a document is now almost out of the picture; we can also omit, in the first place, consideration of the work of editors or abstractors, who are both recipients and (new) originators, but who also do not come directly into the picture for the investigation of information handling. The important factor in the retrieval system is the *indexer*. If the indexing is automated, the resulting secondary information is still something created by rules prescribed by some designer. If the indexer is a person, the original information will have been communicated to him as a recipient, interpreted by him, and converted to the indexed format of secondary information, and this conversion is not necessarily, or even probably, made by any fixed rules (except in a relationally indexed system). The use of a thesaurus provides the possibility of some standardization of terms, but does not necessarily control the *choice* of terms. A title and abstract of a paper, if stored, is unstandardized information, and in a free-text searching system the question has to be elaborated with numerous possible synonyms of question terms. The user, or the indexer acting for him, will also present a converted (indexed) form of his question to the system. The matching process is mechanical, and its study will not elucidate the information problem. Even in the case of fully automated original text searching, there are some rules of grammatical interpretation, truncation of terms, and omission of stopwords which will distort meaning to some extent; in fact, the words omitted as stopwords are important, since they are those which provide the meaningful structure in language. The output, usually in the form of references and/or abstracts, is however virtually original information, especially if the recipient will look up the original documents. The meaning, however, has become what the user interprets it to be.

The efficiency of the retrieval system, considered as comprising the indexing and the matching, thus depends, apart from the mechanics of the system, entirely on the accuracy of the indexing process. This accuracy lies in the attainment of consistency of choice of each indexing word to express a standard meaning, as envisaged by the indexer (or possibly preset by the devices of an automated system), and this accuracy also relates to the indexing of the question. The matching also depends on the depth of indexing (number of terms and coverage of the document subject) and the specificity (level of description) of terms. The depth of indexing of a document should obviously be equal to, or greater than, the depth for the question. The specificities should preferably be at the same level. The user's judgment of the output, which determines recall and precision, is however not part of the retrieval system as outlined. The judgment is made at a later time than that of the document indexing, and changes of terminology or of subject structuring may have occurred in the interval. If the idea of a "system" is enlarged to include the user, then it must be recognized that it immediately becomes much more complex and less analyzable. The document indexing cannot be carried out with anticipation of the user's specific needs, and the matching process is subject to a second selection by the user in an unpredictable manner. In fact, if the user is allowed to vary his question by putting in alternative or additional terms, or by other changes made by feedback methods, any test made will represent the ingenuity or vagaries of the user far more than the characteristics of the system (as an indexing and matching procedure). As a corollary, it will be seen that recall and precision, although individually representative of user satisfaction at a given time, are not valid measures of the restricted "system," and are subject to a number of reservations even in relation to the wider system.

The improvement of retrieval therefore rests on the possibility of controlling the indexing so as to achieve uniformity for both document indexing and question indexing, and on the possibility of making the indexing more exact in expressing a given subject. There is however no yardstick of meaning which can be applied to achieving this. Research is needed on the changes which information undergoes in all these processes. In this respect, the main purpose of Relational Indexing[4,5] has been to achieve greater exactitude, both in the depth of indexing and the structuring, or interrelation of the words used, so that matching will be more exact. New investigations of aspects of relational indexing are in hand.

Further Considerations

On the above basis, it will be very different again to consider "information" in a still wider, general social context. The task of relating the actions of the recipient of information to the original information may be very complex. In few cases will there be immediate, observable action by a recipient of information; in most cases, the information will be converted to stored knowledge, and eventual action may be long delayed, and difficult to trace. With publicly distributed information, such as even a headline in a scientific news journal (which might be much more reliable than a newspaper headline), influences of mass psychology may contribute to the ultimate results.

It is however urged here that defining the term "information" as a physical surrogate of knowledge provides at least a positive starting point for investigation and for construction of an information *science*. The mental states and possible actions arising from the information can then be examined, defined and possibly measured in terms of changes involved. This will need much experimental investigation and the development of suitable methodology. New terminology will be needed to designate the various mental states. Philosophical speculations, and other highly generalized formulations, will not advance our treatment of information science, and mathematical models are useless unless they can incorporate experimental data and predict factual outcomes which can be verified experimentally. The plain truth is that we do not yet have any experimental data which will quantify, or even qualitatively order, the different derivations of the initial information. The provision of this, and associated theory, is the task for the future.

Notes

1. J. Farradane, "Towards a True Information Science," *Information Scientist*, 10 (1976):91–101.
2. N. Belkin, "Information Concepts for Information Science," *J. Documentation*, 34 (1978):55–85, cf. p. 79.
3. *Perspectives in Information Science* (Leiden: Noordhoff, 1975), Chaps. 1, 2.
4. J. Farradane, "Concept Organization for Information Retrieval," *Inf. Stor. Retr.* 3 (1967):297–314.
5. P.A. Yates-Mercer, "Relational Indexing Applied to the Selective Dissemination of Information," *J. Documentation* 32 (1976):182–197.

Useful Theory for Librarianship: Communication, Not Information

BRENDA DERVIN

Assumptions

Implicit in the focus on the measurement of library activities are a number of assumptions. The most obvious is that there is something of value to be obtained as a result of measuring library activities. This assumption is seldom contested, in that the measurement of any institution's "activities" can provide data useful in a number of ways, including planning, promotion, and accounting. Behind the variety of ways in which such measurements might be used rests an even more central assumption—that library "activities" are in themselves of value. Again, few would contest the point.

Yet, perhaps the point should be contested. The very term, *the measurement of library activities*, conjures up a fairly consensual image of libraries and their "activities." The mind's eye sees libraries doing what libraries do and somehow in the process being measured. Notice that the user or the potential user does not get star billing in this mental picture. And, this is the crux of the problem. It is assumed that the library's activities are of value. It is assumed that the library is the initiator. It is assumed that the way the patron uses the library is the way the library intends and that the patron can, thus, be tapped as one of those library "activities" along with all the other library "activities."[1]

True, this set of assumptions is not often presented in such blatant brevity. Yet, these assumptions guide the delivery and measurement of not only library service but virtually all human service delivery systems in the United States. And, ironically, these assumptions prevent these

Reprinted from Drexel Library Quarterly 13(3), July 1977: 16–32 systems from asking the kinds of questions which need to be asked about the very entity (the user or potential user) who is the *raison d'etre* for the institution in the first place. While we know a great deal about such things as cost accounting and acquisition planning, we know very little about how people make use of libraries or, for that matter, how they make use of the prime collateral* of libraries—information. It is probably safe to estimate that more than 90 percent of the attention in library research is focused on the library and its activities, assumes these activities have value, and looks at the user or potential user only in this context.[2]

The kinds of questions that one is able to ask are constrained, of course, by the kinds of answers one already has. The assumptions which hamper question-asking in library research themselves grow out of a set of pervasive and internally consistent assumptions about the nature of people and how they cope and the nature of information and how it helps. What is needed, then, is not simply a change in the kinds of questions that we ask in order to yield measures of library activities but a change in something more deep-rooted, a change in the very way we view the nature of library services. This paper, then, focuses less on the measurement of library activities per se and more on what kind of view we need to take of library activities in order to generate useful measures.

The Current View[3]

Some of the long-held assumptions about the nature of library service are today being challenged. There is a move away from books to other media and a move away from inside-building activities to outreach.[†] These aspects of library service are, in actuality, only the packages within which the real collateral being exchanged in library service is wrapped. Increasingly, there is agreement that the real collateral is information. Yet, while libraries are more often dealing with a larger variety of packages, the basic premises about the collateral—information—

---

*The choice of the word *collateral* is purposive. One point is to differentiate it from the word *utility* to be used later in this chapter. The intent is to separate the finding or construction of information from its uses.

†Books and buildings can be seen as structures developed because they seemed, at some point in time, useful means of implementing some needed functions. Books were once the available technology for the transmission of ideas across time and space. Library buildings were once seen as means of protecting books from piracy and other dangers. The difficulty with structures invented to serve purposes at one point in time is that they live beyond their function. Soon, systems feel constrained to define their functions in terms of the available structures, forgetting that structures are inventions.[4]

remain unchanged and are the same premises that pervade Western civilization.

Information is essentially seen as a tool that is valuable and useful to people in their attempts to cope with their lives. Information is seen as something that reduces uncertainty. As the individual moves through time and space (i.e., the time-space continuum that makes up a life), it is assumed that information can both describe and predict that reality and thus allow the individual to move more effectively. It is in the context of these premises that libraries and other information delivery systems are mandated to collect information, store it so it can be retrieved, retrieve it when necessary, and disseminate it as needed.

The pervasive model of service can be illustrated with an analogy to the delivery of health care. The patient comes to a doctor with an ailment. It is the doctor's job to classify that ailment into a known disease and then to treat it with known and normatively successful methods. The patient is relatively unimportant in this process. The disease is of interest. The information involved in the process allows the doctor to diagnose and treat the disease.[5]

The analogy is extreme but appropriate. Just as the uniqueness of the patient's particular time-space is seen as relatively unessential in the practice of medicine, the uniqueness of the user's particular time-space is seen as relatively unessential in the conduct of library activities. The user comes to the library with a request and it is assumed that there is some universal truth value about the user's situation. The user's unique situation, then, is treated as a typical or normatively defined situation and is thus made amenable to a match in an information system designed normatively. When pushed to this extreme, this view of information suggests that, given enough information and given perfect retrieval of that information, every situation would have a perfect informational match. It is in the context of such assumptions that more and more attention is placed on bigger and bigger storage and retrieval systems.

There are many signs, of course, that this normative view of information and service does not work. Perhaps most obvious is the increasing demand by users of systems that they be treated as individuals. In responding to this demand, libraries and other information systems are increasingly resorting to the employment of user profiles drawn in terms of various demographic variables. Thus, there are evident attempts to describe what kind of information and service are needed by different population subgroups.

While the use of such "community" portraits does have value in some contexts, their use does not really speak to the increasing demand by users that they be treated as individuals. In fact, the irony of the use of across time-space demographic profiles as a means of attempting to individualize service is that it is a normative response attempting to correct the damages of a normative approach. In the normative approach, the individual is treated as irrelevant to the situation. In the use of across time-space demographic predictions, the situation is treated as irrelevant to the individual for it is assumed that groups of individuals (e.g., males, in their thirties, Caucasian, middle-class) behave the same across time and space.

An additional irony of the use of demographic profiles as a means of individualizing service is that collecting data on library activities in this context is in itself an information overload. Assume, for example, that there are only 20 important demographic attributes which describe users and along which user intersection with library activities meaningfully varies. It is not difficult to generate 20 such attributes (e.g., race, age, sex, social class, education). Also assume that each of these attributes has only two values (e.g., old and young, rich and poor). In this scheme, there would be 1,048,576 different types of people intersecting with library activities.

The discussion above suggests, then, that the normative approach which guides the measurement of library activities is very much constrained by a number of untenable but widely accepted assumptions. The core assumption is that information exists independent of human action and that its value lies in describing reality and therefore in reducing uncertainty about reality. This assumption is surrounded by offshoot premises. Because information is seen as helpful, libraries and other agencies that have possession of it are seen as helpful simply because they can supply it. Information systems can be designed "normatively" for the "average" citizen because information has its own order and organization in its own right and diverse citizens must bend to the information in order to use it. Some concessions to diversity can be made by developing specialized services to meet the different needs of specialized demographic groups who differ in life context (and therefore in the topical category of their needs) and in education (and therefore in their ability to handle information).

In the context of these assumptions, questions are now asked that guide the measurement of library activities. Typical questions include: What information needs do citizens have? What information resources do citizens want? What is the best way of storing information for efficient retrieval? How can users be taught to use retrieval systems more effectively? Which library activities are most used? Which subgroups of citizens like which activities?

The series of assumptions that now guide library research and, in particular, the measurement of library activities, are so deep-rooted and internally consistent that they are hard to break. They prevent the asking of a different kind of question that would allow a focus on library activities at the point where it really matters—at the point of use by users. These "different" questions must, of necessity, challenge the long-held assumptions: What is information? What is information used for? How can you meaningfully predict information behaviors? How can libraries help? In the context of the pervasive approach described above, each of these questions has an assumed answer. Information describes reality. It reduces uncertainty and allows people to cope better. Information behaviors can be predicted on the basis of demographic attributes of people. Libraries can help by providing the "right" information at the "right" time.

Measurements of library activities generated by this set of answers can only tautologically support themselves.[6] The average user is as captivated by this view as the researcher. Information is assumed to be useful so if you ask people if they want more, they say "Yes." On the basis of this evidence, more and more comprehensive and complex information systems are organized using more and more sophisticated technology. In the meantime, support for library activities dwindles and study after study shows that, despite their allegiance to the value of objective information, very few citizens use libraries in order to obtain that valuable commodity.

An Alternative View[7]

An alternative way of thinking about information and service is suggested below. This view sees people as being involved in an information process quite different from the one now commonly assumed.

What Is Information?

The current view of information, as described above, is one that theoretically implies a view of the world as a place in which there is complete order. Information is but a description of the order. To the extent that an order is not described, information is somehow missing and must be found. Despite the prevalence of these assumptions, observations about the nature of man and the nature of his environment do not correspond. This view of information posits man as a totally adaptive creature, using information about reality to adapt to reality.

Pushed to the absurd extreme described above, this view of "information" is clearly untenable because it disregards the fact that man creates as well as adapts. Man's creations make maladaptive many of the adaptive behaviors of yesterday. Information grows old and useless, for no amount of information will ever describe the totality as long as unseen forces (human or natural) have the freedom to move freely.

It appears, then, that information ought to be looked at broadly—as something which applies to adaptive *and* creative behavior. In this context, it is useful to make a distinction between objective information (Information$_1$) and subjective information (Information$_2$).

Information$_1$ is defined as information which describes reality, the innate structure or pattern of reality, data.

Information$_2$ is defined as ideas, the structures or pictures imputed to reality by people.

In the most general sense, Information$_1$ refers to external reality; Information$_2$ refers to internal reality. When such distinctions between "external" and "internal" reality have been made in the past, however, the intent has been somehow to devise methods by which a campaign could get around the selectivity barriers of "internal" reality, thereby aligning internal reality more closely with external reality.

The approach suggested here is radically different. Here internal reality becomes a legitimate informational input in its own right. Since no observer can say how "reality-bounded" an individual is, Information$_1$ is assumed to be incomplete.

In this context, the Information$_1$-Information$_2$ distinction is most useful axiomatically. It forces our attention to the notion that information can be whatever an individual finds "informing." It moves our attention away from "objective" information, toward assessing the "cognitive maps or pictures" of an individual. What kind of picture does this person have of his situation? What kind of picture is he trying to make? What kind of picture does he require to control self and movement? What kind of "information" could be helpful?

The utility of the Information$_1$-Information$_2$ distinction goes beyond replacing a focus on Information$_1$ with a focus on Information$_2$: The distinction forces us to recognize that objective reality and internal reality are two different realities. Whenever an individual interacts with reality, he is selectively perceiving aspects of reality (Information$_1$) and making pictures (Information$_2$). We can never know which came first. Nor can we assess the accuracy of the Information$_2$ against the Information$_1$ because such an assessment simply is not meaningful. But, we know that an individual is dealing with reality (Information$_1$) everyday as he moves through his own time and space; we also know that he moves and acts on the basis of his own pictures (Information$_2$) because that is all he has. The question then becomes: How does the individual move between

Information$_2$ and Information$_1$ or vice versa? How does he impose sense on reality when he finds none there? How does he find sense in reality when he goes on looking? These "how" questions focus our attention on the behaviors or procedures by which people get what they do not know, "how" they get informed, "how" they get instructed. Both an individual's selection and use of Information$_1$ *and* his creation of Information$_2$ result from some kind of behavior. It is suggested here that these behaviors are in themselves legitimate informational inputs: Information$_3$.[8]

The utility of Information$_3$ can best be described by example. A particular individual, finding himself in a particular situation, may approach that situation by decision*ing*. He screens his "reality" for alternative means. He looks for relevant comparison attributes. He completes his decision matrix. He makes a decision. Decisioning is a familiar information processing approach,˙ one which seems "right" because it fits nicely with "objective information is valuable" assumptions. In a view of the world which posits Information$_1$ as being able to reduce all uncertainty, decision matrices are useful reduction mechanisms.

The view presented here, however, posits decisioning as merely one possible approach. Another individual may use a liking-disliking procedure, searching his internal pictures and/or environment for the first available "tolerable" means. Yet another individual may look to the advice and counsel of others—a "relating to others" strategy. The important point is that alternative behavioral approaches are obviously being used. In other words, take any given slice of Information$_1$ (a slice of "reality" or a constructed message): Any two different individuals will create different Information$_2$ pictures in the same Information$_1$ context.

While individualized perception has become almost a commonplace tenet of a relativistic age, most information systems adhere to structures that ignore the tenet. Thus, for example, in measuring library activities, it is assumed that fiction imparts entertainment and not information. The user is not asked what kind of picture he was able to make as a result of his use of a library resource. Further, since Information$_1$ has been assumed to be equal to Information$_2$, little attention has been focused on how people make sense both by creating and by using information. Yet, when a user intersects with a library, the theoretic rationale presented above assumes that there must be behavioral connections between the Information$_1$ (the library's resources) and Information$_2$ (the user's expectations for and use of these resources).

˙It is probably not unreasonable to estimate that roughly 90 percent of the available work relating to "human information processing" assumes a decisioning model. Yet, the little direct actuarial evidence there is suggests that decisioning may be a relatively rare approach.[9]

The ignorance we have of how people create and use information is more than mere oversight. It is in this arena that we can begin to understand how citizens make sense out of their worlds if they are not using formal information systems and libraries. It is in this arena that we can begin to understand how to design alternative library activities that can intersect with individuals in more useful ways.

This alternative perspective on information should both free library researchers from inaccurate premises leading to overinflated expectations of the value of Information$_1$ and guide the planning of activities that are communication-based rather than simply information-based. While the latter is activity that is premised on the movement of Information$_1$, the former is activity that is premised on the helpful intersection of the librarian in the informing processes of the individual.

This alternative approach also focuses the library researcher on the kinds of questions he should ask to guide the measurement of library activities. Past research has typically focused on Information$_1$: How many books were circulated? How much use was made of nonfiction books? Who checked out what kinds of materials? Research generated by the alternative perspective would ask instead: Did the user learn, come to understand, or find out something as a result of intersecting with a library activity? What library resource served as impetus? What kind of sense did the user make? How did he make that sense?

What Is Information Used For?

The discussion of information presented above leads logically to another important ramification for library research. Traditionally, it has been assumed that the value or utility of information is that it reduces uncertainty and allows better adaptation to reality. The issue of information utility, then, has been one for which we have operated on an assumed constant answer.

Clearly, in the context of the Information$_{1,2,3}$ discussion presented above, this is a constraining approach. First, if one rejects the notion that Information$_1$ can completely describe reality, then the whole premise of adaptation becomes tenuous. The concept of function or utility, then, must also become a relativistic concept. If each individual has his own "reality" (Information$_2$) and on the basis of that "reality" uses procedures (Information$_3$) for assessing the reality (Information$_1$), then the functions or utilities of the "informations" are also his to decide.

The question, then, becomes "How did the individual find the information useful?" A given piece of Information$_1$ may help one individual calm down and get self-control. For another, it may provide motivation to continue on an arduous road. For another it may provide a sense of not being alone in a difficult situation. For another it may help in making progress toward some goal. For another it may provide a respite or retreat from reality. The same information obtained or created by the same means can serve different functions.

The point is an important one. By essentially assuming that information has value in its own right (i.e., the constant value of uncertainty reduction), library researchers have left untapped a whole realm of library activities. While for the library, functional utilities may be to circulate books or transfer information, for the individual user the functional utility is more likely to be instructions, clarifications, reinforcements, answers, ideas, companionships, confirmations, assistances, escapes.[10]

In sum, if some form of information proves useful to an individual, the question suggested by the perspective offered above is "How?" How did it allow the individual to move, to cope, to control self? How did it allow the individual to make sense? How did the individual use it? How can the librarian deliver to the individual the "something" which will be functional for him?

This alternative perspective suggests that the library researcher needs to ask if different "informations" helped a user as he tried to cope. The answer to this question is not important in itself. More important is determining how information helped or why it did not. It is the answers to these questions that will elicit the functional utilities of the user—the basis on which he will judge whether the library is a good one for him. It is reasonable to expect that these functional utilities are the ones against which libraries should assess their effectiveness.

How Can You Predict Information Behaviors?

Libraries go into the prediction business in one way or the other in order to plan the allocation of resources and achieve some kind of control over the chaotic future.* In particular, as resources dwindle libraries want to predict the behaviors of their users and potential users so that they may both plan and promote their activities. As noted earlier, the use of across time-space prediction on the basis of demographic attributes is a commonly used approach. Obviously, this kind of normative approach which accesses a community along demographic dimensions is useful in some contexts. Thus, it is possible to design activities to meet community needs and to be accountable to a community in a normative way, for ex-

*The word *prediction* is not being used in the traditionally accepted way (i.e., if . . . then prediction) throughout this article. Human service agencies now go into the "if . . . then" prediction business. What is being suggested in this article is an alternative that can be labelled "then . . . then" prediction.[11]

ample, by tapping how many members of the community were served in a certain time period in what ways.

The problem is that the success of library activities does not rest on the community: a useful construct for administrators, at best, and a mythical construct, at worst.* Living, breathing individual human beings use library services. Living, breathing librarians must cope with these living, breathing human beings as individuals. When it comes to dealing with individuals as individuals, demographic attributes are but labels imposed by the outside world. The attributes may or may not be relevant to the individual. Furthermore, whether they are relevant or not, attributes are not the reason an individual may intersect with a library at a given point in time. His reasons are situational: He finds himself in a situation in which he feels a library would be useful.

It is suggested, then, that to cope with *individuality* one must also deal with *situationality.*[12] It is also suggested that the only way to deal with *situationality* is through the eyes of a given individual. The rationale emerges from the axiomatic premises that underlie communications research.† Meanings are in people. No message means the same thing to different people. No situation is seen the same by different people. The same message read on two different days will not mean the same thing to the same person. The same person in the "same" situation on two different days will not see that situation the same way.

In this context, then, library research ought to be developing a different kind of prediction theory—a kind more useful to the realities of library service. Now, the typical questions about users are: "What kinds of people need what kinds of service?" "What kinds of people are library-using people?" The alternative perspective suggested above leads to different questions: "In what kinds of situations do people seek information or use libraries?" "What kinds of situations lead to use of different kinds of information?" "What do people do to make sense of different kinds of situations?" It is in the context of such questions that libraries can understand much more about what happens to their products.

---

*A *community* is a collection of individuals who may or may not have any formalized power to act as a single entity. A *city* may be a community, in which case the individuals have the power to vote and thus decide as a single entity, or the *community* may be elusively the neighborhood around an information and referral center. In either case, there are problems in designing systems on the basis of *community* data when the system will end up being accountable to individual members.

†Despite the clarity of the "relativity of meaning" generalization in communications literature, much of the communications field has also persisted with the across time-space attribute approach.[13]

How Can Libraries Help?

In summary, it has been suggested that while libraries are designed for serving *communities*, accountability rests in the long run on the ability to "help" individuals. It is here that a major focus of library research should be placed.

In trying to cope with individuality, libraries have used an "attribute prediction" approach in which the practitioner is expected to know in advance enough about the relationship between various attributes of individuals (e.g., demography) and behaviors (e.g., use of the library, preferences for system services) so that the librarian can predict how to operate. This approach is seen as not useful since attributes do not describe the locations of individuals in time and space and it is at the points of these locations that something called *information* will be used.

The situationality approach is further reinforced by the alternative perspective to information presented in this paper. In order to be useful, the librarian must acknowledge and deal with the actuality of information processing. Each individual not only collects, stores, retrieves, and uses information, he creates it as well. Indeed, he *must* create it, because information about reality is not enough. To control self and move through time and space, each individual must make his own sense. No outsider can impose sense.

Libraries, along with other human service delivery systems, have essentially accepted a persuasion model of service rather than an intersection or intervention model. Thus, it has been assumed that Information$_1$ is valuable and that one job of the library is to convince potential users of its value. The model suggested in this article is quite different. It assumes that the user is in control of his own sense-making processes and will attend to messages that might help him in these processes. He will find libraries useful to the extent that they are helpful to him in this regard.

This perspective suggests that a major purpose of library research must be focused on the question of how libraries can intervene usefully in individual sense-making processes. Since the individual user of the library cannot be predicted in advance, the librarian cannot be expected to have a perfect system match ready and waiting for each unique user. The librarian can be aware, however, of alternative strategies for interacting with users, for getting their pictures, determining how to intervene usefully, and intervening usefully. The word *alternative* is important. Diverse users in diverse situations at diverse points of time and space require diverse alternatives.

What is suggested here, then, is that library research needs to place a major focus on a little-studied aspect of library activities. In particular, library research needs to ask how the librarian can intervene usefully with users presenting different situational needs at different points in time. How can the librarian intervene? What questions can he ask? How can he enter the user's informing processes? What can he deliver that will be "informing" to that unique individual?

These are the kinds of questions that library research needs to ask in order to assist libraries in developing activities which can cope with individuality in an individual, interactive way rather than a normative, inflexible way. Data generated by asking such questions will help planners create library activities that are communication-based rather than merely information-based.

The assessment of library activities solely within the context of an information model results in assessments which focus on the collection, storage, retrieval, and dissemination of Information$_1$. Using such a model, there is a danger of reifying the existence of the library as a structure regardless of whether that structure and the activities included therein are meaningful to users and potential users. The assessment of library activities within the context of a communication model results in assessments focused on how libraries can help people inform themselves, create their own orders, and establish their own understandings. Using such a model, there is little danger of reification because the research is centered on the entity—the user or potential user, who gives the library its real reason for being.

Notes

1. For discussion of this and related points, see: Douglas Zweizig and Brenda Dervin, "Public Library Use, Users, and Uses—Advances in Knowledge of Characteristics and Needs of the Adult Clientele of American Public Libraries," *Advances in Librarianship* 7 (1977): 231–255. Douglas Zweizig, "With Our Eye on the User: Needed Research for Information and Referral in the Public Library," *Drexel Library Quarterly* 12 (nos. 1 & 2, January–April 1976): 48–58; Douglas Zweizig, "Predicting Amount of Library Use: An Empirical Study of the Role of the Public Library in the Life of the Adult Public" (Doctoral dissertation, Syracuse University, 1973).
2. Zweizig found only 16 studies which he could call "user" studies using his criteria in a search of the public library literature. See Zweizig, "With Our Eye on the User," p. 48.
3. Both the critique of the current view and the development of the alternative view presented in this article rest heavily on the theoretic work of Richard F. Carter. See, in particular: Richard F. Carter, "A Journalistic View of Communication," Paper presented at the Theory and Methodology Division, Association for Education in Journalism Annual Meeting, Carbondale, Illinois, August 20–23, 1972; Richard F. Carter et al., "Application of Signalled Stopping Technique to Communication Research," in Peter Clarke, ed., *New Models for Mass Communication Research* (Beverly Hills, California: Sage Annual Reviews of Communication Research, Vol. II, 1973), pp. 15–44; Richard F. Carter, "A Journalistic Cybernetic," Paper presented at the Conference on

Communication and Control in Social Processes, University of Pennsylvania, Philadelphia, October 31–November 2, 1974; Richard F. Carter, "Toward More Unity in Science" (School of Communications, University of Washington, 1974); Richard F. Carter, "Elementary Ideas of Systems Applied to Problem-Solution Strategies," Paper presented at the annual meeting of the Far West Region of the Society for General Systems Research, San Jose, California, October 23–24, 1975.

4. A helpful discussion of this issue is provided in: Carter, "A Journalistic Cybernetic" (see note 3 above).

5. This portrait of the service model in health delivery systems comes from: Brenda Dervin and Sylvia Harlock, "Health Communication Research: The State of the Art," Paper presented at the International Communication Association Annual Meeting, Portland, Oregon, April 1976.

6. This is a major reason why the literature on citizen use of information resources, including libraries, is beset with contradictions. For a review of that literature and its contradictions, see: Brenda Dervin, "The Everyday Information Needs of the Average Citizen: A Taxonomy for Analysis," in Manfred Kochen and Joseph Donohue, eds., *Information for the Community* (Chicago: American Library Association, 1976), pp. 19–54. See also: Dervin, "Designing Everyday Coping Information Services."

7. In addition to the writings of Richard F. Carter (see note 3 above), the author has relied heavily on the thinking of several other scholars in developing this alternative view. See, in particular: Jerome Bronowski, *Nature of Knowledge: The Philosophy of Contemporary Science* (New York: Science Books, 1969); Jerome Bronowski, *The Ascent of Man* (Boston: Little, Brown, and Company, 1973); Roderick Gorney, *The Human Agenda* (New York: Simon and Schuster, 1972); and Kaarle Nordenstreng, "From Mass Media to Mass Consciousness: Current Thinking in Scandinavia," in Yrjo Littunen et al., eds., *Approaching Mass Media Education Through Communication Research* (Tampere, Finland: Institute of Journalism and Mass Communication, Research for Social Sciences, University of Tampere, 1974), pp. 33–54.

8. A number of theorists have developed related typologies of information. For fairly comprehensive reviews see: Brenda Dervin, "Communication Behaviors as Related to the Information Control Behaviors of Black Low-Income Adults" (Doctoral dissertation, Michigan State University, 1971); Dervin, "The Everyday Information Needs of the Average Citizen"; Clyde Morris, "A Proposed Taxonomy for Communication Research" (Doctoral dissertation, Michigan State University, 1969). The Information$_{1,2,3}$ formulation presented here relies heavily, but not entirely, on the "knowing-finding-making" typology of Carter (Richard F. Carter, personal communication, 1975). The approach to Information$_3$—the making-sense behaviors or procedures—also rests heavily on Carter. For relevant citations, see listings in note 3 above.

9. See, in particular, Dervin, "The Development of Strategies for Dealing with the Information Needs of Urban Residents: Phase I—Citizen Study."

10. For a more complete explanation of the concept of functional utilities or functional units, see Dervin, "Strategies for Dealing with the Information Needs of Urban Residents: Information or Communication?"; Carter, "Application of Signalled Stopping Technique to Communication Research"; Carter, "A Journalistic Cybernetic." For an example of a research project which successfully incorporates the idea of the usefulness of information input from the perspective of the user, see Alex Edelstein, *The Use of Communication in Decision-Making: A Comparative Study of Yugoslavia and the United States* (New York: Praeger, 1974).

11. Carter suggested the phrase "then . . . then" prediction (Richard F. Carter, personal communication, 1976). Dervin refers to the "if . . . then" versus "then . . . then" distinction as "across time-space" versus "situationality." See, in particular, Brenda

Dervin, "ICA Top Three Minus One: A Critique," Critique presented at the International Communication Association Meeting, Portland, Oregon, April 14–17, 1976.

12. For more discussion of the need to focus on "situationality," see: Carter, "Toward More Unity in Science"; Dervin, "Strategies for Dealing with the Information Needs of Urban Residents: Information or Communication?"; Edelstein, *The Use of Communication in Decision-Making.*

13. For a review of the paradoxes that have resulted in the communications field from the use of across time-space approaches, see: Dervin, "Strategies for Dealing with the Information Needs of Urban Residents: Information or Communication?"

Information Science: What Is It?

H. BORKO

Introduction

Now that the American Documentation Institute has voted to change its name to the American Society for Information Science, many of us have been forced to try to explain to friends and colleagues what information science is, what an information scientist does, and how all of this relates to librarianship and documentation. Those of us who have tried to make such explanations know that this is a difficult task. As an exercise I decided to prepare an answer to these questions at leisure rather than under the pressure of a direct inquiry. Let me state at the outset that I don't think I have *the answer.* It is hoped that this paper may provide a focus for discussion so that we can clarify our thinking and perhaps be more articulate about who we are and what we do.

Definition

The term "information science" has been with us for some time. In his chapter on the "Professional Aspects of Information Science and Technology"[1] in the *Annual Review,* Robert S. Taylor provides three definitions of information science. These have many points in common as

Reprinted from *American Documentation* 19(1) (January 1968): 3–5.

well as some differences in emphasis. The definition that follows has been derived from a synthesis of these ideas.

Information science is that discipline that investigates the properties and behavior of information, the forces governing the flow of information, and the means of processing information for optimum accessibility and usability. It is concerned with that body of knowledge relating to the origination, collection, organization, storage, retrieval, interpretation, transmission, transformation, and utilization of information. This includes the investigation of information representations in both natural and artificial systems, the use of codes for efficient message transmission, and the study of information processing devices and techniques such as computers and their programming systems. It is an interdisciplinary science derived from and related to such fields as mathematics, logic, linguistics, psychology, computer technology, operations research, the graphic arts, communications, library science, management, and other similar fields. It has both a pure science component, which inquires into the subject without regard to its application, and an applied science component, which develops services and products.

If this definition seems complicated, it is because the subject matter is complex and multidimensional, and the definition is intended to be all-encompassing.

Obviously information science is not the exclusive domain of any one organization. Traditionally, the American Documentation Institute has been concerned with the study of recorded, that is, documentary, information. This is still our main emphasis; however, the work is now embedded in a larger context. Librarianship and documentation are applied aspects of information science. The techniques and procedures used by librarians and documentalists are, or should be, based upon the theoretical findings of information science, and conversely, the theoretician should study the time-tested techniques of the practitioner.

The Need for Information Science

Information science as a discipline has as its goal to provide a body of information that will lead to improvements in the various institutions and procedures dedicated to the accumulation and transmission of knowledge. There are in existence a number of such institutions and related media. These include: *books* for packaging knowledge; *schools* for teaching the accumulated knowledge of many generations; *libraries* for storing and disseminating knowledge; *movies and television* for the visual display of knowledge; *journals* for the written communication of the latest technical advances in specialized fields; and *conferences* for the oral communication of information.

These institutions have served, and continue to serve, very useful functions, but they are inadequate to meet the communication needs of today's society. Some of the factors that contribute to their inadequacies are:

1. The tremendous growth in science and technology and the accelerated pace at which new knowledge becomes available and old knowledge becomes obsolete;
2. The fast rate of obsolescence of technical knowledge, so that the old graduate must go back to school and update his skills;
3. The large number of working scientists and the large number of scientific and technical journals which exist today;
4. The increased specialization which makes communication and the exchange of information between disciplines very difficult;
5. The short time lag between research and application that makes the need for information more pressing and more immediate.

As a result of these pressures, the existing methods for exchanging information have been found wanting. Information science has not kept pace with other scientific developments, and now there is a need to concentrate efforts in this field and to catch up. If communication and information exchange procedures are not improved, all other scientific work will be impeded; the lack of communication will result in a duplication of effort and a slowing of progress.

The importance of information science and the reasons for the current emphasis upon this discipline are thus clear: The need to organize our efforts and meet the new challenges finds a concrete expression in the American Society for Information Science.

Information Science Research and Applications

As was pointed out in the definition, information science has both a pure and an applied aspect. Members of this discipline, depending upon their training and interests, will emphasize one or the other aspect. Within information science there is room for both the theoretician and the practitioner, and clearly both are needed. Theory and practice are inexorably related; each feeds on the work of the other.

The researcher in information science has a broad field in which to pursue his investigations. A glance through the 566 pages (excluding the Glossary and Indexes) of the last issue (No. 14) of *Current Research and Development in Scientific Documentation*[2] shows a staggering range of projects being studied. The 655 project statements are organized into nine categories as follows:

1. *Information Needs and Uses*
   Behavioral studies of users; citation studies; communication patterns; literature use studies.
2. *Document Creation and Copying*
   Computer-assisted composition; microforms; recording and storing; writing and editing.
3. *Language Analysis*
   Computational linguistics; lexicography; natural language (text) processing; psycholinguistics; semantic analysis.
4. *Translation*
   Machine translation; translation aids.
5. *Abstracting, Classification, Coding and Indexing*
   Classification and indexing systems; content analysis; machine-aided classification, extracting and indexing; vocabulary studies.
6. *System Design*
   Information centers; information retrieval; mechanization of library operations; selective dissemination of information.
7. *Analysis and Evaluation*
   Comparative studies; indexing quality; modeling; test methods and performance measures; translation quality.
8. *Pattern Recognition*
   Image processing; speech analysis.
9. *Adaptive Systems*
   Artificial intelligence; automata; problem solving; self-organizing systems.

In essence, information science research investigates the properties and behavior of information, the use and transmission of information, and the processing of information for optimal storage and retrieval.

Theoretic studies should not, and in fact do not, take place in a vacuum. There is a constant interplay between research and application, between theory and practice. As in most every scientifically based discipline, the researchers form a small but vocal minority. The bulk of the membership is applications oriented. These members deal, on a daily basis, with the problems and practices of information transfer. They are responsible for making the system work in spite of all inadequacies, and they develop improvements within an operational context.

They need to be informed about the new techniques being developed and when these are proven, they need to apply them and evaluate them under operating conditions. Yet, it is important to recognize that, particularly in information science, there is no sharp distinction between research and technology. It is a matter of emphasis, and all members share a concern over a common set of problems.

Every scientific discipline needs an academic component, and so it is important to note that information science is now a recognized discipline in an increasing number of major universities. The subjects taught vary from school to school, probably more as a function of available professorial skills rather than any real difference of opinion about what should be taught. Such diversity is desirable. The field is too young, and it is too soon to standardize on a single curriculum, for a variety of programs encourages exploration and growth. As students graduate, they will exert a unifying and maturing influence on the educational program.

Summary

By way of a summary, I will restate the questions and answers that led to this essay on information science. Again, I would like to add the caveat that these are not meant to be final answers but rather to serve as foci for further discussion and clarification.

What is information science? It is an interdisciplinary science that investigates the properties and behavior of information, the forces that govern the flow and use of information, and the techniques, both manual and mechanical, of processing information for optimal storage, retrieval, and dissemination.

What then is documentation? Documentation is one of many applied components of information science. Documentation is concerned with acquiring, storing, retrieving, and disseminating recorded documentary information, primarily in the form of report and journal literature. Because of the nature of the collection and the user's requirements, documentation has tended to emphasize the use of data processing equipment, reprography and microforms as techniques of information handling.

What does an information scientist do? Information scientists may work as researchers, educators, or applications specialists in the field of information science; that is to say, they may do research aimed at developing new techniques of information handling; they may teach information science; and they may apply the theories and techniques of information science to create, modify and improve information handling systems.

Information science is an important emergent dicipline, and the information scientist has an important function in our society.

References

1. TAYLOR, R.S., Professional Aspects of Information Science and Technology, in C. A. Cuadra (Ed.), *Annual Review of Information Science and Technology,* Vol. 1, John Wiley & Sons, New York, 1966.
2. NATIONAL SCIENCE FFOUNDATION, *Current Research and Development in Scientific Documentation,* No. 14, Office of Scientific Information, NSF-66-17, Washington, D.C., 1966.

Theory in Information Science

A.J. MEADOWS

Information scientists often see their subject as severely practical. However, the range of theory being applied in information science has expanded considerably over the past thirty years. The basic question now is not whether applicable theories can be found to fit the various branches of information science, but rather whether the existing range of theories can be brought together to provide an integrated theoretical picture of the whole subject.

Introduction

Sir Thomas Browne began his book *Religio Medici* with the words: "For my religion, though there be several circumstances that might persuade the world I have none at all (as the general scandal of my profession, the natural course of my studies . . .)." Substitute the word "theory" for "religion" and this might be regarded as a fair description of information

Reprinted from *Journal of Information Science* 16(1) (1990): 59–63.

science by many practitioners. In fact, most information scientists would concede, on reflection, that theory does crop up from time to time in their subject. The real question is whether that theory is sufficiently well developed to provide a genuine foundation for practice.

In some academic subjects, the theory and practice are obviously intertwined. For example, theory and experiment have been recognized as the twin components of physics since its early days in the seventeenth century.

In nonscientific disciplines, defining the theoretical basis of a subject has often proved harder than defining the practice. In sociology, for example, radically different theoretical bases for studying the same phenomenon are still propounded by different groups of practitioners. Equally, vocational subjects have often found it hard to define their theoretical foundations. Sometimes this has led them to doubt whether a theoretical framework is either necessary or possible. Nineteenth-century British engineers, for example, were avowedly empirical in their approach, and were often highly suspicious of any attempt to import theory into their work. The fact that their contemporaries on the Continent were trained in theory, and that this approach is now entirely accepted in the UK, is a reminder—if such is needed—that the role of theory in vocational training may change with both place and time. The role of theory in information science needs to be studied with this point in mind. Present-day information science suffers from the joint disadvantage of being a vocational subject which has at least some of its roots in the social sciences. Hence, reaching agreement on any theoretical framework will be predictably difficult.

Early Developments

One useful way of examining the role of theory in information science is to consider the historical development of the subject. The original thread was essentially practical. It reflected the needs of special libraries, which were recognized in the years between the two World Wars to differ from those of public, academic or national libraries. The main differences were identified as lying in the areas of bibliography and what came to be called "documentation." Exactly what the differences between these new "documentalists" and traditional librarians were was not altogether well-defined. However, there was general agreement that documentalists were concerned not only with the physical handling of documents, but, to a much greater extent than traditional librarians, with the exploitation of the information contained in the documents.

This practical thread generated some of its own theory, a noticeable example being Bradford's law of scattering. After the Second World War, it was joined by a much more distinctively theoretical thread. To some extent, the main stimulus for this came from the publication of Shannon's information theory in 1949. His ideas were taken up rapidly over a range of subjects, including the nascent information science. Unfortunately, it soon became evident that the ambiguity of the word "information" had triumphed. Whereas for Shannon any signal was "information," for an information scientist "information" was what was relevant to a user's needs. The new theory had nothing to say about this problem. As it happened, Shannon's work coincided with a growing interest in the quantitative characteristics of information in the sense that information scientists used the word. Consequently, though Shannon's approach proved something of a dead end, modern information science actually did begin to develop during the 1950s.

The same emphasis on quantitative methods appeared over a range of the social sciences after the Second World War. It derived both from the new prestige of scientific methodology and from the development of new methods of handling data. The name "information science," like the "social sciences," reflected this trend. We may note the trend against this in recent years, which has led, amongst other things, to the British Social Sciences Research Council being relabelled the Economic and Social Research Council.

As Cuadra observed[1], the emphasis on the word "science" reflects not only a desire for professional status but also the hope that it will be possible to develop the solid underpinnings of theory and tested fact characteristic of the other sciences.

The key figure in these new quantitative studies was Price, whose writings, especially *Little Science, Big Science*[2], had a major impact on thinking about the growth and evolution of scientific journals. In part, he drew together ideas already under discussion. For example, the rapid growth in the amount of scientific literature had been debated by librarians and others since the First World War. Similarly, but separately, there had been work on relevant statistical distributions, such as Lotka's work on scientific productivity and Zipf's on word distributions. Price extended this earlier work to provide an integrated, quantitative picture of the scientific literature.

One important area of Price's work covered the applications of citation analysis. In this, he relied on the contemporaneous activities of Garfield in developing the concept of a citation index. This area of study has subsequently burgeoned, and the techniques applied have become increasingly sophisticated. The appearance in the 1970s of the now well-established journal *Scientometrics*, and the regular publication of relevant articles in other journals (including the *Journal of Information*

Science), is a clear demonstration that these quantitative methods are now an accepted part of information science. A scan back through the literature indicates that, for example, the work on statistical distributions (where Brookes' own writings should be mentioned) has interested statisticians, as well as information scientists.

Computers

These developments, however, only affected part of information science. Since the results are basically statistical, they cannot be related directly to the information characteristics or needs of the individual. In addition, since many of the basic data derive from the activities of R&D specialists, the results apply only to the part of the community served by modern information scientists. Consequently, these theoretical developments had only a marginal impact on many practitioners. For them, the advent of the computer was much more important.

Hanson[3], writing in 1971, remarked that information science seemed to have two meanings in practice.

> On the one hand, "information science" can be used to imply the exploitation of scientific and technical information of all kinds (not only documentary) and by all means (manual as well as mechanized) for the benefit of scientists and technologists. On the other hand, it is often used to imply the application of science and technology, particularly via mechanization, to handling information generally, not only scientific and technical information.

The computerization of information-handling progressed rapidly in the 1960s and 1970s. As Hanson noted, this development did not only affect the R&D specialists. In the latter part of the 1970s and into the 1980s, computerization combined with telecommunications led to the explosive emergence of information technology. The impact of IT on the practice of information science is obvious enough: but what impact has it had on theory?

Much important work on the theory of information retrieval was carried out before computers became everyday affairs. Not surprisingly, computers have greatly stimulated such work; particularly because they have allowed a jump to types of retrieval which would not previously have been worth considering. One example is searching techniques based on the three-dimensional structures of complex chemical molecules[4]. The level of sophistication now reached in investigations of information retrieval is such that some information scientists would consider retrieval research offered *the* theoretical basis for their subject.

However, computers have also led to a differing kind of emphasis in information science. This relates to the idea of information handling as contributing to a "system." The interest here ranges from applications of systems analysis to the role of expert systems in the acquisition of information. Whereas much of the theory of information retrieval has been developed by information scientists, most systems theory has been imported from other disciplines. Indeed, one feature of the 1980s has been the blurring of the division between information scientists and computer specialists as the former become increasingly interested in computers and the latter in information.

The Human Factor

A similar overlap has appeared in the past decade between management studies and information science. Interest in information management has also been stimulated by the growth of information technology, both because it offers a means of controlling information, and for its potential contribution to enhanced productivity. The term "information management" first appeared in a strictly practical context. It derived from an attempt by the United States Federal Government in 1978 to control the amount of paper in circulation. But information management covers a wider range of topics than just computerization. Earlier theories of communication in organizations are now merging with newer ideas of how information should be managed. Most of these ideas have originated outside information science; but, as with systems concepts, they are rapidly being incorporated into the basic theory taught to information science students[5].

Information management spans the information needs of both groups and individuals. The same is true of another recent growth area in information science—the study of human-computer interaction (HCI). This study, which also acts as a link between computer and management interests, also has its main roots outside information science (especially in psychology and ergonomics). Yet, in another sense, it is merely an extension of the user studies that have long formed a part of information work. Correspondingly, HCI is an area where information scientists are already making useful contributions. The difference is that the theoretical basis of user studies was always open to debate, whereas the current rapid development of cognitive studies suggests that some general theoretical basis for treating the individual, the information and the technology may appear in the not-too-distant future.

Indeed, looking forward to the 1990s, new developments in information handling may be expected to generate yet further theory. An example is the current growth area of retrieving and handling graphics.

Specific Theories or General Theory?

Even such a brief survey as this of the evolving picture of information science raises immediately a number of questions. Different areas of theory seem to have arisen at intervals in a rather random way. Does this mean that information science has no systematic theoretical base? It is certainly true that there is a "bandwagon" element in the development of information science. The early quantitative studies marked the heyday of scientific influence, whilst the information management of recent years reflects the climb to prominence of management and business studies. It is not difficult to predict that, if the next bandwagon in the information arena is (say) cognitive studies, then corresponding theories will flourish in information science. This is not at all the same as saying that the new theoretical structures are entirely conditioned by the way they originate. Nor is it true that new theories displace the old. Rather, the scope for theory in information science has been broadening; so, whilst some of the older theories may have been refurbished and extended, the more important trend has been the appearance of new areas of theory. Indeed, some management models view information handling itself as a series of vistas that have broadened with time[6]. Perhaps the simplest picture is to see information science as a wide-ranging subject in which various sectors develop a theoretical foundation as, and when, they become ready to do so. The latter would certainly be a reasonable description of the development of a subject such as physics. It is, perhaps, suggested in part by the observation that many theoretical themes in information science have often been discussed in principle long before they are finally established as part of the practical information scene. In either case, new theoretical developments can be seen as supplementing, rather than replacing, earlier insights; so, though the order in which theories have appeared may have been guided by environmental factors, this does not affect their applicability.

Other questions stem from the extent to which information science depends on external sources for its theoretical base. One concern is whether information science has any theoretical base of its own at all. It has been suggested, for example, that information science simply represents the intersection of a number of existing disciplines—linguistics, psychology, computer studies and so on. In this view, information scientists simply bring to their work background knowledge of a variegated bag of topics, and are themselves correspondingly diversified. Cronin[7] has suggested that:

> There is no information profession as such. There is, however, a large, scattered and heterogeneous population of professionally qualified people who, for the sake of convenience, can be classified as information workers. This community is so diffuse that it makes little sense to speak of a fraternity or federation of information workers.

Clearly, a case can be made for such an argument. The problem is that rather similar statements might fit a number of other professions. Substitute "engineering" for "information" in the above quotation, for example, and it still makes sense. Yet engineers nowadays, if not in the past, see themselves as very definitely forming a fraternity. Certainly, it seems to worry them very little that the theoretical basis of their work often derives from other areas, such as physics. Information scientists seem to be more perturbed by their theoretical borrowings from other disciplines than most professions.

A rather different approach is to assert that information science does exist as a separate entity, but that it should be defined primarily in terms of the skills or competencies required to practise it. This approach is particularly common where the educational requirements of information scientists are considered in terms of the jobs they can, or might, do (see Brittain[8] for a discussion). In this case, the tendency is to suppose that each area of the subject has its own particular theoretical basis depending on the activity concerned.

Again, this approach can be supported, but it sometimes overlooks the coalescence of different strands of information science which is already occurring. One effect of information technology has been to blur the distinctions that previously existed between different areas of information handling. For example, retrieval of existing information and creation of new information are now drawing much closer together. Hence, one possibility is that even if they are now distinct, the various areas of information science will ultimately come together. In the process, their distinctive theories will merge, so providing a general theoretical basis for information science as a whole.

A particular danger of this type of approach is that emphasizing the needs of practice may actually make theorizing more difficult. Over twenty years ago, Fairthorne[9] considered how a theory of information science might come about. He felt that it must start by defining

> what matters it will study explicitly. These matters must then be studied and talked about in their own terms, not in terms of their possible applications.

Similarly, Brookes has recently noted how important it is that information science should not be regarded by employers as "a collection of practical skills without underlying theoretical coherence"[10].

The final approach, of course, is to assert that a general theoretical backing for information science is feasible. It might be argued, for example, that pathways leading to an over-arching theory have already been identified, but they are too complicated to lead immediately to the creation of a comprehensive theoretical framework. For example, Saunders[11] suggested over ten years ago that all information scientists require a foundation course in human communication. If this really is the essential topic, then perhaps a comprehensive theory of how humans communicate will provide the theoretical foundation needed by information science once the relevant human sciences have developed far enough. The main problem here is disagreement over which activities or concepts are the fundamental ones. Nevertheless, attempts, such as that by the Vickerys[12], to provide an integrated view of information science do suggest that this approach is worth pursuing further. One of their comments is worth quoting:

> It has become increasingly clear that only by widening its "knowledge base" can information science establish a solid foundation for future development.

Clearly, even if the Holy Grail of a generalized theory of information science is possible, we still have some way to go before we can attain the vision.

Notes

1. C.A. Cuadra, "Identifying Key Contributions to Information Science," *American Documentation* 15 (1964):289–295.
2. D. de Solla Price, *Little Science, Big Science* (Columbia University Press, New York, 1963).
3. C.W. Hanson, *Introduction to Science-Information Work* (Aslib, London, 1971).
4. P.J. Artymiuk, D.W. Rice, E.M. Mitchell and P. Willett, "Searching Techniques for Databases of Protein Secondary Structures," *Journal of Information Science* 15 (1989):287–298.
5. T. Wilson, "Towards an Information Management Curriculum," *Journal of Information Science* 15 (1989):203–209.
6. M. Broadbent and M. Koenig, "The Convergence of Management Attention upon Information: Lessons for Librarianship," *IFLA Journal* 15 (1989):218–232.
7. B. Cronin, "Nichemanship for the Nineties," *Education for Information* 5 (1987):321–325.
8. J.M. Brittain, "Curriculum Development in the Library Schools to Meet the Challenge of Information Technology." *Infomediary* 1 (1985):177–198.

9. R.A. Fairthorne, "Morphology of Information Flow," *Journal of the Association for Computing Machinery* 14 (1967): 710–719.
10. B.C. Brookes, "Personal Transferable Skills for the Modern Information Professional," *Journal of Information Science* 15 (1989):115–117.
11. W.L. Saunders, *Guidelines for Curriculum Development in Information Studies* (Unesco, Paris, 1978).
12. B.C. Vickery and A. Vickery, *Information Science in Theory and Practice* (Butterworths, London, 1987).

Additional Readings for Chapter 1

BECKER, JOSEPH. "The Rich Heritage of Information Science." *Bulletin of ASIS* 2(8) (August 1976): 9–13.

BELKIN, NICHOLAS J. "Information Concepts for Information Science." *Journal of Documentation* 34 (March 1978): 55–85.

BELKIN, NICHOLAS J. and ROBERTSON, STEPHEN E. "Information Science and the Phenomena of Information." *Journal of ASIS* 27(4) (July–August 1976): 197–210.

BRITTAIN, J. MICHAEL. "What Are the Distinctive Characteristics of Information Science?" In *Theory and Application of Information Research*, 34–47. London: Mansell, 1980.

BUCKLAND, MICHAEL K. "Information as Thing." *Journal of ASIS* 42(5) (June 1991): 351–360.

DERR, RICHARD L. "The Concept of Information in Ordinary Discourse." *Information Processing & Management* 21(6) (1985): 489–499.

FARRADANE, JASON. "Towards a True Information Science." *Information Scientist* 10(3) (September 1976): 91–101.

FOX, CHRISTOPHER J. *Information and Misinformation: An Investigation of the Notion of Information, Misinformation, Informing, and Misinforming.* Westport, CN: Greenwood Press, 1983.

HARBO, OLE, and KAJBERG, LEIF. "Theory and Applications of Information Research." In *Proceedings of the Second International Research Forum on Information Science*, 3–6 (August 1977): Royal School of Librarianship, Copenhagen.

HARMON, GLYNN. "On the Evolution of Information Science." *Journal of ASIS* 22(4) (July–August 1971): 235–241.

HERNER, SAUL. "Brief History of Information Science." *Journal of ASIS* 35(3) (May 1984): 157–163.

HOFFMANN, ELIAHU. "Defining Information: An Analysis of the Information Content of Documents." *Information Processing & Management* 16 (1980): 291–304.

KOCHEN, MANFRED. "Information Science Research: The Search for the Nature of Information" *Journal of ASIS* 35(3) (May 1984): 194–199.

LANGLOIS, RICHARD N. "Systems Theory and the Meaning of Information." *Journal of ASIS* 33(6) (November 1982): 395–399.

MACHLUP, FRITZ. *Knowledge: Its Creation, Distribution, and Economic Significance.* 3 vols. Princeton, NJ: Princeton University Press, 1980–84.

MOHRHARDT, FOSTER E. "Documentation: A Synthetic Science." *Wilson Library Bulletin* 38(9) (September 1964): 743–749.

PRATT, ALLAN D. "The Information of the Image." *Libri* 27(3) (September 1977): 204–220.

SCHRADER, ALVIN M. "In Search of a Name: Information Science and Its Conceptual Antecedents." *Library & Information Science Research* 6(3) (July–September 1984): 227–271.

SHAW, DEBORA, and DAVIS, CHARLES H. "Entropy and Information: A Multi-Disciplinary Overview." *Journal of ASIS* 34(1) (January 1983): 67–74.

SHERA, JESSE H., and CLEVELAND, DONALD B. "History and Foundations of Information Science." In *Annual Review of Information Science and Technology* 12 (1977): 249–275.

WELLISCH, HANS. "From Information Science to Informatics: A Terminological Investigation." *Journal of Librarianship* 4(3) (July 1972): 157–187.

WERSIG, GERNOT, and NEVERLING, ULRICH. "The Phenomena of Interest to Information Science." *Information Scientist* 9(4) (December 1975): 127–140.

YOVITS, M. C. "Information Science: Toward the Development of a True Scientific Discipline." *American Documentation* 12 (1961): 191–197.

YUEXIAO, ZHANG. "Definitions and Sciences of Information." *Information Processing & Management* 24(4) (1988): 479–491.

2

The Transformation of Society

Although information has always existed and been of value, it has only recently come to be regarded as so important as to represent the very symbol of our society—the information age. Since World War II the capital and material bases of most western economies have been gradually replaced by new economies based on information and information-processed goods and services. The 1956 United States census showed that for the first time white-collar workers outnumbered blue-collar workers, and as early as 1967 the landmark study by Marc Porat had identified a "primary information sector" in the U.S. economy that he estimated employed roughly 25 percent of the workforce. The numbers of people employed in the information-providing sector (publishing, consulting, online services, and so on) is small (probably around 5 percent). But a wider definition of the information sector, including banking, insurance, government, and education suggests that around three-quarters of today's workforce is directly involved with the processing of information. Apart from these information workers who provide the largest part of the GNP (Gross National Product), we are all users of information at one time or another so there is no one who has not been touched by the information revolution.

Developments in the ways in which we transmit and process information have been drastically altered by the meshing of new technologies.

41

Interactions between the fields of computers, the mass media, and tele-communications have increased not only the speed of information processing but also the volume and accuracy of the information being processed. This has, in turn, increased the market for information products which have come to underlie nearly all other production and distribution services. The significance of information in an information society has been compared to the role of raw materials in an agricultural society or capital in an industrial society. This idea has led a number of writers to suggest that there may be some developmental continuum from an agricultural society relying on products grown from the land, through an industrial society relying on extractive and manufacturing industries, to a society dependent on information services and products.

In the last quarter century we have moved from an environment of relative information scarcity to one of overwhelming abundance as scientific publication rates have been doubling every five and a half years. Most of the new service industries are highly automated and information-intensive. But it is apparent that the trends which Harvard sociologist Daniel Bell tried to encapsulate when he coined the phrase "information society" cannot be explained solely in terms of increased amounts of information and the use of technology for its processing. Nor can it be explained in changes in the ways in which people spend their working lives. A transformation of society, such as Bell envisaged, would require information values to permeate the whole of society and provide the formative force for developments in a wide range of regulatory, commercial, technological, and human areas.

It is possible to identify three stages in the development of such a new economy based almost entirely on the production, storage, and retrieval of information. In the first stage changes occur in the primary information sector—the information producing and distributing industries which are responsible for building the new high tech infrastructure (i.e., information as a raw material). This sector is dominated by a small number of large international corporations (such as IBM, AT&T, or Maxwell) but also includes a group of highly innovative small firms that tend to stimulate the research front or the "cutting edge" of technological development. In such a semi-monopolistic situation it is necessary to guard against the potential for unscrupulous control and manipulation, either through the selective provision of access to information or by the presentation of a biased viewpoint.

In the second stage of development changes occur in the secondary information sector of the economy—the commercial users of information (i.e., information as a facilitator). Information is used to speed up bureaucratic operations and make the control process more efficient. Already many service organizations, such as banks, educational institutions, and health agencies, depend extensively on the new technology. Computer systems make more information available to assist management decision-making and data may be transferred almost instantaneously over electronic networks on a worldwide basis. In this situation the location of work becomes independent of natural or human resources or access to transportation for delivery. Many workers need to be retrained and some may prefer to work from their homes instead of traveling to a central workplace. This stage of development raises concerns over policies for the control of information, for the security of data, for the rights of access to information, and for personal privacy.

The third stage involves the development of a mass market for high technology information services based on home computers, television sets, and telephone or data networks (i.e., information as a consumer product). When society enters this stage, lifelong learning moves from formal educational institutions into an environment that adds a whole new innovative dimension to research and creative thinking. As these facilities become available to more people the information environment will become more flexible and information gathering will become self-service. The concerns raised by this stage of development will focus on individual social principles—the effect of pricing on the equality of access to information, the availability of appropriate education, and the need to guard against feelings of alienation among disadvantaged groups.

This breakdown into three stages suggests that most developed countries today are, in fact, only part way along the road toward becoming information societies in the fullest sense. Nevertheless, it is clear that the everyday life of all citizens worldwide is being affected by the availability of increasing amounts of information. Television via satellite transmission, electronic banking, computer databanks, online airline reservations, and computer library catalogs are information sources in everyday use in the developed world.

The escalating rate of these changes has been cumulative and diffusive, with ramifications affecting all sections of society. Technical developments have led to changes in the nature of work itself and the location of employment. They also require a more highly educated workforce skilled in the new information processing technologies. The United States Labor Department, in its report *Workforce 2000,* projects that by the turn of the century, over 30 percent of all jobs will require four or more years of college education. Furthermore, the fastest-growing areas will be those which require even higher mathematical, language, and reasoning skills.

When viewing these changes we need to strike a balance between the optimism generated by the potential of technological development and the pessimism generated by some of the ways in which it is being applied. Possible developments in the future might include (1) a meritocracy of information workers, (2) the rise of a new deprived class based on lack of access to information, (3) a global village resulting from the pervasiveness of the mass media and telecommunications, (4) drastic measures of educational reform, and (5) the problems of increasing disparities between the information-rich nations of the world and the less technically developed nations. Of particular concern is the question of who will set the social directions and policies in this complex new information environment. It seems that a partnership is needed to reflect a balanced relationship between technological developments, economic constraints, and social justice. Although the new technologies may expand lifestyle options, allowing for more shared responsibilities and rewards, these technologies could also lead to political alienation and social unrest. So far, Western democratic capitalism has (almost unwittingly) diffused the gospel of modernization worldwide and this unstructured social propaganda has appeared to be far more influential than either politics or religion. Its agents are as varied as Hollywood movies, Levi jeans, IBM computers, technology transfer, export subsidies, and protectionist prices for raw materials.

The modern world is rapidly developing into a more complex information and communication environment that will provide a qualitative shift in the thrust and purpose of present-day society. We are dealing with a wide range of converging technologies that have not only changed almost every aspect of our lives but have also highlighted the interactions between political, economic, and social effects resulting in changes such as glasnost and perestroika. This chapter, then, presents an overview of some of these developments—many of which will be discussed in more detail later.

The Information Society

BLAISE CRONIN

Introduction

An information society is one in which labour has been intellectualised; one in which the expression "to earn one's daily bread by the sweat of one's brow" sounds decidedly anachronistic. Employment in the information sector of the economy is growing apace—counterpointing stagnation and decline in the traditional manufacturing industries. Soon, terms such as information worker, knowledge engineer, ideas processor, symbol manipulator will be as common as weaver, cartwright, and miller once were. As if to underscore this trend, the US Bureau of Labor recently reclassified the white-collar work-force as "information workers." The *soi distant* information society has come of age. What began life as a sociological construct and then became a feature of futurologists' patois before degenerating into a media cliché, has finally achieved respectability through endorsement by economic and political analysts. How has this come about and what does it portend?

The Nomenclature of Novelty

From the vantage point of the mid-1980s it is possible, applying social wave-front analysis, to chart global shifts in economic emphases and occupational distributions over time. Long-wave analysis was the approach used by Alvin Toffler in his book *The third wave*. Toffler identified three rolling waves of change, corresponding to the agrarian, industrial and information revolutions. Each of these successive (though not mutually exclusive) waves coincided with periods of fracture or discontinuity in social patterns and economic activity.

The history of "economic man" is, of course, considerably more complex than Toffler's three-wave analysis might seem to imply, but the approach has the virtue of highlighting fundamental, structural changes in socio-technical activity. Mainstream economists and business analysts

Reprinted from *Aslib Proceedings* 38(4) (April 1986): 121–129.

have also tried to unearth cycles in economic activity. Perhaps the best known long-wave cycle is that proposed in the 1920s by Kondratieff, a Russian economist, who, working on a battery of indicators from 1880 onwards, detected three long waves with a mean cycle of fifty-four years. Others have seemingly found evidence to support the view that economic activity displays regularity, periods of growth and recession following one another—as day follows night. Noteworthy cycles of business activity have been proposed by Juglar, Schumpter, Kitchen and van Duijn. There is, additionally, evidence to suggest that the frequency of basic innovation occurring in developed nations reveals a pattern of highs and lows, and, interestingly, that there is an inverse relationship between economic performance and level of innovation.

At the risk of oversimplifying, the major innovation associated with the third of the waves identified by Toffler has been the development of the computer—more particularly the development of microprocessor-based technologies and products. However, it would be misleading to supplant Toffler's preferred term "the information revolution" with the expression "computer revolution." The former is a more precise characterisation of what is happening, though the developments and changes implied thereby would not have been so marked but for the advent of the computer.

Ultimately, it is not terminology which matters, but our understanding of the major changes which Toffler and many others have sought to elucidate is arguably not helped by the shifting nomenclature. The term "information society" seems to have first been used in the late 1960s. Other common rubrics include: "the information age"; "the micro-millenium"; "post-industrial society"; "the computer revolution"; "the infosphere"; "knowledge society"; "service society"; "leisure society"; "technetronic society", "electronic age." Each of these highlights a particular dimension, or cluster of dimensions, but lacks the comprehensiveness of "information society."

The Information Explosion

Before the term "information society" lodged itself in the vernacular, a number of writers, most notably Derek de Solla Price, at the end of the 1950s, had begun to look at the growth, structure, and organisation of science. Price took a particular interest in the growth of formal communications in science. He looked at the increase in the number of scientific journals worldwide from the year 1665 onwards, and noted that "the enormous increase in the population of scientific periodicals has proceeded from unity to the order of a hundred thousand with an extraordinary regularity seldom seen in any man or natural statistic."[1] He further concluded that by about 1830 the "process had reached a point of absurdity: no scientist could read all the journals or keep sufficiently conversant with all published work that might be relevant to his interest."[2]

Price also looked at the growth of scientific manpower and found a not dissimilar picture. Writing more than twenty years ago he was able to say that "some 80 to 90 percent of all scientists that have ever been, are alive now."[3] Assuming another couple of centuries of "normal" growth of science he was forced to conclude that this would mean 'dozens of scientists per man, woman, child, and dog of the world population."[4] The implications of unchecked growth of this kind are both obvious and absurd.

Price was a founding father of the discipline known as "scientometrics." He was the first to quantify the growth of science and to highlight the excesses (in terms of output) of post-war "Big Science." He also diagnosed science's "illnesses," one of these being the "superabundance of literature": a pathology which is even more problematic today than it was in Price's time. Science, for a long time, has been suffocating beneath its own output, a situation which has not really altered, despite advances in information science and despite orders of magnitude increases in the power and sophistication of information handling and communications technologies.

To some extent, the growing pains of adolescent "Big Science" were alleviated by the development of computer-based information storage and retrieval systems. In the post-war years the character of science changed dramatically. The scale and level of funding changed significantly, as research became mission-oriented, multidisciplinary, and matrix-managed in character. The utilisation of an ever-expanding corpus of research findings from an array of fields required new techniques for locating, retrieving, and integrating information.

Information Science and Knowledge Filtration

The majority of early information scientists were former researchers or career scientists who had deserted the bench in favour of a career in information management and control. During the post-war years, this élite among the information professions, pioneered many technical, procedural, and operational developments to improve the efficiency and effectiveness of the information systems and services routinely used by their bench-tied colleagues.

The earliest developments in computer-based information storage and retrieval were in such fields as aerospace research, defence, and medical research. Lockheed DIALOG, the major "supermarket" online host (offering the user access to more than 200 databases/databanks from a wide variety of disciplines) was in fact created as an in-house research support facility for Lockheed Aerospace Division, and attracted such interest from the outside world that it "went public" as an information utility. Today, Lockheed DIALOG is an independent trading company with a worldwide customer base in excess of 50,000. The natural history of Lockheed DIALOG's online service is a microcosm of developments in the rapidly expanding (and, for some, lucrative) online/electronic publishing business.

The application of computers to information storage and retrieval was one of the earliest attempts to, if not staunch the flow of scientific and research information, to improve control and access. The exponential growth in the volume of recorded information is reflected in the proliferation of online, commercially-available databases. In crude terms, there are more than 2,000 online databases publicly available today, containing, at a conservative estimate, in excess of 80 million records and growing at a rate of 8 million records per annum. The use of online databases is likewise on the increase, from unity in the early 1960s to many millions of user accesses per year. Even allowing for the short half life of much scientific literature and the irrelevance of much that is published, this still represents an almost insuperable challenge for the information science profession.

The real problem is not that of storage (though the associated costs here can be prohibitive), but that of sorting out the wheat from the remorselessly-expanding mountain of chaff. Studies carried out by bodies such as the Institute for Scientific Information (ISI) have starkly shown that the great majority of published articles are rarely, if ever, cited during their active life. In other words (and assuming that citation is an indicator of impact or relevance), the bulk of the articles, reports and monographs published by the academic/research world is of minimal import. According to Eugene Garfield, the pioneer of citation indexing and president of ISI, the company which markets the *Science Citation Index (SCI)*, "some 25 percent of the scientific papers published are never cited even once and . . . the average citation count for papers that are cited is only 1.7."[5] If highly cited papers could be identified in advance and only these included in databases and libraries, the work of scientists, librarians, information scientists, and others would be much easier. The problem, of course, is that we have no reliable means of predicting which papers are likely to be heavily or frequently cited. A Lotka or Pareto-like distribution seems to govern the scientific research community's use of recorded information. And, contrary to popular belief, the work of a small élite in science accounts for virtually all significant discoveries and advances. In an ideal world, we would concentrate on those authors whose work makes an impact and store only those papers which are likely to be cited at a significant level. In practice, this is impossible and the problem of information overload seems unlikely to find a solution in the new technology.

Technology the Amplifier

In strict chronological terms the information explosion predates the much vaunted computer revolution. It was a direct consequence of the institutionalisation and professionalisation of science, the growth in funded research, and the expansion of the tertiary education system. The computer was not the prime cause. However, in the intervening years the situation has changed in a number of important respects. The outpourings of scientists (and many other professional, administrative, and lay constituencies) has continued to grow, but now growth is positively facilitated by advances in computing and telecommunications technologies.

Information technology ("telematics" to use the French neologism) is the foot on the accelerator which is driving societies into a post-industrial mode of economic functioning. The impact of the inappropriately labelled "new technologies" on information processing and dissemination activities is pervasive and pronounced. Integrative information technologies ("computications" to use another neologism) do not simply enable traditional operations to be performed more efficiently, more cheaply, or more cost-effectively: they can change what is done, how and why. In particular they are altering classical divisions of labour, deregulating professional life, and opening up new wealth-creating opportunities for entrepreneurially-inclined technocrats. Control of the wealth-producing technologies is slipping, to some extent, from the traditional industry barons and conglomerates into the hands of (to use Toffler's expression) a "new cognitariat."

There is a complex of reasons and explanations, but it may be helpful to consider some macro-level changes in social and organisational interactions, access and control mechanisms and occupational ratios attributable to microprocessor-linked developments.

The Socio-Economic Impacts of Information Technology

Amplification

Technology allows us to store more information, access more information, send more information more quickly than was previously the case. It is an energy amplifier—whether we are talking of computer-aided design, flexible manufacturing processes, image enhancement systems or word processing. Real reductions in labour-related costs can be attributed to information technology investments in a wide range of functional activities. In commercial terms this raises output, improves quality control, allows for customised manufacturing/service provision and gives high tech companies competitive edge over their more manually based market competitors. In the information business/information industry the availability of electronic databases linked via global telecommunications networks and gateways will increasingly marginalise traditional print-based repositories of information (e.g., libraries).

Globalisation

The growth of packet-switched networks and satellite communications and the associated cost-reductions in high-volume data transmission make a mockery of national boundaries. Information distribution has become a global activity, reinforcing McLuhan's vision of a global electronic village. Markets for information services and products are increasingly defined in international rather than national, regional, or local terms. This both increases market opportunity and competitiveness. It has also created a host of new problems relating to ownership and control, and the flow of data across national borders.

Acceleration

Instant access to information (most notably financial, commodity, or futures) is having a profound influence on the way banks, stockbrokers, speculators, and investors conduct their affairs, and is likewise creating new problems for regulatory bodies. In the business and commercial sectors the wide availability of information (particularly value-added or proprietary information) is reducing the time required for decision-making and policy formulation. Decision-making is facilitated by easy access to electronic information stockpiles and, additionally, by the availability of a new generation of "psychological" software designed for executive-level personnel.

Massification

The railroad and press barons of yesteryear have been replaced by a new breed of electronic information barons. Within the electronic information market, buy-outs, mergers and vertical integration are commonplace. Many companies, including blue-chip organisations like IBM, are moving into the electronic information business. Progressively, control and ownership is being vested in a relatively small number of resource-rich organisations. This has important, long-term social implications. An oft-cited fear is that, in the absence of explicit government regulation, a two-tier information society may emerge, consisting of a privileged, informationally literate élite and a disenfranchised information poor.

Decentralisation

Electronic access, distributed processing, teleshopping and flexi-working are encouraging a trend to de-massification, local control and individualised work patterns. The predicted growth in electronic cottage industries may be slower than originally envisaged, but the signs are nonetheless there. In time, patterns of work and social interaction will change as the liberating effects of the new technologies percolate throughout society.

Mystification

It is still the case that the majority of the population is informationally and technologically illiterate. The pace of developments in leading-edge organisations is so vastly different from the rate of absorption of the new technologies at the grass roots level that the bulk of the population will be excluded from participation in the so-called "wired society." This situation may disappear in time; may be a generational problem, but this will not come about without considerable government-inspired initiatives and greater stimulation of the domestic market in terms of its use of public information services.

Transformation

Technology changes jobs. It also creates new employment opportunities. The introduction of gas lamps had an impact on the candle-making industry; the advent of the electric light bulb in turn had a negative impact on the gas-light industry. Technology clearly does eliminate jobs, but also (though not necessarily to an equivalent degree) creates new jobs and opportunities. Structural unemployment, however, would seem to be here to stay. The progressive mechanisation, automation, and robotisation of work functions will continue to result in the displacement of labour. Governments are faced with the challenge of finding alternative work, educational, or leisure opportunities for those dislocated by the introduction of the new technology. The new, flourishing high tech industries are creating a new stratum of professional wealth. This further exacerbates the gap between the unwaged and the *nouveau riche*. How can this new wealth be redistributed in such a way as not to dissipate motivation and entrepreneurism, yet avoid inequitable distribution of national income?

Intensification

One of the effects of technological change has been the creation of a heightened information awareness throughout society, but especially within the business community and government itself. The realisation that information is an important personal, organisational, and social resource, which can be capitalised, which has a market value and which requires effective management has begun to shift attention from the hardware to the content of information systems and the uses to which information can be put. The "technocentricity" of the 1970s and early 1980s is, it seems, being counterbalanced by a new-found information awareness. Information may be intangible, but the market now recognises that information can, in some respects, be treated like any other commodity. It is, however, an unusual commodity: one which does not deplete on consumption, which can have multiple life cycles, which can be easily replicated or mass produced, which violates some of the basic rules of ownership, which can have positive externalities and which, perhaps most importantly, has the features of a social good. It is this last aspect which necessitates some form of government information policy or legislative framework to ensure that the rights of access of Everyman are protected in a free-market economy.

Commercialisation

Until recently information was almost invariably treated as an overhead expense. The real costs of generating, storing, and retrieving information were rarely quantified. The introduction of computer-based information retrieval systems and the development of value-added services and networks, with their highly visible costs (subscription; volume-use;

time and telecommunications costs; royalty payments; capital equipment costs; associated staff and training costs) has led to a fundamental change in outlook and budgetary practices.

The application of cost-accountancy and overhead value analysis techniques to the management of the information resource is slowly but surely becoming the norm. On the supply side, this intensifies the pressure for high-quality, added-value, real-time, exclusive information services. Producers and vendors are increasingly conscious of the need for perceived high quality services in an extremely volatile and competitive marketplace. "Nichemanship" is the order of the day in the information industry.

A disbenefit of this situation is that public sector information utilities are less able to compete and may find themselves pushed to the periphery in the face of competition from private sector companies or cartels. Institutions, such as the public library, are ill-equipped to compete in the high tech, high cost information market, not simply because they lack cash reserves to launch new ventures, but also because they are not traditionally producers or generators of information. Traditionally, they have stored and showcased third-party products. As the penetration of computers into professional and domestic life continues, it is quite conceivable that information providers will choose, in some circumstances, to bypass the intermediary community and market their wares direct to the ultimate user/consumer. It would be in the interests of the population at large, if public sector agencies involved in the information supply business were to enter into partnership with commercial organisations in order to bring onstream new services and products to improve their revenue base. In a fully fledged information society, great care and attention will need to be given to demarcating the lines between the public and private sectors, if one is not to stifle or overpower the other, thereby worsening the quality and range or services available to the less advantaged sections of society.

The Information Workforce

Since the publication of Marc Porat's landmark study on the composition of the US labour force[6], much has been made of the statistic that more than 50 per cent of the economically active in the US are information workers. The effect of this statistic has been to galvanise awareness and interest within and outside the academic community. Porat's figures have been questioned on the basis of the classification employed, but the effect has nevertheless been to bring about a perceptible shift in public appreciation. The term "information worker" is now just about an accepted part of speech. In some respects, it is not that the information worker population suddenly and inexplicably multiplied many times overnight, but that our analysis of the core functions of many professions and occupations has highlighted the informational components.

In dissecting occupational roles, it is clear that a great deal of time is spent by a great number of people "doing something to or with information." Tangible, physical outputs are often not associated with contemporary work roles. Activity is cerebral (be it at a low or high level). Inputs and outputs are "soft." Just as it is legitimate to see many organisations as information-processing entities, so, increasingly, is it legitimate to see society as an information/knowledge processing organism.

The effective management of information flows, the creation of new ideas and knowledge, the promulgation of computer-enhanced human cognitive processing, the development of a strong information industry and improved marketing of value-added information systems, services and products will in the years ahead be the critical determinants of successful economic functioning.

The panoply of statistics, indicators and growth curves, for countries as different as the USA, Eire, Venezuela and Sweden reveal a consistent picture. The percentage of the workforce engaged in information occupations is rising; more specifically, greatest growth is to be found among information occupations in information industries. An exaggeration it may be, but information has the hallmarks of the new capital.

Notes

1. Price, Derek De Solla, *Science since Babylon* (New Haven: Yale University Press, 1961).
2. *Ibid.*
3. *Ibid.*
4. *Ibid.*
5. Garfield, Eugene, *Citation Indexing: Its Theory and Application in Science, Technology and the Humanities* (New York: Wiley, 1979).
6. Porat, Marc, *The Information Economy: Definition and Measurement* (Washington, D.C.: US Department of Commerce, 1977).

Some Questions for the Information Society

MICHAEL MARIEN

New knowledge has created the cluster of technologies described as the "communications revolution," and has resulted in the new social condition presently called Information Society. It also raises a number of serious questions. This article seeks to provide an overview and some sense of the range of future possibilities by providing an interrelated set of broad questions, as well as some brief and tentative answers. It is hoped that this initial inventory of questions will stimulate a better list, continuously updated and addressed in depth as new conditions generate new questions.

In addition to urging better questions, this article also urges better answers. Most of the questions raised here can only be roughly and tentatively answered, even when applied to present conditions. When considering the future, there are of course no firm answers, but only rough estimates, probabilities, and speculations. We should not be ashamed of such fuzziness and imperfection, nor should we turn away from questions about the future. As noted by French political philosopher Bertrand de Jouvenel (1967), it is natural and necessary to have visions of the future.

But three types of preconception should be avoided. The first, and most widespread, is the uncritical, euphoric stance that is expressed by commercial interests which invariably emphasize only positive attributes of new technology. This same preconception is frequently found in the narrow worldview of the technician (that cannot imagine any negative consequences), and in the utopian passion of wanting to help people with this or that technology.

A second type of oversimplified view is the opposite of the first: the hypercritical, pessimistic stance that perceives all modern technology as a human disaster, or focuses solely on growing corporate or government control of information systems. This pessimistic stance can bring

Reprinted from *The Information Society* 3(2) (1984): 181–197.

forth some important truths (e.g., see Schiller, 1981; Woodward, 1980), but it seldom offers guidance for positively shaping an Information Society.

The third oversimplified view acknowledges both of these positions, and concludes that there are opportunities for good and evil, centralization and decentralization, freedom and oppression, wealth and poverty. But this balanced view is often expressed superficially, merely concluding, for example, that we must choose between Computopia or a Big Brother society. The reality, however, is likely to be complex and ambiguous, requiring many critical choices over time and incorporating elements of simultaneous euphoria and gloom that fluctuate in their balance.

Because ambiguity and uncertainty are highly probable, it is important that we continually ask the right questions, supply the best possible answers, and share these answers across national boundaries. The following questions illustrate the type of concerns that ought to be addressed, and the type of answers that might follow.

Will We Live in an Information Society?

The first question is too often assumed as a given. It is now a fact that in the industrially developed nations of the world the bulk of the labor force is engaged in some manner of producing or disseminating information. Yet, ironically, these very nations are *under*developed insofar as being information societies. Moreover, this dominant characteristic of the society and its labor force, will not necessarily continue into the future.

Fashions, values, or insights may change, or society itself may change in such a way that "Information Society" is clearly inappropriate as a societal label. The term "Information Society" has only been used for about a decade, superseding the less specific label "Service Society," and the even more ambiguous "Post-Industrial Society." Information Society was apparently first used in Japan in the late 1960s,* and was the focus of the 1972 *Plan for an Information Society* (Masuda, 1981). Forerun-

*Kenichi Kohyama, "Introduction to Information Society Theory," *Chuo Koron*, Winter, 1968. Cited by Yoneji Masuda in Yoshihiro Kogane, (ed.), *Changing Value Patterns and Their Impact on Economic Structure* (Tokyo: University of Tokyo Press, 1982), p. 174. (Distributed in U.S.A. by Columbia University Press.)

ners to Information Society include the terms "Age of Cybernation" (used widely in various forms during the 1960s), "Electronic Age" and "Age of Information" (both proposed by Marshall McLuhan in 1964), "Knowledge Society" described by Peter Drucker in 1969, and the ungainly "Technetronic Society" suggested by Zbigniew Brzezinski in 1970.

But societal labels come and go, and hundreds have been proposed in recent years. Why should Information Society necessarily last to 2000, or even to 1990? A new variant might come into usage, such as "Telematic Society" (proposed by Nora and Minc and adopted by James Martin) or even the "Age of Infoglut," which focuses on the pervasive condition of information overload (Marien, 1982). Unemployment caused by the automation of office work and other informational services may be extensive and, if not compensated by an equal number of new jobs in the information sector, could result in a labor force no longer dominated by information-related occupations. The major activity of society would then be some other occupation, or even involuntary idleness—the lack of any occupation—a condition which already characterizes some Third World nations.

It should also be acknowledged that there are other concurrent technological revolutions which could have an even greater impact on society than the new information technologies. The biological revolution could retard the aging process and lengthen human life spans so that we become, essentially, a Society of Immortals (albeit a crowded one). Advances in solar cell technology could bring a "soft path" revolution in energy use. The spread of armaments in general, and nuclear weapons in particular, could lead to a cataclysmic detonation of weapons, either through accident or design. (Either instance, ironically, could be seen as a profound failure of communication.) In fact, the EMP or electromagnetic pulse of a single high altitude nuclear blast could burn out a nation's electrical systems (Broad, 1983). In the wake of such a grim scenario, Information Society would seem in retrospect to be the ultimate illusion of modern man.

Although the nuclear threat is still present, most experts think it unlikely that we will experience a nuclear Armageddon. Nevertheless, there is an increasing possibility of serious disruption by war or terrorism (O'Heffernan et al., 1983). If we survive, it is likely that we will have an information society of some sort, although we might not call it that. An intelligent approach to assessing the future would acknowledge the potential for changing images. We must consider the many ways in which we may not have an information society, as well as the many ways in which it may be realized, if we hope to shape such a society to the greatest benefit of the greatest number of people.

Will We Experience a Communications Revolution?

Similar to the first question, a "revolution" in communications is widely assumed. But this, too, should be posed as a question. The phrase "revolution" has been used promiscuously in recent years, even among those whose scientific training would seemingly inhibit rash statements about technical and social developments. Consider, for example, the proclamations in the late 1960s about the Green Revolution—new crops that would solve the world's hunger problems. Similar assertions were also made at that time about communications. In 1970, Isaac Asimov, the prolific author of science fiction and popularized science books, announced a Fourth Revolution of electronic communications (following speech, writing, and the printing press), which when truly established would bring worldwide electronic literacy, the library of mankind available to any person at any time, a personal immediacy to justify the sense of a global village, lessened differences among people, and cities spreading out and disappearing. Shortly thereafter, in 1972, the Carnegie Commission on Higher Education also proclaimed a Fourth Revolution brought on by electronics. A decade later, there are still intimations of such a revolution in higher education and the entire world. But one can hardly say that it has taken place.

Remarkable developments have occurred in the cluster of technologies comprising the "communications revolution." These include not only the notable reductions in computer size and cost, combined with dramatically enhanced capability, but also the expanded use of satellites, cable television, home information services, and the many applications of microchips. And the string of inventions has by no means run its course; in the words of Adam Osborne, an innovative designer and manufacturer of computers, these new technologies are "running wild."

It is impossible to forecast the ultimate configuration of this rapidly evolving cluster of complementary and competing technologies, or to assess their multiple impacts on human life. The best that can be done is to engage in systematic technology forecasting and assessment. Developments in technology can to some degree be anticipated, especially by procedures of collective thinking such as the Delphi method, which assembles expert forecasts, refining and revising them with two or more rounds of questioning (e.g., Pelton, 1981). The potential impacts of individual technologies can be assessed (e.g., Nilles on the personal computer, Tydeman et al. on teletext and videotext, and Wise et al. on microcomputers). The French government has sponsored a study of the impacts of computerization on society (Nora and Minc), and the Science

Council of Canada has expressed concern about planning for an information society. Wilson Dizard has described what the United States should do to understand and control the potentially dehumanizing and antidemocratic effects of this "massive technocratic drive."

Unfortunately, no effort has been made to collect all of these forecasts, assessments, speculations, and warnings, to determine what is known and not known, identify areas of agreement and disagreement, and establish the range of proven and unproven policies that might be pursued. Ironically, in the midst of an inchoate revolution in communications technology, this relatively simple act of communication between researchers and responsible policy-makers has not occurred.

A cautious approach to the "communications revolution" would be to withhold such a label for the present. In contrast to the changes wrought by other technological revolutions in the past 200 years— railroads, the telegraph, telephones, electric power, automobiles, radio, and television—the new cluster of communications technologies has yet to profoundly shape the lives of most people. Still, these new technologies are likely to be immensely influential in the next few decades, if nuclear weapons have not obliterated much or all of humanity, and if a worldwide economic collapse (which would probably retard the development of the Information Society) is avoided. The development and dissemination of new technologies will probably not be as rapid or as widespread as many enthusiasts today believe. But the "revolution" will proceed, for there is little or no public opposition, and governments at best have only been able to influence it somewhat. The nature of the revolution—how it affects the way we communicate and our lives in general—remains problematic.

Will We Communicate Better?

The question of whether we will communicate better—and even whether we are communicating better today then we did in the recent past—appears obvious and simple. But it is a complex question with deep significance, and little or no attention has been paid to it. The failure to consider this question may stem from the trained incapacity of communications experts to consider big questions, or from the twin assumptions that new technologies of communication will necessarily improve communication, and that all attempts to communicate are realized. Rather, it is important to recognize that while error-free communication is an ideal, non-communication in modern society appears to be widespread (Marien, 1982). Examples include failed communications (important messages not sent or received), flawed communications (wrong messages sent as a result of unintentional error or intentional lying or distortion), miscommunication (messages not understood or believed, or resulting in an unintended effect), and junk communication (trivial messages that are received, but are of no importance).

The new communication technologies will greatly multiply capacities for storage, transmission, and manipulation of information. But will they improve human communication, or inadvertently make it more difficult? To sketch some tentative answers to this question, it is useful to briefly examine a few prospects in eight general situations in which people communicate.

- *Work.* Major changes in the workplace are likely, with many jobs eliminated and new jobs created. Robots in factories will presumably perform many tasks that are dangerous or boring. Automation of office work will displace a large part of the female labor force (Menzies, 1981), but, presumably, will also enable better communication within and among organizations, and allow some degree of decentralization of workplaces to rural areas and individual homes (as suggested by the romantic image of the "electronic cottage," proposed by Alvin Toffler).
- *Commerce.* Relationships between buyers and sellers may be improved with the advent of teleshopping (the display of wares on the home video screen), which would give consumers better information on alternative products. Credit cards activated by thumbprints should be a further advance toward a cashless society.
- *Health.* Computerized communications already offer physicians better access to medical knowledge, and the computerization of personal medical histories (with proper safeguards, one hopes) can supply valuable patient information. Individuals will also have much better access to medical information for their own self-care, with new devices to monitor body processes, worn on the wrist or implanted in the body. Microprocessor implants, for example, could detect the first sign of malignant cells being generated. New developments in microelectronics promise at least some degree of hearing for the deaf and sight for the blind, and computers might even act as psychotherapists (Evans, 1980).
- *Entertainment.* Many people will surely have more electronic options for their pleasure, including videogames and simulated experiences, extra channels of cable television, cheap collector dishes enabling access to increasingly sophisticated communication satellites, and/or videocassette recordings. Some or all of these will be accompanied by greatly improved presentation in the home, such as wall-size television displays, improved high definition pictures, and stereo sound. It remains to be seen, however, whether this will result in an abundance of

high quality options or merely a multiplication of banality, a vibrant
free market between entertainers and audiences or cultural monopoly
and control by governments and information conglomerates.

- *Education.* It is doubtful that any information utility will be a completely free service, as utopians imagine. Nevertheless, the potential
for electronic access to the world's knowledge and for computer programs of instruction, multiple cable television channels devoted to education, instructional videotapes, and more, offer enticing possibilities
for an educational revolution, both within and outside of schools and
colleges, that would affect the learning of both children and adults. But
the general caveat for all aspects of the communication revolution—
not as much, nor as soon—is especially applicable to education. Educational institutions serve many functions other than learning, and
they are difficult to change. Extensive self-directed adult learning is
possible, but serious utilization of information abundance must compete with the many enticements of nonserious entertainment. Indeed,
the mind-deadening influence of television is a major explanation for
the steady decline in test scores among American high school students
over the past 20 years. Sober analysis of who is learning what as a result
of the new technologies will be required. It may well be found that information technology will further widen existing divisions between
the rich and poor, and create a new generation gap between the
computer-literate young and their print-literate elders.

- *Politics.* Equal caution should be applied to predictions of enhance-
ments in political communications. The new communications technologies offer many promising ways to make societies more democratic:
e.g., electronic plebiscites and opinion polls, teleconferencing with
representatives, cable television channels devoted to legislative proceedings, and better voter information on candidates. But these possibilities will not necessarily be realized, and could be more than offset
by a dossier society utilizing a centralized data bank, improved surveillance capabilities, new lie detector technology, and narrowcasting of
political messages enabling candidates to say different things to different groups of voters. Automatic language translators might facilitate
intercultural communication and lessen the tensions of world society,
but Western and particularly American culture may very well increase
its dominance over the Third World, leading to more angry but un-
heeded calls for a New World Information Order (MacBride, 1980;
Smith, 1980).

- *Intergroup Relations.* Both within and between nations, the new abundance of information, and its further fragmentation to meet the needs
and interests of myriad racial, ethnic, religious, intellectual, political,
commercial, and leisure interests is unlikely to facilitate intergroup

harmony and sharing. Mass broadcasting lacked diversity and generally aimed at the lowest common denominator, but it did at least provide a shared experience. The de-massification of the media enhances the virtue of greater variety, but the dark side of this trend is a chaos of specialized interests. And to the degree that one finds ample entertainment and education in the home, people will spend more time in their living rooms, and less time with their neighbors or in public places.

• *Families.* Relations between men and women, husbands and wives, and parents and children may be enhanced by the imminent spread of mobile telephones and the possible development of two-way wrist video devices (popularized for many years in the "Dick Tracy" comic strip). But the multitude of specialized entertainments may nevertheless serve to strain these intimate relations. Another important factor affecting communications within families will be the amount of leisure time available, which may or may not be improved by productivity increases at work and decentralization of workplaces (thus reducing commuting time or enabling more work at home). Involuntary leisure forced by unemployment often places a major strain on family relationships.

To summarize this cursory survey of basic communication nexuses, it is difficult to say whether human communication has been improving or will improve in the future. It appears likely that the new communications technologies will produce overall improvements in work, commerce, health, and entertainment. These technologies also offer considerable potential for improving education and politics, but we should be very cautious in making forecasts and assessments. Communications between groups and within families could improve, but are perhaps more likely to worsen. In all these areas considerable monitoring will be required to provide a reasonably comprehensive answer to the question of whether we are communicating better.

Will Our Lives Be Better?

Will the new information technologies lead to improvements in the quality of life? One must immediately ask, improvements for whom? There will surely be winners and losers, within and among nations. Economic abundance may result from the information revolution; Paul Hawken, for example, postulates that we are in the midst of a tumultuous transition from the mass economy of the industrial age to the "informative economy," where information increasingly replaces mass as a factor in production, resulting in better goods and services. But this does not necessarily lead to more equal sharing, or to enhancement of the *median* benefit. Will all nations benefit from an expanded economic pie (as some argue), or will rich nations increase their share of a relatively limited economic pie (as argued by others)? Will illiterate peasants of the Third World benefit in any way from the new abundance of information? Even within the richer nations, the unemployed and underemployed may not benefit, unless economies expand enough to fund a more generous welfare state.

One must also ask how "quality of life" is measured, which is no simple matter. There may be a growing maldistribution of work, with the current worldwide problem of surplus, unemployable populations aggravated by further advances in automation. The promise of many technologies, and information technology in particular, is that they will be labor-saving, allowing more people to have more leisure. But what is to be done with those who have involuntary leisure forced upon them? And among the employed, voluntary leisure in a technological age can prove illusory, as pointed out by the Swedish economist Steffan Linder (1970). Many professionals today find their workloads increasing, rather than decreasing. New ways to process information may only add to the chaos, much as superhighways have inadvertently led to more traffic congestion.

Besides economic indicators of quality of life, one must also assess political and human indicators. Will information technologies increase or decrease the threat of nuclear war? Can we maintain and expand democratic forms of governance (Wicklein, 1981)? Will nondemocratic governments be strengthened by the new technologies (as now seems likely)? Will we spend more time in pleasant and productive interaction with people, or will our interaction with machines increase to the point where computers become our most important teachers and our best friends?

Who Has to Learn What?

Every society requires a minimum standard of competence for its members. The Information Society will demand a new standard of literacy, well beyond merely knowing how to use a computer. To survive in any civilized fashion, we must learn to cope with what Alvin Toffler refers to as our "blip culture" of immense diversity, contradictory fragmented images, and shattered consensus. The new literacy will require the ability to distinguish between knowledge and mere information, and to seek out wisdom amidst abundant knowledge (Work, 1982). Lifelong learning has been extolled for many years, but the new economic literacy will require an ability to learn, and a willingness to retrain for new occupations. Finally, the new civic literacy must include an understanding of global affairs, for the new technologies of communications, combined with such problems as pollution, access to ocean resources, monetary chaos, and the arms race, are accelerating the process of globalization.

But, in contrast to these needs, what do we in fact know? Victor Ferkiss (1969) asserts that technological man does not yet exist, and neoprimitive man continues to be trapped in a technological environment, in which things—not human beings—are in control. In introducing his notion of "meaning lag," Canadian sociologist Orrin Klapp (1982) warns that meaning formation (the limited human capacity for processing information) is slow and inefficient, compared with the speed and amount of information now accumulating in society.

We must recognize that we live in an Age of Ignorance, where the learning needs of all age groups are outracing their attainments. Our nation is indeed at risk. However, the most important learning needs are not among children, but among adults—especially our political, intellectual, scientific, corporate, and religious leaders—the decision-makers who will be shaping the Information Society over the next two decades. Their decisions, for better or worse, will largely determine whether the Information Society is humane, just, productive, free, participatory, and safe, or whether it is a society characterized by greater inequalities, more centralization, accelerating dangers, and further alienation.

Such a reorientation of educational priorities is unlikely, though—at least during the next few years. We still fail to recognize our widespread ignorance and the need to focus on adult learning because the academic degrees that many of us hold convince us that we are well-educated as individuals and as societies. We wish to appear knowledgeable and sophisticated, and this image is reinforced by the sophisticated technologies at our individual and collective command—tools such as computers and automobiles that many are able to use, although comparatively few really understand them very well. The citizens of the industrialized countries live in a society that is *developed* in manufacturing era terms—but *overdeveloped* when assessed by humane and ecological measures, and *underdeveloped* as an Information Society. Our society is underdeveloped because of the gap between our present abilities and our need to learn new skills and shape new worldviews. This "ignorance gap" appears to be growing.

As with the previous questions about the Information Society, this question also points to the need for empirical research—in this instance, research into what people in all age groups in all nations know. And some global standard of Information Society literacy must emerge from this sobering assessment.

Who Will Address These Questions?

The questions raised here are presumably of central importance to all individuals and nations. They could be considered as a matter of national security, deserving the funding equivalent to that now invested in a single battleship or aircraft, let alone the modern arsenals that every nation seems compelled to have. Worldwide, an estimated $650 billion was spent on military preparations during 1982 (Palme). It is doubtful whether even 0.01 percent of this amount ($65 million) has been devoted worldwide to considering questions about the Information Society. Annual spending on this aspect of national security is probably less than 0.001 percent ($6.5 million). Whatever the figure, our societal investment priorities appear to be grossly distorted.

Several hundred books have been published in recent years, dealing with some aspect of the Information Society. Yet there is little communication among those who address some aspect of this subject. This is largely due to our obsolete industrial era colleges and universities, which encourage attention to small and "manageable" questions, technical questions that result in "hard" answers, and questions that conform to the configurations of the established disciplines and professions.

The fragmentation of perspectives increasingly found in the wider society is reflected in the subject of communications itself, which is studied by the professions of journalism, education, and information science (formerly library science), and such cross-disciplinary areas as computer science, management science, behavioral science, language and area studies, and future studies. Adding to this intellectual tumult, researchers in the social sciences often specialize in the economics, politics, and sociology of information and communications. Occasional government studies attempt to provide some overview, but little or no effort has been made by governments, foundations, research institutes, or leading universities to systematically try to overcome the rampant bureaucratization of knowledge in general and thinking about communications in particular.

People in all nations need the best and most up-to-date answers to the most important questions about the Information Society. The "national security" benefits of stimulating inquiry, refining and synthesizing the plethora of observations and policy proposals, and encouraging public understanding and dialogue would certainly be great. The cost, in contrast to these benefits, would be miniscule.

Ideally, we need schemes such as the World Brain, proposed by H. G. Wells in 1938, to bring together the scattered mental wealth of the human race and make it universally accessible. Such a reorientation of education and information has been updated by the concept of WISE, the World Information Synthesis & Encyclopedia (Kochen, 1975). Similarly, to deal intelligently with questions of the future, we need an ongoing surmising forum, as advocated by Bertrand de Jouvenel, to bring together and debate the many "futuribles" about what might happen and what ought to happen.

Will anything of this sort take place? Appeals to higher and wider vision, such as this essay, are easy to make. Creating and sustaining the institutions needed to promote such vision will be far more difficult. Even with the help of such coordinating and synthesizing organizations, evolution to the Information Society will not be an easy one, but only made a little less turbulent than it would otherwise be. Continuing the status quo of informational chaos greatly heightens the likelihood that we will not realize a viable and humane outcome. Most countries have avoided choices, with the expectation of muddling through (Nanus, 1982). In such an event, the Information Society will arrive stillborn—if it arrives at all—due to our failure to wisely generate and employ information.

References

ASIMOV, ISAAC. "The Fourth Revolution," *Saturday Review* 24, (1970):17–20.

BROAD, WILLIAM J. "The Chaos Factor," *Science 83*, 4:1, (1983):40–49. Also 1981.

BRZEZINSKI, ZBIGNIEW. *Between Two Ages: America's Role in the Technetronic Era.* New York: Viking, 1970.

Carnegie Commission on Higher Education. *The Fourth Revolution: Instructional Technology in Higher Education.* New York: McGraw-Hill, 1972.

DE JOUVENEL, BERTRAND. *The Art of Conjecture.* New York: Basic Books, 1967.

DIZARD, WILSON P. *The Coming Information Age: An Overview of Technology, Economics, and Politics.* New York: Longman, 1982.

DRUCKER, PETER F. *The Age of Discontinuity: Guidelines to Our Changing Society.* New York: Harper & Row, 1969.

EVANS, CHRISTOPHER. *The Micro Millennium.* New York: Viking, 1980: (Published in Britain in 1979 as *The Mighty Micro.*)

FERKISS, VICTOR. *Technological Man: The Myth and the Reality.* New York: George Braziller, 1969.

HAWKEN, PAUL. *The Next Economy.* New York: Holt, Rinehart and Winston, 1983.

KLAPP, ORRIN E. "Meaning Lag in the Information Society," *Journal of Communication* 32:2 (1982):56–66.

KOCHEN, MANFRED (ed.). *Information for Action: From Knowledge to Wisdom.* New York: Academic Press, 1975.

LINDER, STEFFAN BURENSTAM. *The Harried Leisure Class*. New York: Columbia University Press, 1970.

MACBRIDE, SEAN, et al. *Many Voices, One World: Communication and Society Today and Tomorrow*. New York: Unipub (1980) (Final report of the UNESCO International Commission for the Study of Communication Problems.)

MARIEN, MICHAEL, "Non-Communication and the Future," in Howard Didsbury Jr. (ed.). *Communications and the Future*. Bethesda, MD: World Future Society, 1982.

MARTIN, JAMES. *Telematic Society: A Challenge for Tomorrow*. Englewood Cliffs, New Jersey: Prentice-Hall, 1981. (First published as *The Wired Society* in 1978.)

MASUDA, YONEJI. *The Information Society as Post-Industrial Society*. Bethesda, MD: World Future Society, 1981.

MCLUHAN, MARSHALL. *Understanding Media: The Extensions of Man*. New York: McGraw-Hill, 1964.

MENZIES, HEATHER. *Women and the Chip: Case Studies of the Effects of Informatics on Employment in Canada*. Toronto: The Institute for Research on Public Policy, 1981.

NANUS, BURT. "Developing Strategies for the Information Society," *The Information Society Journal* 1:4 (1982): 339–356.

NILLES, JACK M. *Exploring the World of the Personal Computer*. Englewood Cliffs, New Jersey: Prentice-Hall, 1982.

NORA, SIMON, and ALAIN MINC. *The Computerization of Society: A Report to the President of France*. Cambridge, Massachusetts: MIT Press 1980. (First published in France in 1978.)

O'HEFFERNAN, PATRICK, AMORY B. LOVINS, and L. HUNTER LOVINS. *The First Nuclear World War*. New York: William Morrow, 1983.

OSBORNE, ADAM. *Running Wild: The Next Industrial Revolution*. (Berkeley, California: Osborne/McGraw-Hill, 1979.

PALME, OLOF. "Military Spending: The Economic and Social Consequences," *Challenge* 25:4(1982):4–21. (Chapter 4 of the report of the Independent Commission on Disarmament and Security Issues, *Common Security: A Blueprint for Survival*. [New York: Simon & Schuster, 1982.]

PELTON, JOSEPH N. "The Future of Telecommunications: A Delphi Survey," *Journal of Communication* 31:1 (1981): 177–189.

SCHILLER, HERBERT I. *Who Knows: Information in the Age of The Fortune 500*. Norwood, New Jersey: Ablex, 1981.

Science Council of Canada. *Planning Now for an Information Society: Tomorrow Is Too Late*. Hull, Quebec: Canadian Government Publishing Centre. Report #33, 1982.

SMITH, ANTHONY. *The Geopolitics of Information: How Western Culture Dominates the World*. New York: Oxford University Press, 1980.

TOFFLER, ALVIN. *The Third Wave*. New York: William Morrow, 1982.

TYDEMAN, JOHN, et al. *Teletext and Videotext in the United States: Market Potential, Technology, Public Policy Issues*. New York: McGraw-Hill, 1982.

WELLS, H. G. *World Brain* New York: Doubleday, Doran, 1938.

WICKLEIN, JOHN. *Electronic Nightmare: The New Communications and Freedom*. New York: Viking, 1981.

WISE, KENSALL D., et al. *Microcomputers: A Technology Forecast and Assessment to the Year 2000*. New York: Wiley-Interscience, 1980.

WOODWARD, KATHLEEN (ed.). *The Myths of Information: Technology and Post-Industrial Culture*. Madison, Wisconsin: Coda Press, 1980.

WORK, WILLIAM. "Communication Education for the Twenty-First Century," *Communication Quarterly* 30:4 (1982): 265–269.

Additional Readings for Chapter 2

ARTANDI, SUSAN. "Computers and the Post-Industrial Society: Symbiosis or Information Tyranny?" *Journal of ASIS* 33(5) (September 1982): 302–307.

BELL, DANIEL *The Coming of Post-Industrial Society.* New York: Basic Books, 1973.

BENIGER, JAMES. "Origins of the Information Society." *Wilson Library Bulletin* 61(3) (November 1986): 12–19.

CAWKELL, A. E. "The Real Information Society: Present Situation and Some Forecasts." *Journal of Information Science* 12(3) (1986) :87–95.

CLEVELAND, HARLAN. "The Twilight of Hierarchy: Speculations on the Global Information Society." In *Information Technologies and Social Transformation,* 55–79. Washington, D.C.: New Academy Press, 1985.

CRONIN, BLAISE. "Telematics and Retribalisation." *Aslib Proceedings* 39(3) (March 1987): 87–95.

GARFIELD, EUGENE. "2001: An Information Society?" *Journal of Information Science* 1(4) (October 1979): 209–215.

KALTWASSER, FRANZ GEORG. "Dangers for Modern Information Society in the Information Age." *IFLA Journal* 13(2) (May 1987): 111–119.

MACHLUP, FRITZ. *The Production and Distribution of Knowledge in the United States.* Princeton, NJ: Priceton University Press, 1962.

MARTIN, WILLIAM. "The Information Society—Idea or Entity?" *Aslib Proceedings* 40(11/12) (November/December 1988): 303–309.

MILES, IAN. "From the Service Economy to the Information Society—and Back Again." *Information Services & Use* 7(1) (January 1987): 13–29.

NAISBITT, JOHN. *Megatrends: Ten New Directions Transforming Our Lives.* New York: Warner Books, 1982.

NAISBITT, JOHN, and ABURDENE, PATRICIA. *Megatrends 2000: Ten New Directions for the 1990's.* New York: William Morrow, 1990.

NANUS, BURT. "Developing Strategies for the Information Society." *The Information Society* 1(4) (1982): 339–356.

PORAT, MARC U. "Defining an Information Sector in the US Economy." *Information Reports and Bibliographies* 5(5) (1976): 17–31.

SUMMIT, ROGER K. "Problems and Challenges in the Information Society—the Next Twenty Years." *Journal of Information Science* 1(4) (October 1979): 223–226.

TOFFLER, ALVIN. *The Third Wave.* New York: William Morrow, 1982.

WILLIAMS, BRUCE. "The Information Society—How Different?" *Aslib Proceedings* 37(1) (January 1985): 1–8.

3

Technology and Information Work

We have seen how the "explosion" in the production of information has permeated our cultural environment and become an essential part of all aspects of our social life. As the new technologies have encouraged the flow of and the demand for more information products and services, additional demands have been made on the communications infrastructure. It is the convergence of the new electronic technologies with the long-standing telephone network that has accelerated the pace of these changes. Although the new technologies were initially used for the automation of basic clerical operations, the emphasis, today, is on access to and delivery of information, often from remote locations. Such access implies connectivity between different systems and requires the development of a standardized set of national and international network protocols.

These information networks are handled by highspeed, digital transmission systems that are computer-controlled. The use of electronic switching equipment means that these systems can be programmed to perform new tasks without requiring physical modification. Now that direct dialing has become firmly established, it is possible to interconnect computers as well as people and to carry pictures and data as well as voices. Advancing technology has also extended the numbers of access points and increased the speed of data transmission, making long distance connections more economically viable. With digitization, a variety of media—broadcasting, film, audio and video recording, cable, print, and mail—have become transferable so that messages, sounds, and images can be selected and combined to produce customized materials in mixed formats.

The industries that produce and distribute the most information are the media—both the traditional media (publishing and television) and the newer media (such as, fax, teletext, and the computer networks). We have seen that these new media have had a profound effect on society by the alteration of public perceptions of time and space through the telescoping of geographic distance. The physical base of these new information industries is the manufacturing and sale of computers, their components, and the electronic transmission equipment that they use. The information that they process and transmit—which is the rationale for their existence—is stored in the form of computerized files known as databases.

These files of information are frequently very large since machines can be linked together to provide almost unlimited storage capacity. For example, a single file from the Education Resources Clearing House (ERIC) contains over seven hundred thousand bibliographic references for journal articles and reports. Meanwhile, the Online Computer Library Center's (OCLC) cooperative catalog file lists over twenty-two million records and is growing at the rate of two million a year. Other new information formats, such as microfiche and CD-ROM, are also capable of storing massive amounts of data. The availability of such databases provides access to large stores of information of many different types—monographs, journals, newspapers, legal cases, census data, graphics—in the form of either reference citations, full text, or as raw data. Access for researchers is no longer restricted to local library catalogs and the availability of materials is not limited geographically, since union catalogs showing the holdings of groups of libraries and computer access to remote databases have become the norm for information seeking.

The searching of these vast files of information would be endlessly time-consuming in a manual situation. Fortunately, although computers are less flexible than humans in many ways (including searching), they more than compensate for that deficiency by their speed of scanning and matching. The same search takes roughly half the time when a computer search system is used as when it is performed manually. Computers can also be very helpful for the indexing of bibliographic records at the time they are being input to the database, through their ability to identify "keywords" taken from the titles or text. Using computers to assist the information retrieval process in these ways gives greater depth to document indexing and enables greater specificity in searching due to the ability to combine search terms using logical and proximity operators.

Most database searching is now done online, with large numbers of human searchers connected directly to a central computer system via an international telecommunications network. Searching online enables the almost instantaneous transfer of information from computer to computer (or terminal) regardless of distance. The data networks involved in this process are central to almost every aspect of information transfer today. Network use ranges from routine operations such as electronic funds transfer to interlibrary lending of materials and the answering of individual search requests. Although early computer communication systems used ordinary telephone lines to provide these links, the deregulation of long-established monopolies in this country, and the "convergence" of electronics, computing, and telecommunications have spawned a plethora of competing communications networks, services, and products. Satellite communication, cable television, cellular radio, and videotex are revolutionizing the ways in which we receive our entertainment, keep up with the news, and the way that we work.

This new telecommunications infrastructure has become essential to all types of businesses. Instead of transmitting information via traditional mail, phone calls, and telex messages, American business organizations now transfer huge volumes of company data at high speeds, transmit facsimiles of blueprints, and conduct video conferences without ever leaving their desks. Most office automation systems now include an electronic mail facility. And, although most such systems are internal, some companies (especially computer companies) have extended them worldwide. The use of such networks are an area of particular interest in view of the increasing need to maximize the use of limited and expensive information-handling resources. These networks enable the distribution of work to remote sites where economic conditions are advantageous or to the homes of individual workers (telecommuters) with a reduction in corporate overheads.

Moving from business to the home environment, experiments using two-way information systems based on television sets have been taking place for a number of years—though they have so far failed to gain widespread acceptance. Other so-called "end-user" information retrieval systems have fared little better even though system vendors have targeted professional groups. It seems that the general public has not, as yet, recognized that information is valuable and is not amenable to the idea of paying for it.

Nevertheless, these new technologies have had a fundamental impact on the way in which scientific researchers use and disseminate scientific and technical information. They now use sophisticated methods to retrieve and manipulate data in machine-readable form, to produce visual images of processes previously represented by long numerical printouts, to process in days data what would have previously required months, and to communicate research results to colleagues. The most recent, and possibly the most exciting, technological development for researchers has been what is known as a "Scholar's Workstation." This is a micro-computer-based linking of a number of the new technologies into a single interface designed to provide an information processor for the individual research worker. Such a machine provides access to the user's private files as well as to publicly-available databases, both local and remote, incorporating information in various forms—text, graphics, bibliographic citations, and sound—and also the ability to select, combine, store, and rearrange data. Such a research aid was first envisaged as long ago as 1945 but is only now becoming a reality. This idea of combining different formats has become known as "hypermedia" and many libraries are now collecting more visual materials and offering access to different versions of such multipurpose workstations.

It seems likely that to achieve this level of integration in an economic fashion will require the use of knowledge engineering to incorporate some elements of artificial intelligence into the computer system. "Expert systems", as these systems are called, are intelligent computer programs that can make decisions, learn from their mistakes and experience, and even make some adaptations to the individual user. Developments of this type seem particularly important in light of the expected shortage of skilled manpower and the greater competition for trained staff as we move into the next century.

The first reading in this chapter is a seminal paper written almost fifty years ago by the famous American scientist and researcher Vannevar Bush. The author sets forth a visionary, imaginative description of an ideal information system—the Memex—for use by the individual science researcher. We will recognize the relationship of his ideas to current systems for searching online and on CD-ROM, and to microcomputer-based database management systems for the organization of downloaded data. Although few people currently maintain such personal desktop information retrieval systems, it is easy to imagine their future development and understand their attractiveness. (See more on these ideas in chapter 4.) The following reading updates us with some of the complications involved in information transfer in today's computerized environment.

As We May Think

VANNEVAR BUSH

This has not been a scientist's war; it has been a war in which all have had a part. The scientists, burying their old professional competition in the demand of a common cause, have shared greatly and learned much. It has been exhilarating to work in effective partnership. Now, for many, this appears to be approaching an end. What are the scientists to do next?

For the biologists, and particularly for the medical scientists, there can be little indecision, for their war work has hardly required them to leave the old paths. Many indeed have been able to carry on their war research in their familiar peacetime laboratories. Their objectives remain much the same.

It is the physicists who have been thrown most violently off stride, who have left academic pursuits for the making of strange destructive gadgets, who have had to devise new methods for their unanticipated assignments. They have done their part on the devices that made it possible to turn back the enemy. They have worked in combined effort with the physicists of our allies. They have felt within themselves the stir of achievement. They have been part of a great team. Now, as peace approaches, one asks where they will find objectives worthy of their best.

1

Of what lasting benefit has been man's use of science and of the new instruments which his research brought into existence? First, they have increased his control of his material environment. They have improved his food, his clothing, his shelter; they have increased his security and released him partly from the bondage of bare existence. They have given him increased knowledge of his own biological processes so that he has had a progressive freedom from disease and an increased span of life.

Reprinted from *Atlantic Monthly* 176 (July 1945): 101–108.

They are illuminating the interactions of his physiological and psychological functions, giving the promise of an improved mental health.

Science has provided the swiftest communication between individuals; it has provided a record of ideas and has enabled man to manipulate and to make extracts from that record so that knowledge evolves and endures throughout the life of a race rather than that of an individual.

There is a growing mountain of research. But there is increased evidence that we are being bogged down today as specialization extends. The investigator is staggered by the findings and conclusions of thousands of other workers—conclusions which he cannot find time to grasp, much less to remember, as they appear. Yet specialization becomes increasingly necessary for progress, and the effort to bridge between disciplines is correspondingly superficial.

Professionally our methods of transmitting and reviewing the results of research are generations old and by now are totally inadequate for their purpose. If the aggregate time spent in writing scholarly works and in reading them could be evaluated, the ratio between these amounts of time might well be startling. Those who conscientiously attempt to keep abreast of current thought, even in restricted fields, by close and continuous reading might well shy away from an examination calculated to show how much of the previous month's efforts could be produced on call. Mendel's concept of the laws of genetics was lost to the world for a generation because his publication did not reach the few who were capable of grasping and extending it; and this sort of catastrophe is undoubtedly being repeated all about us, as truly significant attainments become lost in the mass of the inconsequential.

The difficulty seems to be, not so much that we publish unduly in view of the extent and variety of present-day interests, but rather that publication has been extended far beyond our present ability to make real use of the record. The summation of human experience is being expanded at a prodigious rate, and the means we use for threading through the consequent maze to the momentarily important item is the same as was used in the days of square-rigged ships.

But there are signs of a change as new and powerful instrumentalities come into use. Photocells capable of seeing things in a physical sense, advanced photography which can record what is seen or even what is not, thermionic tubes capable of controlling potent forces under the guidance of less power than a mosquito uses to vibrate his wings, cathode ray tubes rendering visible an occurrence so brief that by comparison a microsecond is a long time, relay combinations which will carry out involved sequences of movements more reliably than any human operator and thousands of times as fast—there are plenty of mechanical aids with which to effect a transformation in scientific records.

Two centuries ago Leibnitz invented a calculating machine which embodied most of the essential features of recent keyboard devices, but it could not then come into use. The economics of the situation were against it: the labor involved in constructing it, before the days of mass production, exceeded the labor to be saved by its use, since all it could accomplish could be duplicated by sufficient use of pencil and paper. Moreover, it would have been subject to frequent breakdown, so that it could not have been depended upon; for at that time and long after, complexity and unreliability were synonymous.

Babbage, even with remarkably generous support for his time, could not produce his great arithmetical machine. His idea was sound enough, but construction and maintenance costs were then too heavy. Had a Pharaoh been given detailed and explicit designs of an automobile, and had he understood them completely, it would have taxed the resources of his kingdom to have fashioned the thousands of parts for a single car, and that car would have broken down on the first trip to Giza.

Machines with interchangeable parts can now be constructed with great economy of effort. In spite of much complexity, they perform reliably. Witness the humble typewriter, or the movie camera, or the automobile. Electrical contacts have ceased to stick when thoroughly understood. Note the automatic telephone exchange, which has hundreds of thousands of such contacts, and yet is reliable. A spider web of metal, sealed in a thin glass container, a wire heated to brilliant glow, in short, the thermionic tube of radio sets, is made by the hundred million, tossed about in packages, plugged into sockets—and it works! Its gossamer parts, the precise location and alignment involved in its construction, would have occupied a master craftsman of the guild for months; now it is built for thirty cents. The world has arrived at an age of cheap complex devices of great reliability; and something is bound to come of it.

2

A record, if it is to be useful to science, must be continuously extended, it must be stored, and above all it must be consulted. Today we make the record conventionally by writing and photography, followed by printing; but we also record on film, on wax disks, and on magnetic wires. Even if utterly new recording procedures do not appear, these present ones are certainly in the process of modification and extension.

Certainly progress in photography is not going to stop. Faster material and lenses, more automatic cameras, finer-grained sensitive compounds to allow an extension of the minicamera idea, are all imminent. Let us project this trend ahead to a logical, if not inevitable, outcome. The camera hound of the future wears on his forehead a lump a little larger than a walnut. It takes pictures 3 millimeters square, later to be projected or enlarged, which after all involves only a factor of 10 beyond present practice. The lens is of universal focus, down to any distance accommodated by the unaided eye, simply because it is of short focal length. There is a built-in photocell on the walnut such as we now have on at least one camera, which automatically adjusts exposure for a wide range of illumination. There is film in the walnut for a hundred exposures, and the spring for operating its shutter and shifting its film is wound once for all when the film clip is inserted. It produces its result in full color. It may well be stereoscopic, and record with two spaced glass eyes, for striking improvements in stereoscopic technique are just around the corner.

The cord which trips its shutter may reach down a man's sleeve within easy reach of his fingers. A quick squeeze, and the picture is taken. On a pair of ordinary glasses is a square of fine lines near the top of one lens, where it is out of the way of ordinary vision. When an object appears in that square, it is lined up for its picture. As the scientist of the future moves about the laboratory or the field, every time he looks at something worthy of the record, he trips the shutter and in it goes, without even an audible click. Is this all fantastic? The only fantastic thing about it is the idea of making as many pictures as would result from its use.

Will there be dry photography? It is already here in two forms. When Brady made his Civil War pictures, the plate had to be wet at the time of exposure. Now it has to be wet during development instead. In the future perhaps it need not be wetted at all. There have long been films impregnated with diazo dyes which form a picture without development, so that it is already there as soon as the camera has been operated. An exposure to ammonia gas destroys the unexposed dye, and the picture can then be taken out into the light and examined. The process is now slow, but someone may speed it up, and it has no grain difficulties such as now keep photographic researchers busy. Often it would be advantageous to be able to snap the camera and to look at the picture immediately.

Another process now in use is also slow, and more or less clumsy. For fifty years impregnated papers have been used which turn dark at every point where an electrical contact touches them, by reason of the chemical change thus produced in an iodine compound included in the paper. They have been used to make records, for a pointer moving across them can leave a trail behind. If the electrical potential on the pointer is varied as it moves, the line becomes light or dark in accordance with the potential.

This scheme is now used in facsimile transmission. The pointer draws a set of closely spaced lines across the paper one after another. As it moves, its potential is varied in accordance with a varying current received over wires from a distant station, where these variations are produced by a photocell which is similarly scanning a picture. At every instant the darkness of the line being drawn is made equal to the darkness of the point on the picture being observed by the photocell. Thus, when the whole picture has been covered, a replica appears at the receiving end.

A scene itself can be just as well looked over line by line by the photocell in this way as can a photograph of the scene. This whole apparatus constitutes a camera, with the added feature, which can be dispensed with if desired, of making its picture at a distance. It is slow, and the picture is poor in detail. Still, it does give another process of dry photography, in which the picture is finished as soon as it is taken.

It would be a brave man who would predict that such a process will always remain clumsy, slow, and faulty in detail. Television equipment today transmits sixteen reasonably good pictures a second, and it involves only two essential differences from the process described above. For one, the record is made by a moving beam of electrons rather than a moving pointer, for the reason that an electron beam can sweep across the picture very rapidly indeed. The other difference involves merely the use of a screen which glows momentarily when the electrons hit, rather than a chemically treated paper or film which is permanently altered. This speed is necessary in television, for motion pictures rather than stills are the object.

Use chemically treated film in place of the glowing screen, allow the apparatus to transmit one picture only rather than a succession, and a rapid camera for dry photography results. The treated film needs to be far faster in action than present examples, but it probably could be. More serious is the objection that this scheme would involve putting the film inside a vacuum chamber, for electron beams behave normally only in such a rarefied environment. This difficulty could be avoided by allowing the electron beam to play on one side of a partition, and by pressing the film against the other side, if this partition were such as to allow the electrons to go through perpendicular to its surface, and to prevent them from spreading out sideways. Such partitions, in crude form, could certainly be constructed, and they will hardly hold up the general development.

Like dry photography, microphotography still has a long way to go. The basic scheme of reducing the size of the record, and examining it by projection rather than directly, has possibilities too great to be ignored. The combination of optical projection and photographic reduction is already producing some results in microfilm for scholarly purposes, and the potentialities are highly suggestive. Today, with microfilm, reductions by a linear factor of 20 can be employed and still produce full clarity when the material is re-enlarged for examination. The limits are set by the graininess of the film, the excellence of the optical system, and the efficiency of the light sources employed. All of these are rapidly improving.

Assume a linear ratio of 100 for future use. Consider film of the same thickness as paper, although thinner film will certainly be usable. Even under these conditions there would be a total factor of 10,000 between the bulk of the ordinary record on books, and its microfilm replica. *The Encyclopœdia Britannica* could be reduced to the volume of a matchbox. A library of a million volumes could be compressed into one end of a desk. If the human race has produced since the invention of movable type a total record, in the form of magazines, newspapers, books, tracts, advertising blurbs, correspondence, having a volume corresponding to a billion books, the whole affair, assembled and compressed, could be lugged off in a moving van. Mere compression, of course, is not enough; one needs not only to make and store a record but also be able to consult it, and this aspect of the matter comes later. Even the modern great library is not generally consulted; it is nibbled at by a few.

Compression is important, however, when it comes to costs. The material for the microfilm *Britannica* would cost a nickel, and it could be mailed anywhere for a cent. What would it cost to print a million copies? To print a sheet of newspaper, in a large edition, costs a small fraction of a cent. The entire material of the *Britannica* in reduced microfilm form would go on a sheet eight and one-half by eleven inches. Once it is available, with the photographic reproduction methods of the future, duplicates in large quantities could probably be turned out for a cent apiece beyond the cost of materials. The preparation of the original copy? That introduces the next aspect of the subject.

3

To make the record, we now push a pencil or tap a typewriter. Then comes the process of digestion and correction, followed by an intricate process of typesetting, printing, and distribution. To consider the first stage of the procedure, will the author of the future cease writing by hand or typewriter and talk directly to the record? He does so indirectly, by talking to a stenographer or a wax cylinder; but the elements are all present if he wishes to have his talk directly produce a typed record. All he needs to do is to take advantage of existing mechanisms and to alter his language.

At a recent World Fair a machine called a Voder was shown. A girl stroked its keys and it emitted recognizable speech. No human vocal chords entered into the procedure at any point; the keys simply combined some electrically produced vibrations and passed these on to a loud-speaker. In the Bell Laboratories there is the converse of this machine called a Vocoder. The loud-speaker is replaced by a microphone, which picks up sound. Speak to it, and the corresponding keys move. This may be one element of the postulated system.

The other element is found in the stenotype, that somewhat disconcerting device encountered usually at public meetings. A girl strokes its keys languidly and looks about the room and sometimes at the speaker with a disquieting gaze. From it emerges a typed strip which records in a phonetically simplified language a record of what the speaker is supposed to have said. Later this strip is retyped into ordinary language, for in its nascent form it is intelligible only to the initiated. Combine these two elements, let the Vocoder run the stenotype and the result is a machine which types when talked to.

Our present languages are not especially adapted to this sort of mechanization, it is true. It is strange that the inventors of universal languages have not seized upon the idea of producing one which better fitted the technique for transmitting and recording speech. Mechanization may yet force the issue, especially in the scientific field; whereupon scientific jargon would become still less intelligible to the layman.

One can now picture a future investigator in his laboratory. His hands are free, and he is not anchored. As he moves about and observes, he photographs and comments. Time is automatically recorded to tie the two records together. If he goes into the field, he may be connected by radio to his recorder. As he ponders over his notes in the evening, he again talks his comments into the record. His typed record, as well as his photographs, may both be in miniature, so that he projects them for examination.

Much needs to occur, however, between the collection of data and observations, the extraction of parallel material from the existing record, and the final insertion of new material into the general body of the common record. For mature thought there is no mechanical substitute. But creative thought and essentially repetitive thought are very different things. For the latter there are, and may be, powerful mechanical aids.

Adding a column of figures is a repetitive thought process, and it was long ago properly relegated to the machine. True, the machine is sometimes controlled by a keyboard, and thought of a sort enters in reading the figures and poking the corresponding keys, but even this is avoidable. Machines have been made which will read typed figures by photocells and then depress the corresponding keys; these are combinations of photocells for scanning the type, electric circuits for sorting the consequent variations, and relay circuits for interpreting the result into the action of solenoids to pull the keys down.

All this complication is needed because of the clumsy way in which we have learned to write figures. If we recorded them positionally, simply by the configuration of a set of dots on a card, the automatic reading mechanism would become comparatively simple. In fact, if the dots are holes, we have the punched-card machine long ago produced by Hollorith for the purposes of the census, and now used throughout business. Some types of complex businesses could hardly operate without these machines.

Adding is only one operation. To perform arithmetical computation involves also subtraction, multiplication, and division, and in addition some method for temporary storage of results, removal from storage for further manipulation, and recording of final results by printing. Machines for these purposes are now of two types: keyboard machines for accounting and the like, manually controlled for the insertion of data, and usually automatically controlled as far as the sequence of operations is concerned; and punched-card machines in which separate operations are usually delegated to a series of machines, and the cards then transferred bodily from one to another. Both forms are very useful; but as far as complex computations are concerned, both are still in embryo.

Rapid electrical counting appeared soon after the physicists found it desirable to count cosmic rays. For their own purposes the physicists promptly constructed thermionic-tube equipment capable of counting electrical impulses at the rate of 100,000 a second. The advanced arithmetical machines of the future will be electrical in nature, and they will perform at 100 times present speeds, or more.

Moreover, they will be far more versatile than present commercial machines, so that they may readily be adapted for a wide variety of operations. They will be controlled by a control card or film, they will select their own data and manipulate it in accordance with the instructions thus inserted, they will perform complex arithmetical computations at exceedingly high speeds, and they will record results in such form as to be readily available for distribution or for later further manipulation. Such machines will have enormous appetites. One of them will take instructions and data from a whole roomful of girls armed with simple keyboard punches, and will deliver sheets of computed results every few minutes. There will always be plenty of things to compute in the detailed affairs of millions of people doing complicated things.

4

The repetitive processes of thought are not confined, however, to matters of arithmetic and statistics. In fact, every time one combines and records facts in accordance with established logical processes, the creative aspect of thinking is concerned only with the selection of the data and the process to be employed, and the manipulation thereafter is repetitive in nature and hence a fit matter to be relegated to the machines. Not so much has been done along these lines, beyond the bounds of arithmetic, as might be done, primarily because of the economics of the situation. The needs of business, and the extensive market obviously waiting, assured the advent of mass-produced arithmetical machines just as soon as production methods were sufficiently advanced.

With machines for advanced analysis no such situation existed; for there was and is no extensive market; the users of advanced methods of manipulating data are a very small part of the population. There are, however, machines for solving differential equations—and functional and integral equations, for that matter. There are many special machines, such as the harmonic synthesizer which predicts the tides. There will be many more, appearing certainly first in the hands of the scientist and in small numbers.

If scientific reasoning were limited to the logical processes of arithmetic, we should not get far in our understanding of the physical world. One might as well attempt to grasp the game of poker entirely by the use of the mathematics of probability. The abacus, with its beads strung on parallel wires, led the Arabs to positional numeration and the concept of zero many centuries before the rest of the world; and it was a useful tool—so useful that it still exists.

It is a far cry from the abacus to the modern keyboard accounting machine. It will be an equal step to the arithmetical machine of the future. But even this new machine will not take the scientist where he needs to go. Relief must be secured from laborious detailed manipulation of higher mathematics as well, if the users of it are to free their brains for something more than repetitive detailed transformations in accordance with established rules. A mathematician is not a man who can readily manipulate figures; often he cannot. He is not even a man who can readily perform the transformations of equations by the use of calculus. He is primarily an individual who is skilled in the use of symbolic logic on a high plane, and especially he is a man of intuitive judgment in the choice of the manipulative processes he employs.

All else he should be able to turn over to his mechanism, just as confidently as he turns over the propelling of his car to the intricate mechanism under the hood. Only then will mathematics be practically effective in bringing the growing knowledge of atomistics to the useful solution of the advanced problems of chemistry, metallurgy, and biology. For this reason there will come more machines to handle advanced mathematics for the scientist. Some of them will be sufficiently bizarre to suit the most fastidious connoisseur of the present artifacts of civilization.

5

The scientist, however, is not the only person who manipulates data and examines the world about him by the use of logical processes, although he sometimes preserves this appearance by adopting into the fold anyone who becomes logical, much in the manner in which a British labor leader is elevated to knighthood. Whenever logical processes of thought are employed—that is, whenever thought for a time runs along an accepted groove—there is an opportunity for the machine. Formal logic used to be a keen instrument in the hands of the teacher in his trying of students' souls. It is readily possible to construct a machine which will manipulate premises in accordance with formal logic, simply by the clever use of relay circuits. Put a set of premises into such a device and turn the crank, and it will readily pass out conclusion after conclusion, all in accordance with logical law, and with no more slips than would be expected of a keyboard adding machine.

Logic can become enormously difficult, and it would undoubtedly be well to produce more assurance in its use. The machines for higher analysis have usually been equation solvers. Ideas are beginning to appear for equation transformers, which will rearrange the relationship expressed by an equation in accordance with strict and rather advanced logic. Progress is inhibited by the exceedingly crude way in which mathematicians express their relationships. They employ a symbolism which grew like Topsy and has little consistency; a strange fact in that most logical field.

A new symbolism, probably positional, must apparently precede the reduction of mathematical transformations to machine processes. Then, on beyond the strict logic of the mathematician, lies the application of logic in everyday affairs. We may some day click off arguments on a machine with the same assurance that we now enter sales on a cash register. But the machine of logic will not look like a cash register, even of the streamlined model.

So much for the manipulation of ideas and their insertion into the record. Thus far we seem to be worse off than before—for we can enormously extend the record; yet even in its present bulk we can hardly consult it. This is a much larger matter than merely the extraction of data for the purposes of scientific research; it involves the entire process by which man profits by his inheritance of acquired knowledge. The prime action of use is selection, and here we are halting indeed. There may be millions of fine thoughts, and the account of the experience on which they are based, all encased within stone walls of acceptable architectural form; but if the scholar can get at only one a week by diligent search, his syntheses are not likely to keep up with the current scene.

Selection, in this broad sense, is a stone adze in the hands of a cabinet-maker. Yet, in a narrow sense and in other areas, something has already been done mechanically on selection. The personnel officer of a factory drops a stack of a few thousand employee cards into a selecting machine, sets a code in accordance with an established convention, and produces in a short time a list of all employees who live in Trenton and know Spanish. Even such devices are much too slow when it comes, for example, to matching a set of fingerprints with one of five million on file. Selection devices of this sort will soon be speeded up from their present rate of reviewing data at a few hundred a minute. By the use of photocells and microfilm they will survey items at the rate of a thousand a second, and will print out duplicates of those selected.

This process, however, is simple selection: it proceeds by examining in turn every one of a large set of items, and by picking out those which have certain specified characteristics. There is another form of selection best illustrated by the automatic telephone exchange. You dial a number and the machine selects and connects just one of a million possible stations. It does not run over them all. It pays attention only to a class given by a first digit, then only to a subclass of this given by the second digit, and so on; and thus proceeds rapidly and almost unerringly to the selected station. It requires a few seconds to make the selection, although the process could be speeded up if increased speed were economically warranted. If necessary, it could be made extremely fast by substituting thermionic-tube switching for mechanical switching, so that the full selection could be made in one one-hundredth of a second. No one would wish to spend the money necessary to make this change in the telephone system, but the general idea is applicable elsewhere.

Take the prosaic problem of the great department store. Every time a charge sale is made, there are a number of things to be done. The inventory needs to be revised, the salesman needs to be given credit for the sale, the general accounts need an entry, and, most important, the customer needs to be charged. A central records device has been developed in which much of this work is done conveniently. The salesman places on a stand the customer's identification card, his own card, and the card taken from the article sold—all punched cards. When he pulls a lever, contacts are made through the holes, machinery at a central point makes the necessary computations and entries, and the proper receipt is printed for the salesman to pass to the customer.

But there may be ten thousand charge customers doing business with the store, and before the full operation can be completed someone has to select the right card and insert it at the central office. Now rapid selection can slide just the proper card into position in an instant or two, and return it afterward. Another difficulty occurs, however. Someone must read a total on the card, so that the machine can add its computed item to it. Conceivably the cards might be of the dry photography type I have described. Existing totals could then be read by photocell, and the new total entered by an electron beam.

The cards may be in miniature, so that they occupy little space. They must move quickly. They need not be transferred far, but merely into position so that the photocell and recorder can operate on them. Positional dots can enter the data. At the end of the month a machine can readily be made to read these and to print an ordinary bill. With tube selection, in which no mechanical parts are involved in the switches, little time need be occupied in bringing the correct card into use—a second should suffice for the entire operation. The whole record on the card may be made by magnetic dots on a steel sheet if desired, instead of dots to be observed optically, following the scheme by which Poulsen long ago put speech on a magnetic wire. This method has the advantage of simplicity and ease of erasure. By using photography, however, one can arrange to project the record in enlarged form, and at a distance by using the process common in television equipment.

One can consider rapid selection of this form, and distant projection for other purposes. To be able to key one sheet of a million before an operator in a second or two, with the possibility of then adding notes thereto, is suggestive in many ways. It might even be of use in libraries, but that is another story. At any rate, there are now some interesting combinations possible. One might, for example, speak to a microphone, in the manner described in connection with the speech-controlled typewriter, and thus make his selections. It would certainly beat the usual file clerk.

6

The real heart of the matter of selection, however, goes deeper than a lag in the adoption of mechanisms by libraries, or a lack of development of devices for their use. Our ineptitude in getting at the record is largely caused by the artificiality of systems of indexing. When data of any sort are placed in storage, they are filed alphabetically or numerically, and information is found (when it is) by tracing it down from subclass to subclass. It can be in only one place, unless duplicates are used; one has to have rules as to which path will locate it, and the rules are cumbersome.

Having found one item, moreover, one has to emerge from the system and re-enter on a new path.

The human mind does not work that way. It operates by association. With one item in its grasp, it snaps instantly to the next that is suggested by the association of thoughts, in accordance with some intricate web of trails carried by the cells of the brain. It has other characteristics, of course; trails that are not frequently followed are prone to fade, items are not fully permanent, memory is transitory. Yet the speed of action, the intricacy of trails, the detail of mental pictures, is awe-inspiring beyond all else in nature.

Man cannot hope fully to duplicate this mental process artificially, but he certainly ought to be able to learn from it. In minor ways he may even improve, for his records have relative permanency. The first idea, however, to be drawn from the analogy concerns selection. Selection by association, rather than by indexing, may yet be mechanized. One cannot hope thus to equal the speed and flexibility with which the mind follows an associative trail, but it should be possible to beat the mind decisively in regard to the permanence and clarity of the items resurrected from storage.

Consider a future device for individual use, which is a sort of mechanized private file and library. It needs a name, and, to coin one at random, "memex" will do. A memex is a device in which an individual stores all his books, records, and communications, and which is mechanized so that it may be consulted with exceeding speed and flexibility. It is an enlarged intimate supplement to his memory.

It consists of a desk, and while it can presumably be operated from a distance, it is primarily the piece of furniture at which he works. On the top are slanting translucent screens, on which material can be projected for convenient reading. There is a keyboard, and sets of buttons and levers. Otherwise it looks like an ordinary desk.

In one end is the stored material. The matter of bulk is well taken care of by improved microfilm. Only a small part of the interior of the memex is devoted to storage, the rest to mechanism. Yet if the user inserted 5000 pages of material a day it would take him hundreds of years to fill the repository, so he can be profligate and enter material freely.

Most of the memex contents are purchased on microfilm ready for insertion. Books of all sorts, pictures, current periodicals, newspapers, are thus obtained and dropped into place. Business correspondence takes the same path. And there is provision for direct entry. On the top of the memex is a transparent platen. On this are placed longhand notes, photographs, memoranda, all sorts of things. When one is in place, the depression of a lever causes it to be photographed onto the next blank space in a section of the memex film, dry photography being employed.

There is, of course, provision for consultation of the record by the usual scheme of indexing. If the user wishes to consult a certain book, he taps its code on the keyboard, and the title page of the book promptly appears before him, projected onto one of his viewing positions. Frequently-used codes are mnemonic, so that he seldom consults his code book; but when he does, a single tap of a key projects it for his use. Moreover, he has supplemental levers. On deflecting one of these levers to the right he runs through the book before him, each page in turn being projected at a speed which just allows a recognizing glance at each. If he deflects it further to the right, he steps through the book 10 pages at a time; still further at 100 pages at a time. Deflection to the left gives him the same control backwards.

A special button transfers him immediately to the first page of the index. Any given book of his library can thus be called up and consulted with far greater facility than if it were taken from a shelf. As he has several projection positions, he can leave one item in position while he calls up another. He can add marginal notes and comments, taking advantage of one possible type of dry photography, and it could even be arranged so that he can do this by a stylus scheme, such as is now employed in the telautograph seen in railroad waiting rooms, just as though he had the physical page before him.

7

All this is conventional, except for the projection forward of present-day mechanisms and gadgetry. It affords an immediate step, however, to associative indexing, the basic idea of which is a provision whereby any item may be caused at will to select immediately and automatically another. This is the essential feature of the memex. The process of tying two items together is the important thing.

When the user is building a trail, he names it, inserts the name in his code book, and taps it out on his keyboard. Before him are the two items to be joined, projected onto adjacent viewing positions. At the bottom of each there are a number of blank code spaces and a pointer is set to indicate one of these on each item. The user taps a single key, and the items are permanently joined. In each code space appears the code word. Out of view, but also in the code space, is inserted a set of dots for photocell viewing; and on each item these dots by their positions designate the index number of the other item.

Thereafter, at any time, when one of these items is in view, the other can be instantly recalled merely by tapping a button below the corresponding code space. Moreover, when numerous items have been thus joined together to form a trail, they can be reviewed in turn, rapidly or slowly, by deflecting a lever like that used for turning the pages of a book. It is exactly as though the physical items had been gathered together from widely separated sources and bound together to form a new book. It is more than this, for any item can be joined into numerous trails.

The owner of the memex, let us say, is interested in the origin and properties of the bow and arrow. Specifically he is studying why the short Turkish bow was apparently superior to the English long bow in the skirmishes of the Crusades. He has dozens of possibly pertinent books and articles in his memex. First he runs through an encyclopedia, finds an interesting but sketchy article, leaves it projected. Next, in a history, he finds another pertinent item, and ties the two together. Thus he goes, building a trail of many items. Occasionally he inserts a comment of his own, either linking it into the main trail or joining it by a side trail to a particular item. When it becomes evident that the elastic properties of available materials had a great deal to do with the bow, he branches off on a side trail which takes him through textbooks on elasticity and tables of physical constants. He inserts a page of longhand analysis of his own. Thus he builds a trail of his interest through the maze of materials available to him.

And his trails do not fade. Several years later, his talk with a friend turns to the queer ways in which a people resist innovations, even of vital interest. He has an example, in the fact that the outranged Europeans still failed to adopt the Turkish bow. In fact he has a trail on it. A touch brings up the code book. Tapping a few keys projects the head of the trail. A lever runs through it at will, stopping at interesting items, going off on side excursions. It is an interesting trail, pertinent to the discussion. So he sets a reproducer in action, photographs the whole trail out, and passes it to his friend for insertion in his own memex, there to be linked into the more general trail.

8

Wholly new forms of encyclopedias will appear, ready-made with a mesh of associative trails running through them, ready to be dropped into the memex and there amplified. The lawyer has at his touch the associated opinions and decisions of his whole experience, and of the experience of friends and authorities. The patent attorney has on call the millions of issued patents, with familiar trails to every point of his client's interest. The physician, puzzled by a patient's reactions, strikes the trail established in studying an earlier similar case, and runs rapidly through analogous case histories, with side references to the classics for the pertinent anatomy and histology. The chemist, struggling with the synthesis of an organic compound, has all the chemical literature before him in his laboratory, with trails following the analogies of compounds, and side trails to their physical and chemical behavior.

The historian, with a vast chronological account of a people, parallels it with a skip trail which stops only on the salient items, and can follow at any time contemporary trails which lead him all over civilization at a particular epoch. There is a new profession of trail blazers, those who find delight in the task of establishing useful trails through the enormous mass of the common record. The inheritance from the master becomes, not only his additions to the world's record, but for his disciples the entire scaffolding by which they were erected.

Thus science may implement the ways in which man produces, stores, and consults the record of the race. It might be striking to outline the instrumentalities of the future more spectacularly, rather than to stick closely to methods and elements now known and undergoing rapid development, as has been done here. Technical difficulties of all sorts have been ignored, certainly, but also ignored are means as yet unknown which may come any day to accelerate technical progress as violently as did the advent of the thermionic tube. In order that the picture may not be too commonplace, by reason of sticking to present-day patterns, it may be well to mention one such possibility, not to prophesy but merely to suggest, for prophecy based on extension of the known has substance, while prophecy founded on the unknown is only a doubly involved guess.

All our steps in creating or absorbing material of the record proceed through one of the senses—the tactile when we touch keys, the oral when we speak or listen, the visual when we read. Is it not possible that some day the path may be established more directly?

We know that when the eye sees, all the consequent information is transmitted to the brain by means of electrical vibrations in the channel of the optic nerve. This is an exact analogy with the electrical vibrations which occur in the cable of a television set: they convey the picture from the photocells which see it to the radio transmitter from which it is broadcast. We know further that if we can approach that cable with the proper instruments, we do not need to touch it; we can pick up those vibrations by electrical induction and thus discover and reproduce the scene which is being transmitted, just as a telephone wire may be tapped for its message.

The impulses which flow in the arm nerves of a typist convey to her fingers the translated information which reaches her eye or ear, in order that the fingers may be caused to strike the proper keys. Might not these currents be intercepted, either in the original form in which information is conveyed to the brain, or in the marvelously metamorphosed form in which they then proceed to the hand?

By bone conduction we already introduce sounds into the nerve channels of the deaf in order that they may hear. Is it not possible that we may learn to introduce them without the present cumbersomeness of first transforming electrical vibrations to mechanical ones, which the human mechanism promptly transforms back to the electrical form? With a couple of electrodes on the skull the encephalograph now produces pen-and-ink traces which bear some relation to the electrical phenomena going on in the brain itself. True, the record is unintelligible, except as it points out certain gross misfunctioning of the cerebral mechanism; but who would now place bounds on where such a thing may lead?

In the outside world, all forms of intelligence, whether of sound or sight, have been reduced to the form of varying currents in an electric circuit in order that they may be transmitted. Inside the human frame exactly the same sort of process occurs. Must we always transform to mechanical movements in order to proceed from one electrical phenomenon to another? It is a suggestive thought, but it hardly warrants prediction without losing touch with reality and immediateness.

Presumably man's spirit should be elevated if he can better review his shady past and analyze more completely and objectively his present problems. He has built a civilization so complex that he needs to mechanize his records more fully if he is to push his experiment to its logical conclusion and not merely become bogged down part way there by overtaxing his limited memory. His excursions may be more enjoyable if he can reacquire the privilege of forgetting the manifold things he does not need to have immediately at hand, with some assurance that he can find them again if they prove important.

The applications of science have built man a well-supplied house, and are teaching him to live healthily therein. They have enabled him to throw masses of people against one another with cruel weapons. They may yet allow him truly to encompass the great record and to grow in the wisdom of race experience. He may perish in conflict before he learns to wield that record for his true good. Yet, in the application of science to the needs and desires of man, it would seem to be a singularly unfortunate stage at which to terminate the process, or to lose hope as to the outcome.

Networks: The Telecommunications Infrastructure and Impacts of Change

LARRY L. LEARN

Networks have come to play an ever increasing and vital role in libraries and the organizations and institutions they serve, and this trend is continuing at an accelerated pace. Beyond the scope of the local institution, statewide, multistate, nationwide, and even international networks have evolved or are evolving to play an even more important role in the services libraries perform, and the way libraries provide these services [Gorman, 1987]. Yet, many have found it difficult to keep abreast of developments in this area, and understandably so. The technology is complex and changing at a dizzying pace, and the telecommunications industry structure is undergoing revolutionary change in the wake of the breakup of the Bell System and the substantial and ongoing restructuring of the related legal and regulatory environment. Further, the networks themselves have fostered new relationships and opportunities as libraries expand their institutional and geographic scope [Van Houweling, 1987].

Much of the current library and information systems literature focuses on application of networks, yet it is equally important for the practicing professional to have a current working knowledge of the telecommunications infrastructure upon which these applications are built. This is particularly true since the telecommunications infrastructure is extremely dynamic, and the effectiveness of many network applications will be determined by the form this infrastructure takes in the future. To be optimum, future applications must be targeted toward the environment in which they will exist and operate. At a minimum, they must be able to compensate for change in the environment, especially because of the

Reprinted from *Library Hi Tech* 6(1) (Spring 1988): 13–31.

magnitude of investment required by many of these endeavors. This article focuses on the telecommunications environment—the infrastructure that forms the skeleton of modern networks—and discusses the outlook for future developments. It is intended to provide a foundation for reviewing and assessing current developments and directions within the field of library and information system networking.

Spheres of Influence

The numerous influences currently impacting the area of telecommunications can be generally categorized into four major spheres: (1) Technology; (2) Economics; (3) Politics; and (4) Government (i.e., legislation, adjudication, and regulation).

Technology

The sphere of technology, as this impacts telecommunications, is probably the simplest to understand and extrapolate to likely future developments. The general areas most directly impacted by technology are transmission and switching [Sherman, 1986]. In the area of transmission, the advent of fiber-optic systems has revolutionized thinking and presented several major capabilities with regard to transmission capacity, media size, and costs. Optical transmission is most effectively accomplished using all-digital techniques, in contradistinction to the inherently analog techniques most common to other transmission technologies. Significant implications arise, therefore, for integration of heretofore distinct classes of transmissions (e.g., voice, data, and video), with improved utilization of the facilities and greater economies of scale [Learn, 1984].

Another important inherent characteristic of optical-fiber systems is their potentially unlimited capacity in practical terms—estimated to be several thousand times greater than the fastest systems currently in operation (including currently installed fiber-optic systems) [Morgan, 1986]. The enormous inherent capacity, combined with the significantly reduced physical size and cost, and the inherent imperviousness to interference, corrosion, fire, and unauthorized interception of transmissions, makes the technology extremely attractive [Rutkowski, 1986]. Optical fiber currently runs between $0.50 and $1.50 per fiber meter, and is expected to drop to a few cents per meter within three to four years [Fredricsson, 1986]. As a result, the major costs of implementation have become those of securing rights-of-way and physical installation of the media, as compared to the cost of the media itself. This is not the case with other media—particularly when viewed in terms of cost per unit of capacity [Tibrewala, 1985]. For these reasons, tremendous inherent system capacity is currently being installed, where in the past implementation was geared to short-and medium-term capacity needs.

Satellite transmission technology has presented both opportunities and inherent disadvantages [Solomon, 1987]. Advantages include distance independence and relatively high capacity, particularly when compared with more common terrestrial transmission technologies such as local twisted-pair wire. The disadvantages include its inherent analog nature; signal delays due to the distances involved and the finite propagation velocity of electromagnetic radiation; cost, particularly compared with terrestrial fiber; and the inherent vulnerability of the satellite media to interception and interference [Marcus, 1987].

Satellite capacity must be recognized as an "expendable resource," having a finite life span typically determined by onboard fuel supply [Learn, 1987]. Satellite technology represents, however, an attractive and viable alternative in the intermediate time frame—until other terrestrial technologies such as fiber optics achieve a more dominant position; and in the longer term, as a complementary technology in certain circumstances such as remote locations where: (1) newer terrestrial technologies may not be expected to penetrate for the foreseeable future, (2) local access costs to other media are unusually high, or (3) access facilities provide unacceptable technical limitations. Very small aperture terminal (VSAT) satellite earthstations (i.e., typically less than two meters in diameter) can be expected to provide an attractive alternative in such regions, when data rates are not excessive [Cacciamani, 1986; Griebenow, 1987].

Switching technology has evolved from a primarily electromechanical physical connection, through computer-controlled electronic physical connection, to a totally digital computer-based connection technology [Rey, 1984, pp. 397–438]. This evolution has reduced both switch size and cost, and dramatically improved capability and capacity; and it is expected to continue to do so for the foreseeable future [Rutkowski, 1987]. In addition, the inherent digital nature of the modern switch presents a synergy with the digital nature of optical transmission media. This synergy is a driving force behind the emerging integrated services digital network (ISDN), which is discussed later.

Economics

Within the sphere of economics, technology has driven the cost of both long-haul transmission and switching down dramatically. Recent developments in the area of satellite "space segment" (i.e., satellite links between earthstations) have somewhat tarnished the outlook for continued reduction in space-segment costs. The advent of fiber-optic technology has resulted in some reluctance toward investment in satellite technology. This reluctance combined with the expendable nature of the asset due to limited onboard fuel supplies, the comparatively high risks associated with launch and operation of satellites, and related insurance rates currently exceeding 30 percent of launch value, will result in the erosion of dominance of satellite space segment compared with terrestrial transmission as the most available, economic, and attractive transmission media [*Telecommunications Reports*, Oct. 28, 1985]. Although primarily an economic issue, this shift is predominantly driven by technical factors.

Economics, which will play the predominant role in shaping the future of the telecommunications environment, is inextricably interwoven with technology and regulation. The impact of regulatory change will be a major force acting on the economic elements fundamental to the industry. It is important to note that these economic elements result from the interplay of several closely related but quite separate facets of regulation and regulatory change. Worthy of note is the shift from a situation where certain telecommunications services have historically been offered by the carriers at rates below the cost to provide these services, to a more cost-based structure. Instrumental in this process has been the separation of long-distance carriers from local telephone service providers as a result of Divestiture [United States v. Western Electric, et al., 82-0192 (D.D.C. 1982)]. This cost difference has historically been supported by cross-subsidization from other more lucrative services. An example is local service being subsidized by long-distance services.

Allocation of costs by various regulatory agencies has also resulted in anomalies in price structures. Noteworthy among these is the regulatory allocation of equipment costs between usage-sensitive elements and fixed-cost elements; and further regulatory allocation of these costs between local and long-distance services, and by state and federal jurisdiction (i.e., "separations procedures"). The practice of "averaging" certain costs on a national or regional basis has also had a significant impact on rates.

Still another important economic aspect being significantly impacted by regulatory change is the depreciation of a large equipment base. Historically, both state and federal regulation dictated relatively long depreciation schedules for this equipment—based for the most part on physical life expectancy. This has had a two-fold result: (1) depreciation charges taken into the "rate base" and used by the regulators to determine subscriber rates were smaller than would otherwise result from more common depreciation methods and schedules, and hence resulted in lower subscriber telephone rates; and (2) since the physical rather than "useful" life of the equipment was the basis for depreciation, much of the equipment tended to become obsolete and non-competitive in comparison with that of the evolving competitive providers. With the advent of more competition in the industry, most regulators have recognized the need to move toward less conservative depreciation mechanisms and schedules, but, unfortunately, the various federal and state regulatory jurisdictions have not moved in a common direction with regard to either methodology or schedule. The reduction of this accumulated "depreciation cost surplus" (i.e., the excess of book value over actual value), which has been taken into the subscriber rate base, has nonetheless resulted in higher rates. In addition, accelerated depreciation schedules and ongoing modernization of the network will continue to affect rates in the future. This is true not only because of additional new capital investment due to modernization, but also because replacement of under-depreciated current equipment will result in additional write-offs.

Also not to be ignored is a recognition by federal legislators, particularly those legislators dealing with trade policies and commerce, that timely access to technical information is necessary if the United States is to be highly competitive in a world economy. Federal efforts are expected to promote deregulation and competition within the telecommunications industry, and provide impetus and support for the networks and networking activity necessary to achieve these objectives [Roberts, 1987].

Politics

It is impossible to discuss regulation without recognizing the realities of the American political system. Although many regulatory bodies are not elected, nonetheless they are usually responsive to an elected legislative body. Elected officials are understandably sensitive to the need for reelection and typically focus this concern toward at least two distinct audiences: (1) the respective voter constituency, whose votes are needed to remain in office; and (2) special interest groups, whose financial and other support is necessary to the reelection process. The legislator, and hence the regulator, must walk a fine line between these two audiences.

In the final analysis, however, it is the voter who often prevails when the two groups come into conflict, since the legislator is usually quick to realize that a disenchanted electorate is not conducive to reelection. This political reality is in the forefront of the debate and furor over rapidly rising residential telephone rates—which, interestingly, play a major role in many of the broader issues confronting telecommunications regulators in the current environment. This is particularly relevant in light of the fact that local subscriber rates are substantially subsidized by long-distance and other services primarily supported by the business community—services also often economically available from competing sources.

Regulators thus find themselves confronting a dilemma. On the one hand, if they allow local service rates to rapidly move toward cost, the increased local rates will create a serious political problem. On the other hand, if they regulate local rates below cost, the carrier is forced to recover the shortfall from business customers, making it economically attractive for them to "bypass" the local carrier completely. This further reduces the revenue base of the carrier and forces local subscriber rates up in order to recover the fixed cost of the local network—the very thing the regulators were attempting to avoid. The regulators cannot allow the carrier to incur sustained and massive losses, and government subsidies are not palatable in today's environment. It is this dilemma that has given rise to the "new social contract," a regulatory concept discussed later.

Legislation, Adjudication, and Regulation

The telecommunications industry is subject, as is all industry, to legislative control. This control has generally taken three forms: (1) revenue collection; (2) antitrust; and (3) regulation as a "natural monopoly" and an instrument of public policy [Bernard, 1986]. The last two concepts are fundamentally in conflict. Over the years, this incongruity has pitted the U.S. Department of Justice against AT&T in the courts, and brought the courts and the Federal Communications Commission (FCC) into conflict as the courts have, in essence, entered into the regulatory domain through the mechanism of the Modified Final Judgment (MFJ), or Divestiture Agreement.

It is important to recognize the relationships between the Congress, which passes legislation and creates regulatory agencies, such as the FCC, to carry out "delegated" rule making; the Executive, which is charged with enforcing the laws of Congress and the regulatory agencies; and the Courts, where the inevitable conflicts are adjudicated. Understanding the intimacies of these relationships can be key to predicting the future direction of many developments in the telecommunications environment.

Legal Separations and Jurisdictions

Telecommunications regulation falls under the jurisdiction of the several states, except to the extent that the "ether"—the boundaries of which are not confined within any state, and the use of which is governed by international treaty or interstate commerce—is involved. Thus, use of radio, microwave, satellite, and other such communications which cross state or international borders fall under the jurisdiction of the Federal Communications Commission. All other aspects of telecommunications regulation fall under the jurisdiction of the several state regulatory agencies.

Further, the federal court, under the MFJ, has defined distinct regions called local access and transport areas (LATAs), which may or may not be contained within a single state jurisdiction. The MFJ provides that communications within a given LATA are provided by local exchange carriers (LECs), while communications between LATAs are provided by interexchange carriers (IXCs). An example of a LEC is the Ohio Bell Telephone Co., while AT&T and MCI are IXCs. Communications between states, whether between LATAs or within a multistate LATA are subject to federal regulation. Since the LECs are prohibited by the MFJ from providing interLATA (i.e., long-distance) service, the potential for cross-subsidy between long-distance service and local-exchange service is minimized.

Further complicating the picture is the fact that defining what constitutes interstate communications, and particularly what constitutes equipment or activities related and necessary to interstate communications, is prone to uncertainty and difference of opinion. For example, it is necessary to install local-loop facilities to connect the subscriber's telephone to the local central office, whether or not the subscriber makes any long-distance calls. How the cost of the local loop should be divided between interstate and intrastate jurisdictions can be a subjective issue. These issues are the subjects of ongoing disputes, generally in the courts, between federal and state regulatory agencies, and often between the various carriers and both federal and state regulatory agencies, or sometimes even between the carriers themselves. This is so often the case that the FCC has created Federal-State Joint Boards, composed of FCC commissioners, state commissioners, and limited staff, to help resolve such issues [FCC Docket Nos. 80-286, 83-1376 and 85-124].

In addition to legal and jurisdictional separations within the regulatory process, there are also highly complex accounting rules which result in certain "economic separations." These rules pertain primarily to the "arbitrary" assignment of costs between state and federal jurisdictions and between fixed (so-called nontraffic-sensitive, or NTS) costs and usage (or traffic-sensitive) costs. The allocation of these costs is important in a regulated environment, since these cost allocations represent the basis from which subscriber rates are determined.

In the case of interstate communications, the FCC determines allocation of costs between the interstate and local exchange carriers. The commission further determines allocation of these costs between NTS and traffic-sensitive components. In addition, the commission prescribes certain mechanisms for recovery of these costs by the carriers. The state commissions do likewise for intrastate communications, except to the extent the FCC has preempted the jurisdictional authority of the state commissions.

There are at least three general concepts which are helpful in understanding the application of certain jurisdictional separations: (1) Preemption; (2) Contamination; and (3) Intent. The principle of preemption (federal supremacy) has been established by the FCC through precedent, and asserts that the FCC can rule that certain aspects or elements are related to interstate communications, and hence are subject to regulation by the FCC. The principle of preemption has, however, recently been called into question by a decision of the U.S. Supreme Court [Toth, 1986]. When elements of a telecommunications system are used for both intrastate and interstate communications—albeit at different points in time—these elements, to the extent they cannot be separated, are generally considered to be "contaminated" and subject to regulation by the FCC. Costs related to these elements are often called "joint access costs." Also, if the "intent" of a communication involves crossing a state boundary, then related facilities and equipment are subject to federal regulation [*Telecommunications Reports*, Aug. 19, 1985]. This is true even though the various transmission facilities may not be directly connected, and may reside within the boundaries of a single state. A classic example is a data network consisting of private leased telecommunications lines connecting several computers in different states, at least two of which reside within a single state. Under these conditions, the private line which connects the two computers located within a single state is solely subject to federal regulation if the communications it carries are routinely "intended" to be passed along to a computer in another state; hence, the intent of the communications is interstate, and the interposed computer is merely an incidental switch.

Pricing Principles

As the telecommunications industry has evolved from a highly regulated monopoly toward a more competitive market-based environment, pricing principles and strategies have changed, and they continue to do so. Of the various pricing principles and strategies that have surfaced over the course of time, three are particularly worthy of note. These have often been referred to as: (1) Value-based pricing; (2) Cost-based pricing; and (3) Strategic (market-based) pricing.

Value-based Pricing

In a highly regulated environment, prices were fixed by regulatory bodies to reflect what was considered to be a reasonable and acceptable level for the services rendered. This "value-based" pricing strategy was not necessarily reflective of specific costs related to the provision of specific services, but in the aggregate was targeted by the regulators to enable recovery of the accumulated costs of the carrier with a reasonable return on investment for the carrier's stockholders. In some instances, prices were established with the objective of promoting public policy.

The value-based pricing strategy had several important and interesting aspects. First, as noted above, the carrier's cost to provide a given service was not necessarily directly related to the price for that service. Second, value-based pricing often resulted in averaging of certain costs by the several carriers on a regional or national basis, depending upon service and regulatory jurisdiction. For example, the National Exchange Carriers Association (NECA) non-traffic sensitive (NTS) pool resulted in contributions of NTS related revenues by all carriers to a monetary pool [Hammons, 1984; Miller, 1984]. The pool was then allocated nationally on the basis of designated fixed costs required by each carrier to provide local service (i.e., the FCC attempted to remove accidents of geography and terrain from the provision of local service). An analogy might be to create a monetary pool consisting of mandatory contributions from local heating fuel providers on a national basis, and reallocating the funds on a state-by-state basis depending upon the average winter temperatures experienced by each state.

Third, value-based pricing tended to send inaccurate messages to consumers regarding specific services, and in general often tended to promote inefficient use of facilities and resources. An example of this phenomenon was the pricing of certain private-line services (e.g., multidrop private lines) below the established cost to provide these services. This resulted in organizations such as OCLC, and many others, building their network strategies on the basis of these comparatively inexpensive facilities (so-called "tariff niche" strategies), only to be very unpleasantly surprised when the facilities were later priced to more nearly reflect their actual cost [Learn, 1984]. Additionally, value-based pricing by its very nature required that certain services be priced above their cost to deliver, in order to generate the cross-subsidies required by services which were priced below cost. The regulators tended to "over price" services which were perceived as "luxury services," or services primarily used by large business that could pass the costs indirectly to their customers.

Putting aside the issue of efficient use of resources, the system of value-based pricing worked reasonably well until the monolithic regulated monopoly approach to dealing with the industry began to be broached with the introduction of elements of competition in the provision of these services. It is also important to note that value-based pricing, as implemented by regulation, segmented the market by product or service alone, and not by customer or customer class. With the first advent of competition, the delicate equilibrium necessarily required by value-based pricing was irreversibly upset. Competitors with different, and often more favorable, cost structures—frequently due to selective market participation, and without the requirement to generate certain cross-subsidies—were put at an advantage over the established carriers. Recognizing this inequity in the system of value-based prices, regulators and the industry as a whole soon agreed that a change in the pricing system was needed.

Cost-based Pricing

With the advent of competition, and with the divestiture of the Bell system, it was recognized that the system of value-based prices could no longer be preserved. Since the major cross-subsidies had historically taken place between long-distance service and local exchange service, with long-distance providing substantial elements of support for local service, the FCC moved toward establishing a cost-based pricing structure wherein each service would be priced to at least recover the cost to provide that service. However, this sudden shift to total cost recovery for local service was soon seen to be politically unattractive and probably politically unachievable as well. As a result, the FCC moved toward a more gradual approach to cost-based pricing, wherein certain subsidies would continue to be provided to local carriers from revenues generated by interexchange carriers.

In the absence of a "clean cut" from value-based to cost-based pricing, the FCC was in essence faced with the worst of both worlds. On the one hand, while they had reduced the "threshold of pain" produced by increasing local subscriber rates, they had not nearly eliminated it, and were faced with a continuing assault on all fronts with regard to this issue. On the other hand, they had not eliminated the necessity for subsidies, or the subsidies themselves, and were faced with reshaping, and in fact augmenting, the massive body of procedures and mechanisms for collecting, accounting for, allocating, and disbursing these subsidies among an ever more vocal and increasing number of carrier entities. To complicate matters even further, the FCC found it difficult, if not impossible, to carry out a two-pronged policy of increasing competition within the industry and allowing market forces to come to bear, while at the same time providing effective and consistent mechanisms to collect the required subsidies from myriad new market entrants in an ever more dynamic technologically evolving environment. To add to the complexities of the situation, the FCC is empowered to regulate, and is specifically prohibited from imposing "taxes," which has further restricted its ability to come to grips with the issue of collecting these subsidies.

Beyond the FCC, similar problems confront the several state regulatory agencies. It is not surprising that "Murphy's Law" has prevailed, and the several states have often chosen disparate approaches to the problems with respect to other states and the federal agency. To further complicate matters, in some instances the rules imposed by the states have been mutually inconsistent and are irreconcilable with federally mandated provisions, which has resulted in considerable controversy, not to mention a healthy portion of litigation between state and federal regulators.

The bottom line is that, in theory, cost-based pricing should provide a simple, satisfactory, and easily implemented solution to the problem. The hard truth is that, in practice, it has not been possible to implement. Further, the prospects for success in implementing pervasive cost-based pricing in the near term are optimistically placed at slightly above zero. The legislative, independent regulatory, executive, and judicial bodies at both the state and federal levels, and, most importantly, the carriers, providers, and users alike, would appear to be faced with a completely unsatisfactory situation from the perspectives of all concerned— although there are many different perspectives. Out of the morass appears to be materializing a possible solution for all concerned. Although it has been called by several names, and has not yet completely solidified, it seems to be most frequently referred to as "strategic pricing."

Strategic Pricing

Regulators, particularly certain state regulators, have recognized that were it not for the backlash created by certain immediate consequences of cost-based pricing—most notably rapidly increasing local telephone rates—it would be an appropriate and acceptable solution to the problem. The increases in local rates necessary to cover costs are not necessarily in and of themselves a serious problem. When compared with comparable service in some other countries, or in terms of the prices consumers are willing to pay for other services, these rates would not appear to be greatly out of line. The problem generally is subscriber expectations regarding the value of the service as a result of the message that has been sent with subsidized pricing over many years, and the rate at which the changes have been attempted.

The perceived solution is to provide certain safeguards in the short- to intermediate-term where particular sensitivities are perceived to exist—particularly where these can be expected to produce adverse political ramifications. It is also necessary to recognize that cost-based pricing, in and of itself, is a regulatory concept. In a free market environment, competition forces prices to marginal values based upon cost. Therefore: (1) if steps were taken to control the increase rate of prices for certain services where particular sensitivity to rapid increase has been identified; (2) certain elements which will help enable the subscriber to control to some degree the expenditure for these services in the longer term are employed; and (3) competitive forces are assured in unprotected (i.e., unregulated) areas; then, prices should tend toward marginal costs as regulatory intervention is reduced. The problem is how to realistically achieve (1) through (3) above.

Achieving the situation described above is much more of a political problem than a regulatory one. The problem is to convince the interested parties that their various interests will be served. The political solution that seems to be evolving is focused under what is being most often called the "new social contract" [McCarren, 1985, pp. 7–9]. Under this approach, the regulated carriers are offered the prospect of complete deregulation—usually by specific service segments—in return for temporary guarantees of service availability and price containment of the sensitive service costs according to prescribed limits and schedules. The "old contract," of course, was provided by the Communications Act of 1934 which attempted

> To make available, so far as possible, to all the people of the United States a rapid, efficient, nationwide and worldwide wire and radio communications service and adequate facilities at reasonable charges. [47 U.S.C. §§151–609 (1976)]

The strategic pricing element results from the flexibility given to the carriers to pick and choose how they will recover subsidies to meet the cost/price differential imposed by the agreed-to price conditions on the sensitive services. It is interesting to note at least two important aspects of this approach: (1) in order to achieve the required critical mass of deregulated services necessary to provide the flexibility to recover the needed subsidies, it is in the carrier's best interest to assure that certain elements of competition exist since "regulatory flexibility" and deregulation is typically only permitted where "adequate" competition exists; and (2) the approach allows for market segmentation by customer/customer class as well as service (i.e., does not prohibit "discriminatory pricing"). The second element is essential for the carrier to compete on the basis of geography, customer size, and specific customer requirements and capabilities, and still be able to generate the necessary revenue to cover the regulatory cost elements not imposed on competitors.

It is also important to note that the approach gives little, if any, protection to business customers beyond the attempt to guarantee competitive choices. Business is generally "on its own" to procure telecommunications services as it would any other service necessary to the conduct of business—by negotiation and prudent procurement practices. The problem is that, at the present time, many businesses and institutions may not be well-prepared technically, administratively, or strategically to do this, and the costs for not doing it well can be great. These are particularly salient issues for many libraries and academic institutions, and constitute a major driving force behind the current interest in networks and networking among these organizations.

Bypass

To the extent that pricing principles diverge significantly from underlying costs in the absence of a highly regulated environment, opportunities can arise for a user, or, in some instances, another carrier, to provide alternative facilities at reduced cost to those provided by a given carrier. Use of alternative facilities is often called "bypass," although the FCC has defined bypass in narrower terms

> Bypass is the transmission of long-distance messages that do not use the facilities of local telephone companies available to the general public, but that could use such facilities [FCC, Bypass . . . , 1984, p. 7].

As a specific consequence of Divestiture—the legal separation of the IXCs from the local telephone companies—and the failure to move to substantially cost-based pricing, a significant revenue shortfall for the support of the local telephone network resulted. This shortfall had previously been offset by cross-subsidization from long-distance services which were then within the sole purview of an integrated carrier (e.g., Bell System). To remedy the shortfall, the FCC ordered "access charges" paid to the local telephone company by the IXCs based on their use of the local network to originate and terminate long-distance traffic. In passing, it should be noted that these charges were designed to recover fixed, or so-called non-traffic sensitive (NTS), costs, but were actually assessed on the basis of minutes-of-use by the IXC as a mechanism of prorating the fees among the various interexchange network providers, a point of frequent confusion. Envisioned by the FCC to be a transitional measure that would fulfill the local telephone company revenue shortfall until the local network could be made more self-sufficient with the gradual increase of local rates—thus minimizing "rate shock"—these charges created problems of a different nature.

Not only is it possible for the IXCs to avoid payment of these fees by not using the facilities of the local telephone company but, since the usage is measured in the local telephone company switch, they can also avoid certain of the fees by bypassing the switch, whether or not local facilities are used.

Bypass has generally been divided into three categories: (1) Facilities bypass; (2) Service bypass; and (3) End-to-end bypass. Facilities bypass involves construction of alternative facilities by the user, or procurement of the facilities from other than the local telephone company, in order to gain access to the long-distance network of an IXC. Service bypass is the procurement of such facilities from the local telephone company, but in such a manner as to connect directly to the IXC network, hence bypassing the local telephone company switch. In both instances, certain access fees are avoided, making the alternative financially attractive. Since the local telephone company facilities are generally not cost-based, it is often possible for larger users to construct or procure private facilities at a lesser rate than that charged by the local telephone company, giving an added financial incentive for facilities bypass. End-to-end bypass, such as the use of direct point-to-point satellite links or private fiber-optic or microwave systems, simply bypasses both the local carrier and the long-distance carrier. This has the economic advantages of facilities bypass as well as any economies that the user can generate with regard to the IXC element.

Bypass can also be classified as economic or uneconomic. Economic bypass is characterized, as described above, by economic incentives. There are, however, other reasons that a user might consider bypass. These may include the requirement for capacity or functionality that is not available from the public carrier, or they may reflect an attempt on the part of the user to provide a degree of stability with regard to operating costs or operational flexibility not possible—or not likely—in a regulated environment. Whatever the reason, bypass for other than purely economic reasons is usually classified as "uneconomic bypass."

The issues and elements discussed above have given rise to the telecommunications environment and infrastructure as it exists today, and suggest the likelihood of certain changes important to the future telecommunications environment. Networks, including those used to support library and information system applications, will find it necessary to operate effectively within this environment, both currently and in the future. Some of the more important changes and probable impacts are presented and discussed below.

Special Access

Special access facilities are provided by the local telephone company to connect user communications equipment to long-distance facilities on a dedicated basis. Examples of special access facilities are private-line local channels used to connect long-distance private lines to local user equipment, or dedicated circuits used to connect user equipment directly to a long-distance carrier's network. These facilities can generally be distinguished by the fact that they are not directly connected to the local switched telephone network, although they sometimes carry traffic indirectly to the local switched telephone network through connections to private branch exchanges—PBXs (so-called "leaky PBXs")—or through use of the long-distance carrier's network (i.e., the issue of IXCs not blocking intraLATA traffic). Although the FCC has attempted to recover lost nontraffic-sensitive (NTS) revenue for such use of the local network through imposition of a "special access surcharge" currently set at $25 per end per month (i.e., some special access circuits, such as OCLC multidrop lines, have more than two ends), this mechanism has not proved to be totally effective.

Certain private-line configurations are incapable of "leaking" traffic onto the local switched network. Such is the case with the OCLC circuits. In response to petitions to the FCC filed by OCLC and others, the Commission has allowed exemption from the special access surcharge upon certification by the user that the circuit in question cannot "leak." Exemption from this surcharge currently saves OCLC users approximately one million dollars per year. The exemption process, however, has been ineffective and has resulted in abuse, since in most instances the local telephone company cannot verify the claim of exemption without actually monitoring the use of the circuit, which is prohibited due to privacy considerations. The FCC will likely eliminate, or substantially modify, the special access surcharge in the near future. This could have a negative impact on private networks, since the resulting revenue shortfall would be recovered by some broader-based mechanism, potentially putting an additional cost burden on private networks which are currently exempt from the surcharge.

Special access rates have increased significantly over the past several years. As an example, OCLC users have experienced increases of more than 60 percent in the local access portion of their private-line facilities [Learn, 1987]. Separation of intraLATA and interLATA services under terms of the Modified Final Judgment (MFJ) as a result of the breakup of the Bell system, and the necessary restructuring of tariffs contributed in a major way toward these increases. Prior to this restructuring, elements of local access had been substantially subsidized by interexchange service revenue. With the post-divestiture restructuring, the FCC moved these elements closer to the recognized cost to provide these services. The need to recover more of these costs from the local subscribers and business has resulted in a disproportionate shift of this burden to special access services rather than to the local ratepayer. With the current movement toward deregulation and strategic pricing, small-to medium-sized organizations will probably continue to bear a disproportionate share of this cost burden. In general, special access rates are expected to experience significant increases in the short-to intermediate-term future.

Switched Access

Costs associated with the provision of local telephone service are still significantly subsidized by interexchange services. These subsidies are expected to be reduced substantially, and most probably eliminated, over the next few years. The costs to support the local telephone network will subsequently need to be recovered at the local level. What is not clear at this time is exactly how these costs will be recovered. The author's best judgment is that a proportionate share of these costs will eventually be recovered from the local subscriber (i.e., residential and single-line business subscriber) base, but that this shift will be more gradual than the shift of the costs to the local level. Certain local services (e.g., special access), therefore, may be forced to bear a disproportionate share of these costs early on. However, switched access costs quite clearly will increase significantly over the next three to five years or so.

Furthermore, changes in allowed depreciation practices will result in increased nontraffic-sensitive (NTS) cost elements. Particular changes that will cause this increase will be elimination of "depreciation cost surplus" and application of more appropriate depreciation procedures to the acquisition of substantial telephone plant and equipment which will be needed to modernize many local networks. These changes have resulted in growth of the NTS cost elements in the recent past, and are expected to continue to put upward pressure on switched access rates.

It should also be noted that when the FCC ordered long-distance carriers to pay access charges for connecting to the local switched telephone network, the Commission provided an exemption for "enhanced service providers", including the so-called value added networks (VANs) [FCC, MTS and WATS . . . , 1983]. The reason given by the FCC for the exemption, which it considered temporary, was the fear that such a sudden and significant increase in the cost structure (i.e., "rate shock") for these VANs could cause potentially irreparable damage to emerging information services. Nearly four years later, on June 10, 1987, the FCC proposed to remove this exemption, arguing that the VANs had had ample time to restructure their businesses and that the local ratepayer was in effect subsidizing the VANs' use of the local network, something the Commission could no longer condone [FCC, . . . Enhanced Service Providers . . . , 1987]. Elimination of this exemption—something very likely in the opinion of the author—will have a significant effect on the cost structure of the VANs and subsequently on the prices they will charge their users, many of whom are libraries. The impact is expected to be in the range of $2.60 per hour, but could turn out to be higher under certain circumstances.

Local Measured Service

As state regulators put pressure on local telephone companies to restrain the pace of local-service rate increases, most likely in return for pricing flexibility or deregulation in other areas, this restraint is expected to take the form of usage-sensitive service charges in many jurisdictions. By imposing mandatory local measured service (LMS), the carrier will argue that the local subscriber can control his or her telephone service expenditures and significantly reduce costs. In fact, taken on face value, this is probably the case. There are, however, several inherent problems with mandatory LMS, as compared with flat-rate unmeasured local service (i.e., unlimited local calls), which is currently the more general practice—or at least a subscriber option—in most jurisdictions.

It is straightforward to gauge the impact of rate changes for flat-rate service. With LMS, however, there is significant opportunity for the carrier to manipulate numerous parameters that can impact the overall costs to a particular subscriber in ways that can be complex and difficult to predict. Among the parameters that may be used to determine LMS costs are number, distance, and duration of calls, as well as time of day. Also, business customers tend to place more calls and, where dial-access to computers is involved, the calls tend to be substantially longer in duration; hence, business tends to bear more of the burden for the support of the local telephone network under LMS schemes, even though the NTS costs are by definition not usage sensitive. Business subscribers thus often bear a substantially disproportionate share of the cost to provide, for example, local-loop facilities—even though the actual cost of these facilities is the same, whether they are used to capacity or not used at all. The impact of mandatory LMS on libraries that use the switched network to access information services, and for other reasons, can be potentially devastating.

Local Area Data Transport

Many jurisdictions currently have in place, or are planning to implement, local packet networks—often called local area data transport (LADT) systems. A major element of subscriber access cost is related to "subscriber plant" (e.g., the telephone wires connecting the subscriber to the telephone office). In the majority of cases, this facility is in place, and is typically used less than 5 to 10 percent of the time, and to only a small fraction of its potential capacity [Rey, 1984, p. 125.]. Most of these facilities are capable of carrying information at many times the rate typically used for voice conversations. Through use of modern technology, and with a relatively moderate investment, these facilities can be made to provide simultaneous access to a local packet network. This approach is expected to serve as the foundation for the evolution of various local telephone company-provided LADT services, and will enable the provision of high-speed data access at marginal cost using mostly in-place facilities. LADT is also considered to be an early forerunner of the evolving integrated services digital network (ISDN). LADT networks are expected to provide an economic access alternative to long-distance private and public data networks in some locations in the near term, with increasing availability and more competitive prices in the intermediate term. For example, a VAN or information service may simply connect its network to the LADT network, thus allowing convenient access by LADT subscribers. Long term, LADT is expected to become less attractive as ISDN evolves as a viable alternative.

Long-Haul Capacity

Long-haul capacity will substantially increase over the next few years with construction and operation of significant amounts of new capacity, much of which will be fiber optic [Morgan, 1986]. The outlook for satellite facilities is currently less optimistic. As traffic is shifted to fiber networks from satellite, and as new traffic, particularly on high-density routes, is initiated on fiber networks, investors can be expected to become more apprehensive toward satellite technology. Digital terrestrial fiber facilities are expected to become increasingly dominant through the remainder of this century. Nonetheless, satellite transmission will play an important role with regard to certain aspects of the long-haul market, particularly in more remote areas where fiber has not penetrated, and may not penetrate for some time to come. Very small aperture terminal (VSAT) satellite earthstations can be expected to provide an attractive alternative in these regions where data rates are not excessive.

Competition is expected to force long-haul capacity to the status of a commodity, particularly on high-density routes, where moderate to large units of capacity can be accommodated (e.g., 45 Mbps T-3 and above, and possibly as small as 1.544 Mbps T-1). Even in smaller capacity units, competition along these routes is expected to force prices closer to marginal costs and result in reductions over current long-haul prices. Market segmentation may keep long-haul prices artificially high in some geographic areas for the near future but, in the longer run, downward trends should come to bear on these routes as well. This will offer significant opportunities for organizations (e.g., libraries and institutions) to band together and consolidate their respective telecommunications traffic on common networks in order to take advantage of these high-capacity facilities.

Therefore, reductions are expected in long-haul facilities prices, although the extent of these reductions is expected to vary by market segment. Increasingly, as long-haul capacity becomes more of a commodity, more unbundling of capacity from other services offered by the carrier is expected. Pricing for each of these elements is expected to move toward marginal cost levels, at a rate and to the extent competitive forces dictate. This will put the onus on the user to procure these services effectively.

Deregulation

The author expects to see significant, and in some cases total, deregulation of telecommunications products and services in most jurisdictions over the course of the next five years or so. In fact, the Department of Commerce, the Department of Justice, and even MCI have recommended movement toward deregulation of AT&T [*Telephone News*, July 27, 1987, p. 3]. Several states have already proposed or enacted telecommunications deregulation legislation. Telecommunications markets are also expected to be segmented on the basis of product or service, market area, customer or class of customer, and geography—particularly with regard to dominant competitive forces within a given area. As a result, prices for a given service may vary significantly between localities and customers. With the advent of strategic pricing, carriers will initially attempt to recover "subsidies" for local subscriber service from other products and services when and where competition, or lack thereof, allows. The historical market segmentation by product or service alone is not expected to suffice in the new environment, and multiple levels of market segmentation are expected to result. This segmentation is expected to be particularly important for evolving networks as they formulate their telecommunications-related product and service cost/price strategies.

Procurement

As deregulation proceeds, carriers will increasingly be freed from tariff constraints. With the advent of further deregulation over the next few years, telecommunications and related product and service prices, terms, and conditions are expected to increasingly be negotiated on a case-by-case basis—particularly where the magnitude of potential revenue is large. This will place the onus on the customer to formulate effective procurement strategies and tactics, package procurements effectively, and negotiate optimum results. In addition, the administrative aspects of procurement, operation, maintenance, and so on, of these elements will increase significantly. This will be particularly evident as carriers unbundle support and other administrative services. For example, simply tracking which elements are related to which supplier, and the disparate procedures of various suppliers and their respective contracts, and so on, can be expected to take on significantly greater scope.

As telecommunications equipment and services continue to be deregulated, organizations may no longer be protected by the applicable state and federal tariffs as they were in the past with regard to procuring telecommunications and related equipment and services. Prior to deregulation and competition, there was little or no choice regarding service and equipment rates and terms; the current tariffs, scrutinized by the various regulatory agencies, provided the equivalent of a legal contract between purchaser and supplier. Organizations need to be vigilant to assure that their procurement capabilities and procedures appropriately reflect the changing telecommunications regulatory and market environments, particularly as contractual and legal protection might be a concern.

Modified Final Judgment

The Modified Final Judgment (MFJ) specifically prohibits the Bell operating companies (BOCs) from engaging in interexchange telecommunications, information services, and the manufacture of equipment. These prohibitions are often referred to as the MFJ "core restrictions." The MFJ contains an escape clause, however, that permits the BOCs to obtain waivers of the restrictions from the court. With mounting consensus—in Congress, the FCC, the White House, the Department of Justice, the Department of Commerce, the Bell operating companies, even MCI, and of course AT&T—that relaxation or elimination of some or all of the core constraints is needed, the question appears to be "when and how much" rather than "whether" the MFJ should be reconsidered. A significant presence by AT&T or the Bell operating companies in the provision of information could have a major impact on organizations providing information services, or aspiring to provide these services, including libraries.

Integrated Services Digital Network

Increasingly, users of telecommunications services need to transmit information in a variety of forms including voice, data, image, and video. More often than not, dedicated physical facilities are currently required for each type of communications. The management of multiple application-dependent networks is operationally complex and the redundancies are costly.

Digital switching, digital transmission, and a modern signalling and control subnetwork are the building blocks for what is known as the Integrated Services Digital Network (ISDN). ISDN promises the following benefits for telecommunications users: (1) no need for separate networks; (2) no need for modems; (3) the ability to simultaneously send different types of messages over the same line; (4) faster, clearer, more error-free transmission; and (5) customer control of services available on particular lines.

Two prerequisites of the ISDN are pervasive implementation of digital transmission and digital switching technologies. This implementation is currently occurring at a rapid pace, and the ISDN is expected to be widely available beginning in about 1990, although limited availability in some places is expected sooner.

A ubiquitous, universally available and economic national public voice network has in the past served to relegate private voice networks to a limited domain, though they have generally been found to be effective where large traffic volumes are involved, or special needs (e.g., security) are important. Now, the attractiveness of even these networks is being reduced with the evolution of so-called "virtual private networks" such as the AT&T Software Defined Network offering. Using the inherent intelligence of the network switch, the carrier can provide many of the advantages of a private-line network using the national long-distance network. The user "appears" to have a dedicated private network, while in fact the traffic is actually carried on the public network. This enables the carrier to take advantage of the economies of scope and scale of this network.

On the other hand, the lack of such a national data network has spawned a variety of different private data networks. With the transition from a basically analog switching and transmission infrastructure to an all-digital network, ISDN proffers the evolution of a ubiquitous and widely available integrated public network. The economies of scope and scale ultimately available in such a network would seem to call into question the long-term outlook for many private data networks. Private networks that survive in an ISDN era will very likely have special requirements not readily met by the ISDN network [Herman, 1986].

Impacts

Many changes have already taken place within the telecommunications infrastructure, and still more change is foreseen in the coming months and years. This change has already had significant impact on library and information systems, and additional impact is nearly assured. It may be beneficial to focus on specific impacts expected to be felt by: (1) National online information servers, such as BRS, CompuServe, Dialog, Mead Data Central, OCLC, or RLIN; (2) Local online information providers, including libraries that are now or are planning to be online; (3) Local and interexchange telecommunications carriers, such as AT&T and the Bell operating companies, that may vigorously pursue the business of providing information; and (4) Users of information.

National Information Servers

Most national online information servers deliver their services using either a private data network, value-added network (VAN), or both. The impact of change in the telecommunications arena on these organizations will be both short term and long term.

In the short term, the major impacts will be a substantial increase in the cost of delivering their services and the potential for significant increases in the cost of overhead associated with procurement and operation of their delivery systems. Further cost increases in the range of 25 percent to 50 percent are to be expected for delivery of these services.

The increase in the cost of access to VANs due to the probable elimination of the access charge exemption for these providers is expected to be in the neighborhood of $2.60 per hour or more, about 40 to 50 percent of the direct cost of acquiring these services by the larger national providers. Also, the potentially devastating effects of mandatory local measured service (LMS) on the cost of access to the VANs for computerized applications cannot be overlooked, or underestimated. Significant cost increases for private-line access, foreseen to be upwards of 20 to 30 percent, will be caused by the combined effects of four factors: (1) deregulation; (2) strategic pricing; (3) the shifting of burden for the support of the local network to special access services; and (4) the potential elimination of the special access surcharge and the redistribution of the resulting revenue shortfall.

Although long-distance private-line facilities are expected to decrease in cost along high-traffic-density routes when procured in large volume, most of the national providers are not positioned to be able to use these facilities effectively, nor do they possess the consolidated traffic volumes to take significant advantage of these savings. In addition, rate deaveraging and strategic pricing can result in significant cost increases for certain customers, or in certain locations. These increases could cause business losses on a scale that might not be expected when only average telecommunications cost increases are considered; thus, pricing strategies by these organizations must be considered carefully. Increased overhead costs can also be expected to contribute to increased service prices. Therefore, the short- to intermediate-term impacts on these organizations have a large and negative potential—particularly when considered in light of the emergence of alternative information delivery mechanisms such as local CD-ROM database systems, and so on.

In the longer term, the emergence of ISDN networks could present a more positive outlook for these organizations. It will be to the advantage of these organizations, however, to consider the potential of the ISDN network, which is evolving in compliance with the International Standards Organization (ISO) Open Systems Interconnection (OSI) model, as a primary delivery mechanism in their evolving system strategies, in order to take maximum advantage of this future opportunity [Martin, 1986].

It should also be pointed out that the accommodation and use of shared regional, national, and international telecommunications networks by these organizations could help to "bridge the gap" between short- and long-term. This mechanism offers the opportunity to consolidate traffic as well as support and administrative overheads.

Local Online Information Providers

Local online information providers face many of the same issues as the national systems, to the extent that they utilize the local exchange network for delivery of their services. In particular, the shift of the burden of support for the local network to the local level will result in increased delivery costs. This may be particularly true for local systems, since they generally cannot generate the economies of scale of the larger national systems over which to amortize a proportionately larger fixed administrative and support overhead cost. Mandatory LMS, to the extent it exists in the local jurisdiction, will also contribute to increased cost to deliver online information using the local network.

Improvements in both capability and cost of private institutional networks, such as "the wired campus," brought about primarily by advances in technology, may offer significant potential opportunities for some local online providers. These organizations may be able to take advantage of significant investments made by a parent institution in modern telecommunications technology to deliver information-based online services at marginal cost.

In the intermediate-to long-term, developments in the areas of LADT and ISDN can be expected to offer the same advantages to local providers as to national providers, at least for local access. As with the national systems, these delivery mechanisms should be considered in the planning and design of evolving local online information systems.

LECs and IXCs As Information Providers

A concern on the part of the court that AT&T and the Bell operating companies (BOCs) could use their significant economies of scale and their control of the telecommunications network to inhibit competition in the area of provision of information, as well as a recognition that the modern switching equipment being implemented at ratepayer expense could be used to facilitate these activities, has led to the prohibition against providing these services contained in the MFJ. Both AT&T and the BOCs would appear to have moved judiciously to position themselves for vigorous entry into this area. When the MFJ constraint is lifted, as is likely to be the case, either in part or in whole within the foreseeable future, these companies will likely make an aggressive entry. Initial competitive thrusts are likely to be in lucrative commercial markets. However, if the commercial offerings are successful, the companies will no doubt move towards lower-margin markets as they seek to expand market share. Certainly, current and aspiring information service providers will be well-advised to carefully consider the competitive implications of this entry since many, if not most, of the future developments within the telecommunications infrastructure foreseen by the author are favorable, or at least not as unfavorable, to AT&T and the BOCs.

Users of Information

Much has been written about the impacts of change on users of information [Meadow, 1986]. Advances within the telecommunications infrastructure will move toward enabling the user to gain access to ever-increasing amounts of information in expanding forms and formats. In the nearer term, the likely developments discussed above will contribute to increases in cost for delivery of that information. On the other hand, increases in functionality of terminal and workstation equipment at ever-decreasing cost may help to offset these cost increases to some extent. Also, investment by major institutions in local telecommunications network technology can be expected to facilitate access to information by their users at marginal cost.

In the longer term, evolution of the ISDN network could further empower the user to gain access to a wider body of information at more reasonable cost. Although not within the scope of this treatise, this raises strategic questions for information intermediaries and information providers alike.

Conclusion

Much like a "whirlwind sight-seeing tour," the author has attempted to present a comprehensive—if somewhat superficial—overview of the telecommunications infrastructure, the forces at work remolding it, and some of the likely outcomes and impacts of this process. In conclusion, several points might be made. The telecommunications infrastructure is undergoing revolutionary change and development which will have far-reaching effects. This change might be likened to the kind of change wrought by the evolution of the transportation infrastructure with the development of a nationwide interstate highway system, or intercontinental air service. Existing delivery systems, such as the railroads and steamships, were negatively impacted, while truck, automobile, and airplane design and production, fuel distribution systems, and even population densities were impacted in ways that were often unanticipated [Drucker, 1974, p. 88].

The next three to five years or so are expected to bring turbulent times to information system-related enterprises that depend upon the existing telecommunications infrastructure for access to and delivery of information. Access and delivery costs are expected to increase and, to the extent that these costs form the basis for related service costs, these costs will increase as well. The impact will be proportional to the ratio of delivery to total service costs. Interestingly, this will likely put low service-cost organizations at a comparative disadvantage.

As the transition period passes, and the environment becomes more stable, the overall outlook would seem to be more favorable; however, as was the case with the railroads and trucking industry, the relative positioning, and indeed the existence, of some services may be expected to change. Without a doubt, the present environment constitutes the most exciting and dynamic period in the history of telecommunications. With dynamic change comes opportunity—opportunity to fail, and opportunity to succeed!

References

BERNARD, KEITH E. "Regulatory Development in the U.S." *Journal of the American Society for Information Science.* 37 (6) (November 1986): 409–413.

CACCIAMANI, EUGENE R. and MICHAEL SUN. "Overview of VSAT Networks." *Telecommunications.* 20 (6) (1986): 38–41.

DRUCKER, PETER F. *Management: Tasks, Responsibilities, Practices* (New York: Harper & Row, 1974).

"FCC Again Rules Interstate Service Has Precedence in Joint Jurisdictional Offering." *Telecommunications Reports.* 51 (33) (19 August 1985): 11.

FREDRICSSON, STAFFAN. "Fiber-Optic System for Premises Wiring Applications." *Telecommunications.* 20 (12) (1986): 39–58.

GORMAN, MICHAEL. "The Organization of Academic Libraries in the Light of Automation." In Hewitt, Joe A., ed. *Advances in Library Automation and Networking* (Greenwich, CT: JAI Press) 1 (1987): 151–168.

GRIEBENOW, ALLAN. "VSAT Implementation from the Buyer's Perspective." *Telecommunications.* 21 (6) (1987): 41–58.

HAMMONS, D.M. "Where's NECA Going?" *Telephony.* 207 (7) (1984): 38–42.

HERMAN, JAMES and others. "Wide Area Networks." *Telecommunications.* 20 (9) (1986): 103–108.

"Intec's Barret Says Staggering Losses from Satellites in Last 20 Months Have Reduced Available Insurance Capacity to Less than Half 1984 Levels, Pushes for Risk Realignment." *Telecommunications Reports.* 51 (43) (28 October 1985): 23–24.

LEARN, LARRY L. "The Impact of Advances in Telecommunications on Library and Information Systems." In Hewitt, Joe A., ed. *Advances in Library Automation and Networking* (Greenwich, CT: JAI Press) 1 (1987): 21–56.

LEARN, LARRY L. and MICHAEL J. MCGILL. "The Telecommunications Environment and its Implications for System Design." *Microcomputers for Information Management.* 1 (2) (June 1984): 125–137.

MARKUS, MICHAEL J. "Satellite Security: Legacy of 'Captain Midnight'." *Telecommunications.* 21 (6) (1987): 61–66.

MARTIN, HORST-EDGAR. "ISDNs: The Network Solution of the Future." *Telecommunications.* 20 (9) (1986): 69–82.

McCARREN, V. LOUISE, Chairman (Vermont Public Service Board). "Funding the Future of the Telecommunications Industry: Managing Technological Innovation to Satisfy Consumer Demands. Thoughts on a New Social Contract" (Montpelier, VT) June 1985 (rev. July 1985); 11 pages. (Presented: Rensselaer Polytechnic Institute, Saratoga Springs, NY, 3–5 June 1985).

MEADOW, CHARLES T. "Networks and Distributed Information Services." *Journal of the American Society for Information Science.* 37 (6) (November 1986): 405–408.

MILLER, NICHOLAS P. and W. RANDOLPH YOUNG. "Access Charge Strategies." *Telephony.* 207 (12) (1984): 99–102.

MORGAN, WILLIAM A. "Spotlight on Fiber Optics." *Business Communications Review.* 16 (4) (July–August 1986): 44–46.

"NTIA Proposes Deregulating Most AT&T, Local Special Access Services." *Telephone News.* 8(30) (27 July 1987): 3.

REY, R.F., Technical Editor. *Engineering and Operations in the Bell System.* 2d ed. (Murray Hill, NJ: AT&T Bell Laboratories, 1984).

ROBERTS, MICHAEL M. "The Need for a National Higher Education Computer Network." *EDUCOM Bulletin.* 22 (1) (Spring 1987): 9–10.

RUTKOWSKI, A.M. "Beyond Fiber Optics Versus Satellites." *Telecommunications.* 20 (9) (1987): 112–124.

_____. "Emerging Network Switching Technology and Applications." *Telecommunications.* 21 (2) (1987): 40–50.

SHERMAN, ARTHUR E. "Trends in Telecommunications Technology." *Journal of the American Society for Information Science.* 37 (6) (November 1986): 414–417.

SOLOMAN, RICHARD JAY and LORETTA ANANIA. "Is There a Role for Satellites in a Fiber World?" *Telecommunications.* 21 (6) (1987): 32–34.

TIBREWALA, RAJEN K. "Feasibility and Economics of Alternatives to Local Loop." *Telecommunications.* 19 (9) (1985): 69–74.

TOTH, VICTOR J. "Louisiana v. the FCC: States' Victory with Complex Implications." *Business Communications Review.* 16 (5) (September–October 1986): 31–33.

United States, Federal Communications Commission, Common Carrier Bureau. Amendments of Part 69 of the Commission's Rules Relating to Enhanced Service Providers, Notice of Proposed Rule Making, CC Docket No. 87-215, FCC 87-208 (Washington, DC: Federal Communications Commission, Common Carrier Bureau, 10 June 1987, Released 17 July 1987).

_____. Bypass of the Public Switched Network (Washington, DC: Common Carrier Bureau, Federal Communications Commission, 1984).

_____. MTS and WATS Market Structure, Memorandum Opinion and Order, 97 FCC 2d 682; 1983.

VAN HOUWELING, DOUGLAS E. "The Information Network: Its Structure and Role in Higher Education." *Library Hi Tech.* 18(5)2 (1987): 7–17.

Additional Readings for Chapter 3

BENIGER, JAMES R. *The Control Revolution: Technological and Economic Origins of the Information Society.* Cambridge, MA: Harvard University Press, 1986.

CURTIS, HOWARD. "The Scholar's Workstation: Networking on Campus." *Wilson Library Bulletin* 63(2) (October 1988): 46–51.

DOWNES, ROBIN N. "Resource Sharing and New Information Technology—An

Idea Whose Time Has Come." *Journal of Library Administration* 10(1) (1989): 115–125.

FORESTER, TOM. *The Information Technology Revolution.* Cambridge, MA: MIT Press, 1985.

FORESTER, TOM. *High-Tech Society.* Cambridge, MA: MIT Press, 1988.

FRANKLIN, CARL. "Hypertext Defined and Applied." *Online* 13(3) (May 1989): 37–49.

FRIEDRICHS, GUENTER, and SCHAFF, ADAM. *Microelectronics and Society.* New York: New American Library, 1983.

GUILE, BRUCE R. *Information Technologies and Social Transformation.* Washington, D.C.: National Academy Press, 1985.

JANKE, ART. "The Medium Is the Message II: Videotext." *Technology Review* (January 1983): 74–75.

MCCLELLAND, BRUCE. "Hypertext and Online . . . a Lot That's Familiar." *Online* 13(1) (January 1989): 20–25.

MEADOWS, JACK. *Information Technology: Changing the Way We Communicate.* London: Cassell, 1989.

OETTINGER, ANTHONY. "Information Resources: Knowledge and Power in the 21st Century." *Science* (July 4, 1980):191–198.

RADA, ROY. "Writing and Reading Hypertext: An Overview." *Journal of ASIS* 40(3) (May 1989): 164–171.

RICE, JAMES G. "The Dream of the Memex." *American Libraries* 18(1) (January 1988):14–17.

ROSENBERG, RICHARD S. *Computers and the Information Society.* New York: Wiley, 1986.

TYDEMAN, JOHN. *Teletext and videotext in the United States.* New York: McGraw-Hill, 1982.

WOODSWORTH, ANNE and HOFFMAN, ELLEN. "Information Technology: New Opportunities—New Problems." *Journal of Library Administration* 9(2) (1988): 91–104.

ZORKOCZY, PETER. *Information Technology: An Introduction.* Marshfield, MA: Pitman, 1985.

4

Information Supply

Problems with access to information have existed since the days before writing was invented but they have been exacerbated in recent years by the so-called information "explosion" resulting from the application of technology to information production and distribution. This proliferation is the outcome of a whole chain of historical circumstances, ranging from the invention of first the codex and then the printed book, to the growth of scientific information and the birth of the journal format in the seventeenth century. More recent accelerators have ranged from the use of computers in publishing and administrative control, to the speed of long-distance travel and communication, and to the growth of more sophisticated information needs among a better-educated and more information-conscious user population. This chapter looks at the ways in which technology has affected interactions between the two major groups involved in information provision—the publishing industry as arbiter of the production and distribution of information resources, and the library information professionals as collectors, organizers, and disseminators of those resources.

Information Production

Over the last forty years, the publication and sale of books has been escalating on a yearly basis. In 1984 the Department of Commerce estimated that just over fifty thousand books were published in America and that there were over two thousand publishers. Today, that yearly publication figure has risen to over a million worldwide while the number of individual firms involved has declined. Across the whole spectrum of monograph publishing, new transatlantic conglomerates are taking over and long-established and reputable smaller publishers are finding it increasingly difficult to remain competitive.

Alongside the escalation of monograph publishing, journal literature has also been rapidly growing. Academic journals began as an effort to keep scholars from being inundated by what then seemed to be a sea of books. The new journals were governed by a system of peer review and were regarded as a convenient method for the rapid dissemination of new information. In 1899 approximately five thousand serial publications existed. Today, even by conservative estimates, there are well over thirty-five thousand. At the same time production costs and prices for academic journals have increased, as the number of publishers has declined. Many academic libraries in particular are finding almost their entire acquisitions budget committed to journal subscriptions and the falling value of the dollar overseas has made the situation particularly difficult for libraries in the United States.

As the flood of information has inhibited the search for primary sources, the number of secondary information tools has increased as technology has accelerated the rates of production. Online databases in every academic field replicate the printed versions of the abstract and indexing publications, providing not only faster searching but also printed listings of the search results. Much of the published literature is duplicated in preprints, offprints, new collections, and computerized files. We are drowning in a sea of information making it increasingly difficult to select appropriate materials, to organize them meaningfully, or to retrieve a particular item when it is required.

Information Provision

Faced with this overwhelming tide of information production, the rapidity of technological change, and the pervasive influence of the mass media, libraries as the traditional providers of free information have had to rethink their objectives and priorities. The long-standing role of the public library as a social agency responsible for the preservation and transmission of cultural values and as an adjunct to the formal educational system has been under siege for many years. As the quantities and diversity of new information has become too great and the costs too high for many individuals, or even schools and industries, to afford, libraries have been expected to provide access to everything for everybody.

In fact, the greater availability of information has produced major problems for most libraries over the last twenty years. They have been faced with rising costs of materials and personnel, increasing numbers and expectations of users, and severely straitened budgets. "Uncontrolled and unorganized information is no longer a resource . . . instead it becomes the enemy of the information worker".[1] The amount of important information that a good library is now expected to be able to provide has long since grown beyond the reach of even our greatest public and academic libraries. The Alexandrian model of unlimited acquisition and growth is dead. Faced with this situation, the emphasis in all public and most private institutions has moved from the role of comprehensive collection and storage, to that of providing access, regardless of where the information may be located or who may own it. The only reasonable long-range solution appears to lie in cooperation for collection development, document use, and preservation. As long ago as 1979 the report of the National Enquiry into Scholarly Communication recommended a number of nationwide cooperative efforts involving both computerized networks and new regional resource centers. Although cooperation among libraries has increased since then, their recommendations have yet to be implemented on the nationally-organized level that was envisioned. At this time the chief cooperative activity among libraries remains the traditional interlending of materials—now expedited through the use of computerized networks such as the Online Computer Library Center (OCLC)—and the production of increasing numbers of shared (union) computer catalogs that are useful for the swift location of materials on a local basis.

But the increased amount of information has also meant a diversification of organizations involved in the provision of information products. After hundreds of years as the major provider of public information, libraries now face fierce competition. The profit sector (formerly represented mainly by publishers, booksellers, and library jobbers) has expanded and changed almost out of recognition in the last twenty years. The technological developments discussed in Chapter 3 have given rise to a host of new information products in a variety of formats involving many different types of information production and dissemination. The market for print products is declining and publishers are developing new products in response to the markets being opened up by the new technologies. Much of this computerized information is generated as a by-product of computer type-setting but even products still being produced in print format are being repackaged to become parts of electronic secondary sources. As the perceived value of information and the means to process and duplicate it efficiently have increased, so has interest in its potential as a commercial product.

This commercialization of information work has caused not only the rise of a whole new sector of information agencies, but also the development of a new entrepreneurial approach to information delivery. The large numbers of publishers, database producers, and online vendors who entered the expanding information market during the 1960s and early 1970s is currently declining and the publishing trade is becoming dominated by a handful of mega-corporations. This has resulted in the concentration of the control of not only newspaper, magazine, and book publishing, but also of many radio and television stations, of film studios, of the content of and access to online databases, and of many software and hardware development companies. At the same time the public sector is being further eroded by recent moves towards the privatization of much of the federal publication program, resulting in increased costs to users. This profit motive has also been reflected by the introduction of costs for certain library services (such as online searching) which, in effect, restricts services to some groups of potential users. (See more on this in Chapter 5). This centralization and privatization of large amounts of information offers an undesirable potential for the control of pricing and the power to shape the content and presentation of information.

The very different agendas of the public and private sectors have tended to polarize the information marketplace. The public sector, represented by government agencies and the state and public library systems, offers information either free or at subsidized rates, while the commercial sector is offering it on a profit basis. This competitive situation has occasioned considerable discussion regarding the most appropriate role for the public library to play. Some writers suggest that drastic adaptation will be needed if libraries are to survive into the next century and they will need to take a more aggressive attitude toward publicizing and marketing their services. Others argue that there is room for both types of systems—that the production, management, and sale of information to a paying customer is very different from the provision of a free service. Others believe that libraries should not try to compete with the entrepreneurs of the information marketplace, but should rely on their traditions of impartial information provision and professional service. Such writers emphasize the role of the library as a service organization and suggest that it should use the new technology and its products as a means of developing new types and levels of service.

The readings selected for this chapter put forth the arguments for these opposing points of view and suggest that Bush's Memex is not necessarily so far-fetched. It is perhaps not inappropriate to suggest that a variety of different agencies can have meaningful roles to play in an information-rich environment, where information comes from many sources, in many forms, and can be used in many different ways by a great variety of information-seeking users.

Notes

1. Naisbitt, John. *Megatrends: Ten New Directions Transforming Our Lives.* (New York: Warner Books, 1982):24.

Information Technology and Libraries: Toward the Year 2000

SUSAN K. MARTIN

A wise man once said, "We should all be concerned about the future because we will have to spend the rest of our lives there."[1] Of course, in an exercise of prediction, it doesn't really matter too much whether you are accurate or wrong about the future; by the time we all get there, no one will remember what you said, so you receive neither the credit for your wisdom nor the mockery for your folly.

The year 2000 is now clearly within reach, and individuals and institutions of all kinds are using it as a benchmark on which to hang special celebrations, and special sets of predictions. This gives the occasion for some old predictions, whose authors sincerely wish everyone would forget, to reemerge. A recent issue of *Life* (February 1989) previews the world in 2000 and beyond. Publishing that issue gave the editors the delight of recalling Thomas Watson's words in 1943, when the future chairman of IBM predicted a "world market for about five computers."[2]

Forty-five years later, this author sat comfortably at home in front of an IBM-AT clone with 20 megabytes of storage, a color monitor, and an internal modem, keyboarding her words. In fact, libraries were already experienced users of data processing equipment and computers within twenty years after Watson spoke. Even earlier, Ralph Parker had created

Reprinted from *College and Research Libraries* 50(4) (July 1989): 397–405.

a circulation system for the University of Missouri-Columbia.[3] Librarians in the 1960s used second-generation hardware and software to create catalogs and circulation systems. Where today's average PC has 640 kilobytes of memory, the computers of the 1960s had 8, or perhaps 12.

Prognosticators cause us to vacillate back and forth, between feeling that change is rapid and has the characteristics described by Toffler's *Future Shock,* and believing that change is more evolutionary than revolutionary.[4] Under both scenarios, much attention must be paid to the way in which our society deals with change. We know that change is difficult for most people; as librarians, we also know that we often lead our users into changes involving information technology. But we cannot lead them faster than they are ready and willing to go; if we try, we will lose them.

What will information technology be like in the year 2000? Will some major hurdles of today be overcome? If so, how accurate is the scene hypothesized by designer Philippe Starck: "We'll be able to transmit physical objects. The fax machine is the start. We won't have to move about any more. People will become like big brains connected to a global knowledge. . . . Since all communications will travel by satellite, those who own satellites will control the world."[5] Farfetched? Maybe, in part, but we must increasingly consider those members of our society who work in their homes, either in their own businesses or as telecommuters; there are 23 million people in this category, and many of them are connected to the outside world by fax and satellite.

Library Technology: The Move From the Back Room to Public Services

What are some of the analogous changes that have taken place in libraries? How is information technology likely to proceed in the future? In talking about automation in our society, John Diebold defined three stages: (1) you automate what you have been doing manually; (2) you find that what you do changes; and (3) society changes in response to these forces.[6]

Is this farfetched? No. In fact, we are already in the middle of the third stage. In the 1960s and 1970s, we automated what we had been doing manually. In the late 1970s and 1980s, what we have automated has been changing the way our libraries work. Quite recently, we have become part of a changing world of information technology in which the users of the information are beginning to access and use information differently than they did in the past.

We are a bit worried about this. We are concerned that libraries may be left behind; that they may become museums; that users will find their information needs satisfied through the information marketplace and will not want or need to come to the library any more. In a sense, these worries are amusing. In the past, we worried that we would not reach this stage; many advocates of information technologies and of libraries urged a more rapid adoption of technologies and warned that libraries were imitating in machine-readable form what they had been doing by typewriter or by hand.[7] In fact, the use of technology in libraries has usually been somewhat ahead of most of the rest of the world. It is with a sudden shock that we are now able to look around us and see that the general populace is becoming acquainted with many of the arcane and mysterious methods to which only we and a few others have been privy.

Focus on User Needs

Whether we want to or not, we are being brought into the twenty-first century. Some of us are kicking and screaming, some are welcoming the future and all it holds, and probably most of us are cautiously optimistic, with some caveats in very specific areas.

The back-room technologies, as applied to libraries, need no further discussion. We know how to do it. We can catalog locally or through networks, we can order and pay for materials online, we can check in serials and circulate books. To be sure, there are functions that have not yet been automated or that require improvement, but we know that this is just a matter of time, not of capability.

Much more interesting and far more to the point is information technology as applied to the user. After all, what are libraries for? Librarians? Of course not. Library collections and services are provided for the users, and the market that publishers and database services address is an intricate combination of users as filtered by library decision makers in their purchase of automated systems and databases.

We began to look at information technologies and their relationship to users when we started to evaluate online catalogs and their "friendliness." Before that time, we had catalog and circulation products; we did not, however, consider their impact on the user. The online search services were geared to the user, but the development of these systems was out of our hands; we merely made the decision whether to offer the service, and if so, whether to subsidize it.

Library research, notoriously inadequate in any case, has so far offered no assistance in the question of how best to provide information services to users in an age when information is being made available in an increasing number of formats, for differing costs and with differing results. Let me paint a verbal picture for you:

Professor B., a member of the history department faculty, sits at his PC, located in his departmental office and linked to the campuswide local area network (LAN), to consult the library catalog by scanning the holdings for definitive works in his area of interest. He finds that three items are on the shelf and sends a computer message to the library requesting that they be charged out and delivered to his office. Finding that a fourth item is already charged out to another user, he places a hold on it. He is disturbed to find that two desired books are not in the collection, so he files an order request with the acquisitions department. Another book is not in the local catalog, but he is able to switch his request to a national database, where he locates the item at Princeton. He then places an inter-library loan request. He also finds an article in a journal held by the University of Michigan and requests telefacsimile transmission of the article. Without setting foot in the library building, Professor B. has thus perused the holdings of dozens of libraries, has made arrangements to secure desired material, and has received a copy of a pertinent article—all in a matter of minutes. Indeed, he continues by using the library's online system as a gateway to external full-text databases of interest to him.

Most of that scenario comes from a document written in the early 1980s. That is why there is no mention of CD-ROM databases or networks and little mention of gateways and links to other systems. But otherwise, it is neither out of the realm of possibility nor obsolescent: it is just about where the technology, the providers, and the users are right now. Because monetary resources rather than technology are the restraining factor, most of the next decade will be spent in putting these pieces into full working order in the largest and most affluent libraries and in beginning to provide such services in less wealthy environments. Just that, however, is a major step forward, and one that finally begins to address what many have been calling for during the past two decades—libraries that are oriented to the future rather than to the past.

In fact, it would be more precise to say that the goal is libraries that are oriented to both the past and the future. The collections developed by libraries over the years are reflections of our culture; they cannot be swiftly put aside, and by no means is all information available electronically through some new information technology. Instead of putting aside one approach to information and replacing it with another, libraries must add to their responsibilities by providing access to data in computer-readable form. This approach places stress on the budget as well as on staff who must adjust by assuming new information roles.

In addition to funding, implementors of information technologies must deal increasingly with a chaotic environment in which there are few standards and no clear guideposts toward the "true" future answer to present-day problems.

Products and Services That Bypass the Library

Inevitably, there will be products, services, and access to information that bypass the library. The minor panic we feel when we think about the future of information technology is really the fear mentioned earlier, namely, that users will find information on their own, without relying on us; that publishers will aim directly at end users, bypassing us; and that we will become museums rather than active information centers.

Part of this fear is justified and should spur us to action; part of it is unreasonable. After all, it has always been possible for users to seek and find their own information, and publishers and purveyors of information have always had direct contact with their readers or users. Why are we afraid? Because in the age of information technology, we believe that someone might discover that libraries are unnecessary.

Ability to Offer Traditional and Innovative Services

Often, the impression is that librarians are not willing to take up the challenge to become twenty-first-century information providers and servers. This impression stems in part from the fact that while many libraries have automated the backroom functions, relatively few seem to have begun to plan for a solid transition to an institution that could provide both the traditional and the innovative information service.

The recent experience of Apple with its program called "Apple Library of Tomorrow," in which they awarded Macintosh systems to organizations that qualified with the best proposals, demonstrates that the popular impression is far from accurate. Apple expected to receive 250 or 300 proposals; they received 1300 in competition for the twelve systems to be awarded. They were stunned by the numbers, which reflected a large number of good, solid proposals and ideas.

If this response is an indication of people's thinking and planning, then the fault in the system does not lie with lack of imagination or creativity among the librarians.

Fiscal Uncertainty

Rather, it is a fiscal matter. The question is not one of replacing one type of service system with another, but instead of adding on to an already burdensome budget. Thus, libraries are finding it increasingly difficult to find resources to make the next leap, from the library-oriented information technologies to the user-oriented information technologies.

Typically, a library that is a user of a bibliographic utility such as OCLC or RLIN, and has invested in its own local circulation system/online catalog, will have asked its parent institution to devote unusually high levels of funding toward these efforts. Some situations are made worse by a decision maker's belief that automation would ultimately save money, a hope that can only be borne out in relative terms, not in absolute dollars spent. With a history of this kind of expenditure, librarians may be less than successful in persuading the powers that be to invest in the next major step toward full implementation of information technology.

The image of the library in the eyes of user and funder alike tends to be consistent: libraries are good, many people need them, "our library" should minimize its costs by taking advantage of as many resource-sharing programs as possible, and "my material" should be on the shelf whenever I need it. A persistent problem can be described by the statement that the library is everyone's second priority. Everyone's first priority is his or her primary field of work. But if one assumes that accurate and up-to-date information is an increasingly important requirement for many professions and activities within twentieth century society, it stands to reason that the library or information service may well be everyone's most important support function—after the primary funding needed to get the task done.

In moving the library toward the twenty-first century, the librarian can and should be able to take advantage of the novelty and sparkle of the information technologies. Decision makers at the corporate level want their entire institution to be in the forefront, and if the new services proposed by the library are also desired by the users of the library, a significant barrier can drop. Where automation of cataloging and circulation procedures can make a nonlibrarian's eyes glaze over with boredom, the concepts surrounding the ability to use innovative technologies to access any kind of information located anywhere in the country or the world are appealing to the visionary instincts of many institutional leaders.

Changing Systems

There are several technological issues that will loom large during the next decade or two for libraries. One that has already begun to be a problem for larger organizations is the obsolescence of the library's "first" system. That is, circulation systems created in-house in the 1960s, or turnkey systems purchased in the early 1970s, while both satisfactory performers, are no longer practical or economical for continued use.

Industry's rule of thumb used to be that a computer system would last about seven years, or at least be amortized in that period of time. In fact, industry often changes systems much more frequently, taking a faster depreciation of the hardware and software. Also, in the last few years there have been such rapid changes that it is unclear if the old rule of thumb can be applied to the real world any longer. Particularly with the entrance of microcomputers and their generations of both hardware and software, bets seem to be off concerning the prediction of a system's lifetime.

It was only in the 1970s that libraries in large numbers were able to participate in the computer revolution. Only during the past two or three years has much attention been paid to the need to change automated systems and how to go about doing it. In libraries that developed their own systems, the changes and upgrades are fully within their control. Most librarians, however, bought turnkey systems from vendors, and many of these vendors have cleverly managed to persuade the libraries to upgrade over the years to more sophisticated hardware and software—at a price, but not a steep one-time cost.

As not-for-profit institutions, libraries are woefully undercapitalized for coping with major change in the tools that they use. Computers are obviously no exception; in fact, their existence and developmental path demonstrate the inadequacy of library budgets and boards to deal with the concept of continuing change. Change management is essential. The library administrator must not only make appropriate technical decisions, but also ensure that the library keeps on working as smoothly as possible, that staff are comfortable with the change, and that users and members of the community have some understanding of what is taking place.

Specific Technologies

Specific areas of technological development will be of particular interest during the coming decade and into the twenty-first century. To repeat an earlier generalization: the pace of change in information technologies is far faster than institutions and individuals can easily cope with; the changes are chaotic, with relatively little being truly standardized; the marketplace is offering more, newer, different products every day, and buyers are purchasing whatever appeals to them, often without carefully thinking through the implications of becoming involved with one kind of technology or another.

To become involved with a specific technology is to make a major commitment. Think about the PCs you have bought and then the decisions you made about word processors or database management systems. You may be happy with your decision, but the instant that decision was made you were locked into a situation that made it difficult or impossible for you to share information or move files easily. Ostensibly there are programs that convert from one language, one set of control codes, to another; it is true, nonetheless, that these techniques rarely work as smoothly as advertised.

The analogous problems with mainframes and other kinds of technologies are only more difficult and expensive to deal with. Much of the next decade will be spent in implementing new and interesting applications and taking advantage of higher density storage and more telecommunications. But simultaneously a great deal of time will be spent trying to sort out the problems that arise from a combination of rapidly changing technology and marketplace-based systems.

CD-ROM

Obviously, CD-ROM is a current favorite in terms of developing technologies. Increasingly, information will be made available on some optical medium. However, the process of assimilating this technology into the range of document delivery services is much slower than most ever thought. Remember that we began talking about the potential of optical disk in the mid to late 1970s. Only now, in the late 1980s, are optical disk products available either on 12-inch optical disk or CD-ROM. Most of the products currently on the marketplace are information-locating tools—indexes to periodical and other literature.

Why hasn't the technology moved more rapidly? There are several primary reasons.

1. *Cost.* Despite the fact that optical disk subscriptions may be more economical than online searching for many users, these subscriptions are still beyond the reach of most medium-sized libraries. Also, librarians cannot disregard the impact upon users, who may now be asked to pay in order to access a supplemental online database or to search an optical disk file and print out abstracts.
2. *Lack of standards.* Until recently hardware manufacturers used dif-

fering standards. Now the High Sierra standard seems to be making it easier for software publishers to deal with the equipment.

3. *Logistics.* Possibly the most daunting issue for the future is logistics. Now libraries are purchasing standalone dedicated computers, one for each CD-ROM subscription. It does not take long for the finances to become unwieldy, the reference room to become overcrowded, and the patrons to become confused about the lack of interchangeability of workstations. The multiuser, multi-CD-ROM jukebox may present a partial solution. In the course of the next decade, however, online access and the associated telecommunications costs will once more put online electronic access in the forefront of information delivery.

4. *Content of disk.* Even a five-inch CD-ROM contains more than 500 megabytes. This is a lot of information, and publishers are having some difficulty determining logical groupings of information to assemble on a disk.

5. *Graphics and color.* Only now are graphics and color beginning to be available.

6. *User readiness.* Users are not yet ready to move from the printed page exclusively to electronic data.

7. *Validity.* Articles solely in electronic form are not yet perceived as valid contributions in the publish-or-perish cycle; they may not have the same stringent scholarly review and they are not yet trusted by the scholars.

8. *Copyright.* The Copyright Act of 1976 did not address emerging information technologies. The library and publishing communities are attempting with only some degree of success to effect a compromise between the interests of the two groups. The copyright issue will become even more intense as full-text documents are increasingly available in electronic form.

9. *Physical restrictions.* The need to place single-purpose terminals in public areas or to identify exactly what one wants in a jukebox system makes CD-ROM, while appealing in many ways, difficult to work with. Also, tests indicate that the lifetime of data on a CD-ROM disk may be at most ten years.

Online

Recent studies have been conducted, primarily in the United Kingdom, to assess the effectiveness of retrieving information online as opposed to searching other source tools. Surprisingly, researchers are finding that of the various mechanisms available, hardcopy is the most successful tool, with online searching coming in a distant third or fourth.[8] For various reasons, there will be increasing use of electronic publishing of a wide variety of materials—although not the novel or even necessarily the article that one wants to read straight through. CD-ROM's current economic advantage will be found to be of limited applicability, and a combination of lower storage costs and better telecommunications structure will refocus our attention on gateways, remote databases, and electronic publishing by the end of this decade.

Copyright Issues

That, of course, brings us to the issue of copyright, a question that is not even close to resolution. The current copyright law can be applied to electronic data, but it requires a juggling act to do it. Publishers—especially traditional print publishers—have determined that whatever is in the computer can be counted. Some publishers are talking about charging for browsing, a scenario that librarians could not easily tolerate. One reasonable approach is to assume that an electronic document belongs to the publisher. That publisher can charge minimal royalty fees for access to the data on a screen; when the data are downloaded or otherwise taken as a separate physical copy, the user can then be charged, just as though the copy were purchased from a store.

This issue will take a long time to sort itself out. We will be dealing with questions of copyright and fairness, and fair use, well into the twenty-first century.

Telecommunications

Standards

The problems of standards as they relate to computers apply with a vengeance in the area of telecommunications. For example, with the Linked Systems Project the library community has been able to come to some agreement about what needs to be done and how it should be accomplished, and in fact has made major strides in achieving these goals.

The problem arises when we wish to communicate, or network, with other pieces of the world. For example, the university library system really needs to be a part of the university's local area network and needs to be able to provide access for users to remote databases in their fields. However, most academic installations use a different telecommunications standard: TCP/IP. Now it is necessary to link an OSI system (as defined by the Linked Systems Project) with a TCP/IP system. Although academic computing centers will indicate that TCP/IP will be supplanted by OSI, there is no evidence of movement in that direction. The only reason for organizations successfully running on TCP/IP to change is if there is some external force, usually in the form of regulations or money or both, to cause such a change.

Gore Bill

In the last session of Congress, Senator Gore introduced a bill in which he proposed to establish an information highway system for the country, just as his father had introduced legislation for the interstate highway system.

If Gore reintroduces his bill in the 101st Congress and it passes, it stands a good chance of being one of the forces that would create standardization in telecommunications. Gore envisions a nationwide system that would allow researchers and educators to communicate using supercomputers as large nodes and all other kinds of computers as lesser nodes on the network. As can be imagined, EDUCOM is very interested in this bill, wants to support it, and has met with LC's Network Advisory Committee to state its position and attempt to draw support from the library field.

Except for the fact that the proposed costs are immense, the Gore bill could be a fascinating solution to the telecommunications standards question.

Relationship Between Libraries and Computer Centers

One of the possible focuses of change in the next decade revolves around the relationship between the library and the computing center. On the one hand, organizations change slowly, especially universities. On the other hand, there seems to be a moderate amount of movement toward the establishment of "information czar" positions, not only within universities but elsewhere. The business of information resource management is drawing much attention within the government. Information resource management pulls together telecommunications, administrative records, computing, and almost everything one can think of in the way of information except libraries and archives. Some additional movement will occur in this area, but the inherent conservatism of large institutions will prevent wholesale change toward the merging of libraries and computing centers. In addition, librarians are beginning to learn that such a combination is not necessarily advantageous; in many instances they are making good cases to their administrations for remaining separate.

Local Systems and Networks

Clearly within our control is the library's use of local systems, and it is unlikely that there will be major surprises in the coming years. There are successful local integrated systems; there are local systems that have failed or are failing. We will continue to be provided with a wide variety of choices of hardware, software, and all sizes and types of systems for all sizes and types of libraries. Local public access catalogs may become the primary focus of CD-ROM production for libraries. The bottom line is that the primary functions that librarians wanted in a local integrated system have been provided in several different kinds of products. This means that the goal stated by Bill Axford at Florida Atlantic University 25 years ago has been reached.[9] The task for the individual institution is to determine its own needs, weigh the various products on the market, make its decision, and work within that structure.

Within the next few years, however, the need to link local systems to other local systems, bibliographic utilities, and remote databases will become critical. The most valuable task that librarians can perform is to ensure that the local systems they specify and purchase have the capability of using OSI protocols to communicate outside the institution. At the present time, this goal generates lip service but very little action. Action, however, is needed, and librarians control the dollars that will finally cause vendors to produce the desired product.

Telefacsimile

The surprise of the year has been telefacsimile. It is almost a matter of "now you don't see it, now you do." A few years ago the author purchased telefax machines for the libraries at Johns Hopkins University, only to find that there were relatively few institutions to communicate with. Even at Hopkins, people were not thrilled with the process or the output.

A major change has occurred in just twelve or eighteen months. Many of us have become dependent on telefax; now we are routinely putting people's telefax numbers alongside their telephone numbers. The technology is inexpensive, the process is much faster than it used to be, and the functionality of the more sophisticated fax machines is appealing. The group IV machines promise even more improvements. This is a simple case of combining several convenient technologies to create an extremely useful product. What will the decade bring? Certainly the ability to copy from books without first photocopying the pages. Probably faster and better quality output, and more management information.

Image of the Library

One objective for librarians in the coming decade is to retain the image of motherhood and apple pie, but to add a modern and functional twist to ensure that potential users become actual users, traditional users are not frightened away, and funders perceive the value of the library's functions to their institutions.

Using innovative information technology wisely and carefully is one way to meet this objective. As information technologies become more widely available, libraries must adopt them. In no case can they replace the traditional functions of the library; the new information technologies are an add-on costing more in time, staff, and equipment, but the value will be considerable. Otherwise, library users will spend those same dollars elsewhere, getting the same products but from a different source.

Librarians cannot become so carried away by information technologies that they are far ahead of their users. That is another good way to lose users. Librarians must remember the influence that changing generations will have on library services. Right now, the adults in our libraries grew up with books. Ten years from now, the adults will have grown up with computer games and computers in school labs. The entire environment and receptivity, and expectations, will have changed. We may remain the same, but our users will not.

Information Policies

The government is responsible, directly or indirectly, for many of the changes we see in our lives and in our institutions. The Paperwork Reduction Act, the Copyright Act of 1976, the Freedom of Information Act, the MARC format, communications regulations, and the General Agreement on Trade and Tariffs (GATT) are only a few of a vast and almost undecipherable set of information policies that make up our country's information policy. Within the next decade we will have either the reauthorization of LSCA or a new Library Improvement Act, the Gore bill, the reauthorization in some form of the Paperwork Reduction Act, reexamination of the Government Printing Office and its role, and unquestionably a rethinking of intellectual property issues.

These represent mammoth policy issues. They are at once daunting, challenging, and fun. Librarians should be in a good situation to look at them carefully and have a major impact in those areas that relate particularly to libraries, because it is expected that early in the 1990s there will be a second White House Conference on Library and Information Services (WHCLIS). At the first WHCLIS, technology was discussed; at the second, we will be able to approach earlier issues with the wisdom gained through experience and to make a real difference for the future. All librarians should become participants in this process in which librarians and information professionals of the country put on a major conference for users, elected officials, and taxpayers. Discussions held and decisions arrived at in that forum are likely to have a pervasive impact well into the twenty-first century.

Notes

1. Charles S. Kettering, On His Seventeenth Birthday (Aug. 29, 1946).
2. "Visions of Tomorrow," *Life* 12 (Feb. 1989): 77.
3. Ralph Parker, "Not a Shared System; An Account of a Computer Operation Designed Specifically—and Solely—for Library Use at the University of Missouri," *Library Journal* 92 (Nov. 1, 1967): 3967–70.
4. Alvin Toffler, *Future Shock* (New York: Random, 1970).
5. Philippe Starck, "Starck Truth," *Life* 12 (Feb. 1989). 72.
6. John Diebold, *Making the Future Work: Unleashing Our Powers of Innovation for the Decade Ahead* (New York: Simon & Schuster, 1984).
7. Frederick G. Kilgour, "Evolving, Computerizing, Personalizing," *American Libraries* 3 (Feb. 1972): 1141–47.
8. "British Library Report Claims Online Searches Ineffective," *On-Line Review* 12 (Aug. 1988): 234–35.
9. *Proceedings of the LARC Computer-Based Cost Studies Institute (University of Texas, Austin, Sept. 16–17, 1971)*, ed. by William Axford (Tempe, Ariz.: LARC, 1972).

Whither Libraries? or, Wither Libraries

F. WILFRID LANCASTER

The problems confronting libraries, particularly research libraries, have received much attention in the last few years. It has frequently been said that libraries face a "crisis." The causes of this crisis are already identified. A typical academic library, while doubling its expenditures in less than a decade, finds itself with a budget that buys proportionately less and less of the newly published literature, because the cost of this literature and of personnel to handle it are both increasing much faster than general indicators of inflation in the economy. At the same time the literature continues its inexorable growth, and many libraries, despite being unable to "keep up" with this growth, face acute shortage of space.

These problems have been addressed by many writers, some of whom have suggested what the library needs to do, now or in the future, in order to cope with them. The implications of escalating costs of periodical subscriptions, for example, are dealt with by Fry and White[1] and, less thoroughly but more entertainingly, by De Gennaro.[2] The space problems are discussed by Gore,[3] and Baumol and Marcus have provided a rather comprehensive analysis of the economics of academic libraries, highlighting the labor-intensive nature of library activities.[4]

Proffered solutions to these problems include increased sharing of resources through networking and other cooperative activities, deliberate curtailment of library growth (the "zero growth" library), more "scientific" approaches to the selection and retirement of materials, and increased reliance on library automation.

All these solutions assume that publications, the raw materials with which libraries deal, will continue to exist in much the same form in which they have appeared for the last five hundred years, i.e., as print on paper or as micrographic images of print on paper. Library automation is seen only as the application of computers to the manipulation of ma-

Reprinted from *College & Research Libraries* 39(5) (September 1978): 345–357.

chine-readable records for documents in print on paper form. In the librarian's view (see, for example, Josey[5]), the library of the future looks only cosmetically different from the library of the present.

Salton, one of the most outspoken critics of library operations and approaches to their automation, seeks a solution in the form of a "self-reorganizing" library but is still preoccupied with the handling of documents in print on paper form; only their representations are manipulated by computer.[6] Licklider is one of the very few writers to come close to a realistic vision of what the library of the future may really look like.[7] But Licklider has not been taken too seriously by the library profession.

It is my belief that the prevalent view in the profession of the library of the future, and how this library will handle the problems already besetting it, is myopic in the extreme. This view ignores the significance of many social, technological, and economic trends, quite evident in the world around us, that point unambiguously to the fact that many types of publication, perhaps the great majority, are highly unlikely to exist indefinitely in print on paper form. The National Science Foundation has stated the case rather clearly:

> The limits of what can be communicated by printing, mailing, storing, and retrieving pieces of paper may be at hand. Certainly, for any real improvement in the accessibility and usefulness of information an alternative must be found.[8]

Whether we like it or not, society is evolving from one whose formal communication has, for centuries, been based almost exclusively on print on paper to one whose formal communication will be largely paperless (i.e., electronic). Why this evolution, which is a completely natural process, appears inevitable, and what an electronic communication system may look like, will be discussed in the remainder of this paper.

Paperless Systems

Publications exist, presumably, as a means of transmitting messages from one individual (writer), or a few individuals, to a great many other individuals (readers). The message may consist of results or opinions based on scientific or humanistic research, industrial or commercial experience, or some other facet of professional practice. Such messages are disseminated for their potential value as sources of information. Other types of messages, such as poetry and novels, are presumably disseminated for their potential value as sources of entertainment or inspiration.

They are disseminated as documents in the form of print on paper because, for many types of message at least, there has been no other convenient way of reaching a wide audience. This situation is now changing. It is now possible to transmit messages in a completely electronic mode. The message is keyed at some on-line computer terminal and transmitted, probably by regular telephone lines, to many other terminals at which it can be read. The message can be stored "electronically" by the recipient, who can also do many other things to it (e.g., index it, add to it, annotate it, redistribute it) without in any way generating paper copy.

In an electronic environment of this kind, paper does not need to exist at all. It seems highly probable that, in the future, the great majority of "messages" now created and distributed as print on paper will no longer be created and distributed in this form. Instead, they will be distributed electronically. This is likely to apply to all types of message now transmitted for their information content (but not necessarily those designed for entertainment), including indexing and abstracting services (which will undoubtedly be the first to disappear in printed form), handbooks, directories, technical reports, patents, standards, the science journal, and journals in the social sciences and the humanities.

The implications of this for libraries are obviously of the greatest significance. The library problem will no longer be one of inadequate space. It may not even be one of inadequate financial resources. Rather, it is likely to be one of justification for existence and simple survival. Will libraries be needed in an electronic world in which documents exist in machine-readable rather than printed form and any such document can be accessed by any individual who can reach a terminal wherever that document happens to be stored?

Before a document can be disseminated electronically, two requirements must be satisfied: (1) It must exist in a machine-readable form, and (2) the audience to whom it is directed must all have receiving terminals readily accessible to them. Clearly, these requirements are not satisfied at the present time, although it is very likely that they will be satisfied, for a wide range of documents and users, in the future. Moreover, the requirements are now beginning to be satisfied in some rather specialized applications. The most notable example is the defense/intelligence community. A large part of the documentation of intelligence interest—perhaps in excess of 60 percent—is already transmitted "electrically" through wire communications devices.

If the majority of the intended recipients have on-line terminals readily accessible to them, there is no need to generate paper copy at the point at which the message is received. Instead, the message can be disseminated to a user terminal, read there, put into an electronic file, redirected, or disposed of in some other way. In point of fact, the intelligence community in the United States is moving rapidly towards such paperless systems. Many components already exist. So do prototype systems in which documents are generated, transmitted, used, stored, indexed, and retransmitted in a completely paperless mode.

The intelligence community is in an unusually fortunate position in terms of the implementation of electronic systems of this kind. In addition, its need for such systems exceeds, perhaps, that of any other community: the volume of documents disseminated is extremely large (several thousand each day), and these must be distributed and acted upon very rapidly. But there is no reason to suppose that paperless systems will be restricted to defense/intelligence applications. Indeed, it seems almost certain that they will emerge in virtually all fields of human endeavor.

Take, as an example, the publication system by which the results of scientific research and technological experience are formally transmitted. The health of this science communication system is of great importance to all of us. Economic, social, and industrial progress are all dependent on scientific discovery and technological invention. These, in turn, depend heavily on the ability of the science community to assimilate the results of previous research, since modern science is a social activity in which progress is made through group endeavor and a process of gradual accretion, one group building on the work of another.

But the results and interpretation of completed research can only be assimilated by the science community if they are properly reported and the reports efficiently disseminated throughout the community. Authors, publishers, librarians, information scientists, indexers, abstractors, and many other individuals all play very important roles in this communication cycle. A breakdown in the cycle could have very serious consequences. Science itself would stagnate if its own achievements were no longer reported, disseminated, and assimilated in an efficient manner.

I believe that the formal science communication system, still heavily dependent on a science journal that has changed relatively little in 300 years, is already showing signs of breaking down. Some channels are almost closed. Others are beginning to close. As long as we continue to disseminate the results of science research as print on paper, the situation will inevitably deteriorate further. These results are becoming increasingly less accessible to that part of the population that relies on the printed word. There is no long-term solution to this problem through publication and distribution of information in print on paper form.

Present Problems in Science Communication

Why do I feel it necessary to paint such a gloomy picture? There are now many problems involved in the use of the literature of science and technology, especially in the "current awareness" aspect of its use. One obvious problem is simply that of growth. As the field of science and technology itself grows, there are more research results and practical experiences to be reported. The literature grows, then, in step with scientific and technical growth and at a very rapid pace.

This "information explosion" really has two dimensions. This can be seen if we consider the distribution of documents as essentially a packaging problem. The dimensions of growth then become: (1) growth in the number of packages and (2) growth in the size of the packages.

Growth in the number of packages is well exemplified by the growth in the number of published journals in science and technology. Best available estimates indicate that there are now about 50,000 journals in scientific and technical areas published throughout the world and that this number is steadily increasing at a compound rate in the range of 2 to 4 percent a year (the rate of growth has not been established precisely to everyone's satisfaction).

If this were the only dimension of growth, the problems created would be less serious than they actually are. But the size of the packages, as well as their number, is increasing. That is, each journal tends to increase in size as more papers are written and submitted for publication. For example, Sandoval et al. have reported that *Biochimica et Biophysica Acta* has been growing at an approximately logarithmic rate since its foundation in 1947. This journal now doubles in size about every 4.6 years.[9]

Besides growth in number and size of journals, of course, we have growth in numbers of technical reports, patents, dissertations, films, videotapes, and other documentary forms. This growth in the volume of literature published creates great problems for anyone who wants to keep up to date in any field of specialization. The problem is simply this: The literature of the field grows rapidly, but the time that any individual has to read it remains more or less the same. A hypothetical scientist spends 10 percent of the working day in "keeping up with the literature," and this proportion is the same in 1976 as it was in 1966. Yet, twice as much is published in 1976 as was published in 1966. Thus the scientist must either fall further and further behind in current awareness activities or must improve efficiency by using better methods of surveying the literature.

Since secondary publications are guides to and synopses of the primary literature, it is obvious that these too must increase at approximately the same rate as the primary literature. Once more, we have increases in the number of secondary publications as well as increases in the size of these publications. It has been estimated by Ashworth that there are about 3,500 such publications in existence in the world and that about 1,500 of these are in scientific and technical fields.[10] The "internal growth" of secondary publications was demonstrated by Ashworth in the following remarkable data on the number of years it took *Chemical Abstracts* to publish successive millions of abstracts:

First million	32 years (1907–38)
Second million	18 years
Third million	8 years
Fourth million	4.75 years
Fifth million	3.3 years

Clearly, if the primary literature of chemistry continues its pattern of exponential growth and if *Chemical Abstracts* continues to attempt to keep up with this growth, we are rapidly approaching a time at which *Chemical Abstracts* must publish a million abstracts in a single year.

A problem closely related to the growth of the literature is the *dispersion* or *scatter* of the literature. The more a particular subfield of science grows the more dispersed the literature is likely to be. In a typical field of research, all the papers published are likely to be scattered among a great number of journals, although quite a high proportion may actually appear in a relatively small number of "key" journals in the field.

To take a hypothetical case, there may be 375 papers published in a particular subject area in a single year. These are widely scattered over 155 journals. A small number of journals, only five in fact, contribute about a third of all the papers, and as few as thirty journals may contribute two-thirds of all the papers, but the final third is distributed over as many as 125 journals.

A hypothetical scientist who routinely scans five journals in his or her field of specialization, if lucky enough to choose the most productive five, might cover as much as one-third of the published papers. The scientist would need to routinely scan very many more journals—about thirty in this example—to increase coverage to two-thirds of the published literature and could do this only if fortunate enough to scan the most productive thirty journals. Very few scientists scan this many journals. In fact, a typical scientist is likely to scan only five or six regularly.

The only way to keep up to date effectively, then, is by scanning secondary publications or, better yet, participating in a current awareness service in which a computer is used to search this secondary literature. It is no longer possible to keep well informed simply by scanning a small sample of the primary literature. Even through the use of secondary services scientists are unlikely to discover every paper of potential relevance to their interests, but they might be able to push their coverage up to, say, 90 percent, which is a great improvement on what one could expect to achieve by scanning only the primary literature.

Another problem is that there are quite substantial delays involved in the publication of primary and secondary literature. There may be a delay of several months, and perhaps more than a year, from the time a paper is submitted for publication to the time it actually appears in print. There will also be some delay from the time a research project is completed to the time a paper describing the project is submitted for publication. Thus the paper published in the science journal is likely to report research completed many months earlier.

As more papers are written and submitted for publication, publication "backlogs" develop and greater delays occur because many papers are competing for the limited publication space available. Roistacher, for example, quotes the case of the journal *Sociometry,* which in 1974 received 550 manuscripts for review but had space to publish only 39 of them.[11] As publishing space becomes increasingly scarce, because publishers restrict growth in an effort to contain price increases, publication delays increase.

It is a delusion to regard the science journal as a reflection of current science research. Indeed, it is more archival than current, reporting research concluded many months ago and perhaps begun years earlier. Information from this research has long ago been disseminated to those well integrated socially within the science community. Professionals who want to keep at the forefront of their fields cannot rely on the science journal alone but must also use other types of documents (e.g., technical reports) and, more importantly, turn to informal channels of communication.

The final problem that should be mentioned is that of cost. The publication process is a very expensive one, and publication costs have been increasing extremely rapidly because of increasing costs of labor, materials, and physical plant. The cost of publications to the buyer must also increase to keep pace with these inflationary elements in production. The problem is particularly severe in that not only are production costs increasing but the amount to be published is also increasing. Publication costs would increase even if the amount published remained the same. But when the amount published and production costs both increase, the resulting price increases to the buyer become very serious.

The most severe price increases have affected the secondary publications. Some of these have experienced price increases of 850 percent in a ten-year period. In 1940 *Chemical Abstracts* could be purchased for only $12 a year. In 1976 it cost $3,500 to subscribe to this publication! The primary literature of science has also experienced great price increases. The average subscription price for a chemistry or physics journal in the United States, for example, went up from $18.42 in 1965 to $65.57 in 1975, and further substantial increases are forecast. De Gennaro mentions the case of *Inorganica Chimica Acta*, which was available to libraries at an annual subscription of $26 in 1970 but cost $235 in 1975, a staggering increase of 804 percent.[12]

The implications of these price increases are obvious. The cost of some science publications increased several hundred percent in a period in which the rate of inflation in the economy (as measured, for example, by the Wholesale Price Index) was only 60 percent. *Psychological Abstracts*, to take but one example, increased in price from $20 in 1963 to $190 in 1973. The accessibility of this publication is thus greatly reduced unless the average salary of a psychologist increased by a comparable 850 percent in the same period, which is clearly not the case. The trend is unambiguous. The secondary publications of science have, to a very large extent, priced themselves beyond the pocket of the individual scientist. They have become available only in libraries.

But the greatly increasing costs of at least some of these services are putting them beyond the reach of the smaller institutions. Thus they become available only in the larger, wealthier institutions. The same fate is in store for the science journal. The ratio of institutional to individual subscribers is changing, slowly but surely, in favor of the former. Baumol and Ordover point out that "a growing proportion of scientific journals have virtually no individual subscribers but are sold almost exclusively to libraries,"[13] and De Gennaro claims that "many commercial publishers have lost interest in personal subscribers and no longer quote rates for them in their advertising copy."[14]

The primary literature of science will soon be accessible only in libraries; later, the more expensive journals will be accessible only in the larger libraries. If scientific publication continues in its present form, it seems inevitable that primary journal subscriptions will continue to move to the institutional subscriber, while the major secondary services will move increasingly out of the reach of the smaller or less wealthy libraries. The general accessibility of the literature declines as a result.

The fact that the cost of science publications is increasing at a much faster rate than general indicators of inflation in the economy is very largely due to the fact that the printing and publishing industry is still very labor-intensive and, unlike many other industries, has not been able to increase its productivity substantially through automation. The industry lags far behind most others in this respect. This is evident from an examination of the Industrial Production Index. Between 1967 and 1974, U.S. industry as a whole increased its productivity by some 24.8 percent. The rubber and plastics industry increased its productivity by 64.4 percent. But productivity in the printing and publishing industry grew only 12.3 percent in this same period.

Libraries, as suggested earlier, find themselves in an unusually adverse situation in this economic picture. Libraries constitute a labor-intensive industry that is dependent for its raw materials on another labor-intensive industry. This causes the problems identified earlier: budgets growing rapidly but dwindling in purchasing power relative to total expenditures. Thus figures prepared by Dunn et al. indicate that the mean expenditures of fifty-eight major research libraries increased 103 percent between 1965 and 1972.[15] In this same period, mean expenditures for materials and binding increased only 78 percent, and these libraries were adding only 35 percent more volumes in 1972 than they were in 1965. As Baumol and Marcus have shown, the cost of operating libraries increases rapidly even in a period of comparative stability in the economy as a whole.[16]

The only long-term solution to all these problems appears to lie in a greatly increased level of automation in the complete system through which the results of research (in science, the social sciences, technology, the humanities) are disseminated, stored, retrieved, and used. In other words, the only solution, in these fields as in the intelligence field, lies in completely paperless (i.e., electronic) information systems.

The Achievements of Automation

Considerable improvements in access to sources of scientific, technical, and other information have already occurred through automation. The two major developments have been the rather phenomenal growth of machine-readable data bases and the equally impressive spread of on-line systems to make these accessible. It is reasonable to accept the MEDLARS data base of the National Library of Medicine, dating from 1964, as the first such data base to be widely used in the provision of information services. It is now estimated that there are in excess of 500 data bases or data banks used routinely in the provision of various types of information service, and more and more of these are becoming readily accessible on-line.

MEDLARS provides a good illustration of the increasing accessibility of information sources through automation. In 1965, when the MEDLARS retrospective search service was just beginning, virtually all of the expertise in searching this data base was concentrated in a handful of search analysts on the staff of NLM itself, and the volume of searches that could be conducted in the United States was severely limited, perhaps to something on the order of 3,000 a year.

When the MEDLARS off-line network was fully developed at the end of the decade, the situation had considerably improved. Through the establishment of a network of regional MEDLARS centers and through the training of information specialists on the staffs of these centers, the number of qualified MEDLARS analysts increased considerably, to perhaps fifty active searchers, and the number of searches handled in the United States rose to about 20,000 a year.

The move to on-line processing, in the 1970s, caused a further dramatic improvement in the situation. In 1975 there were about 300 MEDLINE centers operating in the United States, the number of trained searchers had increased to perhaps 500, and the number of searches conducted had grown to about 20,000 each month in the United States alone, with many additional searches occurring elsewhere in the world.

The cost of access to information sources on-line has also declined dramatically. In 1970, when I began to demonstrate on-line search capability at the University of Illinois, the cost of a one-hour demonstration was estimated to be about $50, of which about $3 was actual computer time and the remainder was communications costs (a regular telephone call to California). Now, through TELENET, the data communication network operated by the Telenet Communications Corporation, the same demonstration can be conducted at a total communication cost of $3.

In 1977 Bibliographic Retrieval Services was quoting on-line connect costs as low as $10 per hour for high-volume users (about eighty hours per month). For use of data bases for which no royalties are charged, these rates bring the cost of an average on-line search down to something in the neighborhood of $2.50 to $3.50, exclusive of terminal rental or purchase costs (minimal when amortized over many searches), the time of the searcher, and cost of printing citations off-line. Even with a royalty charge of $15 per connect hour, the total on-line costs for a search could be as low as $5.75 to $8.50.

On-line access to many data bases is already cheaper than the purchase of printed access. It costs $3,500 a year in subscription alone, ignoring storage and handling costs, to make *Chemical Abstracts* accessible on library shelves. But an on-line search of this data base might be conducted, through Bibliographic Retrieval Services, for $10 or less and is likely to be much more effective than a search of the printed tool. A library would need to do 350 searches a year in *Chemical Abstracts* to bring the per-search cost of data base access in printed form down to the per-search cost of access on-line.

Machine-readable data bases and on-line technology change the entire economics of access to information sources. Purchase of access to a data base in printed form requires a capital outlay in subscription, in storage, and in handling costs. This investment can only be justified if the annual volume of use of the data base is sufficient to bring the cost per use down to a reasonable level. But on-line services make data bases accessible in an on-demand, "pay as you go" mode, and their costs are much less dependent on volume of use. In fact, they make data bases readily accessible to libraries that could not afford to purchase access to the printed equivalents.

In summary, the growth of machine-readable data bases, and of on-line access to these, has had the effect of: improving the availability of information sources, drastically reducing geographic distance as a barrier to communication, making information sources as readily accessible in a small community as they are in a major city, and significantly reducing the cost of access to these resources.

It would be true to say, in fact, that the electronic accessibility of information resources is improving as rapidly as the accessibility of printed sources is declining and that the cost of electronic access is falling as rapidly as the cost of printed access is climbing. Moreover, and this is the most important point, cost and accessibility though electronics will continue to improve, while cost and accessibility through print on paper can only get worse and worse.

A Scenario for the Future

Significant achievements in automation have occurred, then, in the publication of secondary services, in the resulting growth of machine-readable data bases, and in the rapid increase in information services derived from these data bases. Other achievements, although less impressive, have occurred in the automation of acquisitions, cataloging, circulation, and other library activities.

Automation has so far had much less impact on primary publication and almost no impact on the distribution and use of primary literature. Yet, major improvements in the dissemination and exploitation of information will only come when the entire communication cycle—from the composition of a document to its distribution and use—is automated. In other words, these major improvements depend on the emergence of completely paperless information systems. I believe that such systems will emerge; indeed, they are inevitable. What, then, is a science communication system likely to look like in, say, the year 2000?

There are, of course, some basic assumptions underlying any discussion of a paperless future. These assumptions are that computers will continue to increase in power and decline in cost, that methods of data transmission will become more efficient and less costly, that new storage devices will make it economically feasible to hold extremely large volumes of text in a readily accessible form, and, most important of all, that computer terminals will be reduced in price to a point at which every scientist will have such a device in the office and, very likely, in the home. All of these developments, which seem highly probable, will produce the communication "structure" that will permit the substitution of the electronic medium for many of the activities and institutions that we now take for granted as operating largely on the basis of print on paper.

The scientist of the future will use a terminal in many different ways: to receive text, to transmit text, to compose text, to search for text, to seek the answers to factual questions, to build information files, and to converse with colleagues. The terminal on the desk will provide a single point of entry to a wide range of capabilities that will substitute, wholly or in part, for many activities that are now handled in different ways: the writing of letters, the receipt of mail, the composition and distribution of research reports, the receipt of science journals, the collection of documents into personal files, the searching of library catalogs and printed indexes, the searching of handbooks of scientific data, visits to libraries and other information centers, and even certain types of professional "conversations" now conducted through the telephone or face-to-face encounter. In brief, the scientist (or, indeed, other professional) will use some form of on-line terminal to compose text, transmit text, receive text, conduct searches for data or for text relevant to a particular research problem, and build personal information files.

We can reasonably assume that the scientist will use a terminal as a type of electronic notebook in which details and observations on ongoing research are recorded. These informal notes, recording background to the study, equipment and methodology used, results achieved, and interpretation of these results, can be entered at any time into a designated "ongoing project file." It is from these informal notes that the scientist will construct research reports.

The reports themselves, both those that must be submitted regularly to a sponsoring agency and those to be made more widely known through some more formal publication process, will be written at the terminal. In the process of composition, the author will, of course, draw from the notes in the electronic notebook. Some rather sophisticated text editing programs will make it very simple to make alterations in the text—transposition of sentences or paragraphs, deletions and corrections, and even the wholesale substitution of one word for another throughout the report. In addition, there will be available various online reference tools, including dictionaries and data banks of various kinds, which will make the task of accurate reporting so much easier. Presumably, too, the author will have the capability of electronically copying into a report any quotations, tables, or bibliographic references to be drawn from reports already accessible in machine-readable files. In an electronic environment, the problems of checking bibliographic references will be an order of magnitude more simple than is true at present.

When reasonably satisfied with what has been written, a scientist may decide to have the report reviewed, in an informal way, by some professional colleagues. The scientist will submit the draft to these colleagues, within his or her own institution or far beyond it, electronically. This may mean that the text is copied from one's personal files (which no one else may access) into some controlled access file. A message, addressed to those colleagues who are to review the report, is put into the communication system. The message asks these individuals if they would examine the draft and gives the information (including a password) that will allow them to access the text. When one of these scientists next goes into a "mail scan" mode at a terminal (which could conceivably be seconds after the message is entered), that person will see the message and, when ready to do so, call up the text for examination. The comments of the reviewers are transmitted to the author in the same way.

The author, of course, may choose to modify the report on the basis of the comments received. When it reaches its final form, the report may be transmitted electronically to its final destination. This may be the files of a sponsoring agency, or it may be the publisher of some electronic journal.

I suggest that the publication of primary literature in the year 2000 may in fact be a more or less direct electronic analog of the present system. Descriptions of ongoing research projects will get into on-line files similar to those now maintained by the Smithsonian Science Information Exchange. Patents will be stored in machine-readable patent files, dissertations in dissertation files, standards in standards files, and so on. Unrefereed technical reports would be accessible through data bases maintained by government agencies and other sponsors of research.

Science "journals" would continue to be published by professional societies and commercial enterprises. By this I mean that these organizations would build machine-readable data bases, in special subject areas, that would be roughly comparable to the present packaging of articles into printed journals.

Thus I can visualize the existence of an applied physics file, maintained by the American Institute of Physics; a heat transfer file, maintained by the American Society of Mechanical Engineers; and so on.

Refereeing would continue, but all communication among referees, authors, and editors would take place electronically. The allocation of reports to referees could be handled more efficiently through on-line directories of referees, through automatic scheduling and follow-up procedures, and perhaps through some profile-matching algorithm, which allocates each report to those available referees whose interests and experience coincide most closely with the scope of a particular article. Acceptance of an article into a public data base implies that the article has satisfied the scientific review process and received the "endorsement" of the publisher.

In the electronic world, however, space considerations are less likely to be a major constraint on how much is accepted for publication. This may mean that more articles can be accepted by the first source to which they are submitted, resulting in greatly reduced delays in making research results widely accessible. It may also mean that acceptance for publication need no longer involve a binary decision. Instead, as Roistacher suggests, the refereeing process may lead to the allocation of some type of numerical score to a paper, the score reflecting the judgment of the referees on the value of the contribution.[17] Every article having a score above some pre-set value would be accepted into the data base, the score being carried along with the article. Even the articles falling below the required value might, with the permission of the authors, be accepted into a second-level data base.

Once the articles become accessible to the scientific community at large, a form of "public refereeing" becomes possible. The system itself can record the degree of use that a particular item receives, readers can assign their own weights to an article, using some standard scale, and they can place their comments (anonymous or signed) into a public comment file, with comments linked to the identifying numbers of articles. The electronic system, then, may allow an author, whose contribution received a low initial rating from the referees, to be "vindicated" by the reaction of the wider community of scientists.

The processes by which an article is submitted, reviewed, and accepted for publication may not, then, be radically different in the year 2000 than they are in 1977. It seems more likely, however, that a paperless system may force rather sweeping changes in the way the science literature is distributed and paid for. It would certainly seem undesirable if the distribution procedures of the electronic system are more or less direct equivalents of the present situation.

If a scientist is expected to subscribe for the privilege of accessing one or two data bases, a major defect of the present system—the rather inefficient way in which reports of science research are packaged—would simply be perpetuated. Obviously preferable would be some immense

SDI service through which scientists are automatically notified of any new report, added to any accessible data base, that matches a stored profile of their interests. They could then use a terminal to access the full text of any item brought to their attention by the SDI service that they wish to pursue further.

The implementation of a global SDI service of this kind is technologically feasible right now, but it raises major questions relating to organization, administration, and division of responsibility. How many SDI services should exist in the electronic environment, and who should manage and maintain them? It would certainly seem inefficient if each publisher of primary data bases must maintain its own SDI program. Perhaps this function would become a prime responsibility of the present publishers of secondary services. Thus we might expect to see the emergence of national and international on-line SDI services, based upon discipline-oriented and mission-oriented secondary data bases.

Individual users would be billed for the amount of SDI service they receive, the great size of the population served bringing the cost per individual down to a figure that could become rather insignificant. The SDI services used would bring the scientists citations, and perhaps abstracts, of new literature (from all types of sources) matching their interest profiles. For each item brought to their attention in this way, the system will be able to provide, on request, an indication of how they can access the full text and how much it will cost to access it. A scientist who chooses to access the complete text of any item, which would be maintained in the files of a primary publisher, must presumably pay for the privilege of doing so. The paperless communication system is likely to be much more a "pay as you go" one, with individuals paying for just as much as they choose to use rather than subscribing to conventional journal packages, a large part of the contents of which may not be directly relevant to their interests.

The secondary publisher would presumably continue to be involved in the indexing and abstracting of the primary literature, although most of the abstracts would simply be those provided by authors and primary publishers. All indexing, of course, will be carried out on-line.

The "scope" of a secondary data base, however, would no longer be defined in terms of a list of journals (or other sources) covered. Instead, I foresee the need for various levels of SDI within the communication system. The interest profiles (gigantic ones) of the secondary publishers would be matched against updates of primary data bases so that items of potential interest would be disseminated to these secondary services rapidly and automatically.

The customers of the secondary publishers, and/or of information centers, would in turn have their interest profiles matched regularly against the data bases of these institutions. This, of course, is just one possible "model" for a dissemination system of the future. The model may seem a rather radical departure from the ways in which primary publishers, secondary publishers, and information centers now operate. But, if we are indeed moving into an electronic age, such radical departures from tradition are almost inevitable.

Scientists, then, can have their interest profiles matched regularly against one or more SDI services operated by secondary publishers or by some form of information center. These services, to which they or their institutions subscribe, will draw their attention continuously to new literature of all types—research reports, journal articles, dissertations, patents, standards, regulations—corresponding to their current professional interests. I use the term "continuously" deliberately, because I view this as an operation in which the scientist can reasonably expect to get a few things each day in the mail, rather than receiving a much larger output at weekly or monthly intervals.

Any item for which there is no use can be disposed of immediately simply by depressing an appropriate key. Items that appear to be of some interest can be pursued at once. Alternatively, the scientist may choose to read off the bibliographic data into his or her own private electronic files for later action. An item viewed in its entirety can also be placed into private files in much the same way that an article may be photocopied and placed in the paper files of an individual.

In the electronic world, the machine-readable file of resources replaces the paper file. But in the private electronic file an item can be indexed in any way, and with as many access points as the user wishes. The paperless personal file will have infinitely greater search capabilities than the paper files it replaces, and it will occupy virtually no space (since, conceptually at least, a report need exist physically in only one file, its "existence" in other files being achieved through the use of pointers to master files of primary text).

So far we have considered only input to an electronic communication system, dissemination of items within this system, and the building of files of these items. The scientist will also need to search for information—both factual data and text describing particular phenomena of interest. At present, the scientist will seek information of this kind through personal files or conversations with colleagues or consultants. Sometimes (but frequently as a last resort) the scientist will visit a library or other formal information center. In the electronic system, all these approaches to information seeking may be conducted through the same terminal.

The terminal, of course, gives access to one's own information files (and, possibly, the information files maintained by colleagues or by one's department). If these files fail, the terminal will provide an entry point to a vast array of outside sources. Accessible on-line will be machine-readable files that are the electronic equivalents of printed handbooks, directories, dictionaries, encyclopedias, almanacs, and other reference tools. The scientist will also have access to on-line indexes to primary text, presumably built and maintained by those same organizations that provide SDI services. Scientists will be able to use a "widening horizons" approach to their information seeking in this environment, going from personal files to institutional files to national and international resources. And any useful item of data or piece of text that they uncover during the search can, of course, be added rather easily to their personal information files.

But not only *files* will be accessible through the terminal. Human resources will also be available. On-line conversations (in "real time" or somewhat delayed) can be carried out with consultants, professional colleagues, and information specialists located at information centers or information analysis centers (which may, in fact, be 10,000 miles distant). The electronic mailing system can be expected to displace the present mailing system for much, if not all, professional and business correspondence. In the electronic world the distinction between formal and informal channels of communication is likely to be much less distinct, and attempts to meld the two forms (e.g., the formation of information exchange groups) will become much more practicable, through rapid and efficient communication processes, than they are in the present print on paper environment.

In my opinion, there is no real question that completely paperless systems will emerge in science and in other fields. The only real question is "when will it happen?" We can reasonably expect, I feel, that a rather fully developed electronic information system, having most if not all of the features mentioned, will exist by the year 2000, although it could conceivably come earlier.

The implementation of the system will involve the coming together, or rather the deliberate "putting together," of a number of separate services, activities, and experiments already in existence. Major steps towards a paperless system have already occurred through the growth of machine-readable data bases and data banks and the increasing accessibility of these resources through on-line technology.

We can reasonably expect a continued growth in the number of available data bases, with rapid developments occurring in the social sciences and in the humanities as well as in the sciences, and the achievement of even greater levels of accessibility through the further implementation of information networks. We can also expect to see increasing bodies of primary text becoming available in machine-readable form as more and more publishers convert to computerized operations.

The "editorial processing center," as described by Bamford among others, may provide the opportunity for even small publishers to automate their production processes.[18] At the same time, significant further improvements will undoubtedly occur in computer and communications technologies, and these developments will result in greatly reduced costs for the storage, transmission, and exploitation of textual material in very large quantities.

Computer text-editing capabilities were already quite advanced in 1971 when Van Dam and Rice reviewed the state of the art,[19] and many improvements in this technology have occurred since then. In the business world, "word processing" is replacing "typing," and the paperless office (see, for example, Yasaki[20]) is becoming a reality. Computer conferencing, as described by Price,[21] is developing rapidly, and some business organizations are already relying on this form of communication to replace the conventional mail service for intracompany correspondence. We are also beginning to see the establishment of a few small, experimental "journals" in electronic form.

On-line systems to support the building of personal information files have been available at several universities in the United States for some years. It would not be an exaggeration, then, to say that all the features of the model described could be implemented today if these various technologies and experiments were brought together to form a new science communication system.

I do not wish to give the impression, however, that no problems of implementation exist. Elsewhere, I have identified various technological, intellectual, and social problems of implementation and suggested that this sequence is one of increasing complexity.[22] It is not my intention to repeat the discussion of these problems here. It is sufficient to say that, while some of these problems may appear "thorny," they are certainly not insoluble.

Conclusion

We are moving rather rapidly and quite inevitably toward a paperless society. Advances in computer science and in communications technology allow us to conceive of a global system in which reports of research and development activities are composed, published, disseminated, and used in a completely electronic mode. Paper need never exist in this communications environment. We are now in an interim stage in the natural evolution from print on paper to electronics. Now the computer is used as an efficient means of typesetting, but the resulting publications are still distributed, through the mails, as print on paper. Machine-readable data bases exist side by side with printed data bases but have not yet replaced them. This situation will undoubtedly change.

When on-line terminals are sufficiently commonplace that the great majority of potential users of a publication have ready access to them and when the volume of use of machine-readable data bases is large enough to assume their complete financial support, we will witness the transition to electronic distribution and use of information sources, that is, we will achieve completely paperless systems.

This brings me, at last, to the real point of my paper. Can libraries survive in a largely electronic world? Will they be needed when the raw materials with which they have traditionally dealt are no longer available in printed form but are all readily accessible, on demand, to anyone with a terminal and the ability to pay for their use? If libraries and librarians will be needed, what functions will they perform, and how will they perform them?

Folk, in his description of a future electronic system, suggests that "libraries would also wither away, their historic duty done."[23] It is not my intention to investigate here the credibility of this statement. But a thorough analysis of the potential role of libraries in an electronic society is long overdue.

The profession seems to have its head in the sand. The paperless society is rapidly approaching. Ignoring this fact will not cause it to go away. The profession, if it is to survive, should now be devoting energy to the serious study of how it can adapt to life in this society. Unless it now faces up to the question "Whither libraries?" it will indeed face the prospect of "wither libraries."

Notes

1. Bernard M. Fry and Herbert S. White, *Publishers and Libraries: A Study of Scholarly and Research Journals* (Lexington, Mass.: Lexington Books, 1976).
2. Richard De Gennaro, "Escalating Journal Prices: Time to Fight Back," *American Libraries* 8 (Feb. 1977): 69–74.
3. Daniel Gore, ed., *Farewell to Alexandria: Solutions to Space, Growth, and Performance Problems of Libraries* (Westport, Conn.: Greenwood Press, 1976).
4. William Baumol and Matityahu Marcus, *Economics of Academic Libraries* (Washington, D.C.: American Council on Education, 1973).
5. E. J. Josey, ed., *New Dimensions for Academic Library Service* (Metuchen, N.J.: Scarecrow Press, 1975).
6. Gerard Salton, *Dynamic Information and Library Processing* (Englewood Cliffs, N.J.: Prentice-Hall, 1975).
7. J. C. R. Licklider, *Libraries of the Future* (Cambridge, Mass.: MIT Press, 1965).

8. National Science Foundation, "Request for Proposal 75–136, A Systems Analysis of Scientific and Technical Communication in the United States" (Washington, D.C., 14 Aug. 1975),1.

9. Armando M. Sandoval and others, "The Vehicles of the Results of Latin American Research: a Bibliometric Approach." Unpublished paper presented at the thirty-eighth World Congress of FID, Mexico City, 27 Sept.–1 Oct. 1976.

10. Wilfred Ashworth, "The Information Explosion," *Library Association Record* 76 (April 1974): 63–68,71.

11. Richard C. Roistacher, "The Virtual Journal," *Computer Networks* 2 (Jan. 1978): 18–24.

12. De Gennaro, "Escalating Journal Prices: Time to Fight Back," 70.

13. William J. Baumol and Janusz A. Ordover, "Public Good Properties in Reality: The Case of Scientific Journals." Paper presented at the annual conference of the American Society for Information Science, San Francisco, 1976 (Available on microfiche as part of the *Proceedings of the ASIS Annual Meeting*, 1976): 460.

14. De Gennaro, "Escalating Journal Prices: Time to Fight Back," 71.

15. Oliver C. Dunn and others, *The Past and Likely Future of 58 Research Libraries, 1951–1980: a Statistical Study of Growth and Change* (1970–71 ed.; Lafayette, Ind.: Purdue Univ., 1972).

16. Baumol and Marcus, *Economics of Academic Libraries.*

17. Roistacher, "The Virtual Journal."

18. Harold Bamford, Jr., "The Editorial Processing Center," *IEEE Transactions on Professional Communication* PC-16 (1973): 82–83.

19. Andries Van Dam and David C. Rice, "On-Line Text Editing: a Survey," *Computing Surveys,"* 3 (1971): 93–114.

20. Edward K. Yasaki, "Toward the Automated Office," *Datamation* 21 (Feb. 1975): 59–62.

21. Charlton R. Price, "Conferencing Via Computer: Cost Effective Communication for the Era of Forced Choice," in Harold A. Linstone and Murray Turoff, eds., *The Delphi Method: Techniques and Applications* (Reading, Mass.: Addison-Wesley, 1975).

22. F. W. Lancaster, *Toward Paperless Information Systems* (New York: Academic Press, 1978).

23. Hugh Folk, "The Impact of Computers on Book and Journal Publication," in J. L. Divilbiss, ed., *The Economics of Library Automation: Proceedings of the 1976 Clinic on Library Applications of Data Processing* (Urbana, Ill.: Univ. of Illinois, Graduate School of Library Science, 1977): 79.

Whose Computer Revolution Is It?

VINCENT MOSCO

The subject of information access is critically important because how librarians answer the question of who has access to what information will go a long way toward answering a more fundamental question. Librarians are literally on the front lines in the political dispute over who wins and who loses in the information society and play a major role in answering that question, Whose computer revolution is it?

In spring 1988 the importance of librarians was brought home to me when I woke up on a Saturday morning to a front-page headline in Canada's national newspaper, the *Toronto Globe:* "Cash-short universities ponder sale of libraries." The University of Ottawa had already sold its library on a leaseback agreement with a private information services company. Four other universities, including the University of Toronto, were in various stages of completing their deals. The universities would retain access to the collections, but ownership would shift to the banks and trust companies underwriting the deals. The deals were justified on the grounds that books are commodities and, like any commodity, can be sold and leased back to raise cash. The president of one participating university used the example of airline companies that have been selling and leasing back their fleets for years. All the stock responses came to my mind immediately: you can't do this. Libraries are not airline hangars; they are the core of our cultural heritage and must remain as public resources and not private commodities. But a librarian at the University of Calgary put it better than I ever could. Responding to a question about why Calgary turned down an offer from a private company, Alan MacDonald said, "It's the institutional equivalent of selling your daughter." Similar responses from other librarians, particularly the Canadian Association of Research Librarians, helped to overturn the Ottawa University deal, and the others are on hold.[1] Thanks in part to these librari-

Reprinted from *Information Technology and Libraries* 7(4) (December 1988): 341–348.

ans, universities retain full control over access to their libraries. This is
enough to convince me that librarians are central to how our society answers the question, Whose computer revolution is it?

Since the subject of this article is access to information technology, it
is important for me to begin by noting a significant anniversary. Just one
hundred and fifty years ago Samuel Morse and Stephen Vail exchanged
the first message by telegraph. We have come a long way in a relatively
short time. But all of the many changes should not lead us to lose sight of
how the telegraph established a pattern of development that was generally reflected in subsequent technologies, including the telephone,
radio, and television. The pattern encompassed furious early competition among inventors, rapid growth of monopolized corporate control,
considerable government assistance to strengthen monopoly control,
and a public interest movement that forced government and business to
pay at least token attention to such values as fairness and equity, alongside the dominant concern about profitability. Others have noted this
pattern in the history of information technology. Communications historian Willard Rowland has referred to it as "the process of reification."[2]
Actually, one of my childhood heroes, former baseball star and street
philosopher Yogi Berra, put it best when he said, "It's like déjà vu all
over again." Well, here we are in the information age, and perhaps the
most important question we face, turning Yogi's statement into a query,
is Will it be déjà vu all over again? History teaches us that technology
alone does not guarantee access. For us to make this a revolution for
everyone, we, the public—especially those of us on the front lines of the
computer revolution—need to fight for the fullest possible democratic
control over the production, distribution, and use of information
technology.

Nowadays, everyone seems to have a catchword for the new technology. There is a veritable industry of titles to capture the spirit of this new
age: we have tentative ones—the post-industrial society—and more explicit ones—the information age, microelectronics revolution, age of the
computer, etc. Then there are the numerical ones—the second self, the
third wave, the fifth generation. Each tends to capture some dimension
of technological change; however, they also tend to glorify the technology and gloss over the problems it creates. I like to call them
"pushbutton fantasies." To correct this bias, I've decided to enter this
name-the-future contest with a term that better captures the spirit of
computer communications today. I call it the "Pay-per Society"—I like
the pun on *paper* because it unnerves my high-tech friends who, ignoring the evidence on their desks, think that paper is on the way out.[3]

We see evidence of the Pay-per Society all around us. There are pay-
per-call telephones, pay-per-view televisions, and pay-per-bit, -per-

minute, or -per-screenful-of-data information businesses. Advertisers refer to pay-per reader, -per viewer, or -per body when they place an ad. In the workplace, data entry and word processing clerks know about pay-per keystroke, and so on.

Basically, new technology makes it possible to measure and monitor electronic communications and information transactions and to package and repackage information and entertainment in a marketable form. Business and government see this as a means to making money and to improving organizational and social management, and the result is a Pay-per Society. A closer look at these developments is needed.

First, there are developments in technology. Principally, these involve integrating digital computers for processing information with cable, microwave, and communication satellite systems for distributing it, using high-definition screens for displaying information.

This global process of technological integration, the creation of what one analyst calls "the global grid," is primarily driven by large business, but with the assistance of government, mainly the Department of Defense in the United States.[4]

Business stands to gain simply by turning the general resource of information—information in the form of a public good—into a marketable commodity. Though information has been a commodity throughout modern history, new technology makes it easier to deepen and extend this process by reducing information to bits that can be manipulated or packaged and repackaged in an infinite variety of ways and by moving these packages at the speed of light over global communication highways. As a result, business can use information technology to transcend space and time boundaries imposed on the ability to measure and monitor information transactions and to package and repackage information products. Therefore, a newspaper story can be sold in a number of forms, including radio, TV, cable, teletext, magazines, computer databases, educational "courseware," etc. Electronically monitored transactions like credit purchases or employee performance records can be similarly packaged and resold.

The Pay-per Society has resulted in major changes in industry and major social problems. I will address these changes and problems and conclude by sketching out some principles that might guide the development of socially beneficial solutions.

As far as the industry goes, one can identify three fundamental changes: in the stakes—what is gained in the Pay-per Society; in the players—who are the major driving forces in the industry; and in the arena—what is the industry that produces, packages, and distributes the goods in the Pay-per Society.

One of the fundamental reasons why there is so much interest in information technology is because it expands opportunities for profit and control. The financial stakes have grown in the information business. Commentators now refer to information as a strategic form of capital, but information technology is more than the raw material for expanding the sale of commodities. Information technology is also a tool for organizational control. It enables companies like Citibank or even General Motors to centralize and concentrate the flow of strategic information while decentralizing their operations to offices all over the world. Hence, information vital to the big decisions a company makes (for example, whether it should expand into a new market) can be concentrated in the hands of key managers; and far-flung operations can carry out the routine business.

Information technology is the spinal cord of transnational business. Indeed, information technology has opened the way to a truly international division of labor by enabling businesses to take advantage of the lowest cost and most easily managed sources of raw materials, capital, and workers, with fewer and fewer space and time constraints. Boeing can link engineers in Seattle and Tokyo for real-time aircraft design work. American Airlines can hire data entry workers for $1 an hour at satellite-linked remote processing centers in Barbados. Information technology expands both the financial and organizational stakes in the Pay-per Society.

It also changes the pecking order among the major players who contend for control and access to these increasingly valuable stakes. Traditionally, the field of information and communications technology was firmly controlled by a few large providers of facilities and services, chiefly AT&T, IBM, RCA, and a few others. Over the years, however, as users of the technology—the largest banks, oil companies, retail firms, etc.—came to realize that their business depended more and more vitally on the best use of the technology, they pressed for greater and greater large-user control of the Pay-per Society. National and international user lobbies representing the largest companies in the world have pressured government regulatory and policy agencies in the U.S. and abroad to eliminate regulatory constraints on their ability to take advantage of the growing stakes in information technology. The combined clout of these users has resulted in a global movement to deregulate and privatize communication and information systems worldwide. As a result, even a company as large as AT&T, once renowned for its ability to maintain tight control over the telephone network, was forced into a major breakup.

Large users want computer communications systems tailored to meet their needs for instantaneous global transmission of massive amounts of voice, data, and graphic information at the lowest possible price. They saw AT&T and other large providers as insufficiently responsive to meet these needs. They *were* unresponsive but principally because large providers were legally bound to respond to more than the needs of the largest of users. Over the years, a combination of public pressure and corporate policy led to a regulatory system that guaranteed the public universal telephone service at affordable rates. In return, the Bell System maintained its monopoly and a guaranteed return on its investment. A regulator, the FCC, and the Congress served as watchdogs over this arrangement. The system worked well until both a growth in the stakes and the rise of the large user constituency succeeded in changing the system. The upshot of the breakup and deregulation is that market power with diminishing government oversight governs the communications system. As a result, large users get their global data highways and the public gets higher phone bills. This will be covered more fully when I discuss problems, but first, I'll turn to the third and final change in the information technology arena.

It was once possible to speak about separate and distinct industries in the communications and information arena. There were, for example, the broadcasting, telephone, film, print, and, later, computer industries. Each was identified with a specific configuration of technologies, and though there were overlaps, most were shaped by a different set of players. This is all changing: changing technologies, stakes, and players are altering fundamentally the information domain, turning it into one large "electronic services arena." At its technological base, the integrated electronic services arena results from the integration of telephone and computer technology. Simply put, telephones contain computer microprocessors; computers can now communicate. Moreover, since the producers are involved in creating and distributing generalized information products that flow through what used to be called discrete industries (broadcasting, print, etc.), there is no economic ground to distinguish these industries. Finally, the major players are now dominant across these industries. Old broadcasters are information providers: IBM is building a global business-telephone network; AT&T sells computers. Perhaps more importantly, a few large users, with no history of information industry activity, are now major participants across the spectrum of this arena's activities. Sears, American Express, General Motors, and Citicorp are major players in the electronic services industry.

In essence, there is no sector of the U.S. or the global economy that is not directly involved in electronic services. Some see it as the driving force of the contemporary world economy. This is heady stuff for me. I don't know if I feel any better, having gone from teacher to information services professional. It must be heady for librarians, or are you information resources managers? Whatever we are called, there is a certain exhilaration in being on the front lines of a changing world economy. There is also much to worry about. As I reflect on the significance of financial and control considerations in the Pay-per Society, I can't help but wonder if Yogi Berra was right: maybe it will be déjà vu all over again, only this time with a set of powerful technologies and corporate players who can deepen and extend fundamental social problems. Two such problems are growing disparities and social control.

The American communication and information system has historically steered an uneasy course between the principles of profit and public access. Most of the system is located in the private marketplace, but over the years organized labor, educators, and other supporters of widespread access have put in place the laws, regulations, and institutions to make certain that the democratic principles of equality and participation are buttressed by citizen access to information, irrespective of ability to pay. As a result we have enjoyed public education, public libraries, a public mail service, subsidized local telephone rates, public broadcasting, and a system of broadcast regulation that provided some support for fairness and access. The Pay-per Society threatens to undermine this system of public safeguards.

First, the ability of the technology to measure and monitor information products, users, and transactions undermines the protections we have enjoyed because of the technical difficulty of subjecting every information transaction to market criteria. But now telephone companies can charge by the *second* of use and measure by seconds the number of phone calls telephone operators complete. Television companies can determine the precise demographic composition of its audience and cross-tabulate it with marketing and attitudinal profiles, promoting pay-per view programs to precisely targeted audiences. Information companies can measure the amount of usage in precise time intervals and charge accordingly. The demise of unlimited local dialing and the movement from free TV to pay-per month, pay-per channel, and now pay-per view are steps on the way to using the technology to make every information transaction a market transaction.

But there is a danger here in making the technology responsible for increasing the division between the information rich and poor. The technology does not have to be employed in this fashion. A more democratic response would include a strong political commitment to redressing these technologically induced inequities and to using the technologies to strengthen widespread access. But the general political response has been in precisely the opposite direction. Deregulation, privatization, and the cutbacks in funding for public education, public broadcasting, public libraries, and the public mail system are making it more likely that the potential for the technology to deepen divisions will be realized. Consider these developments.

With the divestiture and telephone deregulation, local rates have increased by 40 percent, or three times the consumer price index over the past three years.[5] While businesses benefit with sophisticated intelligent telephone networks, 25 percent of households below the poverty line make do without a telephone.[6] Since divestiture, more than 200,000 telephone workers, or close to 20 percent of the work force, have lost their jobs to the cost-cutting measures and accelerated automation brought about by deregulation.[7]

In the first six months of cable TV deregulation, rates shot up by 11 percent.[8] Now one company controls over 20 percent of the market for cable subscribers; the top five control 42 percent.[9] All programming restrictions have been lifted. As a result, home shopping firms, which share a percentage of shopping revenues with cable companies, now proliferate.

Meanwhile, restrictions on advertising time have been lifted, and broadcasters no longer have to abide by the fairness rules nor program to serve community needs. In fact, radio stations can renew licenses by postcard.

In the absence of a government program to assist in the equitable distribution of computers, access divides along strict economic lines. While 37 percent of the children in families with incomes of more than $50,000 enjoy computers in their homes, only 3.4 percent of the children in households with income less than $10,000 have the same privilege. Of all white children, 17 percent use a computer at home; only 6 percent black and 5 percent Hispanic children enjoy similar use.[10]

As the gap widens, the Paperwork Reduction Act diminishes or eliminates public access to information collected with taxpayer's dollars. The Reagan Administration has dispensed with one-fourth of all government publications.[11] Moreover, it has transferred to the private sector many government information databases. The result has been that end-user charges have doubled.[12]

In addition, it has raised the specter of private censorship, keeping even those who are willing and able to pay from the information market. Not too long ago the Dunn & Bradstreet Corporation, which operates a data-retrieval service containing basic information on one million companies, cut off more than 200 subscribers, including all labor unions, from access to the service. The company took this action because it did not want unions using the information for collective bargaining and organizing. One is hard-pressed to disagree with those who conclude that this "creates a spectre of database purveyors withholding seemingly public information if there is a hint of an adversarial motive."[13]

All of this is overseen by the Office of Management and Budget (OMB), a White House agency that Orwell would recognize immediately. Even conservative legislators have turned on the infamous OMB. According to Alphonse D'Amato (R-N.Y.), "a good name for OMB would be 'the Office of Disinformation.'" He charges the OMB with "twisting the figures when they see fit, cutting the programs they may disagree with, shirking their responsibilities by failing to communicate forthrightly with the committees and the Members attempting to work something out, but really looking to see how they can sabotage those programs they are opposed to—the ideologs, OMB. They are not elected to run the country."[14]

Meanwhile, the defunding attacks continue against public broadcasting, the public mail service, and public libraries. Reflecting on these developments, I think that only the staunchest of marketplace evangelists could disagree with investment banker Felix Rohatyn when, three months before last October's market crash, he decried "a climate of deregulation pushed to dangerous extremes." In an article with the prescient title "On the Brink," this mastermind of the New York City bankruptcy case summed up his position:

> For the sake of competition we have broken up AT&T and the result has been both bad service and higher prices. We have deregulated the airlines and the resulting price wars did indeed, lower fares. However, one airline after another is on its way to bankruptcy or to being acquired by another. The result will be a few huge airlines, with questionable financial structures, poor service with possibly higher prices, and worrisome safety factors. Deregulation of the financial markets has resulted in an explosion of private debt, unprecedented market speculation, and the sordid abuses in the financial industry that have been coming to light in recent months. Deregulation, as with most things in life, has to be done in moderation; it has been carried too far. The free market is not always right; it surely is not always fair. It should not be turned into a religion.[15]

One is tempted to respond: Amen.

Unless we begin to pay more careful attention to Rohatyn's warning (and it is striking that the market crash took place three months after he warned that we were "on the brink"), we are likely to fall victim to deepening divisions in American society. As the economist Lester Thurow put it,

> A bi-polar income distribution of rich and poor is replacing the wide expanse of the middle class. . . . From the point of view of technical economics, a shrinking middle class is of no concern. One business magazine recently noted that the growth of high-income households would be a great opportunity for companies producing high-income leisure prod-

ucts. They are right. . . . But it is a cause of concern for political democracy.[16]

Also of concern is the threat posed by the new technology of violating fundamental rights to privacy and creating the potential for widespread social management of our lives.[17] Buying into the Pay-per Society means more than instant shopping or dial-up videos. It also means providing private companies and governments with enormous amounts of information on how we conduct our daily lives: what we buy, what we read, how quickly we work, whom we contact, etc. Since it is increasingly essential for us to use the technology to bank, shop, or work, people are paying more and more attention to privacy issues, understandably so. In a society in which companies use card-operated washrooms to monitor break time, the laws that protect consumers and workers are like using pop guns against an elephant.

The concern about individual privacy is laudable. Nevertheless, the problem runs much deeper than this. It is not so much a question of violating individual privacy but of social management. Electronic communication and information systems—including those that measure and monitor phone transactions, bank deposits and withdrawals, credit or debit card purchases, keystroke counts in the workplace, etc.—make it possible to gather massive amounts of information about the choices of large or small, amorphous or precisely defined collectivities to more effectively manage and control their behavior. Such management and control can in fact operate with full protection for individual privacy. Indeed, it is likely that such privacy protections will be provided in order to eliminate public reticence about using electronic communication and information systems.

Major interests in social management include governments that want to determine the best means of controlling social behavior and companies eager to guarantee stable growth in consumption patterns and a cooperative workforce. Examples of social management that we should be concerned about are information systems that chart networks of contacts among telephone and computer users, irrespective of message content. Such contact networks are used to identify cliques and other informal groups that might threaten management. The mathematician who pioneered these "block modeling" techniques, overwhelmed by inquiries from government agencies, corporations, mental institutions, and prisons, now warns of misuse.[18] Such systems can be readily applied to electronic communications among consumers as well. Effective social management also means changing your behavior to conform because you know the technology *can* monitor it, whether or not it is actually doing so. Hence the greater fear may not be that we give up our individual privacy but that we keep it and live in a society in which privacy isn't worth having.

So how do we respond to these fundamental problems? The following four basic principles should guide a social policy for an information society.

First, a social policy alternative is based not on what the market makes available but rather on a determination of people's real communication and information *needs* in a society where these needs are growing and changing. Just as societies assess people's needs for housing, food, clothing, etc., we need to develop a systematic assessment of what mix of communication and information services are vital for a citizenry sufficiently skilled to live and work in a society increasingly dependent on communication-and information-based skills.

Second, an alternative would start from a broadened conception of *literacy*. It is popular to discuss the growing problem of illiteracy in Western societies and the need to enhance reading and comprehension skills. It is also popular to talk about the need for computer literacy, though there is considerable vagueness about what this means. An alternative social policy would include a commitment to verbal, visual, and information literacy.

The commitment to literacy includes the traditional dedication to learning how to read; futurists who argue that computers make reading skills obsolete are essentially calling for deskilling society. But a renewed commitment to literacy means more than this. It means teaching people how to read and to understand the range of visual material we are exposed to regularly. This means teaching how visual material—from video to film, from posters to advertisements—is put together and presented. Visual literacy includes learning the language that video-makers use to say things with the visual. This comprises everything from how one can speak with camera angles to the different messages that different forms of editing transmit. By learning some of the language and skill of the visual, people would be in a better position to understand, question, take apart, and reassemble for themselves the messages that the visual conveys. You do not have to subscribe to a music video channel to appreciate how we would all benefit by education that makes us less taken and taken in by the lure of the video.

Finally, literacy means being able to "read" the systems of electronic communication and information. It is not necessary to learn how a computer is put together or even how to program. Rather, it is important to know what these systems can *do*. How do we communicate with them? What communication possibilities do they enhance or diminish? What information potential is opened or closed by the development of these systems? What is the relationship of these systems to the rest of society?

What are the social costs and benefits of developing them in different ways (the market, the government, the community)?

The third component of a social policy for overcoming disparities in communication and information calls for a strengthened commitment to *universality*. Reliance on market principles is undermining the existing commitment to universal phone service, postal service, library service, and others. The response of those who oppose this trend is often to seek a commitment to universal access to a particular instrumentality like the telephone. One cannot quarrel with a public effort to maintain such access. However, in an age when long-dominant instrumentalities are changing and evolving in symbiosis with others, it is not enough to maintain universal access to the telephone. A useful social policy alternative would broaden the definition of *universal* to account for changes in communication and information systems and the evolving needs of people for access to such systems.

Universal access should mean access at affordable rates to telephone networks that provide a wide range of voice, information, and signalling services. These would include, in addition to local and long-distance telephone use, the availability of basic information about health care, education, and other community services; opportunities to respond electronically to verbal communication; and opportunities to signal for emergency services, information, and other vital communications. Universal service can be defined as access to a public network that provides a range of services. A basket of these services would be available to everyone at an affordable rate. Their composition would be determined by the widest possible public participation and would change with the evolution of needs in communication and information services. Such is the basic principle guiding the development of public education. This principle would serve as a useful alternative to the market in guiding the development of communication and information services.

Finally, we need a new definition of *self-and collective determination* that would restrict the gathering of information to those areas that communities and their elected representatives determine to be in the public interest. Social management requires, and electronic systems make possible, extending surveillance in breadth across an entire society and in depth into what the philosopher Michel Foucault has aptly called the "capillary level" of society.[19] The challenge then is not how to protect individual privacy, but rather, how to reduce the threat to freedom, to a self-managed life, or to a life in which people choose their own form of collective management.

Again, reliance on the marketplace for policy remedies here is only likely to accelerate the process of social management. Current discussions about letting the market set a purchase price for individual privacy eliminates a human right and makes it a marketable commodity, a right for those who can afford it. When information on the group behavior of workers or consumers is made a commodity and marketed to advance profit and control, the fundamental right of self-determination is violated.

The protection of self-determination in a world of electronic communication and information systems is difficult, in part because of the value of individual privacy and the difficulty in seeing harm in the gathering of what appears to be anonymous data. What is the problem? is a typical response. Former Supreme Court Justice William O. Douglas, perhaps less pithy than Yogi Berra, nevertheless provided the best answer:

> As nightfall does not come at once, neither does oppression. In both instances, there is a twilight when everything remains seemingly unchanged. And it is in such twilight that we all must be most aware of change in the air—however slight—lest we become unwitting victims of the darkness.[20]

Human needs, literacy, universality, and self-determination are the building blocks for an information age social policy. They are the first steps toward avoiding the negative lessons of old technologies. They are the first steps toward avoiding a more dangerous version of déjà vu all over again. They are the first steps toward an information society in which all will be admitted, including those who lack the marketplace power that is the required price for admission today.

Notes

1. *Toronto Globe and Mail* (April 30, 1988).
2. Willard D. Rowland, Jr., "The Process of Reification: Recent Trends in Communications Legislation and Policy-Making," *Journal of Communication* 32 (Autumn 1982): 114–36.
3. Vincent Mosco, "Introduction: Information in the Pay-per Society," in Vincent Mosco and Janet Wasko, eds., *The Political Economy of Information* (Madison: Univ. of Wisconsin Pr., 1988): 3–26.
4. Dan Schiller, "The Emerging Global Grid: Planning for What," *Media, Culture and Society* 7 (1985): 105–25.
5. Leland L. Johnson, *Telephone Assistance Programs For Low-Income Households* (Santa Monica, Calif: Rand Corp., R-3603-NSF/MF, Feb. 1988).
6. U.S. General Accounting Office, *Telephone Communications: Cost and Funding Information on Lifeline Telephone Service* (RCED-87-189, Sept. 1987).
7. U.S. Bureau of Labor Statistics, *Employment and Earnings* (Washington, D.C.: BLS, 1987).
8. *FCC Week* (Nov. 30, 1987): 5.
9. *Broadcasting*, (May 2, 1988): 36.
10. *The Economist*, (April 23, 1988): 31.

11. American Library Association, *Less Access to Less Information by and about the U.S. Government: A 1981–1987 Chronology* (Washington, D.C.: ALA, 1988): 88.
12. Ibid., 78.
13. *Ottawa Citizen*, (Jan. 5, 1988):C2.
14. American Library Association, *Less Access:* 87.
15. Felix Rohatyn, "On the Brink," *New York Review of Books*, (July 11, 1987).
16. Lester Thurow, "The Disappearance of the Middle Class," *New York Times* (Sunday, Feb. 5, 1985):F-3.
17. Kevin Wilson, *Technologies of Control* (Madison: Univ. of Wisconsin Pr., 1988).
18. *New York Times* (Nov. 20, 1983):sect. III, p.3.
19. Michael Foucault, *Power/Knowledge* (New York: Pantheon, 1980).
20. William O. Douglas, in *New York Times*, (Nov. 29, 1987):sect. 1, p.38.

Additional Readings for Chapter 4

AITCHISON, THOMAS M. "The Database Producer in the Information Chain." *Journal of Information Science* 14(6) (1988): 319–327.

ALLOWAY, CATHERINE S. "Naisbitt's Megatrends: Some Implications for the Electronic Library." *The Electronic Library* 4(2) (April 1986):114–119.

BRISCOE, PETER, et al. "Ashurbanipal's Enduring Archetype: Thoughts on the Library's Role in the Future" *College & Research Libraries* 46(2) (March 1986): 121–126.

CAWKELL, A. E. "Information Technology and Work." *Journal of Information Science* 6(4) (1983): 123–135.

CRONIN, BLAISE. "Adaption, Extinction, or Genetic Drift?" *Aslib Proceedings* 35(6/7) (June/July 1983): 278–289.

HEILPRIN, LAWRENCE B. "The library Community at a Technological and Philosophical Crossroads: Necessary and Sufficient Conditions for Survival." *Journal of ASIS* 31(6) (November 1980): 389–395.

HOROWITZ, IRVING L., and MARY E. CURTIS. "The Impact of Technology on Scholarly Publishing." *Scholarly Publishing* 13(3) (April 1982): 211–228.

HUBBARD, TAYLOR E. "From Pride to Profit: One Hundred Years of American Trade Publishing." *Drexel Library Quarterly* 20(3) (Summer 1984): 4–27.

HUNTER, KAREN. "Academic Librarians and Publishers: Customer Versus Producers or Partners in the Planning of Electronic Publishing?" *Journal of Library Administration* 9(4) (1955): 35–47.

KUSACK, JAMES. "Librarians and the Information Age: An Affair on the Rocks?" *Bulletin of ASIS* 14(2) (December/January 1988): 26–27.

KUSACK, JAMES. "Libraries and the Information Age: Is Reconciliation Possible?" *Bulletin of ASIS* 14(3) (February/March 1988): 27–30.

LANCASTER, FREDERICK W. *Toward Paperless Information Systems* New York: Academic Press, 1978.

LANCASTER, FREDERICK W. "The Paperless Society Revisited." *American Libraries* 16(8) (September 1985): 553–555.

LEWIS, DENNIS A. "Today's Challenge—Tomorrow's Choice—Change or Be

Changed or the Doomsday Scenario Mk 2." *Journal of Information Science* 2(1) (1980): 59–74.

MASUDA, YONEJI. "The Role of the Library in the Information Society." *The Electronic Library* 1(2) (April 1983): 143–147.

MONTAGNES, IAN. "Perspectives on the New Technology." *Scholarly Publishing* 12(3) (April 1981): 219–229.

ROWLANDS, DAVID G. "Towards an Information Market Model." *Aslib Proceedings* 40(1) (January 1988): 27–30.

SCHUMAN, PATRICIA G. "Reclaiming Our Technological Future." *Library Journal* 115(4) (March 1, 1990): 34–38.

WALES, JOHN. "Doomsday or Resurrection—Professional Information Management and the Management of Information Professionals." *Aslib Proceedings* 40(7/8) (July/August 1988): 213–216.

WEISKEL, TIMOTHY. "The Electronic Library and the Challenge of Information Planning." *Academe* 75(4) (July/August 1989): 8–12.

5

Information Use

Investigations of information use have traditionally concentrated on the systems themselves—the data they should include, how the files should be organized, and the use of vocabulary for indexing and searching— and (as we have seen in Chapters 3 and 4) the new technologies have provided a variety of new and more efficient ways of storing and processing information. Computer retrieval systems can search more swiftly and provide a greater variety of search keys but the most notable effect of technology has been to increase the amounts of information available and to help organize and control it more efficiently. The effective collection and dissemination of information presupposes a knowledge of the information needs and information-seeking behavior of the group of people to be served. But most computer retrieval systems operate under a set of assumptions that bear little relation to the reality of the ways in which users behave when seeking information.

There is little consensus regarding the scope of the phrase "information use" and an exact definition of "information needs" has proven almost as elusive as the definitions of "information" and "information science" that we discussed earlier. The idea of information as something that has a constant meaning and some element of correspondence to reality is related to the focus on the mechanics of the systems. This is obviously an unacceptable oversimplification. The problem of defining the human and cognitive aspects of information-seeking has been compounded by the multiple variations in four aspects of the information retrieval process:

171

1. The interface between the system and the user has become more varied as technology has provided new physical forms of access, expanded the content of searchable records, and increased search options.
2. The users themselves provide almost infinite possibilities for variation, though, attempts are usually made to systematize them into groups based on demographic, social, personal, and cultural factors.
3. The situations when information is needed can vary in terms of the time frame involved, the type of problem, or the stage of a research project.
4. The type of information need can also vary, but is usually grouped for convenience using variables such as the use to be made of the information (educational, recreational), or the amount of information required (high recall or high precision searches).

Most user studies carried out during the 1970s tended to assume that system use was a reflection of information need and that the external behavior of different user groups could be used to help identify patterns of use. The objective of this research was to try to define the distinguishing traits of different groups of users and link them to different types of information need and methods of information provision. Such an approach ignores the reality that information use is not necessarily a reflection of information needs, and takes no account of the fact that a problem situation does not automatically lead to information-seeking activity. Not all behavior is driven by a stimulus that leads to action that can be translated into input-output sequences expressed in rules and formulas. Professor James Krikelas of the University of Wisconsin–Madison divides information-seeking behavior into two distinct classes: first, the satisfaction of immediate needs identified as "information-seeking" and second, those associated with deferred needs as "information gathering."

A considerable body of information has been built up regarding the information-seeking behavior of certain groups of information users (i.e., blue-collar workers, scientists, psychologists, historians, engineers, and so on), though less is known regarding the population in general. It has been established, for example, that scientists are mainly interested in the journal literature, while scholars in the humanities read more monographs and engineers read very little at all. Scientists and social scientists both tend to work in teams and rely heavily on informal channels within the "invisible colleges" of their own disciplines. Conferences, casual conversations, and the exchange of preprints are their preferred forms of communication and currency is seen to be vitally important. The people who are sought out as sources of information (the "gatekeepers") appear to have access to a greater variety of information sources and to publish more frequently. Researchers in the humanities, on the other hand, usually work alone and rely less on informal sources and more on older primary materials.

The traditional approach to the study of information use sees the information itself as the objective and the users as merely input-output processors. It starts with the system, focuses on externally observable behavior and events—useage, user attitudes, satisfaction, and so on—and categorizes results along sociological and demographic dimensions. More recently, a broader approach has developed that regards information as something constructed by the user within a given situational framework regardless of the use (or nonuse) of any particular system. This cognitive view of information use seeks to understand and explain individual experience and behavior during the search process. It assumes that information use behavior extends beyond the immediate user-system interaction to include the identification of the problem that first gives rise to the need for information, the user's perception of ways to solve it, and the possible usefulness of available information sources. It is seen as progressing through levels or phases, initially activated either in response to a particular event or when uncertainty is identified within one of a wide range of information-need situations.

Information Scientist Robert S. Taylor of Syracuse University has categorized four types of search questions linked to these different stages of information seeking:

1. Visceral need—a vague sense of dissatisfaction, often unexpressed.
2. Conscious need—an ambiguous and rambling expression of the information need.
3. Formal need—a more defined expression of the information need, often in concrete terms.
4. Compromised need—a translation of the user's request into the vocabulary of the system.

Once a need for information has been recognized there will be an ongoing negotiation between the user's knowledge and the expression of the information need, as the search moves through the four stages of problem resolution. (Review Dervin's ideas in Chapter 1).

This type of cognitive approach makes the information need (rather than the user's behavior with the system) the focus of attention and attempts to determine how people try to make sense of a problem situation by a study of their communication patterns. In this context users are viewed as being in an "anomalous state of knowledge" (ASK) and their attempts to explain what is wrong are analyzed. The search process is seen as a complex combination of thoughts, actions, and feelings. The objective is to isolate the fundamental dimensions of the user's information need in order to link them to appropriate cognitive strategies for resolving the problem. Methodologies using this cognitive approach to problem solving can provide data for incorporation into the computer-based knowledge systems we mentioned earlier, in an attempt to replicate human decision-making processes.

The first reading attempts to give an idea of the range of material available by an overview of early studies in the field of information-seeking and information use. This is followed by a paper that introduces the cognitive approach to an analysis of the information needs of users based on the situational dimensions of the problems involved.

On User Studies and Information Needs

T. D. WILSON

Apart from information retrieval there is virtually no other area of information science that has occasioned as much research effort and writing as "user studies." Within user studies the investigation of "information needs" has been the subject of much debate and no little confusion. The aim of this paper is to attempt to reduce this confusion by devoting attention to the definition of some concepts and by proposing the basis for a theory of the motivations for information-seeking behaviour.

Information

Part of the difficulty with "information needs" lies with the troublesome concept "information." Numerous definitions have been evolved, seeking to distinguish, for example, among "data," "information" and "knowledge," and recently there have been attempts at a single concept of information for information science.[1-2]

However, the problem seems to lie not so much with the lack of a *sin-*

Reprinted from *Journal of Documentation* 37(1) (March 1981): 3–15.

gle definition as with a failure to use a definition appropriate to the level and purpose of the investigation. The word "information" is used, in the context of user-studies research, to denote a *physical entity* or phenomenon (as in the case of questions relating to the number of books read in a period of time, the number of journals subscribed to, etc.), the *channel of communication* through which messages are transferred (as when we speak of the incidence of oral versus written information), or the *factual data*, empirically determined and presented in a document or transmitted orally.

The situation is further complicated by the fact that distinctions may or may not be made among "facts," "advice" and "opinion." The distinction, of course, is that the first of these is assumed (not always correctly) to be free of value judgements, whereas value judgements almost certainly affect advice and opinion.

These multiple uses of the term "information" cause confusion because researchers sometimes fail to distinguish between one sense and another, or simply leave the reader to discover which sense is meant by reading the paper or report. Even then it is sometimes unclear which of the senses the researcher had in mind when setting the research objectives.

User Studies

Fig. I presents a way of thinking of the field, "user studies"; its aim is not to "model" information-seeking behaviour but to draw attention to the interrelationships among concepts used in the field. The figure suggests that information-seeking behaviour results from the recognition of some need, perceived by the user. That behaviour may take several forms: for example, the user may make demands upon formal systems that are customarily defined as information systems (such as libraries, on-line services, CD-ROM or information centres), or upon systems which may perform information functions in addition to a primary, non-information function (such as estate agents' offices or car sales agencies, both of which are concerned with selling, but which may be used to obtain information on current prices, areas of "suitable" housing, or details of cars that hold their secondhand value).

Alternatively, the user may seek information from other *people*, rather than from systems, and this is expressed in the diagram as involving "information exchange." The use of the word "exchange" is intended to draw attention to the element of reciprocity, recognized by sociologists and social psychologists as a fundamental aspect of human interaction.[3] In terms of information behaviour, the idea of reciprocity may be fairly

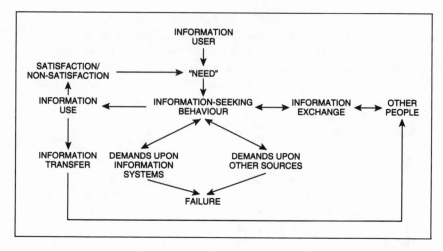

FIGURE I. Interrelationships among areas in the field of user studies

weak in some cases (as when a junior scientist seeks information from a senior but hierarchically equal colleague) but in other cases may be so strong that the process is inhibited, as when a subordinate person in a hierarchy fears to reveal his ignorance to a superior.[4]

In any of the above cases of information-seeking behaviour, "failure" may be experienced: this is indicated in the diagram for the use of systems but, of course, it may also be experienced when seeking information from other people.

Whatever the source of the information it will at some point be "used," if only in the sense of being evaluated to discover its relationship to the user's need. That "use" may satisfy or fail to satisfy the need and, in either event, may also be recognized as being of potential relevance to the need of another person and, consequently, may be "transferred" to such a person.

Although all of these areas are of potential interest to the field of user studies, attention has been given in the past chiefly to the demands people make upon formal information systems. Curiously, information use (which ought to point most directly to the needs experienced by people) is one of the most neglected areas; and "information exchange" as defined here has tended to fall within the sphere of interest of sociologists and organizational theorists rather than within that of information scientists.

"Information" in the figure may be understood in any of the senses mentioned earlier. Thus, in information exchange, an individual may be looking for facts, advice or opinions, and may receive any of these either in writing or orally. Sometimes the channel itself may be of overriding significance, as when orally given advice may be *preferred* over anything in writing. Again, a user may be interested in a specific document as a physical entity, as in the expression of a need to view variant copies of an incunabulum. In information transfer it may be a fact, an opinion or a piece of advice that is transferred orally, or a physical document "containing" the fact, opinion or advice may be given to another person. We can choose to study the facts, ideas, advice or opinions, or the nature and distribution of the documentary "containers." In any event, when the term "user study" is employed the specific sub-field should be specified, and the aspect or aspects of "information" under consideration should be defined.

Information Needs

Within the field of user studies the investigation of "information needs" has presented seemingly intractable problems. If we date user studies from 1948 and the Royal Society Scientific Information Conference, with its several surveys of users' information-seeking behaviour,[5] then the progress towards some theoretical understanding of the concept of "information need" has been slow. This fact is recognized by virtually every commentator on the subject from Menzel[6] and Paisley[7] through the various authors in the ARIST volumes,[8] to Ford's review of 1977.[9] As well as drawing attention to this fact, the authors have tried to discover why it is so and have generally concluded that the reason lies in inadequate methodology and the failure to do research that is "cumulative." Attention has also been paid to the definitional problem of "information need"[10] and the difficulty of separating the concept from "wants," "expressed demand," "satisfied demand" and so on. However, while much of this work is very useful, the problem remains generally unresolved.

Partly, this is the result of a failure to identify the context within which information needs investigations are carried out. Fig. 2[11] is an attempt to show some of the possible contexts. (Fig. I may be thought of as a subgraph of Fig. 2, centred on the user.) It is difficult in any two-dimensional diagram to convey the complexity of the "real" world and abstract elements of that real world. The "universe of knowledge," for example, is an abstract concept which embraces all knowledge-related objects, events and phenomena and, as such, clearly interacts with the "physical universe." To show the complex interactions of the physical and abstract universes, however, would involve a multi-dimensional diagram which would be extremely difficult, if not impossible, to express upon a sheet of paper. Accepting that difficulty, however, the "user's life

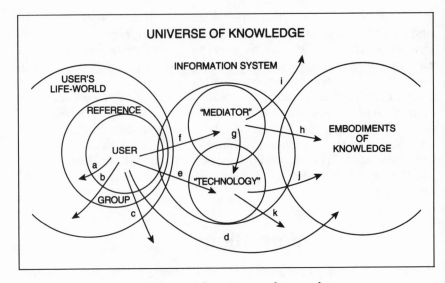

FIGURE 2. Information-seeking paths

world" can be defined as the totality of experiences centred upon the individual as an information user. Within this life-world one important sub-world will be the world of work, within which will exist various "reference groups" with which the user identifies: fellow professionals, the peer group within an organization and so on.

The user will be in contact with a variety of "information systems," only one of which is shown in the diagram, hence the indicated overlap with the user and his life-world. Within the information system two subsystems are shown: the "mediator" (generally a living system, i.e. a human being) and the "technology," used here in the general sense of whatever combination of techniques, tools and machines constitute the information-searching subsystem.

The information system must have access to various "embodiments of knowledge," phrased in this general way to indicate that such embodiments may be documents or living people.

The lettered paths on the diagram are intended to show some of the possible search paths that may be used by the information seeker directly or used on his behalf by the information system and its subsystems. The paths are not comprehensive of all possible search paths; however, they do identify four relevant groups:

• paths a, b, c and d identify search strategies by a user independent of any information system, and will be referred to as 'Category A' paths;

- paths e and f identify search paths involving either a mediator or an information system's technology (manual card file, computer terminal etc.)—Category B paths;
- paths g, h and i identify search strategies employed by a mediator to satisfy a user's demand for information—Category C; and
- paths j and k identify strategies employed by a sophisticated technology on behalf of either the user or the mediator—Category D. As an example of this latter category, a system could be envisaged in which a computer network could be searched at the initiative of any computer which is a member of that system. The network might include files of knowledge in the process of creation, such as research data files, computer conference files etc.

If we choose to investigate any of these categories of search strategies we are clearly investigating "information-seeking behaviour" rather than the user's *need* for information. Equally clearly, our motives for investigating search processes may be to make inferences about need, or it may be to uncover facts relating to *other* variables related to the design, development or adaptation of information systems.

Thus, we may wish to investigate Category A strategies to discover whether they are undertaken in ignorance of formal information systems, or because they are more efficient (for example, simply in terms of speed of delivery of a response) or more effective (for example, in terms of the quality of the information provided, or its currency). Such studies may never address the central question of "information need," that is, *why* the user decides to seek information, what purpose he believes it will serve and to what use it is actually put when received. However, the data derived from such studies may be of considerable use in discovering whether it is possible to redesign existing formal information systems so that they are more efficient or more effective.

Similarly, the search processes involved in Categories B and C may be studied to find out how efficiently the mediator, or the "technology," is performing, and Category D searches may be studied for similar reasons.

As noted above, the study of information-seeking behaviour can stand on its own as an area of applied research where the motive for the investigation is pragmatically related to system design and development. A different motivation is involved if we wish to understand *why* the information seeker behaves as he does. This is an area of *basic* research and, although the resulting knowledge may have practical applications, there is no *necessity* that it should.

However, many (if not most) "information scientists" are practitioners in information work or information systems management, and they look to studies of information "needs" for guidance on aspects of systems design, development and operation. A confusion then arises between what is *intended* by information needs research and what is *expected* of such research. As a consequence, basic research may fail to be funded because referees do not find in the proposals indications of potential practical applications which were never intended by the researcher.

There is another confusion, possibly more basic, in the association of the two words "information" and "need." This association imbues the resulting concept with connotations of a basic "need" qualitatively similar to other basic "human needs." However, if we examine the literature on human needs we find that this concept is divided by psychologists[12] into three categories:

- physiological needs, such as the need for food, water, shelter etc.;
- affective needs (sometimes called psychological or emotional needs) such as the need for attainment, for domination etc.;
- cognitive needs, such as the need to plan, to learn a skill etc.

It will be quickly recognized that these three categories are interrelated: physiological needs may trigger affective and/or cognitive needs; affective needs may give rise to cognitive needs; and problems relating to the satisfaction of cognitive needs (such as a failure to satisfy needs, or fear of disclosing needs) may result in affective needs (for example, for reassurance). These interrelationships are shown in Fig. 3 which suggests that, as part of the search for the satisfaction of these needs, an individual may engage in information-seeking behaviour. Indeed, it may be advisable to remove the term "information needs" from our professional vocabulary and to speak instead of "information-seeking towards the satisfaction of needs."

This is not to suggest that some affective or cognitive need will *immediately* "trigger" the response of information-seeking. Many factors other than the existence of a need will play a part: the importance of satisfying the need, the penalty incurred by acting in the absence of full information, the availability of information sources and the costs of using them, and so forth. Many decisions are taken with incomplete information or on the basis of beliefs, whether we call these prejudices, faith or ideology. So, information-seeking may not occur at all, or there may be a time delay between the recognition of the need and the information-seeking acts; or, in the case of affective needs, neither the need nor its satisfaction may be consciously recognized by the actor; or a cognitive need of fairly low salience may be satisfied by chance days, months or even years after it has been recognized, or the availability of the information may bring about the recognition of a previously unrecognized

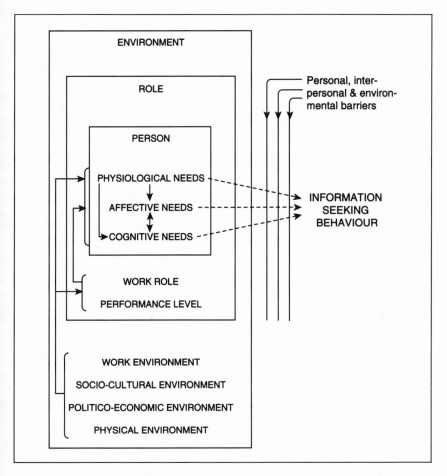

FIGURE 3.   Factors influencing needs and information-seeking behaviour

cognitive need. These factors are crudely represented in Fig. 3 as personal, interpersonal and environmental barriers to information-seeking.

If we take the earlier analysis of the ways in which the word "information" is used we can see that the different senses are more or less related to the above needs. Thus

• the factual data, or subject content, of a document may satisfy cognitive needs, and this is the usual sense in which we think about the use to which information is put. The attempts at single definitions of "information" are also couched solely in cognitive terms. For example, Belkin[1] notes that his concept of an information recipient's "anomalous state of knowledge" leads to "an explicitly cognitive view of the situation with which information science is concerned" (p. 80) and Wersig's[13] view of information as reduction in the uncertainty involved in problematic situations similarly connotes cognitive changes in the recipient of a communication. However, as Hollnagel[14] writes:

> Information science is concerned with the use of information by humans. . . . And it is concerned specifically with the way in which humans search for information, systematically as well as unsystematically. The basis for information science is therefore to be found in our experience of using and searching for information . . . (p. 184).

Because the situations in which information is sought and used are *social* situations, however, purely cognitive conceptions of information need are probably adequate for some research purposes in information science, but not for all. Information may. also satisfy affective needs, such as the need for security,[15] for achievement, or for dominance;

- the channel of communication, particularly the choice of oral channels over written channels, may well be guided by affective needs as much, if not more than, by cognitive needs. For example, in seeking information from a superior, someone may be more interested in being recognized and accepted as a particular kind of person than in the actual subject content of the message; in other words, he may be seeking approval or recognition. The oral transfer of information to others may also be done for affective reasons; for example, to establish dominance over others by reminding them that you are better informed and, therefore, in some sense superior;
- the physical document may satisfy an affective need, as when someone collects rare bindings, or illustrated books, because of their beauty. Under extreme circumstances documents may serve physiological needs, as when the tramp on the park bench covers himself with newspapers to avoid freezing to death.

If, as suggested here, the full range of human, personal needs is at the root of motivation towards information-seeking behaviour, it must also be recognized that these needs arise out of the roles an individual fills in social life. So far as specialized information systems are concerned, the most relevant of these roles is "work role," that is, the set of activities, responsibilities etc. of an individual, usually in some organizational setting, in pursuit of earnings and other satisfactions.[16]

At the work-role level it will be clear that the performance of particular tasks, and the processes of planning and decision-making, will be the principal generators of cognitive needs; while the nature of the organization, coupled with the individual's personality structure, will create affective needs such as the need for achievement, for self-expression and self-actualization.[17] The particular pattern of needs and the resulting form of information-seeking behaviour will be a function of all of these factors, plus factors such as the organizational level at which a role is performed and the "climate" of the organization.[18]

Again, the search for determining factors related to needs and information-seeking behaviour must be broadened to include aspects of the environment within which the work-role is performed. The immediate work-environment and its "climate" has been mentioned above, but the socio-cultural environment, and the physical environment, will all have an impact in particular ways. The relationships will be too numerous to detail here, but examples can be given:

- the economic climate and the differential stratification of resources will define some work environments as "information-poor" and others as "information-rich," with consequent effects upon the probability of information-seeking behaviour and the choice of channel of communication;
- the political system may define certain types of information as forbidden to particular groups (including the general public) and, consequently, the non-availability of this material may affect performance in specific work roles;
- the physical environment will have a clear effect upon the nature of some categories of tasks and upon the consequent cognitive needs. For example, questions emerging out of drilling for oil in the North Sea are likely to differ in many cases from those that emerge out of drilling in Saudi Arabia.

Fig. 3 shows the probable interrelationships among personal needs and these other factors, the aim of which is to suggest that when we talk of users' "information needs" we should not have in mind some conception of a fundamental, innate, cognitive or emotional "need" for information, but a conception of information (facts, data, opinion, advice) as one means towards the end of satisfying such fundamental needs. In the past a great deal of user studies research has suffered from a concentration on the *means* by which people discover information (often analysed in terms of the information researcher's view of how the user *ought* to have been seeking information) rather than upon the *ends* served by the information-seeking behaviour. It is this bias in past research that has led to dissatisfaction with the results of user studies research, since the service implications of the results have been far from clear. There are, of course, exceptions; the Baltimore study of the information needs of the ordinary citizen avoided the means versus ends trap by building the interview schedule around the idea of problems experienced in everyday life, for which information-seeking using formal information systems might or might not be appropriate.[19] What emerges from the Baltimore study is certainly compatible with the view presented in this paper but, again, information needs are presented in largely cognitive terms (although the existence of non-cognitive barriers is recognized) and the affective dimension of the user's situation is lacking.

Consequences

The analysis presented above is not intended to be merely definitional; the aim is to suggest that the analysis may be used as a springboard to research based upon a wider, holistic view of the information user. In such a wider view the individual would be perceived not merely as driven to seek information for cognitive ends, but as living and working in social settings which create their own motivations to seek information to help satisfy largely affective needs. There would need to be a consequent shift in the focus of research from an examination of the information sources and systems used by the information-seeker to an exploration of the role of information in the user's everyday life in his work organization or social setting.

The consequences of a shift in focus could be fundamental for information research in at least three respects. First, there are consequences for the methods to be employed in research. The vast majority of studies of "information needs" has been conducted under a relatively crude conception of the "scientific method," using self-completed questionnaires as the main data-collection instrument. Social researchers of many kinds have become disenchanted with this model of research and are turning increasingly to a consideration of "qualitative research" either as a complete alternative to quantitative research or, at least, as a preliminary.[20] The methods employed in qualitative research overlap to some extent those of traditional "quantitative" research in the social sciences in that they include interviewing, but qualitative research is likely to use less formally structured interviewing procedures and may, in addition, use methods such as observation, free-flowing discussion, and the analysis of documents (personal or organizational) and conversational analysis. Under one school of thought, "Qualitative research ... is concerned with developing concepts rather than applying preexisting concepts,"[21] and given the state of theory in information science (that is, its undeveloped state) it can well be argued that "developing concepts" is what is needed. Qualitative research seems particularly appropriate to the study of the needs underlying information-seeking behaviour because:

- our concern is with uncovering the facts of the everyday life of the people being investigated;
- by uncovering those facts we aim to understand the needs that exist which press the individual towards information-seeking behaviour;
- by better understanding of those needs we are able better to understand what meaning information has in the everyday life of people; and
- by all of the foregoing we should have a better understanding of the user and be able to design more effective information systems.

The second consequence for information research of the proposed shift in focus is that, before a generally applicable theory of information-seeking behaviour can be evolved, the context of the research must be narrowed so that crucial determining factors can be identified and analysed. There can be little use, for example, in a national survey of the "information needs" of any group (chemists, botanists, economists etc.) if members of these groups are undertaking widely differing kinds of tasks in totally different organizations with varying levels of information provision. If we wish to uncover the determining factors of behaviour we must do so by first undertaking in-depth studies of well-defined categories of persons, developing explanatory concepts and then testing these concepts in related but different settings.

The third consequence for research would be a need to widen our conceptual perspectives of the user and his behaviour. It seems unlikely that information-seeking behaviour can be explained by purely "information" concepts. Belkin[1] notes that, "The most commonly proposed information concept for information science . . . is that of Shannon. . . This is hardly surprising, since Shannon's information concept is almost the only formalized, mathematical, and successfully implemented concept ever proposed for any purpose" (p. 66). However, the communication model proposed by Shannon,[22] with its elements source, channel, message, coder, decoder, receiver and noise, was never intended as an information-science model nor as a behavioural science model, and, consequently, can tell us nothing about the information user and his needs. The concepts we need for explanation, or for development within our own emergent discipline, multidiscipline, or whatever it may be, need to be drawn from psychology, social psychology and sociology, as much as from communication theory.

There are other consequences for information science defined here as a multidisciplinary field rather than as a single-discipline, theoretical science. Roberts[23] has drawn attention to the need to pay more than lip-service to the suggestion that, in some respects at least, information science is a social science. The proposed shift of focus suggested here would support that proposition by insisting upon the more intelligent use of social research methods for the development of models from the point of view of the philosophy of social (rather than physical) science. It would require that such models pay more attention to the behavioural and organizational contexts of information-seeking than hitherto, and to the totality of types of information resources and information transfer mechanisms. Information science is likely to make more progress in this way than by seeking to evolve on the basis of physical science notions of a discipline alone.

An "information science" firmly founded upon an understanding of information users in the context of their work or social life is also likely to be of more use to the information practitioner, by pointing the way to practical innovations in information services, and to potentially beneficial associations with other communication/information-related subsystems. It does little injustice to the historic record to suggest that information services have developed more by copying previously existing examples than by genuine analysis of the needs of potential users. In particular, the transfer of techniques from special libraries in science and technology to information units in the vastly different environments of public service bureaucracies, voluntary organizations, business concerns and central government, has been carried on without any serious questioning as to whether these different contexts of information provision require different means of service delivery or, indeed, whether information itself needs re-definition. An orientation towards the user in the true sense, that is, avoiding preconceptions about what *he or she* will perceive to be "information," while concentrating upon the problems that create cognitive and/or affective needs, must result in a greater humility about the potential value of traditional information practices and a greater willingness to innovate and experiment.

The result of a more truly user-oriented, innovative, experimental information profession should be a reduction in the *marginality* of information service. Scientific research generally recognizes the significance of services which provide access to the external research literature, but when such services are adopted by different kinds of organization with little or no adaptation in the light of a proper analysis of the needs of users or of their relationship with organizational communication systems, information services become increasingly marginal to the organization's functioning. Evidence for this can be found in industry, where, when economic pressures have been intense, numerous special libraries and information systems have been abolished or subject to severe staff redundancies.

The answer to this does not lie simply in manœuvring for a more central reporting position in the organization, but in analysing the *total* range of information services that may be appropriate to meeting the needs of members of the organization. In all probability this may mean closer association, to the point of merger, with other organizational sub-systems that have an "information" mission—indeed, as a result of developments in information technology, the trend has already begun.

There are, finally, consequences of all of the foregoing for "information science" as a profession and for professional education in the field. No sooner had information science (in this professional sense) emerged out of special librarianship, than it found what appeared to be the central ground occupied by computer scientists, system analysts, management information system designers, and most recently, data-base entrepreneurs. Soon, office automation through word-processors and other applications of micro-technology will be extending their influence into areas information scientists as practitioners have believed to be theirs. The only sensible response to this is a widening of the concept of the "information profession" and an acceptance of the need for consultation and co-operation with other groups, the better to serve the needs of the information user. That there is potential for this can be seen in the increased disenchantment with crudely designed management information systems and the increased awareness that, in designing such systems, the technology involved is only part of the total system, and that the user, hitherto somewhat neglected, is an important element.[24]

As for the impact on professional education, there are several things to consider. First, if the social situation of the user is as significant as suggested in this paper, and if the need for more care in the use of social research methods (both quantitative and qualitative) is accepted, then curricula should become more concerned with the social and organizational contexts of information-seeking and information use, and should pay more attention to general theories of communication (mass media, organizational, person-to-person), and to social research methods and their philosophical basis.

However, if a shift takes place towards a new information profession, revision of existing curricula in information science will not be enough and, certainly, the mere addition of one or two courses to a curriculum will be far from sufficient. The members of that wider profession will be drawn from many disciplines, and the most fruitful development (and, in these hard times, possibly the most cost-effective) could be the incorporation of "information science" subjects into the graduate schools of a variety of different disciplines. With luck this could be achieved by designing joint programmes with other departments within a teaching institution, coupled with increased service teaching to undergraduate courses in particular fields. If this development does not take place, that is if planning does not begin now or in the near future, the result may be a gradual diminution of the role of schools of librarianship/information science in the education of the new information professional.

Acknowledgments

The ideas in this paper have been developed over a number of years—in fact, since wrestling with the concept of 'information need' with students at the University of Maryland in 1971! Oral presentations of earlier papers were made at an IBICT seminar in Rio de Janeiro and at a research seminar at Sheffield University Postgraduate School of Librarianship and Information Science, both in 1979, and I am grateful to the participants at these meetings for their discussion of the issues. Further, useful comments have been made on earlier drafts of this paper by three colleagues, Professor Wilfred Saunders, Norman Roberts and David Streatfield, and, most recently and very helpfully, by an anonymous referee. I am aware of the imperfections that remain, however, and accept full responsibility for them.

Notes

1. Belkin, N. "Information concepts for information science." *Journal of Documentation* 34 (1978):55–85.
2. Farradane, J. "The nature of information." *Journal of Information Science* 1 (1979):13–17.
3. Gouldner, A.W. The norm of reciprocity. *American Sociological Review* 25 (1960):161–78.
4. Jackson, J.M. "The organization and its communication problems." *Journal of Communication* 9 (1959):158–67.
5. Royal Society Scientific Information Conference, London, 1946. *Report and papers submitted.* London: Royal Society, 1948.
6. Menzel, H. *Review of studies in the flow of information among scientists.* 2 vols. New York: Columbia University, Bureau of Applied Social Research, 1960.
7. Paisley, W.J. *The flow of (behavioral) science information—a review of the research literature.* Palo Alto, Calif.: Stanford University, 1965.
8. *Annual review of information science and technology.* Vol. I–; 1966–. (Various editors and publishers).
9. Ford G. *User studies: an introductory guide and select bibliography.* Sheffield: Centre for Research on User Studies, 1977.
10. See, for example, Line M. B. Draft definitions: information and library needs, wants, demands and uses. *Aslib Proceedings,* 26 (1974):87; Roberts, N. Draft definitions: information and library needs, wants, demands and uses: a comment. *Aslib Proceedings,* 27 (1975):308–13; and, for a philosophical view drawn to my attention by Colin Harris: White, A.R. Needs and wants. *Philosophy of Education Society, Proceedings,* 8 (1974):159–80.
11. An earlier version of this diagram was used by the author in a discussion at IRFIS 3,

Oslo, Norway, 1979, and was modified as a result of the participants' comments. It has been further modified since that meeting.

12. See, for example, the entry for the word NEED in *Encyclopaedia of psychology*, edited by H.J. Eysenck, W. Arnold and R. Meili. London: Search Press, 1972.

13. Wersig, G. *Information-Kommunikation-Dokumentation*. Pullach bei Munchen: Verlag Dokumentation, 1971. (Cited by Belkin, *op cit.*).

14. Hollnagel, E. Is information science an anomalous state of knowledge? *Journal of Information Science*, 2 (1980):183–87.

15. The significance of affective needs was first drawn to the author's attention when carrying out evaluation interviews with the users of a current awareness bulletin; see, Wilson, T. D. Information uses in social services departments. *In: Proceedings of the 3rd international research forum in information science, Oslo*, (1979) edited by Tor Henriksen. Oslo: Statens Bibliotekskole, 1979.

16. It is recognized, of course, that social roles other than work role may influence information system design in other contexts. Thus, a citizens' information service ought to be designed in full awareness of the implications for information seeking of social roles such as house-owner, tenant, parent or voter.

17. See, for a review of the literature on motivation and work: Katz, D. and Kahn, R.L. *The social psychology of organizations*. 2nd edn. New York: Wiley (1978):Ch. 13.

18. "Organizational climate" is a rather fuzzy concept (see, for a review, Payne, R. *and* Pugh, D. S. Organizational structure and climate. In M. D. Dunnette, ed., *Handbook of industrial and organizational psychology*. Chicago: Rand McNally, 1976, 1125–73), and whilst work conducted in some types of organization indicates a relationship between climate and information-seeking behaviour, e.g. Olson, E. E. Organizational factors affecting information flow in industry. *Aslib Proceedings*, 29 (1977):124–9, other work finds no such relationship, e.g. Wilson, T. D., Streatfield, D. R. *and* Mullings, C. Information needs in local authority social services departments: a second report on Project INISS. *Journal of Documentation*, 35 (1979):120–36.

19. Warner, E. S. *et al. Information needs of urban residents*. Washington: U.S. Department of Health Education and Welfare, Bureau of Libraries and Learning Resources (1973).

20. Evidence for this interest has appeared in many sources from the emergence of 'ethno-methodology' in the late sixties (Garfinkel, H. *Studies in ethnomethodology*. Englewood Cliffs, N.J.: Prentice Hall, 1967) to Douglas, Jack D. *Investigative social research*. Beverly Hills, Calif.: Sage publications, 1976; and, more recently, in a symposium on the subject organized by the Social Science Research Council, The analysis of qualitative data: a symposium. *Sociological Review*, New Series, 27 (1979):648–827 (Issue editor, Mildred Baxter) and another symposium, Qualitative methodology. *Administrative Science Quarterly*, 24 (1979):520–671.

21. Halfpenny, P. The analysis of qualitative data. *Sociological Review*, New Series, 27 (1979):799–825.

22. Shannon, C.E. and Weaver, W. *The mathematical theory of communication*. Urbana, Ill.: University of Illinois Press (1960).

23. Roberts, N. Social considerations towards a definition of information science. *Journal of Documentation*, 32 (1976):249–57.

24. See, for example, Lucas, H.C. *Why information systems fail*. New York: Columbia University Press (1975).

Problem Dimensions and Information Traits

SUSAN E. MACMULLIN
ROBERT S. TAYLOR

As our society becomes more information based, the systems that store, organize, and provide information and knowledge will become increasingly critical. We may hazard a guess that one of the major characteristics of the early period of an information society is information glut, i.e., information overload. This doesn't necessarily mean that we have too much information, it means rather that the systems that filter, transmit, and distribute information do not operate well. More important than the systems themselves are the assumptions we hold concerning information and the way we think about the systems that provide the information—what they can do, how they are structured, and indeed why they exist at all.

The major—perhaps only—reason for the existence of an information system is to store and to provide information and knowledge in usable chunks to those who live and work in certain environments, and who, as a result, have certain problems which information may help to clarify or even solve. In this context we view "problem environments" in the broadest sense—from leisure reading to corporate decision-making, from education to scientific research and development, from the need to be informed to the assessment of environmental impact. How we accept, perceive, and structure these systems will have a profound effect on the culture of the information society and on the efficacy of the information-providing mechanisms upon which that society is based.

Historically, our information systems have been technology-driven and content-driven. The former systems first found their base in the book and its technology and today finds it in the computer and associated technologies. These technologies have essentially prescribed the size, shape, dynamics, and even the content of information systems. What is stored in a book or similar artifact, or what is stored and is

Reprinted from *Information Society* 3(1) (1984): 91–111.

manipulable in a computer is perceived as knowledge or information. And the constraints of the book or the computer are the determinants of the technology-driven models.

On the other hand, content-driven models derive from the traditional classifications of knowledge, together with the elaborate schemata that have grown around them over the past 25 centuries. These have established not only a way of organizing knowledge, but also a disciplined way of perceiving knowledge, e.g., the formation of academic departments and the identification and structure of researchable problems. In information terms, it is what is in the package, namely, the subject, and its storage, organization, and retrieval, that has established the boundaries and objectives of content-driven systems.

It is not that these models are poor; it is rather that they are no longer enough. The explosive growth of potentially relevant information in research, managerial, educational, social, and policy contexts is altering the information environment in rather basic ways. The information-providing systems based on these models and their associated assumptions are no longer adequate. The inadequateness is due in part to a failure to understand the contexts from which the need for information arises. The approach suggested in this paper has implications for the way we view information and the systems which provide it in our society.

Information helps people understand their situation through, for example, verifying, clarifying, decreasing uncertainty, and educating.[1] These, the results of effective information use, evolve from information needs which are determined by the problems arising from specific situations. Such a situation is a convergence of environmental variables such as: subject matter; organization type and style; function activity; goals; levels of sophistication; connections with other environments; opportunities and constraints. Within each situation, problems are generated and sometimes defined in order to structure ideas or to trigger action. Under these circumstances, unless the problem is very simple or routine, a need for information is created. However, as discussed above, information systems are primarily content-driven, which means that they are designed from just one of the possible environmental variables, that of subject matter. They tend to ask only one question; "What do you want to know?"—and they respond to this rather well. As we have argued, there are other equally important concerns that need to be responded to: "How do you need to know it?" "Why do you need to know it?" "In what form do you need to know it?" "What do you know already?" "What do you anticipate finding?" "How will this help you?" "What does your problem look like?"

With this as context, this paper suggests the development of additional criteria for the design of information systems. These criteria should include as much of the user situation as feasible. Therefore, problems, not questions (which are only subject based), should be the level of concern, since the problem represents the information use environment more completely than does the question. This approach is not merely interdisciplinary; rather, it requires a different configuration of information and its structure, with different access points and different dimensions.

Between this use environment and the information-providing system, whatever its configuration, there exists what Taylor called the "negotiating space." "The dynamics of this space in a very real sense define the time, effort, initiative, and even dollars a user must invest in order to extract information of use to him from the system."[2] This is the point where a user or client actively seeks or is given information, and where he makes choices based on the criteria derived, consciously or unconsciously, from his problems. The success of the information process therefore depends on two factors: the user's perception of the value (e.g., precision, accuracy, etc.) of the information provided; and how well problem types are anticipated and understood by the designer of the system, and hence reflected in the filtering processes.

This paper then is an early attempt to structure problems in information terms so that information systems of any type can be more responsive to the environments they serve. This is a first and tentative step toward mapping problem dimensions against information traits. This approach considers the client or user of an information system initially as a set of problems generated by a particular environment, and relates those problems to the generation, supply, and provision of information.

Questions, Problems, Sense-Making

Information systems as they now exist are quite good at providing documents in answer to a question about a subject. Presumably, if one is able to ask a question, one has reduced a problem to fragments which are related through the problem framework itself. However, there is a distinction between what is contained in the problem and what is contained in the question. A problem is a compression of the user situation with all of the important elements intact. A question, however, does not retain all those elements that make up a problem. It is not the situation made smaller, but only a part of the situation. By focusing on problems, we are moving on a continuum which proceeds from *questions* to *problems* to *sense-making*.[3] As the actor moves on this continuum, his information needs become less definite and the response to those needs more difficult. The isomorphic information continuum moves from *specifying* to *connecting* to *orienting*.

The *question* is structured in two parts:

(1) *subject:* a term or terms which refers to an object in the world about which some type of determination is being sought, and

(2) *query:* an expression which identifies the particular determination to be made regarding the subject of the question.[4]

The question requires information which is specific. The *relationship* between the subject and a determination is known for a question. The information requirement, then, is to designate that relationship by a specific, but not necessarily unique, answer. For instance, "What was the ratio of intake over outlay last month?" contains a subject and query in a well defined relationship. Question elements are usually not ambiguous.

Questions are the result of the fragmentation of problems and indicate the most precise state of incognizance. A question refers only indirectly to the user's environment. It contains one segment of unknown information which may in itself be simple (e.g., a population count) or complex, such as a known process (e.g., auditing.) The important aspect of a question, for this discussion, is that its connection to a user situation is remote and fragmented.

The *problem* has three definitional components: (1) the initial state; (2) the goal state; and (3) the process(es) which are mental, physical, or perceptual activities required to move from the initial state to the goal state. The relationship between the initial state and the goal state is not specified. The problem requires information which makes *connections* between those states.

The initial state accommodates the definition of a problem situation, that is, how elements of an environment connect in an unsatisfactory way. The initial state is the result of the process of problem definition which in turn is the activity of the third portion of the continuum, *sense-making*.

Although our major concern is with "problems," the concept of problem definition and question formation represents a process of sense-making which begins with an unexamined, unformed need for information.[5] This need is the most abstract point on the problem continuum, and at this stage the need is for information which *orients* so that a problem can be identified, clarified, and understood. Orienting information endeavors to provide a perspective or frame in which to identify problems.[6] Problem definition is a stage of analysis of a situation, and the initial state of the problem is a stage of synthesis. The synthesis brings together all of the crucial elements of a problem that have been defined in the analysis. Problem definition requires that a situation be identified and explicated. The initial state of the problem is the result, the synthesis, of that identification and explication. It is worthwhile to note that all of the assumptions that were used to form the analysis of the problem are carried over to the initial state.

Ideally, the information requirement at this point is the culling of important factors derived from the analysis of the problem situation. In reality, however, probably nothing this systematic takes place, and the delineation between problem identification and the initial state is rather hazy. Information for analysis and synthesis, exploration and definition are all possibilities at this point.

The goal state is also characterized by degrees of definition. In decision-making, goal states are usually very broad and indefinite. For example, the social goal of eliminating poverty is not very useful in an operational sense. Rather, this kind of goal sets a direction for the definition of subgoals which relate directly to the primary goal. The space from the initial to the goal state may be defined, selected, or truncated to form subgoals. This reduction or partitioning is often necessary to make a problem manageable and appropriate information accessible. The danger lies in losing track of how the subgoals relate to the goal. Information can intercede at two possible points, in identifying the subgoals and in defining the relationship of these subgoals to the main goal.

The third component of the problem comprises the processes needed to move from the initial state to the goal state. These processes are specified protocols for achieving the transformation of the initial state to the goal state and may take the form of physical action, perceptual activities, or mental activities. The levels of process specification may vary with the environmental constraints, subject, prior experience, resources available, and knowledge domain.[7] Information is used to choose among alternative methods of affecting a change. One of the most useful types of information during this process is that used to track the change in the initial state and the goal state. A continual process of evaluation would monitor progress as conflicting elements are eliminated by the designated process. This monitoring function would include the following questions: (1) Is the initial state being affected? (2) Is the initial state changing in the direction of the desired goal state? Are things getting worse? Are there unanticipated changes?

It should be noted that there do not seem to be definite boundaries between questions and problems or problems and sense-making activities. Questions require answers, that is, questions are satisfied by the most precise chunks of information that we can provide. Problems require solutions, resolutions, clarification, and compromises (satisficing). Sense-making demands information which provides context and orientation. No strong demarcation exists between the various information forms. As one moves from the most abstract to the most concrete information state (orienting to specifying), there is a continual progression. One passes through gray areas where, for instance, the discontinuity in understanding has been breached, but a problem has not yet been formulated.

Problem Dimensions and Information Traits

Problems can be thought of as surrogates of the use environment, which is the situation that evolves out of aggregated variables such as organizational context,[8] functional role,[9] and societal constraints. Problems represent the use environment and contain enough that is important about it to indicate that the exercise of defining problem dimensions may allow the information professional to infer needs for information in a more structured systematic way. Therefore, the use environment is represented by problem dimensions. In this approach, concentration and interest involve three stages of the information environment: (1) the results from the user environments (i.e., problems); (2) the output from the system environment (i.e., information); and (3) the interface.

The shape and size of the interface where problems and information outputs meet, change with features of problems and information. It is in this interface that the system, however defined, attempts to meet the needs of the user. It is in the interface that the user attempts to define his concerns. It is always dynamic. The idea behind problem dimension/information trait matching is that the activity in the interface evolves to reflect the users from either side (i.e., problems or information). That is, information systems can be built with user specifications beyond the present discipline or system specifications, and, in addition, can provide dimensions and context to subject matter, coming closer to problems in contrast to questions. The interface, then, will be characterized by less uncertainty than it is now.

Information Traits

Information traits are the special attributes that can be used to define the ways that information can be identified and presented. More importantly, these traits can be related directly to the dimensions of a problem. Some traits appear to exist on a continuum, while some seem to be dichotomous and mutually exclusive. Others seem to coexist within a problem area. These are brief descriptions of information traits important to the *need* for information. These traits, which are fairly general, refer to the processes and goals of presenting information.

1. *Quantitative continuum.* Quantitative information is derived from phenomena that can be measured, and is represented numerically. Otherwise, qualitative information is presented, that is, information which is descriptive. Quantitative data are specific and, when aggregated, give an overall picture of a situation, whereas qualitative data may give reasons, assumptions, nuances, and details.

2. *Data continuum.* Data which can be empirically derived can be called *hard data.* Hard data are a result of observation and can be replicated. *Soft data* exist when the data cannot be observed but must be inferred or where assumptions must be made in order to collect the data. As a rule of thumb, data which are not the result of a random sample of a population or a census are soft data. Data derived from measurement scales and tools which are not developed to an acceptably reliable point are also soft data, as are beliefs and values.

3. *Temporal continuum.* Historical (precedence)/forecasting (future modeling). This continuum concerns information on what has been (historical), what will be (probabilities), and what should be (prescriptive). Litigation support systems, for example, consist of historical legal information. Financial business information is a mix of information about past performance and potential performance, the latter projected from formal models.

4. *Solution continuum.* (Single solution/option range). The criteria, which define a situation, yield a distribution of possible good and bad solutions.[10] There may be one desired "best" solution or, in some cases, any number of solutions will do. Satisficing or finding the first solution that meets minimum criteria is the standard operating procedure of the engineer. Gerstenberger and Allen, in their study of engineers and choice of information channel, noted that:

> Engineers, in selecting among information channels, act in a manner which is intended not to maximize gain, but rather, to minimize loss. The loss to be minimized is the cost in terms of effort, either physical or psychological, which must be expended in order to gain access to an information channel.[11]

Information is collected until a reasonably good solution is discovered. There is no need to go beyond this point if cost and functional factors are met. The importance and degree of structuredness of a problem dictate the number of solution possibilities generated. The area of decision-making is a field which has high uncertainty (i.e., unstructured problems) and may require more options before a solution or a goal can be settled on, as the criteria are fluid and not well defined. There is more to this continuum than satisficing and optimizing, then. Generating solution options is also a way of understanding a problem.

5. *Focus continuum.* (Precision/diffusion). The focus continuum is based on the extent to which facts are identified and associated for a situation. Precise information is useful for a situation which is well defined, whereas diffuse information may be more useful for an ill defined situation. Precision necessitates an exactness of information. A fact or other specific piece of information would be needed if a problem was well understood or if a question was being asked. Diffusion is an asset if a problem is not well understood or is in a definitional stage. Brainstorming and idea generation, e.g., the first stage of the design engineering process, produce scattered diffuse information which can be used to gain a perspective on the situation in question, i.e., to orient.

6. *Specificity of use continuum.* (Applied/theoretical). This continuum is concerned with concreteness or specificity of use. Applied information is immediately useful in an operational sense. It tells how to do something, explains processes, or establishes procedures. Theoretical information gives possible reasons or clues as to why/how something works or behaves. The theoretical principles and logic of an event are sought in order to explain and predict.

7. *Substantive continuum.* (Applied/descriptive). This continuum is defined through form and content. Applied information is defined here just as it was above in the *specificity of use continuum.* It is instrumental or operational information which describes the protocol or how to do something. Substantive information seems to be different than theoretical information in that it describes the content and meaning of a phenomenon without necessarily predicting the process or behavior. A theory links the item in question to the environment. Substantive information focuses on the object and describes it.

8. *Aggregation continuum.* (Clinical/census). Information can be presented quantitatively from a sample of one to a population study. Situations which are highly complex and contain variables which are not quantitative can be researched by case studies. This kind of research yields information which has a great amount of depth and detail but cannot be easily generalized or aggregated. On the other end of this contin-

uum are studies done on entire populations, and there is, of course, no need to generalize. Aggregated information, taken from population samples, gives us information on the most central measurement of the population (i.e., mean, mode). This is the center of the continuum. The appropriateness of each type of information is dependent on the tractableness and suitability of a subject to research.

9. *Causal/diagnostic continuum.* Causal information (why something happens) is an implicit need in all problem solving. In some situations, such as those that deal with people and/or complex under-researched variables, causal information is difficult to achieve. Diagnostic information (what is happening) is the information that must be gathered by defining a situation carefully. This is the first step toward causal information.[12]

These information traits are as characteristic of stored information as are subject descriptions. Just as we now have subject classification and subject naming systems, we need to have schemata for locating and classifying these information traits. When we learn how to do this, these traits can be identified and used in decisions about information selection, organization, retrieval, and display. They become legitimate and useful signals affecting user choice in the complex process of selecting relevant information for problems which have certain dimensions.

Problem Dimensions

Problem dimensions are those characteristics that, beyond specific subject matter, establish the criteria for judging the relevance of information to a problem or to a class of problems. Saracevic, in a 1971 paper on relevance, hinted at this in noting that "the human factor, i.e. variations introduced by human decision-making, seems to be a major factor affecting the performance of every and all components of an information retrieval system."[13] We interpret those "variations" to reflect the problem dimensions discussed briefly here, which exist in the non-subject part of the question response by the system. They are presented below as dichotomies, though they probably exist as continua.

1. *Design/discovery:* Discovery is the description of the natural world, the things and processes which are apart from human activities. Discovery is concerned with what exists in the natural world. Natural sciences, such as astronomy and physics, are examples of disciplines which involve the process of discovery, i.e., which describe what is "al-

ready there." In contrast, design concerns those problems which refer to things and processes made by humans. Design problems are ones where a certain state is desired and through effort a change can be effected which creates the desired state. Economics, cognitive psychology, education, and information studies are examples of disciplines which concentrate on problems of design. Man does not create what is "described," but he does create what is "designed." Design is a process of *creation* while description is a process of *explication*.

A manager who is interested in increasing productivity is confronted with a problem of design. Very simply, design and discovery are analogous to the processes of inventing and finding. Information for design would include an option range, while information for discovery would concentrate on a single piece of data. Simon in his book, *The Sciences of the Artificial*, explains this category in terms of the natural and artificial sciences.[14]

2. *Well structured/ill structured:* Well structured problems (WSP) are those which can be solved by application of logical or algorithmic processes. Ill structured problems (ISP) are those which cannot be *resolved* through strictly analytical means. Reasons for the existence of ISP can be that the problem is nonroutine or too complex to be properly analyzed, variables within the problem are not well understood (e.g., human motivation), and therefore may vary over time and space, or that random factors exist in the problem (e.g., weather). WSP tend to lend themselves to the use of hard, quantitative data. However, the assumptions behind the quantitative data and the method of collection may introduce hidden subjectiveness into the information. ISP require decisions based on probabilistic information on how to proceed, e.g., development of a policy for the management of information resources by federal agencies.

3. *Complex/simple:* Complexity of a problem refers to the number and interactions of problem variables. A simple problem is one where a path between the initial state and the goal state is easily defined. Complex problems need to be reduced to manageable blocks. Complexity and structure (well-or ill-structured problems) may influence the choices made as to which problems to attend. An actor may choose to employ selective perception, ignoring things which do not "fit" because connections are unclear.

4. *Specific/amorphous goals:* This problem dimension introduces the use of proxy goals which are substituted when goals are too ambiguous to be operationalized. This may be seen in policy and legislative pro-

cesses as well as in managerial decisions. For example, "office productivity" must be made measurable in order (i) to make specific plans for reaching the goal, and (ii) to recognize when the goal has been reached. Proxy goals are then employed, such as reducing the time needed to compile a report. Information needs begin with an analysis of the goal state which implies an understanding of what is desired and measurable. Specific goals, as we have indicated, are those which can be operationalized in such a way as to be evaluated. Efficiency measures are based on specific goals. Amorphous goals tend to require preference decisions in order to make them in some degree specific. Amorphous goals are an indication of the direction one wishes to go and not the result that one wants.

5. *Initial state understood/not understood:* Initial states, that is, the specific problem state, are confusing because at least some of the interrelationships among the contributing factors are not well understood. This may be because the problem solver is not privy to information that would explain the interrelationships or it may be because the factors are not yet described or because there are too many of them to control.[15] In science, there is no progression unless each step is explained. In many ways, the task of science is to understand a state by observation and description. Social science research is the means by which we attempt to define and understand aggregate behavior and, therefore, the initial state of many policy and managerial problems. Various methodologies and means of analysis have produced too many conflicting and unsupported results to be said to actually describe most initial states in these areas. This means that, in information terms, soft and qualitative data may be of more use in helping to define the initial state. If we shift a bit to problems which use technical information (e.g., environmental problems) there is an interesting difference. Presumably, environmental problems are largely technical and scientific in scope. However, often this type of problem, for example that of acid rain, is not well understood because the number of interactions among the factors is large and the interactions themselves are not clearly defined. Information in such a case is needed to corroborate data, to forecast, and to generate opinions.

6. *Assumptions agreed upon/not agreed upon:* Problems in the management and policy sciences do not have one accepted knowledge base such as those that exist in the natural sciences. Natural laws are largely consistent; axioms that include inferences about human behavior are somewhat questionable. Approaches to economics, for instance, center on contradictory assumptions. Problem definition is made difficult by disparate assumptions which do exist. Barriers to problem definition are

identified by the field of social cognition as perception, information coding, and motivation.[16] Perceptions about the world lead to different basic assumptions which are further diversified by various ways of coding information and the motivation to use it and to make sense of it.

7. *Assumptions explicit/not explicit:* Whether assumptions are agreed upon or not, they often get buried and become normative imperatives which are not taken into account in higher levels of debate. Therefore, a greater range of possible frames for problems is lost the more strictly the normative position is held. Often argument is at cross-purposes because assumptions are not made explicit, and positions are worlds apart from the beginning. This is intensified by packaging and form. Information may seem more objective when represented in certain forms; e.g., statistical tables, data sets, and computer printouts. Numbers and machines carry an authority in themselves at times, with no reference to the possible vagaries of data collection.

This is an opportunity for information systems to be valuable in a substantive way. Analysis and explication of assumptions that are found in the information provided would be of use in clarifying complex issues. Multiple advocacy[17] (soliciting various viewpoints) and dialectic planning[18] (deriving direction by debate and concession) are roles which can be adapted to information systems by increasing the information range and option range provided decision-makers. Because there is so much information in so many forms, synthesis of salient studies and opinion is necessary. Critical/informative summaries, for example, are one way of relieving the burden of the first level of analysis and synthesis from the decision-maker and his staff.

8. *Familiar/new pattern:* Many problems are essentially procedural. Professions such as engineering, medicine, and teaching rely on well established method. For example, patterns of symptoms are investigated in diagnosing a disease. Engineers investigate safety factors, material strengths, and similar phenomena when designing structures. Specifications provide guidelines for the quality of the work, and the literature includes information on how other engineers design. If the problem pattern is familiar, then the information needs are largely procedural and historically oriented. If the problem pattern is new, however, the information needed will tend to be more substantive and future-oriented. The experienced professional has built up a repertoire of analogies which he/she can use to assess problems. The novice needs more information because he is not used to seeing similar problems.

For both familiar and new patterns, option ranges are important. In managerial fields, clinical (one case) information may be useful. For instance, if the problem of office productivity is addressed, useful information could take the form of the experiences of similar offices in raising their productivity. Information which addresses itself to the patterns of problems would have the effect of reducing duplication of effort.

9. *Magnitude of risk great/not great:* This problem dimension is based on the consequence(s) of failure to resolve a problem. Usually it would also be considered with the possible rewards of action. High-risk, high-reward problems would justify expenditure of resources in securing the "best" available information. High-risk, low-reward problems may or may not deserve intensive information-seeking although the implicit assumption is, that by averting risk, there is sufficient reward to mandate information gathering. Some professions tend to be perceived as high-risk situations. The industries which deal with nuclear objects, medicine, engineering, pharmaceuticals are in large part high-risk industries. Therefore, it would be expected that the information which was gathered would be as accurate (precise) and comprehensive as possible. Low-risk industries would be able to tolerate a higher rate of failure and still be able to succeed in the marketplace.

10. *Susceptible/not susceptible to empirical analysis:* Some problems are judgment calls in that no amount of research can evaluate the alternatives fairly. Also, situations exist where an organization may have two competing goals and a choice has to be made between them. These resolutions of problems with this dimension are helped by subjective information, advice of experts, weighing of values and options, and forecasting. Those problems subject to empirical analysis rely on data which are objective and aggregated. Most problems are not purely one or the other but there is often a mix of empirical analysis and judgment in the resolution process.

11. *Internal/external imposition:* Problems either are sought out or they are imposed. If we take an organization as a base point, an illustration of the two ways in which problems are identified can be developed. Problems which are sought out tend to be goal directed. The organization has identified a state it would like to reach and seeks ways to accomplish its self-defined task. A company which decides to increase its market share by X percent in some time period has defined a problem situation.

The other type of problem identification is imposed either from within or from the environment. Internal problems of this kind are caused by dysfunctions in operation, e.g., too many widgets are failing quality control tests. External problems come from the environment, e.g., competitors and government regulations. Information needed at this point generally is that which describes the environment as it impinges on the organization. The environment supplies the stimulus, e.g., new regulations, and the organization must define aspects of the new problem situation (e.g., cost compliance, resource availability, penalties for noncompliance, alternatives) to formulate a response. Organizations generally would like to avoid a stimulus response situation since reactions provide less time, less control, and fewer alternatives than does a planned activity. Therefore, another information need would be one for monitoring the environment in anticipation of outside variables which might affect the organization. To this end, companies employ people who monitor government regulations, competitors, the economy, and legal matters. The information derived from such activities allows management to lobby, plan, and maneuver in such ways as to benefit the organization.

Summary and Implications

When we speak of "the information society" we tend to get lost in the technological details and in the mechanisms to manage these technologies. This is *not* what the information society is all about. We forget, in our love affair with technology, that information itself is the basis of this emerging society. (It says so on the label). The function of information is, among other things, to inform, to activate, to instruct, to provide precision, to generate ideas, to trigger the imagination, and to give pleasure. The diversity of function is immense. Technology and the paraphernalia surrounding that technology are but one factor in the process of providing useful information to widely varying classes of people. A means not an end.

This paper has argued the necessity for two basic shifts in attention. The first is to shift the focus away from the technology and toward information and its uses. The second is the change in perception, from seeing information as only "about something" to perceiving information as "having an effect on." The former is inherent in the information itself, the latter responds to externals.

We have suggested that one way of refocusing our attention is to concentrate on problems, rather than questions. Problems, as described here, are more multidimensional and hence reflect information users and their environments more completely than do questions. Beyond this, the division made in this paper between problems and sense-making tends to be indistinct. Sense-making is not sufficiently understood at this time to be used in the design of information systems. Rather it depends on that large and growing class of interpreters endemic in the information society called consultants, counselors, analysts, instructors, etc.

The listing of information traits and problem dimensions suggested in this paper is an early attempt to provide structure so that clients or users become more central to the process of information provision.

Information traits are seen as important to the *need* for information. These traits, which are fairly general, refer to the processes and contexts for presenting information. Some traits appear to exist on a continuum, others seem dichotomous and mutually exclusive:

- quantitative continuum
- data continuum
- temporal continuum (historical, precedence: forecasting, future modeling)
- solution continuum (single solution: option range)
- focus continuum (precision: diffusion)
- specificity of use continuum (applied: theoretical)
- substantive continuum (applied: descriptive)
- aggregation continuum (clinical: census)
- causal/diagnostic continuum.

Problem dimensions are those characteristics that, beyond specific subject matter, establish the criteria for judging the relevance of information to specific problems or to a class of problems in different contexts. They are presented here as dichotomies, though they probably exist as continua:

- design/discovery
- well-structured/ill-structured
- complex/simple
- specific goals/amorphous goals
- initial state understood/not understood
- assumptions agreed upon/not agreed upon
- assumptions explicit/not explicit
- familiar pattern/new pattern
- magnitude of risk great/not great
- susceptible/not susceptible to empirical analysis
- internal/external imposition.

If we can succeed in developing problem typologies based on these classes or on a refined set of dimensions, specific information traits could then be identified as useful for each typology of problem. Certainly there have been some good discussions about information needs in specific situations already.[19] However, a broader understanding of problems in varying settings would allow us to create criteria for information systems design that would more closely match the needs of the many different types of potential users. Not only can systems be made more responsive but the dual concept of problems and information can have a profound effect on education, on decision-making, on research and development, on policy-making, and indeed for simple coping in the information society.

Empirical research is now needed to confirm or alter the dimensions of problems and the traits of information as presented in this paper, or to establish new ones. The predictive links between the problem dimensions and the information traits must then be established for various types of clients and problems.

Notes

The preparation of this paper was supported by the National Science Foundation, under Grant IST-816080.

1. Brenda Dervin, "Information for Sense Making" (University of Washington, 1976), 3.
2. For a discussion of the interface as negotiating space, see Robert S. Taylor, "Organizational Information Environments," in *Information and the Transformation of Society,* ed. G. P. Sweeney (Amsterdam: North-Holland Publishing Co., 1982), 309–322; Robert S. Taylor, "Benefits and Costs of Information Use," in A. D. Petrarca et al. (editors), *Proceedings of the 45th Annual Meeting of the American Society for Information Science,* vol. 19 (1982), 296–297.
3. For a full discussion of anomalous states of knowledge as related to sense making, see N. J. Belkin, R. N. Oddy, and H. M. Brooks, "ASK (Anomalous States of Knowledge) for Information Retrieval," *Journal of Documentation,* 38 (June 1982):61–71; (September 1982):145–164.
4. Richard Derr, "Questions." (Case Western Reserve University, 1982), 3.
5. Robert S. Taylor, "The Process of Asking Questions," *American Documentation* 13 (October 1962):391.
6. Amos Tversky and Daniel Kahneman, "The Framing of Decisions and the Psychology of Choice," *Science* 211 (January 30, 1981):453.
7. Morton Hunt, *The Universe Within: A New Science Explores the Human Mind* (New York: Simon and Schuster, 1981), 264.
8. Richard Mason and Ian Mitroff, "A Program for Research on MIS," *Management Science* 19:5 (January 1973):475.
9. Colin Mick, George Lindsey, and Daniel Callahan, "Toward Usable User Studies," *Journal of the American Society for Information Science* 31:5 (September 1980):347.
10. For an explanation of five possible theoretical distributions of solutions, see James Meindell, "The Abundance of Solutions: Some Thoughts for Theoretical and Practical Solution Seekers," *Administrative Science Quarterly* 27 (December 1982):670–685.
11. P. G. Gerstenberger and T. J. Allen, "Criteria Used in the Selection of Information Channels by R & D Engineers," *Journal of Applied Psychology* 52 (1968):277.
12. Daniel Kahneman and Amos Tversky, "Prospect Theory: An Analysis of Decision Under Risk," *Econometrica* 47 (March 1979):263.

13. Tefko Saracevic, "Selected Results from an Inquiry into Testing of Information Retrieval Systems," *Journal of the American Society for Information Science* 22:2 (1971):138.
14. Herbert Simon, *The Sciences of the Artificial* (Cambridge, MA: MIT Press, 1969).
15. Herbert Blalock, "Presidential Address: Measurement and Conceptualization Problems: The Major Obstacles to Integrating Theory and Research," *American Sociology Review* 44 (December 1979):881.
16. Sarah Keisler and Lee Sproull, "Managerial Responses to Changing Environments: Perspectives on Problem Sensing from Social Perspectives," *Administration Science Quarterly* 27 (December 1982):548.
17. Alexander George, "The Case for Multiple Advocacy in Foreign Policy," *American Political Science Review* 66 (September 1972):751.
18. Ian Mitroff, James Emshoff, and Ralph Kilmann, "Assumption Analysis—Methodology for Strategic Problem Solving," *Management Science* 25:6 (June 1979):583.
19. See, for example: Thomas Allen, *Managing the Flow of Technology* (Cambridge, MA: MIT Press, 1977); Herbert Brinberg, *The Contribution of Information to Economic Growth and Development* (Paper presented at the 40th Congress of the International Federation for Documentation, Copenhagen, August 18, 1980); and Hedvah L. Schulman, *Information Transfer in Engineering* (Glastonbury, CT: The Futures Group, 1981).

Additional Readings for Chapter 5

BEAL, CHRISTINA. "Studying the Public's Information Needs." *Journal of Librarianship* 11(2) (April 1979): 130–151.

CRANE, DIANA. *Diffusion of Knowledge in Scientific Communities*. Chicago: University of Chicago Press, 1972.

CRONIN, BLAISE. "Invisible Colleges and Information Transfer: A Review and Commentary with Particular Reference to the Social Sciences." *Journal of Documentation* 38(3) (September 1982): 121–236.

DALRYMPLE, PRUDENCE W. "Retrieval by Reformulation in Two Library Catalogs: Toward a Cognitive Model of Searching Behavior." *Journal of ASIS* 41(4) (June 1990): 272–281.

DERVIN, BRENDA, and NILAN, MICHAEL. "Information Needs and Uses." In *Annual Review of Information Science and Technology*, vol.21: 3–33.

FAIRHALL, DONALD. "In Search of Searching Skills." *Journal of Information Science* 10(3) (1985): 111–123.

FINE, SARA. "Research and the Psychology of Information Use." *Library Trends* 32(4) (Spring 1984): 441–460.

FORD, NIGEL. "Psychological Determinants of Information Needs: A Small-Scale Study of Higher Education Students." *Journal of Librarianship* 18(1) (January 1986): 47–62.

HALL, HOMER J. "Patterns in the Use of Information: The Right To Be Different." *Journal of ASIS* 32(2) (March 1981): 103–112.

INGWERSSEN, PETER. "Search Procedures in the Library—Analyzed From the Cognitive Point of View." *Journal of Documentation* 38(2) (1982): 165–169.

KRIKELAS, JAMES. "Information-Seeking Behavior: Patterns and Concepts." *Drexel Library Quarterly* 19(2) (Spring 1983): 5–20.

KUHLTAU, CAROL C. "Developing a Model of the Library Search Process—Cognitive and Affective Aspects." *RQ* 28(2) (Winter 1988): 232–242.

KUHLTAU, CAROL C. "Inside the Search Process: Information Seeking from the User's Perspective." *Journal of ASIS* 42(5) (June 1991): 361–371.

NAJARIAN, SUZANNE E. "Organizational Factors in Human Memory: Implications for Library Organization and Access Systems." *Library Quarterly* 51(3) (July 1981): 269–291.

ROLOFF, M. E. "Communication at the User-System Interface: A Review of Research." *Library Research* 1(1) (1979): 1–18.

SIMON, HERBERT A. "Information-Processing Models of Cognition." *Journal of ASIS* 32(5) (September 1981): 364–377.

STONE, SUE. "Humanities Scholars: Information Needs and Uses." *Journal of Documentation* 38(4) (December 1982): 292–313.

TAYLOR, ROBERT S. "Information Values in Decision Contexts." *Information Management Review* 1(1) (1985): 47–55.

ZWEIZIG, DOUGLAS L., and DERVIN, BRENDA. "Public Library Use, Users, Uses: Advances in Knowledge of the Characteristics and Needs of the Adult Clientele of American Public Libraries." In *Public librarianship: A reader*: 189–205. Littleton, CO: Libraries Unlimited, 1982.

6

Information and the Individual

To the extent that Americans in 1787 thought about privacy at all, they conceived of it in terms of property and the need for protection against undue government search and individual trespass. Freedom of speech and freedom of the press were protected by the First Amendment to the Constitution but these rights were developed within a print-based society. They have since been extended to cover other forms of communication, such as computer data. However, the electronic transfer of information means that information regarding any individual today is scattered among a range of records maintained by federal and state governments, credit agencies, banks, insurance companies, schools, and hospitals. It is almost impossible to live in modern society without leaving an electronic trail.

The concern with these vast dossiers of information is to protect personal information and restrict its use to authorized purposes. The privacy rights that apply to this data are now additionally protected with regard to search, copying, publication, and accuracy by the Fair Credit Reporting Act of 1970 and the Privacy Act of 1974. Nevertheless, tighter restrictions are needed in order to limit access to electronic information and its threat to personal liberty. The idea that information might need to be controlled in order to preserve the rights of individual users is not new, but the automation of most public record systems has made it a matter of more urgent concern. Because computer-based systems increase the quantity of information collected, the effectiveness with which it is organized and stored, and the speed and efficiency with which it can be retrieved, many old problems are being exacerbated and new ones are emerging. They include issues as varied as the regulation of personal data files, federal support for the nation's libraries, and the property rights associated with electronic information products.

Since the passage of the Freedom of Information Act in 1966, information technology has outpaced government policies designed to manage the ever-increasing stores of data. In fact, no overall regulation exists. In summary, current policies governing information issues in this country are a composite of many specific regulations and laws, frequently outdated, and inappropriate for an electronic society. Gradually a partial network of new laws is being developed, though much of this legislation has been influenced by a variety of different interest groups and reflects no single coherent view. Any individual case is likely to be affected by overlapping or contradictory laws or may not be covered at all.

This piecemeal approach sometimes has unintended side effects and may also allow for varying interpretations as policy issues arise from the inherent tensions between the particular values reflected in different laws. In a wider sense conflict also arises between the traditional values of free and equal access for all and the personal right to privacy.

Although the issues involved are frequently overlapping, some attempt at categorization will assist this discussion (see Table 6.1).

TABLE 6.1   Categories of Problems

Level	Character of issues	Examples
content	storage & use	copyright, accuracy
system	design & operation	security & ease
environment	societal & individual	legal rights, fairness

Content

Traditional intellectual property safeguards (patent and copyright laws) are proving inadequate in controlling the new electronic information and its products. The intention of the original copyright legislation was to allow the originator of an innovative work to obtain appropriate economic benefits for a specified period of time. It attempted to balance the intellectual ownership rights of creators of printed information products with the rights of users. Today, we are in a transition period where technology has outstripped our ability to control the reproduction of information and the question of ownership has become much more complicated. The very ease with which some materials (videotapes or computer programs, for example) can be copied makes it difficult to enforce protection based on the old idea of "fair use." Software developers and owners of online databases have recognized their vulnerability with regard to the ownership and copyright of machine-readable information and have tried to protect their products with varying degrees of success. At the same time, a whole new industry in repackaged information has blossomed under the rubric of "value-added" products, thus, further complicating questions regarding the definition of authorship.

The constitutional right of the individual to privacy has also become a major issue as a result of the computerization of record keeping and the development of massive databanks of personal information regarding credit ratings, property titles, driving records, bankruptcy proceedings, and so on. This information has economic value, which at present resides with the owner of the database, though a case could well be made for vesting ownership rights with the individuals concerned. The Privacy Act permits an individual to inspect government records about himself, and to challenge their accuracy if necessary. There is obviously a conflict here between the individual's right to privacy and society's right of free access to information. In addition to the Federal Freedom of Information Law some individual states have passed their own laws regarding rights of access to all official records that incorporate government decisions and policies (except those exempted in the interests of national security).

System

Issues that focus on the information system itself relate mainly to its reliability and security from unauthorized access. Although such issues are mainly of concern to the organizations involved in the operation of the systems, they also have broader societal implications when they impact the public domain. Computer security is concerned with the safety of the computer systems themselves, the information within them, and also . with controlling access to them. It is important regardless of whether the information contained in them is personal (privacy), military (national security), or economic (corporate). In recent years, for example, public attention has focused at different times on the security and reliability of air traffic control systems, military defence control systems, and electronic funds transfer systems, which are all matters of considerable public concern. The issues that arise are associated with the development of a standard framework within which to establish security and assign responsibility so as to mitigate the impact of system failures or illegal access.

Environment

The issues discussed so far are all of current concern, but the escalating use of computers at home and in the workplace also raises issues that may have impacts in the future. The enormous complexity of our new information society and our future economic prosperity, upon which all else depends—security, social services, social cohesion—is becoming ever more dependent on a high quality workforce. Despite current educational efforts, it is projected that there will not be enough people with college degrees or advanced vocational and technological training to provide the optimum workforce needed by the year 2000. In such a society the unskilled and the undereducated will find it increasingly difficult to compete.

It would seem that in this respect technological developments may tend to reinforce the established social hierarchy rather than expand opportunities. Democratic structures such as public education, public libraries, and public television have been built up over the years based on the assumption of equal participation regardless of ability to pay. The increasing importance of technology is eroding these freedoms in both education and the workplace by requiring increased education and imposing costs on access. The political responses of deregulation, privatization, and the cutback in support for public services have only served to increase these social disparities.

Overall, the longterm effects of the changing role of information in American society and the policy decisions that will be made over the next ten years seem likely to limit some of our long-established, democratic freedoms and enhance the power of bureaucratic institutions. Care will need to be taken to preserve the delicate balance between the interests of the individual and the legitimate claims of organizations and society at large. Otherwise, it seems likely that the societal values attached to the idea of personal privacy will erode in the face of more efficient electronic record keeping, instantaneous online access, and the lethargy of our government to challenge the power of the marketplace in order to defend and preserve individual rights. The following readings, then, highlight two areas where conflicting interests challenge our long-established democratic rights—(1) free access to information versus privacy, and (2) ownership versus fair use.

Technology, Privacy, and Electronic Freedom of Speech

FRANCES M. McDONALD

Decisions being made now have the potential of creating a society in which all forms of communications are free or a society in which restrictions on access to information are imposed by legislators and other government officials. Unfortunately, based on precedents set with the regulation of radio and television, technologically uninformed government officials are passing laws without adequate attention to First Amendment freedoms and civil liberties.

> Electronic technology is conducive to freedom. The degree of diversity and plenitude of access that mature electronic technology allows far exceeds what is enjoyed today. Computerized information networks of the twenty-first century need not be any less free for all to use without let or hindrance than was the printing press. Only political errors might make them so.[1]

While technology has made it possible to access information at a rapid pace and in great diversity, current regulations impose a set of interlocking restrictions on that access to information. The morass of court decisions, Congressional legislation, and Federal Communications Commission (FCC) regulations which focus on technology ignore the Bill of Rights. First Amendment freedoms have not been applied to electronic distribution of information. Whether newspapers and other communications transmitted electronically will enjoy traditional press freedoms or be regulated as electronic broadcasting is still open to question. In addition to violating the First Amendment, recent technological advances have led to violations of the Fourth and Fifth Amendments. Using information stored in massive databases, the government, private industry, and individuals invade privacy with impunity.

In this article, five major issues related to the impact of technology on

Reprinted from *Library Trends* 35(1) (Summer 1986): 83–104.

privacy and access to information will be explored. An overview of some of the abuses and the shortcomings of current attempts at regulating electronic communications will be provided.

1. *Regulation and licensing of the press.* The precedent of regulation of the press which began with the Radio Act of 1927 has resulted in almost unquestioned acceptance of regulating any forms of electronic communication today.
2. *Electronic surveillance.* Amassing information in huge computer databases leads to risks of massive governmental surveillance.
3. *Invasion of privacy.* Computers combined with a telecommunications link, provide virtually trackless access to any individual or organization wishing to peek.
4. *Copyright.* Copyright law, based on printed methods of communication, does not work when applied to the ownership of information existing only as electronic impulses.
5. *Policy-making and regulation.* The inability to anticipate the next technological advance leads to a patchwork of laws and regulations governing telecommunications and an incoherent national information policy.

The basis of American communication policy resides in the Constitution and the Bill of Rights.

1. Article I, Section 8 [8] gives Congress power to establish post offices and post roads. (*Common Carrier*)
2. Article I, Section 8 [8] gives Congress the power: "To promote the Progress of Science and useful Arts, by securing for limited Times to Authors and Inventors the exclusive Right to their respective Writings and Discoveries." (*Copyright*)
3. The First Amendment in the Bill of Rights prohibits Congress from passing any law abridging freedom of speech or of the press. (*Freedom of the Press*)

Competing with these rights are the protections provided in two other amendments in the Bill of Rights.

4. The Fourth Amendment provides: "The right of people to be secure in their persons, houses, papers and effects, against unreasonable searches and seizures." (*Privacy*)
5. The Fifth Amendment entitles all individuals to a range of procedural protections known as due process and states that "no person shall be compelled to be a witness against himself." (*Due Process*)

Regulation and Licensing of the Press

Eli Oboler[2] wrote that "the end of licensing of the Press was, of course, the beginning of true intellectual freedom in the United States." However, over the years, three communications models evolved without true intellectual freedom for all forms of communication: a print model free of regulation, a common carrier model with the government assuring nondiscriminatory access for all, and a broadcasting model with the government licensing owners as publishers.[3]

Each of the three models developed in a particular industry and for different types of communications. The press developed free of regulation. Based on concepts of monopoly, the common carrier approach evolved for telegraph and telephone. Then, based on concepts of spectrum scarcity and later on concepts of the public good, the broadcasting model evolved resulting in government regulation of radio and television. Since all media are now becoming electronic, "telecommunications policy is becoming communications policy."[4] Oboler asks in relation to the transformation of print media to electronic media:

> Is the cause of intellectual freedom helped or hindered by the late twentieth-century developments on many fronts of new ways to send, receive, store, and disseminate widely the vast amounts of information now available? Will the censor find new methods for censoring the vital communications so necessary to progress?[5]

Electronic media have never had the eighteenth-and nineteenth-century constitutional protections of no licenses, no special taxes, no regulations, no laws, and no prior restraint. Moreover,

> when wires, radio waves, satellites and computers became major vehicles of discourse, regulation seemed to be a technical necessity. And so, as speech increasingly flows over those electronic media, the five-century growth of an unabridged right of citizens to speak without controls may be endangered.[6]

The questions are: whether information policy will develop under the public interest, good-of-society regulations which now affect broadcast media; whether market conditions and property rights will be allowed to dominate the development of telecommunications policy; whether the common carrier concept will be applied; or whether First Amendment freedoms will prevail in electronic communications. Currently, the government seems to favor diversity as deregulation breaks up communications monopolies. But, deregulation leading to a lifting of restrictions on press freedom appears unlikely.

When regulation began, the government viewed the telegraph as a business machine (like the computer later) and the issue of free speech did not arise. The high cost of sending a few words appeared to preclude the use of telegraphy for debate and expression. The courts concluded that the government had the authority to regulate telegraphy under commerce. Later, as newspapers began to use telegraph lines, the concept of news service developed. At first, carriers could choose not to carry news service traffic. But by 1893, the Supreme Court said telegraph was similar to common carriers requiring access without discrimination. Later, the common carrier concept was extended to telephone. While this appeared sensible since contact required individuals to be on the same line, it allowed a monopoly to develop.[7] As radio grew, the federal government required licenses to be issued in the public convenience, reasoning in terms of common carrier law. Today the same type of reasoning appears in telecommunications licensing.[8]

In 1920, the first radio station, KDKA Pittsburgh went on the air. Issues of scarcity, selective licensing, and free speech dominated the 1924 to 1927 debate leading to the Radio Act of 1927. Three points of view appeared in *The Nation.* David Sarnoff urged that the "same principles that apply to the freedom of the press should be made to apply to freedom of the air. . . . The real danger is in censorship, in overregulation."[9] Hudson Maxim wrote against free speech, although with some hesitation. "I distrust the wisdom of allowing radio broadcasting to be controlled by any private monopoly, but I also distrust the wisdom and the ability and the justice of federal control of radio. . . . Perhaps the control of radio should be made quasi-private and quasi-governmental."[10] In the same issue, Grover Whalen argued for government control.[11] The next year, H.V. Kaltenborn appeared to be favoring a common carrier approach when he predicted that since the government would limit the number of stations, government should compel those stations to sell air time to "all comers on equal terms."[12] Ernst, in 1926, recognized that from the beginning, radio was subject to censorship—by the stations, in the selection of what ideas were broadcast; and by the government, in selecting which groups would be granted licenses to operate stations.[13]

As early as 1925, broadcasters had urged because of scarcity that no more licenses be issued and a common carrier approach to radio be adopted. "Broadcasting is as much of a public service and convenience as the telephone, and ultimately must be subject to the same kind of regulation and control."[14] Over the years, distrust of big business entered into decisions about regulations. Fear of AT&T led to rejection of the alternative of property rights for the new industry and regulation through licensing developed. "Both the motive and the effect of the Radio Act were to install government controls at the ground floor of the new industry before a structure of private rights could develop."[15]

The debate resulted in regulations promulgated on the basis of early use with no awareness of future technological advances. Although uses changed and television broadcasting arrived, regulations did not adjust. The concept of scarcity prevailed and the concept of equal time was introduced. Regulation of content expanded when *Red Lion*[16] established the Fairness Doctrine. While proponents favor the apparent access the Fairness Doctrine promises, critics point out that in practice, access is not enhanced. "The irony of the Fairness Doctrine is that broadcasters can fulfill it by tucking away an interview on a contrary viewpoint somewhere in the schedule."[17] Through licensing, equal time provisions, and the Fairness Doctrine, the government administers the content of broadcasting.

Cable TV and the End of Scarcity

Even before the advent of cable television, scarcity as an argument for continued government regulation had become untenable. Tighter channel spacing and the allocation of new frequencies through compression and multiplexing had increased the number of available channels. With the introduction of improved receivers and advanced telecommunications technology, spectrum scarcity is no longer a reality. Enclosed carriers (cable), the potential of fiber optics, and satellite transmission further diminish the scarcity argument. In addition, electronic memory now allows messages stored on videotape and videodisc to be delivered when convenient.[18] However, regulation continues.

Regulation of cable television has been divided between local franchising authorities and the FCC. Until 1965, the FCC declined jurisdiction creating a favorable environment for the growth of cable, but in 1965, the FCC put a freeze on new subscribers and banned cable television systems in the 100 largest markets from importing "distant signals." No longer wanting to stop growth, the FCC adopted new rules in the early 1970s. These rules which supported cable television were not profreedom for cable television. Cable television was regulated in four areas—(1) signal carriage; (2) required or permitted offerings; (3) technical standards; and (4) division of responsibility between state, federal, and local governments. Signal carriage and required or permitted offerings have First Amendment implications.[19]

Local regulations, in the form of franchising agreements, served to assure access to those who wanted it. Pool called the resistance of the cable industry to requirements for channel leasing "self-serving" and described the "temptation for the cable monopoly to stifle uses that do not interest it" as good reasons for city governments to require nondiscriminatory access as part of franchising agreements. If cable is operated like a common carrier system, all who desire access may have access. When a cable carrier operates as a publisher, the operator may institute restrictions on who uses the system. Separating a carrier from content is both economically unwise and wrong on First Amendment grounds.[20]

Hints of issues of current concern were raised in 1969 when the FCC applied the requirement of equal time to rival candidates if newspaper publishers delivered news over cable channels. The FCC said:

> We do not intend to apply these requirements to the distribution of printed newspapers to their subscribers by way of cable. . . . We have no intention of regulating the print medium when it is distributed in facsimile by cable [but] we do hold that the publication of a newspaper by a party does not put it in a different position from other persons when it sponsors or arranges for presentation of a CATV origin which does not constitute the distribution of a newspaper.[21]

Until recently, cable has been viewed primarily as entertainment. Now, cable performs as a two-way delivery system for all types of electronic traffic—computer data, electronic mail, videotext, information bases, education, security monitoring, teleconferencing, news services, movies, money, meetings, scientific data, opinion polling, manuscripts, petitions, editorials.[22] Two-way interactive television, while appealing in its ability to provide a variety of services, also carries with it dramatic risks to individual freedom and privacy. Burnham identified concerns about personal and collective privacy, uses, and regulation. Personal privacy risks exist when records about banking transactions, stock purchases, shopping patterns, and even the film-viewing habits of individuals are readily available. The ability to define the habits and interests of targeted groups of people through research on individual purchases, viewing patterns, and other uses of interactive television raises the larger issue of collective privacy. When speech recognition becomes possible, the prospect of increased surveillance expands.[23]

The 1984 cable television bill, while setting minimal federal restrictions on the cable industry, gives the franchising authority the power to censor "obscene" programming and allows the cable operator to censor "nonobscene, sexually-oriented programs" if the franchiser thinks the program is in "conflict with community standards."[24] The legislation fails to provide adequate guarantees for freedom of communication for cable. Further, the bill "restricts the import of leased access by limiting its provisions to video programming, thereby excluding computer languages, videotext, and other important and growing areas of cable use."[25] "Cable porn" legislation recently introduced into Congress could severely restrict, by federal mandate, what cable broadcasters would be allowed to transmit.[26]

Ignorance of potential technological advances, distrust of big business, and attempts to deter the development of communications monopolies led to regulation of broadcast media. Regulatory policy rather than information needs determined telecommunications policy. Owen suggested two factors to account for the acceptance of regulation of electronic media.

> First is simple ignorance on the part of courts, commissions, and congressional committees of the economics and technology of broadcasting. . . . The other factor is a certain psychological attitude toward the electronic media. Many people regard television as being too powerful and influential to be allowed freedom from government control.[27]

Solutions

Critics of the current method of regulating broadcast media have offered a variety of proposals. Owen and Brazelon suggested deregulating but charging stations a reasonable spectrum use tax for the right to distribute programs over airways.[28] Kelley and Donway recommended repeal of the Fairness Doctrine and other content regulation, a transfer of current licenses into property rights, and an end to restrictions on entry, ownership, and conduct of business.[29] Wicklein proposed a decentralized common carrier "backbone system" available to everyone on a nondiscriminatory basis with no surveillance and no monitoring.[30] Krasnow believes the public trustee approach is constitutionally suspect and characterizes the regulation/deregulation scenario as applied to broadcasting as "political maneuvering."[31] Irwin suggests the time has come to allow regulation to be done by state governments, not the FCC.[32]

Attempts by Congress to extend First Amendment freedoms to the electronic media have not succeeded because of intensive lobbying by the industry, by the FCC, and by special interest groups. Persons on both sides of the debate over broadcast media and the First Amendment call themselves real protectors of the First Amendment. In 1978, Van Deerlin and Frey introduced legislation to replace the FCC with a Communications Regulatory Commission. This met with intense opposition from all segments of the industry, the FCC, and special-interest groups. After attempting to appease critics by writing and rewriting the proposed legislation, the issue faded by 1980.[33] In the early eighties, Senator Packwood tried unsuccessfully to introduce legislation leading to First Amendment protections for electronic media.[34]

Surveillance/Privacy

While the discussion of regulation/deregulation of electronic forms of communication goes on, the issue of the capability of using electronic forms of communication to monitor the activities of citizens also demands attention. Alan Westin, an expert in issues of surveillance and privacy, pointed out that: "When a powerful (and expensive) new technology such as computers and communication systems is developed, the questions of who will use this new power, for what ends, and under what constraints becomes (once the potential for the new technology is recognized) more a matter of social policy than of technological determinism."[35] The computer has allowed us to create a "dossier society" that invades our privacy and threatens civil rights. Discussion of the threats focuses on how to balance privacy and other social interests with the content and control of computerized databases.[36]

Surveillance is "the systematic collection and monitoring of personal information for purposes of social control."[37] The National Security Administration (NSA) has installed voice-recognition, word-spotting devices that look for key phrases on transatlantic phone conversations. Markoff characterized NSA surveillance as an "invisible electronic . . . net over the entire population." Congressional hearings conducted during the mid-1970s revealed that for decades NSA had been intercepting international telegrams originating in the United States, and later, all radio and telephone conversations linked to this country looking for name and address combinations and trigger words.[38]

The government does not limit surveillance to private citizens but also monitors government employees. Privacy issues occur when the government monitors employee telephone calls using computer software which will spot frequently called numbers, long calls, and calls placed at unusual times. Civil libertarians warn about the chilling effect such monitoring could have on forms of expression and on government whistle blowers. The government considers such surveillance perfectly legitimate pointing out that collecting information does not violate privacy, only disseminating information to third parties does.[39]

Not everyone shares concerns about the uses of government databases. Society approves the use of databases to identify dangerous drivers or to track welfare cheaters. Establishing eligibility for insurance and federal programs, defining and documenting details to meet bureaucratic obligations, determining credit and passport eligibility are accepted everyday uses of bureaucratic databases. While people protest unfair surveillance of themselves, they condone surveillance of others for any purposes they support. However, Rule warns that "we can conceive of no form of personal information which might not, under certain conditions, come to serve the purposes of bureaucracies aiming at some form of social control—brutal or humane."[40]

Computerized Criminal Records

National computerized criminal records are readily available and represent one of the most threatening databases. The criteria and standards enforced by the various states do not provide uniform information. Further, being arrested does not mean having committed a crime. Employers use criminal records to screen applicants for federal employment, the military, workers for government contractors, federal banks, and anywhere licenses and permits are required for a job. In New York, the "use of criminal records by law-enforcement agencies has declined in recent years, while its use by private employers has gone up."[41] Florida opens its records to anyone who will pay the search fee. In California, criminal history records serve to keep people unemployed. In spite of the fact that inaccurate records exist, opening criminal records to the public is not likely to result in innocent individuals checking records since they would be highly unlikely to expect to find a record. Even those who have reason to check are not likely to do so. In California, with 3 million records, only three hundred to four hundred ask to see records each year, and of these, eighty find incorrect information and only forty are successful in forcing California to correct their records. So, one in four who check find discrepancies, and one in ten force the state to make a correction. Further, responses to an Office of Technology Assessment questionnaire indicated that four of five states never conducted audits of the quality of the records.[42]

Privacy Rights

The basic rights involved in access to database records are those of personal privacy, personal access, and public access.[43] The Privacy Protection Study Commission (PPSC) identified five competing societal values in formulating public policy to protect personal privacy: "(1) First Amendment interest, (2) freedom of information interests, (3) the societal interest in law enforcement, (4) cost, and (5) federal-state relations."[44] Three criteria have been developed to protect privacy: maintaining accurate, complete, up-to-date records subject to review; citizens knowing uses which can be revoked; and organizations only using data on a need-to-know principle to attain their goals.[45]

The discussion of privacy and collection of data has "shifted from one of debate over privacy protection to one of elimination of abusive practices."[46] Burnham suggested that the right to see and correct our own records is viewed as the "miracle cure for many of the abuses of the computer age."[47] In fact, most remedies do not address the issue of privacy or the threat of massive surveillance finding its way into law. Recognizing that "freezing and dismantling" the record collection is unlikely, Chaum proposed restructuring major systems that use detailed information in a way that requires less information or using cryptographic techniques to mask individual records.[48] The problem lies in attempts to implement privacy laws without identifying people. Another suggestion, the use of a unique, reliable, personal identification, has itself the potential of leading to the invasion of individual privacy.[49]

Computer Matching

Computer matching is a term that has been applied to a variety of computerized data processing activities where separate files are run through a computer with a program set to detect certain matches. Computer matching is currently "being used to detect fraud and abuse in government programs by linking together formerly independent databases."[50] Westin thinks that banning computer matching is impossible. He thinks that at this point all we can do is monitor the amount of use and build safeguards into matching systems.[51] While warning that computer matching systems carry the potential for privacy and due process abuses, the American Civil Liberties Union (ACLU) also suggests that it is unrealistic to expect the government or organizations not to use computer matching.[52] Burnham stated that "increased sharing of information by all agencies of government gradually may be undermining the constitutional theory of checks and balances."[53] Particularly alarming is the assumption of guilt implied by computer matching. We are "moving from a system relying on voluntary compliance and an assumption that citizens obey the law, to the assumption that citizens cannot be trusted."[54]

The government interprets the use of computer matching for purposes such as detecting welfare fraud and tracking runaway fathers to enforce child support to be legitimate government uses and point out that computer matching encourages efficiency. But Burnham asks whether the system which is so efficient at tracking fathers might actually have headed off other reforms that might have "improved the stability of American families." Once the system is established, what is to prevent it from later being used for the surveillance of other groups who fall into disfavor? If computer matching is successfully used for one kind of debt relationship, how do we assure it will not be expanded to other debt relationships? In a system set up to track segments of the population, inaccuracies present an important hazard.[55] Finally, the ACLU points out the risk of computer matching becoming computer merging resulting in the establishment of a national database?[56]

General computer matching violates our guarantees against unreasonable search and seizure, due process, and the assumption of innocence until proven guilty. To minimize computer matching abuses, the ACLU advocates a procedure called "front-end verification" in which only applicants for government services or a suspect's files would be checked rather than the government conducting general sweeps of databases looking for matches. Additionally, safeguards could be built into the system requiring notice that files are subject to matching, requiring verification of all matches, and requiring a hearing before benefits are denied or terminated on the basis of a computer match. All files created by a match should be destroyed after the match, further reducing privacy risks.[57]

Illegal Computer Access

Once the record collection has been put into place, the question of unauthorized access arises. There are three issues of concern. First, privacy rights of electronic communications; second, illegal computer access; and third, federal regulation of data communications.[58] Privacy rights have been discussed earlier.

Well-publicized activities of computer hackers illustrate how lack of security has made any database—whether educational, medical, or governmental—vulnerable to invasion. Hackers have successfully entered computers at Sloan-Kettering, the Department of Defense, the Florida Department of Education, and the Los Alamos National Laboratory in addition to routinely entering corporate databases. A nineteen-year-old physics major at UCLA was arrested for entering defense department computers.[59] A *Newsweek* reporter's credit file was opened and credit card records distributed in retaliation for a story about bulletin boards.[60] But hackers are not responsible for all illegal computer activity. The San Francisco public defender's office accused police of spying on clients' records kept in a shared computer.[61]

Credit records are among the least secure of the giant databases. Credit bureaus have a "waiver of the nation's privacy laws" and have information about us we would not allow the government or anyone else to keep.[62] A large credit firm was sued to force it to tighten security against illegal access to credit files which contain lists of credit cards, credit limits, amounts owed, social security numbers, and inquiries. The credit company charged that the responsibility for allowing illegal access belonged to careless user companies whose employees are lax in protecting access code numbers and passwords.[63]

Although hackers receive the most publicity, much illegal access involves persons employed by data processing or electronic information companies. A recent survey of members conducted by the Data Processing Management Association revealed that of the 21 percent who said their organizations were victims of computer abuses, only 2 percent reported that the abuses were committed by outsiders. A survey of 130 prosecutors by the National Center for Computer Crime also reported that most computer crime was perpetrated by insiders.[64]

The term *hacker,* when used by computer enthusiasts, refers to people "involved in a wide range of computer related activities." When used by persons alarmed about illegal computer access, the term refers to a "person who often attempts to gain unauthorized access to large systems by using his personal computer equipment."[65] After an arrest connected with his hacker activities, Bill "Cracker" Landreth provided this rationale for unauthorized "exploration" of computers: "We were explorers, not spies." Hackers defend their activities by pointing out that most of them abide by a code of ethics, do not erase or damage files, do not write ridiculous or obscene messages, do not identify others, do not seek publicity, and do not leave tracks. "To hackers, what is known as "browsing" is a (usually) harmless, "educational" pursuit."[66] Sherry Turkle described hackers as intelligent students, mostly male, in "a culture of loners." Turkle's investigations show that from the hacker viewpoint, there is nothing wrong with inspecting (without invitation) programs and data files and that using others' programs is not stealing.[67]

However, the bad image of the hacker and his activities leads to legislative action and the fear that FCC regulation will sharply curtail activities of computer enthusiasts while at the same time doing nothing to deter serious online crime. Publicity about hacker activities led to the passage of the nation's first computer crime law, the Counterfeit Access Device and Computer Fraud and Abuse Act of 1984. The law imposes penalties for "unauthorized intrusion into computers holding electronic funds or national security data" and government-owned computers. Although not likely to pass during the fall of 1985, a bill to extend protection to private computers has been introduced. Over thirty states have computer crime legislation already in place.[68]

Computer Networks

One development of electronic technology which promises to provide information and publishing access for a wide variety of individuals is the communications network. Ranging from small privately operated bulletin boards to giant information databases operated for profit, these networks offer a delivery system for all types of communication. Poetry, fiction, news commentary, and spiritual messages as well as databases are all available through electronic information networks. Bulletin boards have become little newspapers providing publishing outlets for minority points of view.[69]

With the development of communications networks have come abuses. Phone numbers and credit card numbers are routinely listed for sale on "private boards." Computer programs appear in listings and copies are sold illegally and transmitted electronically. A southern California bulletin board operator faces criminal charges because an AT&T number was found on his board. Messages related to child pornography have been disseminated on computer bulletin boards. These activities cause legislators to focus on abuses rather than on protecting the First Amendment rights of bulletin board users. A commonly proposed solution is the requirement that bulletin board operators monitor messages carried on their systems and delete offensive or illegal messages. In California, a bill has been introduced which would make the system operator (sysop) "legally responsible for anything left on his bulletin board." This approach puts the bulletin board operator in the dual role of police and censor. Further, the bulletin board operator risks having the system shut down if illegal activity is found on it. Reacting to flaws in current and pending legislation, a California lawmaker introduced a bill proposing an amendment to the California Constitution which would insure the privacy of electronic communications and provide for electronic freedom of speech.[70]

Electronic Mail

By the year 2000, two-thirds of the nation's mail will be handled electronically. Although the Postal Service insists that its electronic mail system, E-Com, is secure, electronic mail poses potentially serious problems of security and privacy. Electronic mail offers an attractive target to anyone seeking access to individual and corporate information. Intruders can intercept and alter electronic mail. Since electronic mail creates a centralized record of who writes what to whom, the database developed presents the potential for private and government surveillance. Law enforcement officials need a warrant to open standard first class mail. The same letter in electronic form must be made available to officers with a subpeona or on demand of lawful authority, a much weaker restriction.[71]

Legislation has been proposed to protect the privacy of users of electronic mail and "provide legal protection against unauthorized government or private interception of new electronic communications." Electronic mail gives government agencies and others the ability to compile profiles of a highly personal nature on any individual by scanning messages for names, addresses, and topics. Messages are most vulnerable to interception when being held for forwarding or recorded for backup and audit purposes.[72] Because of legal precedents holding that citizens have no privacy rights in records held by third parties, uncertainty surrounds the legal status of electronic mail databases.[73]

During the summer of 1985, the government learned that an individual accused of cocaine trafficking had been exchanging messages with potential buyers and sellers using the electronic mail service operated by The Source. The Source refused to release its files to law enforcement officers on the grounds that messages entrusted to it are not "under its legal control." Since the defendant decided to plead guilty, the issue never went to court and the questions of legal control of files and Fourth Amendment protections have not been decided. However, the U.S. Attorney General's office suggested that since there was no legal precedent in the case. The Source had no grounds for its refusal to reveal its files.[74] Hints that offensive messages had been deleted by CompuServe, another electronic service, resulted in a statement by a CompuServe official that "CompuServe will 'never' engage in such E-Mail censorship."[75]

At the present time there are both private and public electronic mail operations. Bailey suggested that the surveillance problem might be more manageable if the private sector rather than the government ran automated clearinghouses and facilities for sending mail electronically. "In our 10-year effort to get the fair information practice philosophy articulated, we have tended to overlook the extent to which institutional pluralism can be an important safeguard for personal privacy in our society."[76] The ACLU advocates legislation which "protects the privacy of new electronic communication without unintentionally stifling technical or social innovation or inhibiting the free flow of information."[77]

Electronic Publishing

Electronic publishing is an outgrowth of the computer database industry. The prospect of publishing on demand, enabling scholars to have access to important titles, is only one aspect of the appeal of electronic publishing. On-demand publishing also allows the construction of individual profiles of readers' interests for selective dissemination of information. The ability of computers to scan electronic manuscripts for bibliographic information creates immediate databases for researchers. The greatest benefit of electronic publishing is that virtually anyone will be able to publish at will. Finally, electronic publishing allows for lower production costs, fewer errors, formatting standards, speed of production, and submission by electronic mail.[78]

Pournelle predicts the establishment of an "Electronic Village" creating a synergistic effect on the generation of ideas. "When the Founding Fathers wrote freedom of the press into the Constitution, they intended to protect far more than big city newspapers; they also had in mind the smaller-scale activist pamphleteer. Thomas Paine's *Common Sense* was more in their minds than the London *Times*." While publishing a newspaper requires considerable money, a computer network is available to nearly everyone. Pournelle predicts that the ready availability of networks will make suppression of ideas almost impossible.[79]

Unanswered questions about the status of electronic publishing exist. Electronic publishing is a mix of long-term and local storage with telecommunications links delivering information to the user's premises. If electronic publishing is viewed as publishing, traditional press freedoms will apply. But, if electronic distribution of information over telephone lines on cable television is viewed as broadcasting, regulation could occur. "The cause for fear is that when its (electronic publishing or on-demand publishing) technology looks like that of an office the law may see it as commerce, not publishing and thus subject to regulation like any business."[80]

As publishing increasingly becomes electronic, the risk of widening the gap between the information rich and information poor emerges as an issue of social concern. Unless individuals have free access to information regardless of format, those least likely to have access through their own personal computers will have no access at all. Institutions providing access to electronic databases now rarely provide the service without cost.

Copyright

Authority to establish copyright law is embodied in the Constitution. If the concept of copyright is accepted as enhancing the free flow of ideas by stimulating creative work, one must live with the restrictions copyright puts on the use of another's intellectual property. The "laws of copyright are among the most obvious but least condemned restraints on freedom of expression."[81] Pool concluded that the idea of "the objective of copyright is beyond dispute. Intellectual effort needs compensation." But "to apply a print scheme of compensation to the fluid dialogue of interactive electronic publishing will not succeed."[82]

Copyright issues arise in the discussion of all forms of electronic communication. Computer programs generate abstracts and create databases. The programs are copyrightable, but questions exist about who owns the generated text. The "idea that a machine is capable of intellectual labor is beyond the scope of copyright statutes. Can a computer infringe copyright?"[83] Participants in computer conferencing sharing ideas with strangers risk having their individual ideas taken and used. Zientara reports that computer conferencing is largely based on trust and that electronic messages are implicitly copyrighted in the name of the person who inputs them but, if no notice is included, others can use the ideas. If "on-line conferences [are] regarded as databases with their own intrinsic value," who should hold the copyright?[84] Bibliographic control as we know it is also likely to change as the concept of uniform copies changes. As users modify and expand text, different versions will be stored in different locations. In the instance of full text databases, does storage on disk memory for later use violate copyright?[85]

Piracy of Software

The area of copyright and technology receiving the most publicity is the piracy of computer software. The Software Publishers Association (SPA) has had some success in stopping illegal copying of software primarily by personal contact, investigation, and threats of lawsuits. A threatened lawsuit against a school district in Ohio resulted in the school district's promise that policy guidelines would be adopted. Industry officials intend to continue such pressures to stem the tide of illegal copying. Pirate bulletin boards are monitored by the SPA to identify copyright violation for potential prosecution.[86]

Major corporations nationwide are also caught in the illegal software net. Apple computer officials, after conducting an investigation of employees within the company, concluded that employees "regularly distribute pirated software among themselves, as well as outside the company." Officials attributed the copying to "Apple's original 'hacker ethic.'" However, an Apple vice-president concluded that Apple's compliance with copyright and the law is 99 percent.[87] The success of a recent lawsuit against a national corporation by the software company Micropro is expected to have an impact on corporate piracy of software.[88]

Licensing

The software industry has instituted various methods to inhibit illegal copying. Copy protection devices and site licensing are two such attempts. However, questions have been raised about the legality of some of these methods. Licenses include restrictions that go beyond the copyright law. A computer law attorney stated that: "Most of the license forms I've seen fail to distinguish the intellectual property and physical property."[89] Software publishers interpret copyright law to mean that only the purchaser of a program has the right to use the program and then only in one location and on one machine. Strong consumer and legal objections are being heard about the application of copyright to microcomputer software. Software industry interpretations which dictate the users and uses of software and licensing are of special concern.[90]

Software producers offer site licensing as the solution for educational institutions and corporations which require several individuals to use the same program at the same time. Fawcette sees site licensing as an "umbrella to cover general dissatisfaction by corporate micro managers or information center managers with the policies of the software industry." Reflecting the users at large, Fawcette lists the concerns as copy protection, customer support, and network licenses which obstruct the ability to use software on networks.[91]

One of the most controversial of the attempts to limit copying has been the shrink-wrap license. Under a shrink-wrap agreement, the opening of the wrap is supposed to put a contract into effect. Experts hold differing opinions about the legality of the concept of shrink wrap. Of concern to software users is the issue of being held accountable to a contract they had no hand in writing and might not be able to read clearly and understand. Louisiana passed specific legislation making computer software purchasers legally responsible for abiding by the shrink-wrap terms on the package. Louisiana's law is written so that no proof needs to be provided that users consented to the shrink-wrap agreement.[92] A lawsuit designed to test Louisiana's shrink-wrap law was recently dismissed by a district court judge in New Orleans.[93] The industry had anticipated that the decision in the Louisiana case would help to eliminate some of the confusions about the application of the law to microcomputer software.

Other measures have been proposed. One antipiracy scheme would license owners of computers with a unique identification code installed in the computer's hardware. Software writers would have to program traps in software to look for special serial numbers. Since both hardware and software purchases would be known and recorded for the scheme to work, the potential for violation of privacy as well as restraints on purchases exists. Another solution being proposed by the software industry is the attachment of special devices into the computer.[94] Not all software users find the use of such devices reasonable. The publisher of *Info-World* called the introduction of the key device "extremist" and found it unreasonable to use a special port to hook up a hardware key to prevent software copying.[95]

The Office of Technology Assessment recently released a study of new information technologies related to intellectual property rights and is expected to have a publication identifying problems, issues, and gaps in current law.[96]

Conclusion

Certain principles must be applied to electronic forms of communications to insure that First Amendment freedoms, privacy, and access considerations are protected. The First Amendment must be applied fully to all media giving anyone—whether cable operator, major broadcast network, or computer networker—the opportunity to publish without licensing or scrutiny by the government. Prior restraint regulations must not be allowed to dominate electronic publishing. Privacy, due process, and protection from self-incrimination must be built into any regulatory scheme imposed on electronic communications. Copyright enforcement must be adapted to the new technology. "Control of the system, restrictions on freedom of expression, intrusions on privacy, and threats to individual liberty" are issues which must be debated and policies developed at the national level.[97]

Electronic freedom of speech is as essential as print freedoms. Today's corner orator now finds an audience on an electronic bulletin board. The patchwork of existing and pending legislation, drafted in reaction to abuses of the moment, will not serve to build the coherent national policy needed for communication through electronics. At the present time, the FCC is experiencing serious problems trying to fit new technologies into its current regulatory scheme.[98] The "lack of technical grasp by policy makers and their propensity to solve problems of conflict, privacy, intellectual property, and monopoly by accustomed bureaucratic routines are the main reasons for concern.[99] Passing further piecemeal legislation and regulations must be halted until a coherent national information policy can be adopted. Unless this happens, erosion of First Amendment rights and civil liberties will continue.

Notes

1. Ithiel de Sola Pool, *Technologies of Freedom* (Cambridge: Belknap Press of Harvard University Press, 1983):231.
2. Eli M. Oboler, *To Free the Mind: Libraries, Technology, and Intellectual Freedom* (Littleton, Colo.: Libraries Unlimited, 1983):61.
3. Pool, *Technologies of Freedom*, 233.
4. Ibid.
5. Oboler, *To Free the Mind*, 5.
6. Pool, *Technologies of Freedom*, 1.
7. Ibid., 91–96.
8. Ibid., 103.
9. David Sarnoff, "Freedom of the Air: Uncensored and Uncontrolled," *The Nation* 119(23 July 1924):90.
10. Hudson Maxin, "Freedom of the Air: Radio—The Fulcrum," *The Nation* 119(23 July 1924):91.
11. Grover A. Whalen, "Freedom of the Air: Radio Control," *The Nation* 119(23 July 1924):91.
12. H.V. Kaltenborn, "On Being 'On the Air': Behind the Footlights in a Broadcasting Studio," *The Independent* 114(23 May 1925):583–85.
13. Morris L. Ernst, "Who Shall Control the Air?" *The Nation* 122 (21 April 1926):443–44.
14. Pool, *Technologies of Freedom*, 121.
15. David Kelley, and Roger Donway, *Laissez Parler: Freedom in the Electronic Media* (Bowling Green, Ohio: Bowling Green State University, Social Philosophy and Policy Center, 1983):14.
16. *Red Lion Broadcasting Co.* v. *FCC* 89 S. Ct. 1794 (1969).
17. William Small, "Radio and Television Treated Like Distant Cousins," In *The First Freedom Today: Critical Issues Relating to Censorship and to Intellectual Freedom*, edited by Robert B. Downs and Ralph E. McCoy (Chicago: ALA, 1984):319.
18. Pool, *Technologies of Freedom*, 152.
19. Ibid., 157–58; and T. Barton Carter, et al. *The First Amendment and the Fourth Estate: The Law of Mass Media*, 3d ed. (Mineola, N.Y.: The Foundation Press, 1985):642–57.
20. Pool, *Technologies of Freedom*, 239–40.
21. Ibid., 159.
22. Ibid., 167, 227.
23. David Burnham, *The Rise of the Computer State: The Threat to Our Freedoms, Our Ethics and Our Democratic Process* (New York: Random House, 1983):242–49.
24. "Cable TV Bill Passes in Final Hour of 98th Congress," *Civil Liberties Alert* 8(Jan. 1985):6.
25. American Civil Liberties Union, "The ACLU and Cable Television: A Critique of the New Federal Legislation." (Washington, D.C.: ACLU, 1984), p. 3 (pamphlet).
26. Barry W. Lynn, "Testimony Regarding Regulation of 'Cable Porn' and 'Dial-A-Porn.'" U.S. Senate. Judiciary Subcommittee on Crime (31 July 1985) Washington, D.C.: ACLU, 1985.
27. Bruce M. Owen, and David L. Bazelon, "Different Media, Differing Treatment?" in *Free but Regulated: Conflicting Traditions in Media Law*, ed. Daniel L. Brenner and William L. Rivers (Ames: Iowa State University Press, 1982), 44.
28. Ibid., 63.
29. Kelley, and Donway, *Laissez Parler*, 43–44.

30. John Wicklein, *Electronic Nightmare: The New Communications and Freedom* (New York: Viking Press, 1981):249–53.
31. Erwin G. Krasnow, et al., *The Politics of Broadcast Regulation*, 3d ed. (New York: St. Martin's Press, 1982), 21, 27.
32. Manley R. Irwin, *Telecommunications America* (Westport, Conn.: Quorum Books, 1984):126–28.
33. Krasnow, *The Politics of Broadcast Regulation*, 240–70.
34. U.S. Senate Committee on Commerce, Science and Transportation, *News Release*, 97th Cong., 2d sess., 28 Sept. 1982.
35. Alan F. Westin, "The Long-Term Implications of Computers for Privacy and the Protection of Public Order," in *Computers and Privacy in the Next Decade*, ed. Lance J. Hoffman (New York: Academic Press, 1980), 168.
36. Ibid., 167–81.
37. James B. Rule et al., "Preserving Individual Autonomy in an Information Oriented Society," in *Computers and Privacy in the Next Decade*, 68.
38. John Markoff et al., "Federal Court Okays Sweeping Surveillance Privileges," *InfoWorld* 5(4 April 1983):14–15; and _____, "Electronic Surveillance Menaces Personal Privacy," *InfoWorld* 5(11 April 1983):16–17.
39. Elizabeth Tucker, "Would '1985' Have Been a Better Title for '1984'?" *Washington Post*, National Weekly edition (25 March 1985), 28.
40. Rule, "Preserving Individual Autonomy, 71.
41. Burnham, *Rise of the Computer State*, 77.
42. Ibid., 75–82.
43. Gordon C. Everest, "Nonuniform Privacy Laws: Implications and Attempts at Uniformity," in *Computers and Privacy in the Next Decade*, 141–50.
44. Irwin J. Sitkin, "Comment on 'Privacy Cost Research: An Agenda,'" in *Computers and Privacy in the Next Decade*, 61–64.
45. Rule, "Preserving Individual Autonomy," 74.
46. Ibid., 73.
47. Burnham, *Rise of the Computer State*, 81.
48. Michael Swaine, "Taking a Pseudonym Can Prevent 'Dossier Society,'" *InfoWorld* 5(12 Sept. 1983):19.
49. Robert C. Goldstein, "Privacy Cost Research: An Agenda," in *Computers and Privacy*, 51–56.
50. Jerry J. Berman and Lauren Dame, "ACLU Privacy and Technology Project," (Washington, D.C.: ACLU, 1985), 2 (pamphlet).
51. Westin, "Long-Term Implications of Computers," 178.
52. Berman, and Dame, "ACLU Privacy and Technology Project," 3.
53. Burnham, *Rise of the Computer State*, 29.
54. Berman, and Dame, "ACLU Privacy and Technology Project," 13.
55. Burnham, *Rise of the Computer State*, 29–33.
56. Berman, and Dame, "ACLU Privacy and Technology Project," 14.
57. Ibid., 12.
58. Brock N. Meeks, "Telelaw vs. Electronic Freedom of Speech." *LinkUp* 2 (Sept. 1985):22–23.
59. Katherine Hafner, "UCLA Student Penetrates DOD Network," *InfoWorld* 5(21 Nov. 1983):28; Tom Shea, "The FBI Goes After Hackers," *InfoWorld* 6(26 March 1984):38–43; and "Student 'Hacker' Cracks Code, Enters Education Files'" *Education Week* 5(9 Oct. 1985):3.
60. Peggy Watt, "Hack Attack Alarms Hobbyists," *InfoWorld* 6(31 Dec. 1984):17.

61. Hank Bannister, "Police Accused of Computer Spying," *InfoWorld* 7(18 March 1985):15–16.
62. Watt, "Hack Attack Alarms Hobbyists," 17.
63. ———, "Credit Bureau Sued on Security," *InfoWorld* 6(3 Dec. 1984):18.
64. Elizabeth Ranney, "Data Security Violated Mostly on the Inside, 2 Studies Show," *InfoWorld* 7(23 Sept. 1985):1.
65. Bill Landreth, *Out of the Inner Circle: A Hacker's Guide to Computer Security by "The Cracker": The Teenage Computer Wizard* (Bellevue, Wash.: Microsoft Press, 1985):26.
66. Ibid., 207.
67. Sherry Turkle, *The Second Self: Computers and the Human Spirit* (New York: Simon & Schuster, 1984):196–238.
68. Scott Mace, "Computer Bills in Works," *InfoWorld* 7(14 Oct. 1985):10; John Markoff, "Teen-hackers' Antics Prompt House Hearing," *InfoWorld* 5(7 Nov. 1983):26; and ———, "New Laws May Penalize Bulletin-Board Hackers," *InfoWorld* 5(21 Nov. 1983):27.
69. "Here Come the Networkers," *Newsweek* 126(25 Nov. 1985):100.
70. Meeks, "Telelaw vs. Electronic Freedom," 22.
71. Seth Rosenfeld, "Who's Reading Your Electronic Mail?" *InfoWorld* 5(12 Dec. 1983):24–26.
72. Jerry J. Berman, "Testimony on S. 1667 The Electronic Communication Privacy Act of 1985," U.S. Senate, Senate Judiciary Committee, Subcommittee on Patents, Copyrights and Trademarks (13 Nov. 1985) Washington, D.C.: ACLU, 1985 (pamphlet).
73. *United States v. Miller*, 425 U.S. 435 (1976).
74. Doran Howitt, "Court Pries Into E-Mail." *InfoWorld* 7(15 July 1985):26.
75. Paul Berstein and Steve Casman, "Who's Reading the Mail?" (letters section) *InfoWorld* 7(11 March 1985):6.
76. Carole Parsons Bailey, "Comment on 'Privacy in Electronic Funds Transfer, Point of Sale, and Electronic Mail Systems in the Next Decade,'" in *Computers and Privacy in the Next Decade*, 45–50.
77. Berman, "Testimony on S. 1667," 1.
78. Warren J. Haas, "Computing in Documentation and Scholarly Research," *Science* 215(12 Feb. 1982):857–61.
79. Jerry Pournelle, "The Real Electronic Village," *Popular Computing* 4(Oct. 1985):45–49.
80. Pool, *Technologies of Freedom*, 194.
81. Carter, *The First Amendment*, 178.
82. Pool, *Technologies of Freedom*, 249.
83. Ibid., 215.
84. Marguerite Zientara, "Watch Your Words: Who Owns Information in an Electronic Conference?" *InfoWorld* 6(6 Aug. 1984):33–34.
85. Pool, *Technologies of Freedom*, 213.
86. "School Districts Singled Out on Piracy Charges," *Classroom Computer Learning* 6(Oct. 1985):14.
87. Christine McGeever, "Software Piracy Troubles Apple Officials," *InfoWorld* 7(2 Sept. 1985):1.
88. Kathy Chin, "Conglomerate Sued for Piracy," *InfoWorld* 7(4 Feb. 1985):17.
89. ———, "The Software License Quagmire: The Irony of Unenforceable Contracts," *InfoWorld* 6(25 June 1984):34–35.
90. Allan Stein, "License to Own Computers—Projections of a Paranoid?" *InfoWorld* 5(3 Oct. 1983):37–38.
91. James E. Fawcette, "Site Licensing Crucial," *InfoWorld* 7(22 July 1985):5; Jerry

Pournelle, "Of Publishers and Pirates," *Popular Computing* 4(Dec. 1984):59–62; and Gary Becker, "Software Copyright Looks Fuzzy, But Is It?" *Electronic Education* 4(Oct. 1984):18–19.

92. "'Shrink-Wrap' Law to Receive Its First Test," *Tech Trends* 30(Sept. 1985):3; and Elizabeth Ranney, "First Test for 'Shrink-Wrap' Law," *InfoWorld* 7(8 July 1985):22.

93. Elizabeth Ranney, "State 'Shrink Wrap' Piracy Suit is Dismissed by Judge," *InfoWorld* 7(21 Oct. 1985):6.

94. Scott Mace, "Devices Allow Backups Yet Inhibit Piracy of Programs," *InfoWorld* 7(16 Sept. 1985):15.

95. James E. Fawcette, "Fighting Common Sense," *InfoWorld* 7(4 March 1985):5.

96. "The New Agenda on Intellectual Property Rights," *TechTrends* 31(May/June 1986):3.

97. Wicklein, *Electronic Nightmare*, 242.

98. Carter, *The First Amendment*, 657.

99. Pool, *Technologies of Freedom*, 251.

Who Owns Creativity?

Property Rights in the Information Age

ANNE W. BRANSCOMB

In the coming months, a Boston, Mass., federal district court may settle a $10 million lawsuit by deciding who owns the "look and feel" of a popular computer program. The result will only intensify the controversy over the impact of new information technologies on intellectual property rights.

In January 1987, the Lotus Development Corp. filed suit against two small software houses for violating its copyright on the enormously successful Lotus 1-2-3 computerized spreadsheet. The defendants had developed and marketed "work-alike" spreadsheet programs that incorporate the program functions and screen design of 1-2-3 without duplicating the programming code traditionally protected by copyright. Nevertheless, Lotus argued that the work-alike programs are unauthorized copies. The name of one clone is—revealingly—"Twin," and an advertisement for the other boasts that it is "a feature-for-feature work-alike for 1-2-3 . . . designed to work like Lotus . . . keystroke for keystroke." According to Lotus, the essence of a program is not its code but its distinctive "look and feel," which the copyright should protect.

Reprinted from *Technology Review* 91(4) (May/June 1988): 39–45.

The defendants disagreed. From their perspective, the work-alikes are not imitations but innovations, providing all that Lotus offers and more and at a lower price. Indeed, what the defendants have done is not so different from what Lotus did some five years ago when it built upon the first computerized spreadsheet, Visicalc, to create a technically superior product.

Ironically, three months after Lotus filed its suit, the company itself became the defendant in another copyright-infringement case, this time brought by the parent company of the firm that created Visicalc. The claim was that Lotus had borrowed the look and feel of the original spreadsheet.

The desire of individuals—and corporations—to profit from their own intellectual creativity has often clashed with the public's wish for relatively free access to ideas and innovations. Over the centuries, many different legal mechanisms have been invented to strike a balance between the two. However, what suited the age of print and mechanical inventions is proving inadequate to that of the computer program, expert system, and distributed database. The attempt to force these new technologies into outmoded categories can create absurd and contradictory situations that threaten to undermine public confidence in the principle of intellectual property rights itself.

Software is a good example. Copyright is designed to protect literary expression. But what makes a computer program a literary work? Is it the code written to make the program function? Or is it, as Lotus argues, the look of the screen and feel of its commands?

To make matters even more confusing, software manufacturers simultaneously employ other legal protections to safeguard their intellectual property rights, because they are doubtful that any one will prove effective. The principle of trade secrets underlies the "shrink-wrap license" to which every software user supposedly agrees upon opening the package of a new program.

Some computer programs are also eligible for patents, most notably software embedded in computer hardware. And while operating systems that are not built into hardware have traditionally been excluded from patent protection, the U.S. Patent Office has recently been considerably more lenient toward such applications.

As the forms of protection increase, the gap between legal precedent and everyday behavior grows wider. The new technologies make copying intellectual property easier and legal protections much more difficult to enforce. Some degree of unauthorized copying has become accepted social practice—despite the legal prohibitions against it: journal articles are photocopied at universities, recorded music is taped onto blank cassettes, and computer software is commonly reproduced.

Although disputes about technology and intellectual property are usually cast in narrow legal terms, they are intimately related to public attitudes. Realistic legal rules depend upon a social consensus about what kind of behavior is acceptable and what is not.

"To Promote Science and the Useful Arts"

The idea of intellectual property rights has been around since the late Middle Ages, but the roots of U.S. intellectual property law go back to the Constitution: "The Congress shall have Power . . . To promote the Progress of Science and useful Arts, by securing for limited Times to Authors and Inventors the exclusive Right to their respective Writing and Discoveries."

As this language suggests, the fundamental goal of intellectual property rights is not to benefit the creators of works but to further the public good. Authors and inventors are given a limited right to their work as an incentive to create and disseminate ideas and information. Thus, intellectual property law makes protection conditional on public disclosure.

For example, copyright law covers original "works of authorship" as long as they are "fixed" in a "tangible medium" such as a book. Copyright protects the literary expression of an idea, rather than the idea itself, from unauthorized copying for the life of the creator plus 50 years (or, for corporations, for a total of 75 to 100 years). Other authors can make "fair use" of a copyrighted work—for example, quoting a passage in an article or review—without asking the original author's permission. More extensive use requires permission and often the payment of a royalty.

Patent law protects inventions or discoveries that are registered with the U.S. Patent Office. Unlike copyright, a patent protects not only the expression but the actual useful features of a product or process for 17 years. A design receives protection for 14 years. Patent rights grant a monopoly, good against those who independently discover the same design or product. But rights can be licensed to other users.

However, a patent is much harder to get than copyright. To be eligible for patent protection, a work must have distinguishing features that are innovative, useful, and not obvious. And the application process often takes two years or more.

Not all forms of intellectual property protection require public disclosure. The oldest and probably most common form of protection is secrecy. Trade secrets are protected by contracts designed to ensure confidentiality on the part of licensed users. To be enforceable in court, the information considered a trade secret must be used commercially and relevant to a firm's competitive advantage. Also, the firm must have evidence that it has actively attempted to keep the information secret.

The Intellectual Property System Breaks Down

These traditional mechanisms for balancing public and private claims worked relatively well during the industrial era. As long as the publication of books and journals depended on a relatively small number of commercial printers, it was easy to identify copyright violations. As long as most industrial innovations had a relatively long life, the patent process successfully protected their economic value. And as long as most violations took place either within a single nation or between nations with relatively compatible legal systems, effective sanctions could be easily enforced.

Recently, however, three interrelated factors have eroded the effectiveness of traditional protection mechanisms: the development of new information and communications technologies, the globalization of the marketplace, and the privatization of information providers.

The traditional categories of intellectual property law depend on a set of clearly defined "products" or "processes"—literary works, inventions, designs, etc. But with the new technologies, boundaries between media are blurred and intellectual assets become increasingly abstract and intangible. The same work or even parts of a work can be stored and presented in a bewildering variety of forms—not only paper, but magnetic tape, floppy disc, or laser disc. The work can be made available to large numbers of people via broadcasting, computer networks, or telephone lines. Databases can be packaged and re-packaged. Pieces of music or video images can be electronically re-mixed, re-formatted, or otherwise altered. And easy-to-use technologies like video graphics and desk-top publishing allow more individuals and small businesses to enter the information marketplace than ever before, making enforcement of intellectual property rights nearly impossible.

The globalization of the world economy, caused partly by the new technologies, has also contributed to the breakdown of the old system. International conflicts over intellectual property have always been a problem, as developing countries, anxious for economic growth, have been unwilling to extend protection to foreign works. This was true of nineteenth-century America, and it is true of much of the Third World today.

But the increasing integration of the world economy has multiplied both the incentives for international violations of intellectual property rights and the economic harm of such violations. Today, the products of newly industrialized countries such as Korea or Taiwan are sold all over the world. "Borrowing" intellectual property allows these countries to successfully compete in markets for many advanced products without bearing the cost of research and development.

Finally, the growing trend toward using market mechanisms to gather and disseminate information has disrupted the traditional public infrastructure for sharing intellectual assets. For example, before the breakup of the regulated Bell Telephone system, Bell Labs was the equivalent of a national basic-research laboratory, supported by corporate cross-subsidies. Today, institutions like Bell Labs face growing pressures to pay their own way. The federal government has mandated that agencies such as the National Technical Information Service become self-supporting through user fees. And even universities are turning to patent rights and copyright royalties to recoup their investment in faculty research and development.

The High Costs of Copying

Thus, at the very moment when information is becoming a valuable commodity, protecting the economic value of intellectual assets is proving more difficult. While the loss of income is difficult to ascertain, estimates range anywhere from $20 billion to $60 billion each year.

Most serious is the deliberate commercial pirating of both low-and high-tech products in foreign countries. For example, videotaped copies of Hollywood films are often illegally released in foreign markets before the U.S. release. The Motion Picture Association of America estimates the loss at about $6 billion annually. And illegal publishing of books and technical manuals abroad costs the American publishing industry about $1 billion every year. In Korea alone, nearly 1 million U.S. titles have been pirated.

Other violations of intellectual property rights—for personal rather than commercial use—are more difficult to track. The rule of thumb in the software industry is that at least one unauthorized copy exists for every authorized sale of a software program. According to the Software Publishing Association, software manufacturers lost approximately $1 billion in sales to piracy (both for profit and for personal use) in 1986. Lotus claims that over half of its potential sales of 1-2-3 are lost—at a cost of about $160 million every year. And Wordstar estimates that in 1984 it lost $177 million in potential sales, compared with $67 million in revenues from actual sales of the program.

Such reports need to be taken with a grain of salt, as they assume that every user of an unauthorized copy would buy the program in question were the copies to disappear—an unlikely proposition. Still, the numbers suggest the scope of the problem.

Violations of intellectual property also have public costs. Widespread copying is one factor in high software prices, as firms try to recoup their investment in a program as quickly as possible. If unauthorized copying could be eliminated, it is likely that the costs of software could be greatly reduced—a net gain for society as a whole.

Owners of intellectual property have tried a variety of methods to combat unauthorized copying. In some cases, technology itself seems to offer a solution. To stop satellite-dish owners from capturing broadcast signals without subscribing to local cable services, programmers scramble their signals. Today, the most popular programs cannot be received by satellite unless viewers pay a monthly fee to gain access to the special code of each cable channel.

However, technical protections can spawn their own technical countermeasures or result in a consumer backlash. For example, the practice of "copy protection," once widespread in the software industry, has given birth to special programs whose sole purpose is to override copyprotection code. And consumer dissatisfaction with the inconvenience of using copy-protected software has led most software companies, Lotus included, to give up on copy protecting their programs altogether.

On the international front, the federal government has encouraged trading partners to enact intellectual property laws or expand coverage of laws that already exist. Under recent provisions in trade and foreign aid laws, countries whose copyright and patent practices do not conform to U.S. standards can be penalized, even to the point of restricting their imports to the U.S. market. The federal government is also promoting a multilateral agreement on intellectual property as part of the Geneva Agreement on Tariffs and Trade.

So far, such efforts have had only limited effect. The sanctions available to federal trade officials are miniscule compared with the enormous profits foreign companies can make by using U.S. processes and designs in the international market. Even money damages and confiscation of goods are simply absorbed by pirate firms as a cost of doing business.

Copyrighting the User Interface?

In the absence of effective protection, owners of intellectual property have tried to fit their products into any and all of the available legal categories. The results are legally contradictory and confusing to the general public. They also undermine traditional rationales for intellectual property protection.

For years, the legal status of computer programs was unclear. Although the U.S. Copyright Office began tentatively registering software under its "rule of doubt" provision in 1964, many analysts suspected that computer code written to be read by a machine rather than a human couldn't qualify for copyright. And the Patent Office considered most programs a collection of algorithms—which, like other mathematical equations, are excluded from patent protection.

So the computer software industry relied primarily on trade secrecy. This has worked reasonably well for larger computer installations with custom-made software. However, the mass distribution of easily available software made possible by the personal computer created a new legal situation.

Any personal computer user has seen the long and complicated agreement, usually set in type so small that it is barely legible, on the cover or inserted underneath the outer protection of most software diskettes. This is the shrink-wrap license to which the purchaser is assumed to agree upon opening the package. Most such licenses stipulate that the buyer cannot "use, copy, modify, merge, translate, or transfer" the software "except as expressly provided in this agreement."

The shrink-wrap license treats software as a trade secret. This poses an immediate practical problem. To consider a computer program used by millions of people as a trade secret offends common sense—the fact that so much copying takes place indicates how few users take the agreement seriously. What's more, at least one court has held such licenses legally invalid.

In 1980, Congress amended the 1976 Copyright Act to explicitly include software, partly because there seemed no other adequate mechanism for protecting what was clearly a valuable asset. Since then, the courts have steadily extended copyright protection for software. At first, it applied only to the source code, written in a programming language such as Fortran or Cobol. Later court cases established that a program's object code, the sequence of 0s and 1s read directly by the computer, was covered as well. In 1986, the flow diagrams that encapsulate the logic and sequence of the program were also included under copyright.

That same year, in *Jaslow* v. *Whelan*, the Third Circuit Court of Appeals affirmed a lower court ruling that copyright protection extends to certain "non-literal" features of the program. The court decided that the screen design and the commands of the program represented the time and effort the computer software programmer had expended in understanding the needs of the application in question—an inventory system for dental laboratories. The conclusion was that such laborious intellectual analysis should be protected. This has set the stage for the "look and feel" cases currently under consideration.

At the same time that copyright protection is being expanded, software firms are again turning to patent protection. Court cases have redefined the status of computer programs under patent law, considering operating systems just like other industrial processes and therefore eligible for patents. In 1986, the artificial intelligence firm Teknowledge received patents on two new software products.

The Dangers of Ad Hoc Protection

There are a number of dangers inherent in this ad hoc approach. First, it is contradictory to claim that a computer program is a trade secret and yet deserves copyright protection, which assumes broad public dissemination. And saying that the same software can come under both copyright and patent law similarly defies people's sense of what belongs in what category.

Second, ad hoc measures run the risk of shifting the emphasis toward too much protection, even to the point of threatening innovation itself. Protecting the "look and feel" of a computer program could become a serious obstacle to standardizing software applications and could prove extremely costly as well.

For example, should the federal district court in Boston decide that the look and feel of Lotus 1-2-3 can be copyrighted, then every maker of computerized spreadsheets will have to create distinctively different screen designs. This could mean that the techniques and skills acquired by using Lotus spreadsheets wouldn't be transferable to other spreadsheet programs. Individuals and firms would face increased training costs, and even the most innovative software would encounter substantial barriers to entering the spreadsheet market.

Third, as communications technology becomes more complex, the ad hoc approach will become even more cumbersome. For instance, a single "read-only" compact disc (CD ROM) can store a 20-volume encyclopedia. What uses of the CD ROM are permissible within the limits of current law? Can users print the entire 20 volumes, or is this a violation of copyright? If so, how much of the encyclopedia can they reprint? Can portions of the encyclopedia be transferred to another computer, or does this constitute making a copy? Can portions be displayed in the classroom, or might this legally qualify as a performance or retransmission? May the contents be simultaneously networked to many locations, such as different classrooms at a university?

Some lawyers argue that since different mechanisms protect different rights, the proliferation of mechanisms covering the same intellectual asset is both effective and reasonable. So, for example, design of the laser videodisc may be patented; the process by which it is manufactured may be a trade secret; the content of a specific disc can be copyrighted; the commercial name under which the product is marketed will be a trademark; the talent whose performance is captured on the disc will be subject to performance rights; and the work, if retransmitted by a cable system, may be subject to royalties.

The problem is that such an elaborate system is costly and, when it comes to competing in the world economy, a distinct disadvantage. The price of a product must reflect not only the high costs of research and development but also the legal fees necessary to document legal protections and enforce them.

Toward a New Rationale of Protection

As long as the United States depends on the private sector to create and disseminate information, we need a simpler, less costly system for protecting intellectual property. Such a system should recognize that effective protection of intellectual property is not just a legal matter. It is also a function of public attitudes and opinions. No law, no matter how carefully worded, can prohibit widespread practices that the public considers acceptable.

While ethical standards for using new information technologies are still in an early state of development, it seems clear that the public favors flexibility—as long as the original owner of the copied product enjoys no commercial advantage. The rationale seems to be that if you can loan your friends books, why not let them copy your software programs and musical tapes?

A public opinion poll conducted by the congressional Office of Technology Assessment found that 70 percent of those questioned thought copying a record, tape, software, or TV program in one's personal possession is permissible. About half agreed that such copies should be publicly available, for example in a library. However, some 80 percent opposed circumventing commercial offerings such as pay TV or cable television. And nearly all deplored the reselling of databases for personal gain.

Both Congress and the courts have begun to take these attitudes into account. Under the Cable Communications Act of 1984, satellite-dish owners do not have to pay to capture the broadcast signals of copyrighted programs, as long as those programs are not encrypted. And in the now-famous "Betamax" case (*Sony Corp.* v. *Universal City Studios*), the Supreme Court recognized that it would be fruitless to try to turn the tide against the massive purchase of videocassette recorders able to record television programs for later use. Although collecting copied programs for a personal video library might violate the Copyright Act, the Court made a distinction between commercial exploitation and copying for "private use."

Owners of intellectual property are beginning to realize that they must cultivate public awareness and sympathy to protect capital investment. Numerous trade organizations are selecting this route and allocating more dollars to public education than litigation. For example, the Association of Data Processing Service Organizations has initiated a "Thou Shalt Not Dupe" campaign to discourage corporations from copying programs. The association has sent out hundreds of thousands of brochures urging companies to adopt a sample policy statement against copying. Similarly, the recently formed American Copyright Council is launching an advertisement campaign on the legalities of copyright infringement. And in addition to prosecuting flagrant cases of cable piracy, the cable television industry is spending millions of dollars advertising the impropriety of tapping into cable lines.

However, initiatives like these do not address systematic commercial pirating or complicated conflicts between innovation and imitation such as the look-and-feel lawsuits. Here, we need to articulate a new rationale for legal protection.

The starting point should be an understanding that information technology makes the form a product takes easy to separate from the intellectual assets that go into it. This suggests that copyright law, with its focus on the expression of an idea rather than on the idea itself, is inappropriate for protecting what is really valuable in the new kinds of intellectual property.

More suitable would be a system that emphasized the actual use of intellectual assets. For example, the entertainment industry has developed its own legally binding arrangements to determine who benefits from the use of entertainment programs. Standard contracts govern the division of earnings among all those necessary to produce works for continued use on radio, television, and videotapes. Perhaps the software industry could develop similar mechanisms.

Another possibility is a modified form of patent rights with registration procedures, monopoly time limits, and rules for licensing all shaped to the unique realities of the computer industry.

Of course, such efforts may eventually demonstrate that simple and effective protection of new kinds of intellectual property is largely impossible. If so, policymakers will have to reevaluate recent trends toward the privatization of information. When the private creators of intellectual assets cannot be adequately protected for their efforts, then new kinds of public support may be necessary.

Whatever the specific mechanisms for addressing the problems of intellectual property protection, those who are creating the new information and communications technologies—and who best understand their capabilities and limits—need to play a more active role in policy debates. Too often, the lawyers and legislators who write and litigate intellectual property laws have only a superficial understanding of the technology in question.

One possibility would be to create teams of technical experts to serve as negotiators or mediators in complex technological controversies. Or professional associations could develop codes of ethics for what constitutes acceptable—and unacceptable—borrowing of others' intellectual work.

Only when we hear from technologists will we begin to meet the real challenge of intellectual property rights: encouraging creativity while preventing exploitation inimical to investment and the rational allocation of R&D funds.

Additional Readings for Chapter 6

BRANSCOMB, ANNE W. "Law and Culture in the Information Society." *The Information Society* 4(4) (1986): 279–311.

CAWKELL, A. E. "Privacy, Security, and Freedom in the Information Society." *Journal of Information Science* 4(1) (March 1982): 3–8.

CHARTRAND, ROBERT L. "The Role of Government in the Information Society." *Journal of Information Science* 5(4) (December 1982):137–142.

CHILDERS, THOMAS. *The Information Poor in America*. Metuchen, NJ: Scarecrow Press, 1975.

CLEMENT, ANDREW. "Comments on Democracy in an Information Society." *The Information Society* 4(1/2) (1986):109–113.

CLEVELAND, HARLAND. *The Knowledge Executive: Leadership in an Information Society*. New York: Dutton, 1985.

LEVIN, MARC A. "Government for Sale: The Privatization of Federal Information Services." *Special Libraries* 79(3) (Summer 1988): 207–214.

LINOWES, DAVID F., and BENNET, COLIN. "Privacy: Its Role in Federal Government Information Policy." *Library Trends* 35(1) (Summer 1986): 19–42.

LORIMER, ROWLAND. "Implications of the New Technologies of Information." *Scholarly Publishing* 16(3) (April 1985): 197–210.

RUBIN, MICHAEL R. "The Computer and Personal Privacy, Part I: The Individual Under Assault." *Library Hi Tech* 5(1) (Spring 1987): 23–31.

SCHILLER, HERBERT I., and SCHILLER, ANITA R. "Libraries, Public Access to Information, and Commerce." In *The Political Economy of Information*, edited by Vincent Mosco and Janet Wasco. Madison, WI: University of Wisconsin Press, 1988.

SHANK, RUSSELL. "Privacy: History, Legal, Social and Ethical Aspects." *Library Trends* 35(1) (Summer 1986): 7–18.

STERLING, THEODOR D. "Democracy in an Information Society." *The Information Society* 4(1/2) (1986): 9–47.

STERLING, THEODOR D. "Democracy in an Information Society: A Rejoinder." *The Information Society* 4(1/2) (1986): 127–143.

WARE, WILLIS H. "Information Systems, Security, and Privacy." *EDUCOM Bulletin* 19(2) (Summer 1984): 6–11.

WILSON, ALEX. "The Information Rich and the Information Poor." *Aslib Proceedings* 39(1) (January 1987): 1–6.

WOODRUM, PAT. "Censorship and Community Awareness." *Journal of Library Administration* 9(3) (1988): 103–110.

7

Information and Public Policy

The importance of information as a resource has meant that it is no longer of concern solely to individuals in their relationships with one another and with their own governments. Moreover, it has become a basic ingredient of almost all other economic transactions on an international level. The issues involved are complicated by the multitude of both public and private organizations involved and the need to protect the interests of both economic development and national security.

Information has been moving from one country to another for many years in the shape of published materials, telephone and broadcast communication, and other media such as film and video. It has also been subject to regulation for a variety of economic, security, or social reasons. But it is only recently that this "transborder data flow" has been recognized as a major international policy concern in its own right. Its current importance stems from the explosive growth in data transmission during the last decade, not only to meet the needs of international trade, but also to obtain cheaper processing, or to avoid local restrictions on the handling and use of data. For example, it is quite common to have keyboarding carried out in one country for input to a remote database because of economic reasons.

The international movement of machine-readable data covers not only the transfer of marketed data services (such as the online search services), but also the movement of trade-related (banking and stock exchange) data and the flow of in-house data within big multinational corporations. The international issues involved in such transborder flows include, not only the ownership and security of data in transfer, the possibilities for high technology piracy, and the need to protect domestic industry and employment, but even extend to questions of personal privacy and national sovereignty. It is estimated that computer losses in money and information are in the range of a half billion dollars a year in this country alone. Access safeguards range from multiple levels of access and frequent changes of passwords to encryption. But these safeguards are still not entirely adequate. A balance has to be struck between the value of the data, the costs of implementing tight security, and the inconvenience to authorized users caused by the security itself.

This ease of transfer from country to country via international telecommunications networks and satellites has made the question of access an international concern, with the motivations of different states depending largely on their own stage of technological development. Some of the developed countries are seeking to limit foreign competition in order to protect technological developments at home, while others favor an open market in information goods and services so as to gain access to new developments. The United States currently has a head start in the information business due to its early development of machine-readable databases and communications networks and is thus concerned to maintain this high-tech lead and to stave off the competition. Fears in this regard have led to increased protection at home in recent years and to the greater privatization of government information sources and products as a source of additional revenue and control. Restrictions on transborder data flows are seen as a way of curtailing the transfer of high-tech products and lucrative data processing business to cheaper manufacturing and processing centers in the developing world. Nevertheless, it is clear that total control and policing of the export and import of digitized data is not only extremely difficult, but also in violation of the constitutional rights of many democratic countries.

The industrialized nations of western Europe on the other hand, have been moving towards the idea of a common market (the European Economic Community or the EEC), to be inaugurated in 1992 as an attempt to develop an economic base large enough to support successful competition with the United States and Japan. A complete Europe without frontiers may eventually develop since many of the countries of Eastern Europe now appear to be headed toward free-market economics and will probably request entry to the EEC in due course. Japan, the other major producer of high tech products and user of information, also favors free enterprise since it enables them to compete effectively in international markets.

Meanwhile, the newly industrialized countries are working hard to develop indigenous information industries. Some rely on protectionist legislation to limit competition from imported products (e.g., Brazil), while others are adapting the newest ideas and relying on their cheap labor to enable them to compete effectively (e.g., Korea and Taiwan). The least developed nations (such as many of the African countries) are hampered in their desire to transfer the new technology by a shortage of hard currency and by their lack of an appropriate technological infrastructure to support electronic communication systems. Some foreign countries are further constrained by obstacles such as their national language or character set, since English has become firmly established as the "lingua franca" of the information age. It is the language of computers, of diplomacy, and of most international business transactions today.

Some of the least-developed countries feel threatened by the virtual monopoly over information that has been established by the developed world over the last two decades. Their concern is with losing control of their own national information due to its export to countries that offer advanced data processing and more competitive entrepreneurial and managerial skills. Many of the less developed countries have recognized the possibility that those nations that dominate the technology (such as the United States) can also control the content and distribution of information and even possibly modify the culture of another nation through their international media exports. The results of this cultural colonialism are difficult to predict and to control as developments in Iran and Iraq have clearly shown.

It is largely the American fear of Japanese dominance that has fueled protectionist policies regarding the production, access to, and marketing of information products. The result has been the passage of laws that increasingly restrict the free flow of data and information in this country. Laws originally established in an attempt to prevent supranational corporations from dominating information markets at home are now being used to try to prevent scientific and technological information from flowing out of the country. The objective is twofold—to protect the national information industry and to safeguard national security (since most scientific research is government-funded and much of the high-tech market is military). The government has a powerful weapon for control of this publicly-funded information since it is the final arbiter of exactly what is meant by "the interests of national security." The conflicts arising between the constitutional rights of the individual citizen and the control of information in the interests of the nation will have to be more clearly specified in the future to preserve this delicate balance.

The American Library Association and the Information Industry Association, as the official representatives of professional information workers, have been increasingly involved in the fight to limit political control of access to information of all types. They have been concerned particularly with the effects of the commercialization of much government-produced information and with centralized attempts to exclude some individuals and organizations from access to certain types of information. The U.S. government's lack of a comprehensive information policy has resulted in endless ad hoc decision-making frequently influenced by interests of economic advantage or motivated by an obsession with secrecy. This lack of a coherent national policy is typical of many other developed countries, but it will have to be addressed urgently as international policies shift more and more from economics decided by governments to economics decided by the marketplace.

National Information Policy: An Insider's View

TONI CARBO BEARMAN

Scope of the Paper and Framework

This paper presents one individual's view of national information policy in the United States. The paper is not intended as a comprehensive review of information policy; rather it is intended to provide a personal view from someone who has been interested in information policy since 1962 and has had the pleasure of playing a small role in helping to shape it for many of those years. The discussion concentrates on U.S. policy activities within the last decade.

This paper presents a series of trends to set the background and content for a discussion of information policy; discusses the 1976 *National Information Policy (NIP) Report*; reviews clusters of policy issues, including some recent activities of key players; and concludes with a discussion of the implications of policy developments for the library and information community.

Reprinted from *Library Trends* 35(1) (Summer 1986): 105–118.

Information and Society

In "Information and Society," Edwin B. Parker contends that there are

> three basic factors making up our new, largely manmade environment, and hence determining the quality of life. The first is matter, the second is energy, and the third is information. The three factors are related. . . . Investment in the production of information (creation of new knowledge) and investment in widespread distribution of knowledge (e.g., through education) may be the only way to permit continued improvement in the quality of life without large increases in consumption of matter and energy.[1]

He argues that all of society's expenditure on science, technology, research, development, and discovery in all fields can be viewed as investment in the production of knowledge. He further argues that:

> Similarly, all of society's expenditures on education, broadly defined, can be viewed as investment in the distribution of knowledge[2]. . . . In order to identify the information needs of society, both the information needs of individuals and of society as a whole must be included.
>
> Therefore, when viewed from the perspective of the society as a whole, the social need for information may be greater than the aggregate of the individual needs (or demands). . . . Thus, a careful analysis of the information needs of the society should also include an examination of the importance of investment in both generation and distribution of information as a means to productivity gains in the U.S. economy. . . . Pessimists may argue that the views of the economic expansionists and the stability-seeking conservationists are irreconcilable. That debate is likely to continue for the rest of this century. But, social investment in information resources in this decade may be the key to eventual reconciliation.[3]

All policy work should begin with a careful examination of both individual and societal information needs so that policies developed take into account the needs and concerns of the citizens and the society the policies are meant to govern. Of course there are many different needs and these needs are often in conflict with one another. Institutions may pull one way and individuals—or other institutions—another, resulting, for example, in conflicts between a desire by some to provide unrestricted access to most information and a wish by others to restrict access to protect national security or proprietary interests. Policy determination is best described as a question of balance—balancing among concerns and interests. Understanding these concerns, needs, and interests is critical in developing sound policies.

Trends

Influencing individual and societal information needs are changes in U.S. society itself. A brief overview of some of the trends emerging over the last decade provides insights into the information issues resulting from these trends. Dramatic changes have taken place in the United States since the 1960s and, as a result of these changes, several trends are clear. These trends relate to population shifts, technological developments, economic factors, changes in the information profession itself, and a renewed emphasis on consumer interests.

Population Shifts

The U.S. population is becoming older, more ethnically diverse, and is shifting geographically. As an article prepared for the U.S. National Commission on Libraries and Information Science[4] points out, by the end of the decade over 31 million people in the United States will be aged 65 or older. The 1980 census indicates that the four major cultural minority groups in the United States are (1) Black, (2) Hispanic, (3) Asian and Pacific Islander, and (4) American Indian, Aleut, and Eskimo. By the year 2000 almost one-third of the total U.S. population will be composed of these groups.

Another population shift has been geographic, from North to South and East to West. Of the net population expansion during the 1970s, 90 percent took place in the Southern and Western states. Most of this migration was from metropolitan to nonmetropolitan areas. The most rapidly growing counties in the United States are the nonmetropolitan areas in the West. The growth of small towns and rural areas is expected to continue throughout the 1980s with the majority of this growth taking place in the Sun Belt.

These population changes bring with them new and different information needs, such as needs for publications in languages not previously included in databases and library collections and requirements for the integration of technologies to deliver information in new formats to rurally remote areas.

Technology Developments

The most dramatic trends relate to technological developments and concomitant increases in the ease of violating protection of intellectual property or violating privacy. The cliché, "knowledge is power," has taken on new meaning with the increased ability to tap vast databases of information about individuals and organizations. Technology also permits the storage of huge amounts of information, increased ease of manipulating and managing it, and greatly improved delivery mechanisms. These developments have improved society's ability to share resources and to link local area networks to larger national and international networks.

An important related trend is that the perceived center for networks is shifting from networking organizations to the individual's work station; this shift has important economic implications such as the widening gap between information haves and have-nots.

Economic Factors

Economic trends include increasing budget deficits, international trade imbalances, and a growing awareness of the importance of information resources in the economy. With the financial difficulties facing the country coupled with the large portion of the gross national product (GNP) derived from information-related activities, more attention is being paid to information as a valuable resource. The trade imbalances and increased concerns about the need to protect technological information for the nation's defense have led to moves toward protectionism and restrictions on the dissemination of information. In recent years, policymakers within the U.S. government have disagreed over what information should be restricted and what should be disseminated.

Related to this is disagreement over the appropriate role of the government in gathering, managing, and disseminating information. A recent trend has been toward an increasing privatization of information activities previously considered to be inherently governmental. In a recent article, Reinhardt Krause notes:

> Balancing the traditional role of government as the collector, organizer, and disseminator of information with the functions of a $13 billion private industry growing 20 percent annually is getting harder these days. . . . One of the things clear, though is that government is getting out of the publications business. What analogies are appropriate between cooperative agreements instituted with depository libraries with printed material, and what might be necessary now with "on-line" information in a different age needs to be examined.[5]

The current trend in Washington is to increase reliance on the private sector through contracting out of services or by turning activities completely over to the private sector.

The Information Profession

These economic developments are having an impact on the information profession itself. The information profession is changing as the discipline—currently in a period of transition—breaks down into new specialties and combines with other disciplines. In addition, both the public perception of the role of the information professional and the added demands of the job are putting new pressure on educators, employers, and all information professionals to change curricula, improve continuing education, and develop new recruitment programs. With these changes has come an increased awareness of the importance of the information profession and the need for heightened attention to ethical issues such as the protection of privacy.

These trends are expected to lead to a stronger role for those information professionals and graduate schools who can survive—and hopefully thrive—under the increased demands placed upon them. We can expect to see continued attention paid to discussion and perhaps the development of a code of ethics for the information profession.

A related trend is the reshaping of the education system for the information profession. Some graduate library and information science programs have shut down; others have dramatically changed their curricula and faculty. Graduate programs in business, computer science, and other disciplines have moved into the information field. A reexamination of the accreditation process is underway. Links are being made with related professions such as records management, archives, business, and data processing. Continuing education programs are becoming more varied and, in some cases, highly competitive with one another. Studies have recently been completed on the competencies needed by information professionals in the years ahead. All of these factors point to dramatic changes in the education of information professionals in the future.

Consumers' Interests

All of these trends relate back to the information needs of individuals and of society as a whole. Emerging from them is a renewed emphasis on the protection of the consumers' interests. Recent suits, such as the Dalkon shield case and the possible relation between aspirin and Reye's syndrome, emphasize the importance of information in health. Information products and services play a critical role in providing information that consumers need to make decisions and in insuring that the effects of products on individuals and society are known and disseminated. We can expect continued demand for information to help individuals make decisions, govern society effectively, and enhance the quality of life.

These trends—population shifts, rapid technological developments, economic factors, changes in the information profession, and a continued emphasis on protecting consumers' interests—have raised a number of issues and have increased the need for information policies.

The National Information Policy Report of 1976

In reviewing the literature since the 1960s, it becomes clear that many, if not most, of the questions and issues raised in the late 1960s and early 1970s are still facing us today. Also, most of the questions remain unanswered.

First, of course, is the frequently asked question, "Do we need A NATIONAL INFORMATION POLICY, a national information policy, policies for the dissemination of federal information, or none of the above?" The answers are as diverse as the questions. The Rockefeller report on National Information Policy published in 1976 by the U.S. National Commission on Libraries and Information Science, pointedly declares:

> To debate whether there should be a national information policy is pointless. There will be such a policy. . . . It will exist whether or not these questions [raised in the report] are arrived at consciously or unconsciously, by commission or omission, carefully or haphazardly, in a comprehensive or in a piecemeal fashion.[6]

We already do have some policies, such as the First and Fourth Amendments to the U.S. Constitution, the Office of Management and Budget (OMB) Circular A-76 which stresses the need for government agencies to contract with and to rely upon the private sector as much as possible, and the Paperwork Reduction Act (Public Law 96-511) which has had a major impact on the gathering, production, and dissemination of government information. Also, the recent OMB Circular A-130 on the management of information resources provides another major set of policies. National and international information policies have been developed and continue to be developed in a piecemeal fashion, some by legislation, others through executive orders, and yet others through circulars, regulations, and guidelines established by individual agencies.

Information policy has a wide range of connotations to different people. As the *NIP Report* notes:

> All of them, however, have one thing in common—they deal with the pol-

icies which govern the way information affects our society. To the Federal Communications Commission information policy may mean policy dealing with the regulation of information messages over common carrier facilities; to the Justice Department it may mean policy with respect to the implementation of the Freedom of Information Act; to the National Science Foundation it may mean policy concerning the communication of research results to the scientific and technical community in the public and private sector; to the library community it may mean policy with respect to postal rates for the distribution of books throughout the country; and to the businessman it may mean policy affecting the information reporting requirements imposed by federal and state governments.

Although the term *information policy* can have different connotations, the various perspectives which are brought to it are all part of a common family of interdependent and intersecting interests. It is this larger context and the expectation that information policy issues will become more pressing in the future which compel a national information policy. The interrelationships which exist between and among information communications, information technology, information economics, information privacy, information systems, information confidentiality, information science, information networks, and information management have signalled the need for a broader, more comprehensive approach to the problem.[7]

The *NIP Report* reviews five clusters of issues: (1) government information collection, transfer, and dissemination; (2) information in commerce: a resource for public good and private gain; (3) the interaction between technology and government; (4) international implications of information policies and developments; and (5) preparing for the information age. A decade later, most of these issues are still unresolved. The report also recommended the establishment of an Office of Information Policy in the Executive Office of the President, but this recommendation was never implemented.

Although no single agency or office exists to develop and implement a single national information policy, over the last decade considerable attention has been paid in the development of policies.

An Overview of the Issues and the Players

A review of some of the major issues makes it clear that the issues are complex, diverse, and strongly interrelated. The issues can be divided, somewhat arbitrarily, into four areas: technological, economic, sociocultural, and political.[8]

Technological Issues

Technological issues involve those related to the hardware itself or to issues brought about by the hardware. For example, international negotiations about geostationary "parking orbits" for communications satellites or the allocation of spectrum frequencies relate directly to the hardware. The development of international standards to use the technologies raises important related issues such as whether some standards favor certain nations or restrict competition.

Technology has made it much easier to gather and disseminate information, but it has also created new problems in protecting privacy and proprietary or national defense information. Because television signals and data are easily beamed via satellite, methods are also needed to protect these signals from piracy and to encrypt data.

In the United States, billions of dollars are being spent to develop encryption techniques and protect data and to develop the technologies needed both to disseminate and to protect information. Questions have arisen concerning whether companies previously forbidden from certain types of discussions under antitrust laws should be permitted to collaborate to build new generation computers. Some recent policy decisions have been in the affirmative. The impact of the major policy shift resulting in the divestiture of AT&T continues to be significant resulting in new competition, increases in telecommunication costs for library and information networks, and changes in the U.S. telecommunications system. We can expect technological developments to continue to raise information policy issues in the years ahead.

Economic Issues

All information policy issues have economic implications because of the value of information and because of the importance of information management and technology for increases in productivity and in improving the quality of life. The fundamental question is "Who pays?" Increasingly large portions of the U.S. gross national product (many estimate nearly half) are derived from information-related activities. The higher the proportion of a country's information that is stored and managed outside its borders, the greater the loss to the country of jobs and revenue generated from the information-related activities. Although we have no adequate statistics on the world and U.S. markets for information industries, trends from available data indicate that: (1) the sector has grown enormously and has tremendous potential for continued growth; and (2) competition for U.S. and world markets continues to be fierce.

The United States is losing the trade balance with its competitors. For example, in 1983 exports of communications equipment and electronics components from the United States were $11.8 billion, and imports were $19.1 billion. In 1984 the consumer electronics industry represented $40 billion and 1.5 million jobs in the United States. Estimates of the size of the total U.S. information industry in 1985 range from $200 to $300 billion. Clearly this is a sizable industry with great implications for the world's economy.

The economic dimensions are significant and raise a number of issues such as those concerning the need to protect intellectual property, whether trade restrictions are needed, and determining the appropriate roles of the government and the private sector (both for-profit and not-for-profit) in the life cycle of information. Discussions of the appropriate roles of the various sectors have taken place for several decades in the United States. NCLIS issued a major study on this topic in 1982.[9]

In December 1985, the Office of Management and Budget issued Circular A-130 on the management of information resources. This circular, which includes a number of basic assumption statements, seeks to establish broad policies for the entire life cycle of information from gathering or creation to dissemination. Many consider it to be the single most important information policy document since the Paperwork Reduction Act. Comments on an earlier draft came from more than 350 individuals and agencies with more than half from librarians and several from members of Congress.

The circular seeks to strike a balance between protecting the citizen's right to access and a desire to provide information in the most cost-effective manner. The Government Printing Office (GPO) also has responsibility to insure that government information is disseminated. At the time this article was written, staff at GPO and the U.S. Congress' Joint Committee on Printing were drafting guidelines for executive branch agencies on the depositing of publications in depository libraries. Differences of opinion between the executive and legislative branches over the definition of a publication and possible disagreement over roles and responsibilities will have to be resolved. It is clear that increased attention will be paid to determining the government's responsibility for the entire life cycle of information.

Increased attention is also expected to be paid to questions of foreign competition. Decisions by countries to restrict trade and to support research and development aimed at focusing efforts and leap frogging technology to dominate the market have resulted in regulatory controls on telecommunications and information activities, protectionist trade barriers, and government funding in cooperation with industry for research and development (R&D). These activities are being watched closely within the United States. The 1985 decision by the Department of State to establish a Bureau of International Communications and Information Policy within the department reflects the increased attention paid by the administration to these concerns. Among possible U.S. efforts in this area, we can expect to see attempts to work with individual nations and international groups to remove trade barriers and improve reciprocal trade and efforts to enhance the competitiveness of export firms perhaps through tax credits for research and development, export tax credits, or increased federal support for R&D in high-risk areas. Economic issues are expected to receive even greater attention in the months ahead.

Sociocultural Issues

Although many of these issues are international, they must also be dealt with as national issues. When a country's data reside outside its boundaries, national regulatory efforts cannot reach the data and the absence of bilateral or multilateral agreements prevent control by the country over its own data and may limit its return on demand. Such a situation could threaten national sovereignty or even national security. In many countries information products and services have been strongly nationally oriented; the diversity of languages, alphabets, classification schemes, and approaches to organizing information are usually considered assets. Efforts toward uniformity of data storage or the perceived dominance by some countries may be viewed as threatening to national cultural identification and self-images. For example, a proliferation of television programs and advertising from one country may be seen as a threat to another country's culture.

Unrestricted data flows and the location of a nation's data outside its borders lead many nations to fear that they may not have access to their own data when the nation needs them and that the country's cultural heritage may be in jeopardy. Related to these concerns are questions of the preservation of intellectual property rights, privacy issues, and concerns with assistance programs by developed countries for the less-developed nations and their "terms of modernization." The protection of intellectual property and privacy rights has become increasingly difficult because of the power to violate these rights offered by technology. Several ethical issues have been raised concerning the responsibilities of the information profession and are being discussed at conferences of professional societies such as the American Society for Information Science (ASIS).

Determining the kinds of programs for aid needed by less developed countries is equally difficult. Many advanced technologies are unsuitable to meet the needs of developing countries, and databases often have a national cultural bias. Also, shortages of trained experts to implement new programs, the requirement of high capital investments, and countries' concerns about being "locked in" to another country's technology and support requirements all exacerbate the problem of identifying and implementing aid programs.

A final sociocultural issue area relates to the education of information professionals. Determining what our future colleagues need to know to perform successfully as information professionals is very difficult. Several efforts are underway in the United States to define competencies and the resources needed for educational programs. The issues concern who should determine the competencies, what they actually are, and who is responsible for education and training. The United States continues to address these problems and to seek bilateral and multilateral solutions to them.

Political Issues

All of the issues discussed earlier, of course, have political aspects. In addition, other major political issues relate to equity of access, especially by developing nations; to information, disinformation, and propaganda as tools of national policy; and to national security functions. Equity of access is one of the most significant issues facing us today. One futurist has predicted a recolonization of the world based on access to information; information-poor nations will be linked with and increasingly dependent on information-rich nations. The concern is also that those who can find and use information effectively will have great power over those who cannot leading to further inequities in society.

The potential of information and communications technology to create a global communications network is being realized but with the network comes awareness of a conflict between the information ideologies of the developed nations (often conflicting ideologies) and those of the developing nations. Many developed nations advocate the unrestricted broadcast of most information across national boundaries along with the unrestricted access of a private press to all parts of the world with uncensored reporting of whatever the private press wants to report. Recently we have seen some questioning of these principles by the governments of some developed nations. Most developing nations also appreciate the value of information technology yet may wish to maintain some control to avoid an inundation of broadcasting over which they have no control. In part this concern derives from a feeling that reporting is biased and may reflect "developed-nation imperialism." The debate between the need for a "New World Information and Communications

Order" and the need for a firm stand against control of the press is likely to continue in the near future.

National security issues have placed the United States in a bit of a quandary. Although we champion the unrestricted flow of most information, we find ourselves being asked to restrict certain kinds of information, particularly technological information identified as being of strategic importance. Senior officials from the Department of Defense may disagree with those from the Departments of Commerce or State, or with the academic community on determining what information should be disseminated.

Related to this issue are the problems of encryption for secure networking including the availability of encryption and decryption programs and the setting of related standards. Some data must be protected to insure privacy, protect proprietary interests, or safeguard national security. Determining what should be protected, from whom, and how are important issues to be resolved in the years ahead. This overview highlights some of the major information policy issues confronting us in the future.

Implications for the Future

Some of the implications of these issues have been discussed earlier, in particular the need to examine and resolve these issues, the changes in the information profession itself, the dramatic developments in education, and the need for a code of ethics. Information professionals will be called upon to take the lead in these areas and in developing policies. Although many policies have been developed, other policies and perhaps changes in current policies, are needed. In this author's personal opinion, a single National Information Policy is not desirable. Policies for all phases in the life cycle of *government* information are needed.

Determination of these policies must begin with a clear definition of what kind of information is covered by the policy. The NCLIS Public Sector/Private Sector Task Force developed the somewhat awkward but correct phrase *governmentally distributable information* to mean:

> Information brought together for governmental purposes from information in the public domain or within the scope of "fair use," or owned by the government itself, or that the government has obtained rights to distribute, or that is distributable under the Freedom of Information Act, subject only to the statutory limitations (such as national security, personal privacy, etc.).[10]

This distinction is critical to insure that information to which access must be restricted—such as personal information about an individual—is treated differently from that which can and should be made widely available.

In describing the possible content of information policies, the *NIP Report* offered a series of principles as a starting point for debate:

- Encourage access to information and information systems by all segments of society to meet the basic needs of people, to improve the quality of life, and to enable the responsibilities of citizenship to be met.
- Safeguard the use of personal information about individuals and protect their right to personal privacy.
- Encourage systems that foster the creation and dissemination of knowledge.
- Maintain adequate control over the power information provides to government either through checks and balances, through diffusion of control, through decentralization, through federal/state consortiums, or by other means.
- Encourage efficient resource allocation in the development of introduction systems and efficiency in their use through consistency in standards, practices, and procedures, and through encouraging quality and accuracy.
- Maintain pluralism in information systems and strengthen the private sector so that, through competition, innovation can be encouraged.
- Adopt rules which will have some permanence and general applicability so that the private sector will be encouraged to invest in new systems and methods.

Given a clear definition of what information is included, these principles could still serve today as a good starting point for debate. Many will question the need to strengthen the private sector. The question of the appropriate roles and responsibilities of the private sector (both for-profit and not-for-profit) and the government, at all levels—federal, state, regional, and local—deserves much greater attention and debate. In addition, many other principles should be added to this list.

Conclusion

What should information professionals do about information policy? First, become familiar with the issues; read about them; and discuss them, especially with people from different viewpoints. Second, information professionals should make their views known to policymakers, members of Congress, industry leaders, and others who are developing policies. Third, information professionals should work on the actual development of policies. Expert advice from information professionals is needed; and policies will be developed with or without the participation of information professionals. To have effective, realistic policies requires the active participation of knowledgeable information professionals from all sectors.

Notes

Note: The comments reflect the author's own views and do not necessarily represent those of the U.S. National Commission on Libraries and Information Science (NCLIS) or the U.S. Government.

1. Edwin B. Parker, "Information and Society," in *Library and Information Service Needs of the Nation,* Proceedings of a Conference on the Needs of Occupational, Ethnic and Other Groups in the U.S. U.S. National Commission on Libraries and Information Science (Washington, D.C.: USGPO, 1973), 10.
2. Ibid., 11.
3. Ibid., 13–14.
4. Kathleen Falcigno and Polly Guynup, "U.S. Population Characteristics: Implications for Libraries." *Wilson Library Bulletin* 59(Sept. 1984):23–26.
5. Krause Reinhardt, "Policy Shift." *Government Data Systems* (June/July 1985):25–27.
6. U.S. Domestic Council Committee on the Right of Privacy, *National Information Policy: Report to the President of the United States,* (Washington, D.C.: NCLIS, 1976):182–83.
7. Ibid., xi–xii.
8. Some of the following discussions of issues are based on an unpublished paper the author prepared with Congressman George E. Brown. The author wishes to gratefully acknowledge this work and that of John Clement who worked at that time as a science fellow for Congressman Brown and who is now director, Governmental Activities, American Federation of Information Processing Societies, Inc.
9. U.S. National Commission on Libraries and Information Science Public Sector/Private Sector Task Force, *Public Sector/Private Sector Interaction in Providing Information Services,* (Washington, D.C.: NCLIS, 1982).
10. Ibid., 22.
11. U.S. Domestic Council Committee on the Right of Privacy, *National Information Policy,* 202.

Transborder Data Flow: An Historical Review and Considerations for the Future

DAVID R. BENDER

In the 1960s when Marshall McLuhan first spoke of the Global Village, he attributed the phenomenon to television. Little did he know what was yet to come. Since that time, communications technology has advanced and contributed to the shrinking of our Global Village. Today, computer technology, communications satellites, fiber optics, and an entire host of communications technology have been combined to allow for the international exchange of information.

Transborder Data Flow (TDF) is most simply defined as the exchange of information across national borders via telecommunications technology. As simplistic as that may seem, TDF plays a vital role in our global society. However, along with this critical exchange of information comes a variety of international issues that has spurred international debate and has divided the Global Village into the information "haves" and the "have nots."

This article will encompass a review of the significant events which comprise the major points in the history of TDF, a discussion of the current issues surrounding TDF, and considerations for the future.

History

Transborder Data Flow was first discussed at a seminar sponsored by the Organization of Economic Cooperation and Development (OECD) in 1974. At that seminar, the term was used in the context that privacy protection laws could be circumvented if data on citizens in the country

Reprinted from *Special Libraries* 79(3) (Summer 1988): 230–235.

were held in computers located outside the country and remotely accessed by telecommunications channels.[1]

While the introduction of the concept cannot be trivialized, it might be viewed as somewhat myopic inasfar as it was concerned solely with personal privacy and seemed to ignore the greater implications of information transfer.

The debate on TDF quickly evolved into a more serious discussion on security of nonpersonal data in 1977 at a symposium sponsored by OECD in Vienna.[2] While nonpersonal data included a wide range of information, at the heart of the debate was the primary concern that business information was no longer safe. Nations recognized the implications of TDF and began to consider and implement legislative restrictions to safeguard information from the inquiring computers of others.

This marked an important change in the focus of debate on TDF. Discussion of TDF switched from invasion of privacy on a personal level to concerns on the results of transmitting business information from nation to nation. Viewing TDF from a business perspective opened a Pandora's box of issues. Considerations were, and continue to be, made on the impact of TDF on trade, productivity, competitiveness, and employment, not to mention national sovereignty.

These early discussions provoked widespread concerns on the issues of TDF, and, in 1977, the General Assembly of the Intergovernmental Bureau for Informatics (IBI) passed the following resolution:

> The transnational dimensions of information must be recognized as well as its economic and social consequences to national sovereignty, especially when large amounts of data are transmitted abroad for processing and storage, or in cases where foreign interests collect data about a country and its people and do not make it freely available to the government of that country. The need to create a new international order in the field of transnational data flows must be recognized.[3]

In 1978, an OECD Expert Group on Transborder Data Barriers and the Protection of Privacy was established. The goal of the group was to develop guidelines for basic rules governing the flow of personal data and the protection of privacy and to investigate the legal and economic problems related to the flow of nonpersonal data. This led, in 1980, to the establishment of OECD guidelines governing the protection of privacy.

In the United States, TDF first appeared in a background report entitled "International Barriers to Data Flows," prepared for the Committee on Interstate and Foreign Commerce for the U.S. House of Representatives in 1979.

The definition of TDF became more specific and complex. TDF was

defined as "the electronic transmission of data across political boundaries for processing and/or storage in computer files."[4]

Five years had passed since the introduction of the TDF concept. Discussion focused on the impact of TDF at both the national and international levels. The Committee report stated that:

> National governments and international organizations are examining
> some potentially harmful impacts arising from the free international flow
> of information. Apprehension is particularly acute in Europe because of
> the fact that so much data processing, transmission and storage there is
> [sic] frequently performed in a country other than where the data is col-
> lected and used, or where the concerned data resides. Individual govern-
> ments have enacted or are contemplating restrictions designed to
> safeguard the security of personal data.[5]

West Germany and Sweden were among the first countries to enact
laws to protect the privacy of citizens. Since then, the number of countries with laws controlling TDF have grown to more than 20.[6] The impetus for such laws was the belief that, once information was computerized
and moved across national borders, the potential for abuse of that information was tremendous.

International Involvement in TDF

In 1980, OECD formulated a specific set of principles entitled "Guidelines on the Protection of Privacy and Transborder Flows of Data," with
the intent to ensure data protection in both private and government
sectors. In 1983, the Council of Europe enacted a binding treaty with its
members that created a consistent approach to TDF in Western
Europe.[7]

In 1985, OECD initiated a Declaration on Transborder Data Flow,
which recognized the benefits to be derived from the growing use of
TDF and, at the same time, recognized that market forces alone could
not deal with some of the legitimate concerns of governments. OECD
member governments agreed to promote access to data and information
and avoid the creation of unjustified barriers to the international exchange of data and information. They also agreed to develop common
approaches for dealing with the issues and to consider the possible implications for other countries when taking unilateral action. This agreement became the first international effort to address the economic issues
raised by TDF.[8] All OECD member countries have signed this non-
binding agreement.

Glenerin Declaration

In 1987, the U.S., Canada, and the United Kingdom, at the conclusion of a series of meetings on TDF, issued a joint statement which has become known as the "Glenerin Declaration." This statement, which was published in the December 10, 1987, *Federal Register*, stated that:

> The government explicitly recognize its responsibility to maintain public support for the creation and provision of certain information, through such means as the library system in each country, recognizing that there is a minimal level of information which must be available to, and accessible by, all citizens regardless of means.[9]

The National Commission on Libraries and Information Science (NCLIS) participated on behalf of the United States in the formulation of the statement. This attempt at a coordinated response to the issues of TDF seeks a "mechanism for the orderly sharing of information among our three nations and eventually any other who may wish to participate."[10] This statement sets the stage for a review of the current discussion and issues surrounding TDF.

The Current State of TDF

Concerns with personal privacy have long since given way to two major issues: national sovereignty and economic and trade concerns. Both of these points have a number of subsidiary issues which constitute the current discussion on TDF.

The discussion that surrounds issues of sovereignty and culture tends to provoke tremendous debates which are frequently heated and generally less open to compromise. The laws enacted in the late 1970s protecting the privacy of a nation's citizenry are a clear indication that national pride cannot be underestimated, particularly in TDF.

Three issues arise in TDF from a national perspective: (1) loss of control of information; (2) dependency on technology and/or information; and (3) perceived impact on culture.

The control of information becomes critical when information is either processed outside of the originating country (generally for economic reasons) or when information is stored outside of national borders. Despite controls to protect raw data and its resultant information, control over that information can be asserted in a variety of ways. Data can be intercepted without the knowledge or consent of the owner.

Information can be destroyed, either willfully or by an accident or natural disaster. Access to databanks may be denied because of political unrest or opposition to government or interference by nature.

Technology brings both cures and curses to our Information Age. Media coverage of information invasion fuels the fears that technology is not infallible or that information may be accessed by unauthorized personnel.

The overriding fear expressed by most Third World nations and several Second World nations is that of dependency on the "information superpowers"—generally the United States, Canada, and several western European countries. Most nations recognize the need to utilize information and technology to create both economic development programs and prowess. Yet, with an estimated 65 percent of database suppliers headquartered in the U.S.[11] and probably a high percentage of technology vendors in North America, the apprehension is understandable.

Lesser-developed nations are taking actions to build and enhance information technology, while taking actions to limit dependency on the information superpowers. Brazil is one of the most aggressive of a growing number of countries limiting foreign suppliers of technology and related services.

Concerns over dependence on foreign databases led the European community to band together in 1979 to develop Euronet Diane, an information network supplying information from European sources. Since 1979, the network has grown to offer access to more than 500 databases.

Associated with loss of control of information and dependency on foreign sources of information is impact on culture. While no data exist to support the contention that TDF has a negative impact on culture outside the originating country, the perception exists that there is a negative impact, or a threat, from the influx of other—generally Western—cultures throughout the world. The threat, which may appear insignificant on the outside looking in, is a subtle, yet visible, undermining of one country's traditions and mores.

Television broadcasts are the most vulnerable targets to criticism on the impact of TDF on a country's culture. At present, there is no international consensus on worldwide broadcasts. The Soviet Union favors prior review of broadcasts, while the U.S. adheres to the belief that broadcasts should not be restrained. There is no agreement by the worldwide community on this issue although it has been the topic of discussion by the United Nations on more than one occasion.

These issues—loss of control of information, dependency, and cultural impact—constitute a portion of the current controversy on TDF.

Economic and Trade Concerns

In 1988, the world business community recognizes the importance and value of information to keep business productive and competitive. Yet problems arise in trade and commerce that are attributable to TDF. These problems—which involve employment, restraint of trade, productivity, and competitiveness—will continue to be the core issues of TDF until the international community agrees on a resolution to these issues.

Employment and, more importantly, loss of employment is a growing issue. The need for information services continues to grow. It is estimated that the international data processing market will break the $1 trillion point by 1990—less than two years from now.[12] As a result, countries with established data-processing industries are working furiously to capture a share of this rapidly expanding, worldwide market.

This is a natural progression for nations with established information industries. Countries without such industry or with developing information-processing industries may find it cost effective to send such work to those nations with the appropriate expertise. Developed countries have the opportunity to create jobs in this industry and to positively impact their national economy.

On the other hand, lesser-developed countries have taken steps to limit foreign control of the information marketplace. Some countries require in-country data processing, while others limit use of foreign databases or require use of domestic telecommunications satellites. These restrictions enable the "have not" countries to support growth and development of domestic information industries while utilizing outside service providers.

Other non-tariff barriers inhibit foreign industry from establishing a foothold in information services. These barriers can include restrictions on services, prohibitions on the introduction of new products and services, or regulations that require investment in domestic facilities. Non-tariff trade barriers can help assure that nations keep—and hopefully build—jobs in their domestic information industry.

Restraint of trade is another aspect of TDF that is quickly coming to the forefront of discussion. Obviously, the attraction of a multi-million dollar industry is too much for conglomerates to avoid. Tariff-based trade barriers are no small problem. They include price differentials for use of post, telephone, and telecommunications (PTTs) networks or subsidies to the domestic information industry which precludes competition from foreign information providers.

The elimination of flat-rate charges for foreign users of PTT networks has the potential of driving competing industry from certain markets because of escalating fees for use of PTTs. As an alternative, competing industry can develop alternative networks to bypass PTTs or simply pass along costs to users.

Transnational corporations operating in countries with competing industry can fall victim to laws restricting the flow of information from their headquarters. Restricting an organization's access to databanks in a different country will nullify any competitive edge and result in the loss of the ability to compete.

The continued development of technology, in concert with the accessibility to technology, has begun to void some of these problems. The international trading community has come to accept the positive impact of TDF, if for no other reason than the information it provides which enhances their competitive stance and increases productivity and trade.

Future Considerations

The future of transborder data flow, regardless of the past 14 years of international consternation on the issue, can be reduced to two considerations: development and implementation of an international policy, and standardization. Resolving these issues will aid in ending debate on TDF while providing for an equitable solution to the issues of TDF.

As this article demonstrates, international discussion has long focused on TDF, and a variety of international treaties have been enacted which outline conditions, rights, and benefits of TDF. Yet, to date, there has been only limited international cooperation on the issue.

TDF is unique in the sense that there is no precedent upon which to base conclusions or solutions to the variety of problems posed by the issue. Additionally, there is no single international organization which might serve as the focal point for leading and determining the future of TDF for the nations of the world. The United Nations does not recognize all nations and OECD does not have Third World nations as members.

This is one of the challenges of the future—to create an international agreement that will satisfy the needs of all nations and all concerned parties in TDF. Such an agreement would dismiss such longstanding issues as a basic definition of TDF, establish a world-recognized set of legal principles and practices that would encompass all aspects of TDF, protect the rights of information producers and information users, and provide a flexible framework into which future technology and developments would fit.

Problems that must be overcome in order to develop such an international agreement include differences in national legal systems, actual and perceived rights of nations and individuals, and current barriers to information flow.

Issues of trade, economic development, and employment, as well as competitiveness and productivity, must be resolved. While most world-wide organizations agree on the basic premise of free flow of information, many barriers exist to free flow. Any internationally accepted agreement must provide for the removal of barriers to the flow of information. Developing such an agreement, in light of the concerns of privacy and issues of proprietary information, might make tearing down barriers to the free flow—internationally—of information difficult, if not impossible.

Secondly, international standards must be developed that will allow for the anticipated growth in TDF. At present, no unified system for software or hardware exists, but rather a hodgepodge of national standards which may or may not serve as an impediment to the flow of information. Both the International Telegraph and Telephone Consultative Committee and International Standards Organization have been working to develop such a system of standards. Fortunately, the key players in the industry have cooperated and work is advancing in this crucial area of TDF.

Conclusion

Obviously, there is a choice. The Global Village can continue on its current course by taking no action to reconcile the issues of TDF. As history has shown and as practice has proven, by taking no action, the nations of the world act. Regrettably, actions taken in those instances tend to be negative. In the case of TDF, they reduce worldwide cooperation at a time when worldwide cooperation is needed; they restrict the flow of information, which impacts the worldwide economy; and they take a step backward while technology is leaping forward.

Can the Global Village take action and reconcile the problems created by TDF? The answer to that lies in the ability of the world's information leaders to persuade both political and business leaders that finding a solution is critical and to their benefit, as well as to the benefit of all users of the world's information resources.

Notes

1. Meheroo Jussawalla, and Chee-Wah Cheah, *The Calculus of International Communications* (Littleton, Colo.: Libraries Unlimited, Inc., 1987), 159.

2. Ibid.
3. Jean-Luc Renaud, "A Conceptual Frame-work for the Examination of Transborder Data Flows," *The Information Society* 4(1986):145–185.
4. "International Barriers to Data Flows—Background Report." *Report from the Committee on Interstate and Foreign Commerce, U.S. House of Representatives, Subcommittee on Communications.* (Washington, D.C.: U.S. Government Printing Office, 1979).
5. Ibid.
6. Thomas T. Surprenant, "International Flow of Information," *The Information Professional: Facing Future Challenges,* (Washington, D.C.: Special Libraries Association, 1988), 163.
7. Ibid.
8. Peter Robinson, "From TDF to International Data Services," *Telecommunications Policy.* (December 1987):369–375.
9. "National Commission on Libraries and Information Science—Glenerin Declaration; Statement of Policy." *Federal Register* 57 (December 1987):46980–46981.
10. Ibid.
11. John Martyn, "Transborder Data Flow: An Introduction," *IFLA Journal* 12 (1986):318–321.
12. "Reshaping the Computer Industry," *Business Week* (July 16, 1984):85.

The Dangers of Information Control

JOHN SHATTUCK AND MURIEL MORISEY SPENCE

For the past decade, the federal government has established a network of policies that restrict the availability, shape the content, and limit the communication of information. This net includes an expanded classification system, limits on the exchange of unclassified information, the use of export controls to restrict technical data, and restraints on contacts between U.S. and foreign citizens. The architects of the new policy have also curtailed the role of government in both collecting and publishing many categories of scientific and statistical information.

The cumulative impact has been to restrain academic freedom, hamper technological progress, and undermine democratic decision making. Consider the following examples:

• In 1983 the White House issued a directive requiring more than

Reprinted from *Technology Review* 91(3) (April 1988): 62–73.

120,000 government employees with access to classified materials to sign a lifetime agreement: they would submit for prior clearance any material they wished to publish.

- In 1985, the Department of Defense (DoD) required the Society of Photo-Optical Instrumentation Engineers (SPIE) to restrict attendance at a conference where unclassified papers would be presented to U.S. and Canadian citizens and permanent U.S. residents. Scientists allowed to attend had to sign an "Export Controlled DoD Technical Data Agreement," promising that they would obtain an export license before sharing information from the conference with foreign citizens.
- The Federal Communications Commission (FCC) decided in 1986 to publish its proposed actions in the Federal Register only in summary form, making public comment more difficult.
- The FBI has asked some librarians to report library users who might be "hostile intelligence people."
- In 1984, the Department of Housing and Urban Development (HUD) drafted a research contract with a Harvard scholar that would have required him to submit results of HUD-sponsored research for review 6 months before publication. The scholar would also have had to submit results on related work not funded by HUD. The contract would have given the agency the right to demand that the scholar make "corrections" in data, methodology, and analyses. After months of negotiation, Harvard decided to refuse the contract.

The trend toward greater control of information is predictable in some respects: information is an important national resource that the government understandably seeks to manage. Nevertheless, the government's efforts in these areas should be fundamentally different from its management of other public resources: it should be guided by a heavy presumption, based on the Constitution and our national history, that open communication and the free flow of information have great social utility. This presumption should be overcome only in particular cases where the government can show a substantial public necessity, such as a concrete risk to national security.

Advocates of extensive government control of information have relied on two justifications. The first is the need to protect national security—a concept that under the current administration has become nearly limitless. The idea that broad categories of information must be kept from hostile ears and eyes has shaped a growing array of government decisions. This philosophy has supplanted the long and widely held view expressed by Vannevar Bush, President Truman's science advisor, that "a sounder foundation for our national security rests in a broad dissemination of scientific knowledge upon which further advances can more readily be made than in a policy of restrictions which would impede our further advances in the hope that our potential enemies will not catch up with us."

The second asserted justification for restrictive information controls is that the federal government must curtail its deficit spending and excessive regulation. The policies that result, however—including the FCC decision not to publish the complete text of its proposed rules—limit access to much information about government decision making.

The negative effects of these policies could be substantial. As a 1982 report by the National Academy of Sciences (NAS) concluded, the continued health of U.S. science requires open exchanges among researchers worldwide. The Soviet Union's experience illustrates the danger of a restrictive information policy. The American Physical Society cites official controls on scientific communication as the cause of the well-known Soviet lags in solid-state electronics and biology.

Restraints on the flow of scientific information can also hurt the U.S. economy. An April 1987 NAS report indicates that controls on the export of manufactured goods and information cost the U.S. economy 188,000 jobs and $9 billion a year. Exporters report sales losses to Japan and other nations because of these controls. And limits on the participation of foreign citizens in the U.S. economy deprive the nation of needed foreign expertise. For example, 40 percent of all doctoral engineers entering the work force every year are foreign citizens.

A further victim of controls, ironically, is likely to be U.S. security itself, as the long-term technological progress on which it depends is impeded. Finally, if these trends persist, they will erode a long national tradition of free speech and public access to information.

The U.S. Tradition of Openness

The pattern of government information controls is one of historical shifts between openness and secrecy. The U.S. tradition of open communication stems from the Constitution, which guarantees freedom of speech, thought, religion, and the press. It also obliges the federal government to publish regularly information on its spending and taxing activities and their effects on the citizenry.

The late nineteenth century saw the beginnings of a long period of growth in the amount of economic and social data collected and circulated by government. During the first half of the twentieth century Congress repeatedly resisted efforts by the executive branch to impose official secrecy on the expanding number of federal agencies.

World War II ushered in an era of increased consciousness of national security and more restrictive information policies. President Roosevelt instituted procedures for classifying information in 1940, relying on a 1938 statute restricting public access to military installations, equipment, and "information relative thereto." World War II also prompted the founding of a large intelligence bureaucracy. After the war Congress gave agencies such as the Atomic Energy Commission and the Central Intelligence Agency authority to bar communication of some information to protect national security.

A countertrend toward more open government began with enactment of the Freedom of Information Act (FOIA) in 1966. Congress strengthened the FOIA in 1974, and two years later passed the Government in the Sunshine Act requiring federal agencies to open more of their meetings to the public. During the 1970s the Ford and Carter administrations both issued executive orders designed to curb the excessive secrecy of intelligence agencies over the previous decade.

Presidents Nixon and Carter also narrowed the classification system. In a far-reaching 1978 executive order, President Carter stipulated that even if information fell into one of seven restricted categories, it was not to be classified unless its unauthorized disclosure reasonably could be expected to cause "identifiable damage" to the national security. The order also called for documents to be automatically declassified after six years and prevented them from being reclassified. Significantly, information could not be restricted for the first time after an agency received a request for it under the Freedom of Information Act.

Meanwhile, demand for government information mushroomed with the expanding federal role in areas such as civil rights, environmental and consumer protection, public health and safety, and employment relations. This demand was spurred by a technological revolution that enabled both public and private sectors to store and disseminate growing amounts of information. But in the early 1980s, as demand for government-collected information continued to climb, the principles of public access again began to erode—this time to an unprecedented degree.

Expanding the Classification System

The Reagan administration has used a panoramic definition of national security to justify an extensive network of restrictions on many categories of government information. Richard V. Allen, former national security advisor to President Reagan, asserted in 1983 that national security "must include virtually every facet of international activity, including (but not limited to) foreign affairs, defense, intelligence, research and development policy, outer space, international economic and trade policy, and reaching deeply into the domains of the Departments of Commerce and Agriculture."

Supplementing this concept is the theory of an "information mosaic": the idea that hostile elements can use sophisticated search techniques to assemble bits of seemingly harmless information into insights that threaten national security. An often-cited example of how this could be done is the blueprint for manufacturing an H-bomb published by *Progressive* magazine in 1979. The authors of the article amassed their information from unclassified data scattered through scientific journals.

Proponents of the mosaic theory have used it to fashion a broad expansion of the classification system. President Reagan issued a 1982 executive order giving federal officials authority to classify more information than ever before. Instead of having to demonstrate "identifiable damage" to national security, today officials need only point out that "disclosure reasonably could be expected to cause damage to the national security." The order created a new presumption in favor of classification when officials are in doubt about whether secrecy is necessary. It also eliminated the requirement that information be declassified within a prescribed length of time, and gave officials new authority to classify documents already in the public domain.

The Reagan system appears to allow classification to occur at any stage of a project and to be maintained indefinitely. The net effect could be to inhibit researchers from making long-term intellectual investments in fields that are likely to be classified at a later date, such as cryptography and laser science.

Language from a research contract with the Department of Energy reflects this new policy: "If the grantee believes any information developed or acquired may be classifiable, the grantee shall . . . protect such information as if it were classified." This provision places the burden on researchers to determine what data to withold, and does not specify how long they must comply. Such policies have prompted fears, in the words of one scholar, that "academic research not born classified may die classified." There is recent evidence that fears of retroactive classification are justified. In 1987 a federal appeals court upheld the National Security Agency's right to remove 33 documents from a library at the Virginia Military Institute.

New Use for Export Controls

The current administration has used the export-control laws to extend its sweeping view of national security. These laws—particularly the 1979

Export Administration Act—were enacted primarily to regulate the flow of goods and machinery. Yet they are increasingly being used to restrict the flow of intangible items such as unclassified technical information, both domestically and abroad. The asserted justification is that technical data are different from other information protected by the First Amendment because they can be used to create dangerous items such as weapons. And since technical information has immediate economic use, it resembles commodities more than ideas, according to this philosophy.

Such an outlook is new because there have traditionally been only two ways to restrict information. One is the classification system, for information controlled by government. The other is the doctrine of prior restraint, used for information not controlled by government in extraordinary circumstances involving a clear and present danger to national security. The government's burden of proof in such situations is very heavy, as illustrated by its unsuccessful effort to enjoin the *New York Times* from publishing the Pentagon Papers.

The Department of Defense has cited the export-control laws in pressuring scientific societies to limit foreign access to DoD-sponsored research results—as evidenced by the restrictions on the 1985 meeting of the Photo-Optical Society. When the presidents of 12 leading scientific organizations—including the American Association for the Advancement of Science and the American Chemical Society—protested these restrictions, the administration attempted to clarify the situation. The White House issued National Security Decision Directive (NSDD) 189, which exempts unclassified basic research from control—"except as provided in applicable U.S. statutes." But this did not assuage fears. One such statute, of course, is the Export Administration Act. DoD also issued a rule early in 1986 requiring scientists to submit all DoD-funded research for prior review "for consideration of national security at conferences and meetings."

Events at a June 1986 Linear Accelerator Conference, a biennial international gathering of nuclear physicists, revealed that not much had changed. The authors of 13 DoD-sponsored papers submitted them for clearance six weeks before the conference, as required. On the morning of the conference the Defense Department informed the authors for the first time that they could not present their papers—on the grounds that doing so would violate the export-control laws. Conference organizers appealed the decision, and after a hastily called meeting DoD officials cleared 10 of the papers—approving 1 only five minutes before it was delivered. One of the papers not approved had already been published.

To avoid such problems, some societies have informally barred foreign researchers from conferences. These include the Society of Manufacturing Engineers, the American Ceramics Society, and the Society for the Advancement of Material and Process Engineering. Nevertheless, restricted meetings are still more the exception than the rule. According to a 1986 survey by the American Association for the Advancement of Science, two-thirds of scientific societies with policies on foreign participation prohibit restricted meetings.

The Reagan administration's interpretation of the export-control laws has also forced scientists to be wary in their contacts with foreign citizens in classrooms, libraries, and research laboratories. The FBI's notice to librarians that they must report on "hostile intelligence people" is one such example. Another occurred in 1984, when DoD initially told UCLA's Extension Division that it could enroll only U.S. citizens in a course entitled "Metal Matrix Composites" because it involved unclassified technical data appearing on an export-control list. In 1981 the State Department attempted to require universities to report campus contacts between U.S. citizens and Chinese exchange students. Strong objections from universities led the department to abandon the policy.

The administration has also tried to restrict foreign nationals' use of U.S. scientific instruments. Supercomputers are a prominent example. The National Science Foundation (NSF) is the major funder of supercomputers at five universities, which will act as consortia for unclassified basic research. The Defense Department wants the universities to limit foreign scholars' access to these machines. Scientists have reacted with dismay, fearing that such restraints on unclassified work will undermine the quality of their research. Universities object to the prospect of policing researchers on campus.

The NSF has proposed guidelines designed to balance these concerns. Under the proposal, students from all countries could use supercomputers for regular course work. Soviet-bloc scientists could also use the machines for research in fields with no direct links to defense or intelligence functions. Officials from the departments of Defense and State as well as the White House have been reviewing the NSF proposals for more than two years without resolution.

The National Security Agency has designated some scientific fields as inherently sensitive and therefore subject to scrutiny under the export laws. A prominent example is cryptography, which has been so designated since 1981. Many cryptologists now submit their work to NSA for review before it is published to forestall even more stringent controls. The field of nuclear energy is also becoming increasingly secret. In 1981, at the request of the Reagan administration, Congress authorized the secretary of energy to regulate "the unauthorized dissemination of unclassified nuclear information."

By far the broadest category of information targeted for control is that maintained in electronic databases throughout academia, industry, and government. A National Security Council directive issued in October 1986 by John Poindexter, former national security advisor, laid out the policy. The directive sought to restrict unclassified information affecting not only national security but also "other government interests," including "government or government-derived economic, human, financial, industrial, agricultural, technological, and law enforcement information."

Poindexter's directive prompted fears that U.S. intelligence agencies would monitor virtually all computerized databases and information exchanges in the United States. The White House withdrew the notice in March 1987 under pressure from Congress, but the underlying policy—as set out in NSDD 145—is still in place. This calls for "a comprehensive and coordinated approach" to restricting foreign access to all telecommunications and automated information systems. The justification is again the mosaic theory—that "information, even if unclassified in isolation, often can reveal sensitive information when taken in the aggregate."

In December 1987, partially in response to the database controversy, Congress passed the Computer Security Act. This legislation transfers responsibility for developing a government-wide computer-security system from the National Security Agency to the National Bureau of Standards. But the act is silent on whether new categories of restricted information can be introduced as part of the security program.

Prepublication Reviews as Censorship

The federal government's funding of many information-producing activities puts it in a unique position to influence the content of research or restrict its publication. Recent developments show that such restraints can undermine the objectivity of research, and sometimes constitute official censorship.

A 1980 Supreme Court decision set the stage for allowing the government to examine a wide range of documents before they are published. In *Snepp* v. *United States* the Court accepted the government's argument that a former CIA agent's book violated his agreement to give the CIA a chance to determine whether the material "would compromise classified information or sources." This ruling led to CIA review of all proposed publications by current and former employees, not only those necessary to "protect intelligence sources and methods from unauthorized disclosure."

Three years after the Snepp decision, the White House issued NSDD

84 requiring 120,000 federal employees and contractors to agree to life-time reviews of anything they wished to publish. This directive also allowed the government to give employees polygraph tests while investigating unauthorized disclosures of classified information. The new policy further required agencies to set up regulations governing "contacts between media representatives and agency personnel, so as to reduce the opportunity for negligent or deliberate disclosures."

Testifying before Congress on NSDD 84, Thomas Ehrlich, then provost of the University of Pennsylvania, noted that prepublication review would discourage academics from serving in government, depriving the country of their expertise and insight. Ehrlich noted that the policy would also thwart criticism of government, since those "in the best position to provide that criticism"—academics who have served in Washington—would be enjoined from discussing their experience.

Under pressure from Congress, the administration suspended the prepublication-review provision in September 1984. However, it left in place a similar 1981 requirement that government employees with high-level security clearances sign a lifetime agreement—Form 4193—to submit all writings, including fiction, for prepublication review.

A 1986 General Accounting Office report concluded that suspension of the supposedly broader requirement has had little effect. The GAO found that the government had examined 21,718 books, articles, speeches, and other materials as part of the review process in 1984. In 1985, after the policy supposedly changed, the number grew to 22,820. By the end of 1985, at least 240,776 individuals had signed Form 4193. From 1984 through 1985, current or former government employees made only 15 unauthorized disclosures in their books, articles, and speeches.

Restrictions on publication can also be a source of conflict between the CIA and its civilian researchers, many of whom are academic scholars. Until recently, most CIA contracts required consultants and researchers to submit all their writings for prepublication review. Many universities chose to forgo such contracts rather than agree to the restrictions.

In 1986 the CIA narrowed prepublication review to "the specific subject area in which a scholar had access to classified information." But the new rule continues to pose problems for scholars because they are likely to concentrate their research in their fields of specialization. Any later writing they do in those fields will apparently still be subject to CIA review.

Tension between funding agencies' interest in obtaining a certain research product and scholars' desire to avoid constraints are not uncommon, but this tension has risen to new levels. The conflict between

Harvard and the Department of Housing and Urban Development, which wanted to review a scholar's research results for six months before publication, is one example. Harvard also objected to a NASA policy requiring grantees to obtain the agency's permission before copyrighting, publishing, or otherwise releasing computer software produced under contract. Harvard obtained an exception to this rule for one contract, but the underlying policy remains in place.

CIA contracts are a source of tension for scholars because the agency has traditionally required that the scholars not reveal that it funds their research. In 1986 the CIA recognized that a blanket rule would create "misunderstandings and suspicion," so contractors now can name their sponsor unless "public association of the CIA with a specific topic or subject would prove damaging to the United States." But this exception seems to apply to a broad range of circumstances, including where "acknowledged CIA interest in its affairs" would "create difficulty with a foreign government," or where "CIA interest in a specific subject . . . could affect the situation itself." Such secrecy undermines the credibility of academic work.

Reducing Paperwork—and Influencing Policy

A pivotal point in the evolution of government information policy occurred in 1980 when Congress enacted the Paperwork Reduction Act (PRA). The current administration has used the act to cut back to a troubling degree the amount of information agencies collect and publish.

The Paperwork Reduction Act was a response to growing public concern about the burden of complying with federal requests for information, including tax and health-care forms and a wide variety of other required reports. The Commission on Federal Paperwork estimated in 1974 that these requirements cost citizens and government a total of $100 billion a year. Yet as the Senate Committee on Governmental Affairs noted when approving the PRA, the government must collect information to fulfill important national goals, including promoting research, protecting civil rights, ensuring safe working conditions, and—above all—informing the public about the workings of government itself.

To streamline the process of collecting data, the PRA established an Office of Information and Regulatory Affairs (OIRA) within the Office of Management and Budget (OMB). The OIRA director is charged with determining whether the information a federal agency collects is "necessary for the proper performance of its functions," including "whether the information will have practical utility."

Concerned about potential abuse of these provisions, Congress explicitly stated that they do not authorize interference with "the substantive policies and programs of departments, agencies and offices." Such interference, however, has become increasingly common.

An early example was a 1981 OMB directive requiring departments to cut the costs of producing both written and audiovisual materials. In response, the Department of Education created the Publications and Audiovisual Advisory Council (PAVAC), which rejected numerous requests from grantees to publish research results and information for the public. Yet as one research director pointed out, many contracts require grantees to publish the results of their work.

After examining the pattern of refusals, the House Committee on Government Operations concluded that the PAVAC review process was based on vague and content-related criteria—including whether the publication was "essential" or "timely"—that amounted to censorship. Moreover, the committee found that the review process had had no "cost-effective" results.

Since 1981 the administration has taken further steps to transform OIRA—and thus OMB—into a policymaking agency. The administration greatly expanded OIRA's authority with a January 1985 executive order requiring agencies to submit their regulatory plans to OIRA before making them public. OMB then reviews them for "consistency with the administration's policies and priorities." The agency has used this authority to interfere with efforts by the Department of Health and Human Services to require aspirin manufacturers to include warnings about the dangers of Reye syndrome on their labels. OMB has also hampered efforts by the Environmental Protection Agency to ban some uses of asbestos.

OMB has used the criteria of "necessity" and "public utility" in the Paperwork Reduction Act to decide which projects other agencies can fund. A prominent example has been research sponsored by the Centers for Disease Control (CDC)—which OMB must approve, under the PRA provision that it review plans by federal agencies to collect information from 10 or more people.

A congressional committee asked researchers at the Harvard School of Public Health and New York's Mount Sinai School of Medicine to examine this process. After reviewing 51 projects CDC had submitted between 1984 and 1986, the study authors concluded that OMB was more likely to reject projects focusing on environmental or occupational health than those concerned with infectious diseases or other conventional illnesses. Research on reproductive topics, such as birth defects and venereal disease, was also more likely to be rejected. The authors noted that the proposed research had withstood the scrutiny of the peer-review process, and that OMB lacked the expertise to evaluate its practical utility. The authors concluded that the agency showed a "demonstrable bias" in thwarting efforts "to answer public demands for information on serious public health questions."

The administration has also tried to shift the burden of collecting and publishing information to the private sector. According to a 1985 OMB directive—Circular A-130—agencies must see that information is disseminated with "maximum feasible reliance on the private sector" and the use of charges to recover costs. This policy led in 1986 to efforts to scale down the National Technical Information Service (NTIS)—a clearinghouse for a wide range of scientific and technical data. The Commerce Department originally proposed discontinuing the NTIS entirely, selling it to the private sector, or contracting with a private entity for some or all of its functions.

This proposal prompted extensive criticism by legislators, libraries, universities, and industries that rely on the service, as well as by officials in the Public Health Service and the departments of Energy, Agriculture, and Defense. The Commerce Department's own staff concluded that "extensive privatization presents substantial costs and risks for the government, for NTIS customers and for the information industry as a whole." Critics worry that information without commercial appeal might go unpublished, and that private companies might be unwilling to maintain information over a long period of time. Changing the structure of NTIS could also hamper the influx of foreign technical information, which occurs through government-to-government agreements involving the NTIS.

The administration has responded by announcing—in a brief paragraph in the proposed 1988 budget—its decision to offer the private sector "the opportunity to operate NTIS on contract, with the government retaining overall policy direction." This has convinced neither the House nor the Senate. Both have voted in separate legislation to prohibit further privatization of NTIS without express congressional authorization. This prohibition has not yet received final approval.

Congressional dismay over OMB's attempts to manage information has also sparked efforts to cut OIRA's funding. This prompted OIRA director Wendy Gramm to set up a policy of disclosing OMB exchanges with other agencies regarding draft and final regulations. When Congress reauthorized the Paperwork Reduction Act in October 1986, it made this disclosure policy law and included a separate budget line for OIRA to allow close congressional oversight.

Undermining the Freedom of Information Act

The Freedom of Information Act (FOIA) has become an increasingly important tool for gaining public access to government information, but recent actions by the administration have made it harder to use.

In amending the act in 1986, Congress stipulated that fees for searching and reproducing documents could be waived or reduced when "disclosure of the information is in the public interest." The legislators recognized that exhorbitant fees can be a substantial impediment to academic researchers and non-profit groups that apply for information. The legislation's sponsors further specified that "a request from a public interest group, non-profit organization, labor union, library or . . . individual may not be presumed to be for commercial use" unless the information is being sought solely for a profit-making purpose.

Despite these indications of congressional intent, the fee guidelines issued by OMB in March 1987 could significantly raise the cost of requesting information under the act. The new guidelines allow "educational institution(s)" to obtain documents for the cost of reproduction alone, excluding the first 100 pages. However, OMB defines educational institutions as entities that "operate a program or programs of scholarly research." This excludes public libraries, vocational schools, and a wide variety of other educational groups that may not be associated with research. The new OMB guidelines also expressly reject the presumption that a request "on the letterhead of a non-profit organization [is] for a noncommercial request."

The nonprofit National Security Archive has challenged these restrictions in federal district court. The case was argued in late January; a decision is still pending.

Reversing the Trend

A decade of restrictive information policies has significantly affected important aspects of national life. The United States has lost some of its ability to innovate in a world increasingly driven by technology. Excessive secrecy—partly the result of an expanded classification system—has led to compartmentalized federal decision making, manifested in its extreme form in the Iran-contra affair. The public has been deprived of information it has paid for with tax dollars, and important values of free speech, academic inquiry, and democratic participation have been undermined.

The recent race to develop a high-temperature superconductor, in contrast, provides dramatic evidence of the advantages of open communication, especially in science. The two scientists who first succeeded in creating a relatively high-temperature superconductor were German and Swiss nationals working for IBM, an American company, in Zurich. Their research, funded by the U.S. Defense Department, set off a race around the world to develop practical ways of putting the discoveries to use. If federal policies had prevented these scientists from sharing their results, their work might still be unknown.

In mid-March 1987 thousands of physicists from around the world gathered in New York at a meeting of the American Physical Society to discuss the latest developments in this field. Such a meeting would not have been possible if DoD had prevented foreign nationals from attending.

Only one segment of the industrialized world has been left out in the cold during this extraordinarily fertile period of discovery and exchange. The Warsaw Pact nations have played no part in the superconductor frenzy. No one has sought to exclude them, but they are weighted down with bureaucratic restraints on travel, contacts with foreigners, and the use of telephones and copying machines.

Reversing the trend toward more government control of information should be a top priority of the next president. Within the first 100 days, the new administration should issue an executive order on information policy liberalizing the classification and export-control systems, and curtailing OMB's authority over the collection and dissemination of information. The president should also work with Congress to amend the export-control laws, the Paperwork Reduction Act, and the Freedom of Information Act.

The new executive order should establish a presumption that information generated both inside and outside the government will be freely available—except where it can demonstrate a substantial public need, such as a clearly defined threat to national security. The government should not restrict any information based on its speculative relationship with other data: the mosaic theory leaves no chance for practical limits on information controls.

In a democracy, the management of information and ideas must be guided by a heavy presumption that open communication is essential to society's well-being. Experience shows that the free flow of ideas is vital to the fabric of national life, powering the engines of innovation, guaranteeing national security, and protecting personal freedom.

Additional Readings for Chapter 7

ANTHONY, L. J. "National Information Policy." *Aslib Proceedings* 34(6/7) (June/July 1982): 310–316.

BOLLINGER, W. A., and ELLINGEN, D. C. "Evolving United States' Information Policy and Its Effect on the International Access to Online Technical Databases." In *Proceedings 11th International Online Information Meeting.* (London, 8–10 December 1987): 519–527. Medford, NJ: Learned Information, 1987.

BORTNICK, JANE. "National and International Information Policy." *Journal of ASIS* 36(3) (May 1985): 164–168.

CRONIN, BLAISE. "Transatlantic Perspectives on Information Policy: The Search for Regulatory Realism." *Journal of Information Science* 13(3) (1987): 129–138.

DOSA, MARTA. "Information Transfer as Technical Assistance for Development." *Journal of ASIS* 36(3) (May 1985): 146–152.

ERES, BETH KREVITT. "Transfer of International Technology to Less Developed Countries: A Systems Approach." *Journal of ASIS* 32(2) (March 1981): 97–101.

GOULD, STEPHEN B. "Secrecy: Its Role in National Scientific and Technical Policy." *Library Trends* 35(1) (Summer 1986): 61–82.

JACOB, M. E. L., and RINGS, D. L. "National and International Information Policies." *Library Trends* 35(1) (Summer 1986): 119–169.

LEVIN, MARC A. "Access and Dissemination Issues Concerning Federal Government Information." *Special Libraries* 74(2) (April 1983): 127–137.

MAHON, BARRY. "Transborder Data Flow—How It Impinges on the Information Industry." *Aslib Proceedings* 38(8) (1986): 257–261.

MENOU, MICHEL J. "Cultural Barriers to the International Flow of Information." *Information Processing & Management* 19(3) (1983): 121–129.

RELYEA, HAROLD C. "Secrecy and National Commercial Information Policy." *Library Trends* 35(1) (Summer 1986): 43–60.

RENAUD, JEAN-LUC. "A Conceptual Framework for the Examination of Transborder Data Flows." *The Information Society* 4(3) (1986): 145–185.

RUBIN, MICHAEL R. "The Emerging World-Wide Information Economy." *Library Hi Tech* 4(4) (Winter 1986): 79–86.

RUBIN, MICHAEL R. "The Computer and Personal Privacy, Part II: The Emerging Worldwide Response to the Threat to Privacy From Computer Databases." *Library Hi Tech* 6(1) (Spring 1988): 87–96.

RUBIN, MICHAEL R. "The Computer and Personal Privacy, Part III: The Regulation of Computer Records in the United States." *Library Hi Tech* 7(3) (1989): 11–21.

SAUVANT, KARL P. "Transborder Data Flows: Importance, Impact, Policies." *Information Services & Use* 4(1984): 3–30.

SMITH, KENT A., and HEALY, PATRICIA E. "Transborder Data Flows: The Transfer of Medical and Other Scientific Information by the United States." *The Information Society* 5(2) (1987): 67–75.

WIGAND, R. T., SHIPLEY, C. and SHIPLEY, D. "Transborder Data Flow, Informatics, and National Policies." *Journal of Communication* 34(1) (1984): 153–175.

8

Information Ethics

A common theme throughout this volume has been the idea that the emerging knowledge-based society is a technologically-oriented service economy with a workforce dominated by professional groups. The idea of a "profession" is traditionally thought of as denoting an elite group with a shared set of values and attitudes relating to their specialized area of knowledge which is used to assist and advise clients. The emphasis is on the personal nature of the relationship, the confidentiality of the consultation, and the expert nature of the knowledge base. The rise of the information economy has brought with it the growth of a new breed of professionals whose expertize is shared with the client in order to provide relevant assistance. Their professional status is based on their knowledge of the available information sources and the application of information retrieval techniques. This special status is somewhat eroded by the fact that most information professionals are employed within bureaucracies where final authority and responsibility frequently rest outside their control. This situation can lead to a conflict of interest between professional values and organizational regulations and procedures which, in turn, may lead to problems involving ethical decisions. Some of the ethical issues involved in the production and distribution of information have already been discussed in previous chapters (security, privacy, and free access, for example) from the point of view of the information users. This chapter looks at the ways in which ethical issues can also cause problems for the information workers.

Ethics are moral values generated from human experience which are

287

usually defined by cultural norms. Within this broad social framework, ethics are a personal set of values, that vary from time to time and from place to place—changing as circumstances dictate. This variability makes it particularly important for information workers to have agreed standards of professional behavior. In librarianship, for example, service to the client is assumed to be independent of the personal attitudes and feelings of the information professional providing the service. A professional relationship must be based on mutual trust and a respect for ethical responsibility. But emphasis must also include ethics in the wider societal sense, involving the promotion of liberal values through the collection, organization, and provision of free access to the widest possible range of materials. These values are formalized in a "Statement on Professional Ethics" issued by the American Library Association in 1981, and intended as a set of principles to guide professional behavior in support of intellectual freedom and the freedom of access to information. This professional philosophy sets forth the following criteria:

- Maintain the highest levels of service.
- Resist attempts at censorship.
- Respect the user's right to privacy.
- Support due process and equal opportunity.
- Distinguish between personal and professional philosophies.
- Avoid personal advantage at the expense of others.

Barriers to free access can occur on a variety of different levels, beginning with choices regarding the selection of library materials, which can be influenced by many extraneous factors. The availability of more materials from which to select, the restrictions imposed by limited budgets, and the limitations of available space, all mean that every information service is becoming increasingly selective in its acquisitions. We have seen how these cutbacks are normally supplemented by increased sharing of resources among major libraries, so that it is inevitable that there will be a number of different levels of accessibility to materials in any library. In addition to the implicit "censorship" as a result of selection policies, professional information providers will also undoubtedly be influenced by their personal value judgements. It is not uncommon, for example, for material considered to be pornographic to be judged as unsuitable for certain groups of users, such as children. Value judgements are also bound to have a bearing on the materials recommended to users. The idea of deliberate censorship is abhorrent to most information workers, but a number of writers have suggested that liberalizing influences in many schools, libraries, and bestseller lists tend to discriminate against conservative literature and ideas. In a world where choices have to be made, some literature, some ideas, some perspectives will necessarily be favored over others. The information professional needs to be aware of the motivations on which these choices are based and to make explicit any observed biases in the materials. The intention should be, not to exclude materials that conflict with social norms, but to see that opposing points of view are fairly represented so as to provide a balanced collection.

At the same time that information is becoming more widely available, we have seen that increasing numbers of people are being excluded from access by monetary constraints. As more information services, such as online searching, become available only for a fee, certain segments of the population without the means to pay are being excluded. Libraries have traditionally been the havens of middle-class culture and seem to have failed to attract the very people who are most in need of their services and expertise. The premise that information should be free to all citizens lies at the core of library ethics and needs to be defended wherever it is being eroded. For example, much of the previously free information collected using tax-funding is now only available for sale. This privatization of public information has been a major concern to information professionals in recent years, particularly in relation to online information.

At the other extreme, developments in technology have provided a wide range of new equipment that enables privileged individuals to generate personal information products without relying upon outside service agencies. For example, the ability to collect, manipulate, and distribute information in a cottage industry mode enables any individual to "publish" through the telecommunication networks. As clients become more knowledgeable and self-reliant, they also become more demanding, and may well require increasing accountability for professional decisions in the future. Under these pressures, the role of the information professional is changing from one of packager and disseminator of selective information, to that of consultant and advisor to a user who is an independent information-seeker.

The question of professional responsibility for the accuracy of the information provided is also a new development. The principle of vendor liability for the quality and performance of physical goods and many professional services is well established. It has not, however, normally been extended to information, though some information providers have suggested that liability is a prerequisite for professionalism. The problem lies in the nature of information itself and the ways in which it differs from physical goods. Its value is variable and is based on the credentials of the seller and the subjective perceptions of the buyer, as well as the actual information content. The question is whether the buyer or the seller should bear the risk that the information may be incorrect. In general, it appears to have been agreed that since the buyer has the option to accept or reject the information provided, the responsibility is then his (though this attitude may well change in the future).

This chapter looks at some of the moral dilemmas raised by the greater amounts of information being produced, the difficulties involved in gaining access to much of it, possible professional conflicts between confidentiality and social responsibility, and between personal and organizational accountability for the accuracy of the information provided.

Selection and Censorship: A Reappraisal

LESTER ASHEIM

To buy or not to buy, that is the question. None of us can escape either of those responsibilities if we really see ourselves as professionals charged with serving the entire community through the institution for which we are the appointed gatekeepers. Thirty years ago I wrote:

> To the selector the important thing is to find reasons to keep the book. Given such a guiding principle, the selector looks for values, for virtues, for strengths, which will overshadow minor objections. For the censor, on the other hand, the important thing is to find reasons to reject the book. His guiding principle leads him to seek out the objectionable features, the weaknesses, the possibilities for misinterpretation . . .

> The selector says, if there is anything good in this book let us try to keep it; the censor says, if there is anything bad in this book, let us reject it. And since there is seldom a flawless work in any form, the censor's approach can destroy much that is worth saving.[1]

The reason it may be desirable to explore once again the differences between selection and censorship is the fact that in today's climate some serious thinkers, and more importantly many opinion leaders (who unfortunately are not always the same people), are raising the question:

Reprinted from *Wilson Library Bulletin* 58(3) (November 1983): 180–184.

"Why should arrogant librarians be allowed to impose their preferences on materials that are purchased with other people's money?"

The key distortion in this attack is the underlying assumption that the approach librarians take to selection is based upon their own preferences, that books that are not bought are those the librarian happens not to like or care about, and that the collection is a direct reflection of the librarian's own pet peeves, preferences, and prejudices. I cannot say unequivocally that a library collection contains none of the books that the librarian likes to read, but I think I can say that any library in which any kind of professional selection policy is in effect (whether written or not) will contain many works that the librarian does not like or agree with. What the collection reflects is the librarian's view of what readers and users want and need, whether the librarian likes it or not. The librarian's bias is that the collection should be unbiased. But an unbiased collection is precisely what many censors disapprove of.

Which leads us to an interesting dilemma. Selection is as much involved in building a collection that responds to the whole community as in building a collection that caters only to the interest of a special group. To make sure that there is something for everyone, which sounds like "anything goes," requires just as tight a control over purchases as special purpose selection. For one thing, there is only so much money, which means that not everything can be bought; there is only so much space, which means that everything that is published or released in other formats cannot be added. The librarian's duty is to see that the available money and space are used in the best interests of all those who are present or potential users of the library. But while money and space require that selection be exercised, they do not determine which individual items be selected. That is where the librarian's judgment enters.

A Representative Institution

In these days of mass media, Nielsen ratings, blockbusters, and bottom lines, the library has a unique responsibility. The mass agencies of communication think in terms of large, faceless audiences. The common denominator, not the individual differences, becomes the criterion. A library, on the other hand, strives to assure that while the interests of the majority are being met, the interests of the many minorities are being protected. It is characteristic of American democracy that the individual, the special case, has rights too, and the public library is one of American democracy's most representative institutions.

So what we are saying, when we resist the removal of materials that have been selected for the library's collection or take exception to the restriction of materials that have already passed the test of relevance for a particular library, is not that questions may not be raised about the librarian's choices. It is that one segment of the library's total constituency should not be permitted to interfere with another segment's rights and that it is part of our responsibility to protect the rights of all.

The removal of materials threatens the democratic balance that the total collection is meant to represent, and while it is sometimes difficult to bleed, fight, and die for one book in a collection of thousands, there is a long-standing principle involved that should not be heedlessly overlooked in the heat of a momentary reaction to a single word, a private prejudice, or even a strongly-felt provocation. What we are saying is not that a member of the public does not have the right to express his or her opinions of our professional judgment, but rather that there should be a due process, taking all of the pertinent considerations into account, before a professional judgment is overthrown.

The Right to Choose

The response of the censorious, when a demand to remove an item from the collection is not immediately carried out, is: Why should this material, offensive to me, be rammed down my throat? Why are the morals of Las Vegas forced upon the citizens of Pleasantville?

These questions fall wide of the mark. The material picked out for repression sits in the library along with thousands of other books that the censor does not oppose. And there they all do, indeed, sit—approved or not—until someone chooses of his or her own volition to use them. The preponderance of books in a library are beyond criticism by any standard, and if shelf-space were a guarantee of wide public attention, not even the most censorious could complain.

The problem, of course, is not that certain books are forced on readers, but that readers make choices, and sometimes those choices do not coincide with the choices that the censorious would prefer them to have. It is the other person's right to choose that is being questioned by the censor, for even if librarians wanted to force the use of certain materials, they do not have the power to do so. As Samuel Goldwyn is purported to have said: "If the public doesn't come, no one can stop them." The grammar is a bit fractured, but the point is clear: when people have freedom of choice, they exercise it, and neither availability nor hype can make them choose any item they do not wish to choose.

Clearly, the problem is not that readers are coerced by librarians into using certain materials, but rather that people—given democratic freedom of choice—do not always choose as we would like them to. The censor's solution is to take away their freedom of choice. The social responsibility of the library is to preserve freedom of choice, and the selection policies of the librarians are designed to foster it.

If there is to be a confrontation between librarians and some members of the society, then the issue should be properly stated. The issue is broader than *Catcher in the Rye* or *Huckleberry Finn* or *Brave New World*. It is the right of the people in a democracy to have access to the widest possible variety of choices and freely to choose for themselves, on the basis of their own judgment. And notice that proviso: for themselves. Not for everybody else.

Limiting Special Interests

In the program "Are Libraries Fair?" held during the 1982 ALA conference in Philadelphia, Cal Thomas, vice-president of Moral Majority, urged that libraries open up the book selection process to the public. There's nothing wrong with the general principle that ways should be found to learn from patrons about their wants and interests, to tap their satisfactions and their complaints and to be responsive to them. An informal system already works to provide that kind of feedback constantly to the librarian. But in the end, after one patron demands that a certain book be banned and another person insists that a certain book be bought, someone has to be responsible for the interests of the library's entire public, not just the interests of those who are vocal. And that is where librarians are called upon. Because by training, by experience, and through the exercise of professional skills, they are able, as particular interest groups often are not, to recognize and respond to those interests that differ from their own.

For the most part, those who would remove materials are motivated by the best of intentions; to keep what is right and to remove what is wrong, as they see it. I do not question the strength of their conviction nor the sincerity of their belief. But they tend to approach the library's collection as a case of "either/or" when to be truly responsive the library's motto must be "not only/but also."

I do not mean to suggest that any inquiry about the justification of a library's purchase is *ipso facto* censorship. What I am talking about are the actions that have been taken: the removal of books or parts of books, often in the form of theft or vandalism; the occasional but nevertheless actual burning of some library materials; the imposition of restrictions and barriers that reduce the number of ideas to which users may have access. The legal actions brought and the removal of librarians from their positions for doing what they were hired to do are a justifiable reason for concern not only about the specific instances themselves, but even more because of the "chilling effect" (a concept recognized by the courts) on future selection and freedom of access. Remember that the freedom we are talking about is not only our freedom to disseminate ideas; equally important is the public's freedom to receive ideas.

The one thing that reassures librarians that they are probably doing something right when they get into disagreements about the collection is that the protests are as vehement from the Left as they are from the Right, from the pro-somethings as from the anti-somethings. Each special interest group thinks its ideas are underrepresented while all others are overrepresented. It is seldom that any group can make the case that its ideas are not represented at all. The most they can say is that their perception is that ideas of which they do not approve appear to be more heavily represented than those they'd like to promote. And what is disturbing is that it almost invariably comes down to "let's get rid of" rather than "why don't you add?"

New Words, Old Music

At least that's how it used to be, but today some of the censorious groups are getting more sophisticated. They have found, to their dismay, that the direct censorship and removal of materials is now frequently condemned, not only by librarians and other such humanistically-tainted types, but even by many of their own neighbors and fellow-citizens for whom they presume to speak. As a result, they have begun to alter their tone and—at least in the statements they make for public consumption—deny any desire to censor or remove materials. The aim, they say, is only to add the materials they favor in sufficient quantity to bring about a balance that is not now there.

They are also making tactical changes, such as adapting some of the arguments of the American Civil Liberties Union to their own purposes and, in the state of Washington at least, changing the name of the Moral Majority to the Bill of Rights Legal Foundation. It is a smart move, and if they really follow their new rhetoric, things may be looking up. I may be forgiven, I hope, in having some reservations about the sincerity of the new look, which, on the basis of past performance, could turn out to be more skillful public relations than a real change of heart.

Meanwhile, the change in rhetoric may be salutary both for them and for us. For them, because if they find themselves obliged to practice what they now publicly preach, it could change their approach to the materials that carry ideas. And for us, because if they begin to practice what they preach, we may have to do so as well.

We may have to listen to some of their complaints more seriously and look more carefully at what we do in the light of what they say we do. Up to now, we have been able to take refuge behind wisecracks, a sense of our own selfrighteousness, and the assurance that the extremist groups are sure to go just far enough beyond reason to bring ridicule onto their own heads. Making the opposition look ridiculous is a delightful ploy; it is even better when the opposition makes itself look ridiculous with no help from us whatsoever. When the Mothers Against Smut, or some such group, a few years ago created a smut wagon filled with examples of obscenities from books and other sources and drove it around town for everyone to examine, they ended up in the pokey, quite rightly, for disseminating obscene materials. One always gets a certain satisfaction in seeing the biter bitten.

The put-down makes us feel good, of course, but such wisecracks as "The Moral Majority is neither moral nor a majority, and the New Right is neither, either," even if they convey a truth or a partial one, are an inadequate evaluation of the power of those groups. What's more, our satisfaction at getting a laugh can divert us from whatever may be worthy of consideration in what the opposition is saying. I suggest to you that we should pay more attention to those who attack our purposes and our practices for two reasons: because so many people do and because we should be prepared to answer those attacks, if we can.

Asking the Right Questions

I hope you don't think I've gone over to the enemy by suggesting that they might, in some instances, just possibly be right. If, on occasion, they are correct in some of their accusations, we ought to be glad for their help in putting us back on any track from which we may have inadvertently strayed. They have already learned from us and have altered their tactics as a result. Do we now have something to learn from them, something that goes beyond the simple alteration of tactics to a reaffirmation of our basic principles? Insights and truths turn up in all kinds of odd places and contexts.

Phyllis Schlafly (if you'll pardon the expression) back in 1981 suggested a test of libraries to her followers that we might ourselves adopt. In her article, "How to Improve Fairness in Your Library," she supplies a list of forty-eight titles that she feels local public libraries ought to have on their shelves in the categories of pro-life (meaning anti-abortion), pro-defense, pro-family, and pro-basic education. Her charge to her readers is to take this list and check it against their public library catalogs to see how many of them are there and then put the pressure on to add all the ones that aren't in the collection. She even adds a little list of pro-lib books as a check. Notice how sure she is of the library's bias; she's betting that few libraries will have any, or very many, of her preferred list.

ALA's Office for Intellectual Freedom took Schlafly's advice and tried to check the extent to which the titles she recommends are missing from libraries. As you can guess, it is much harder to establish factual evidence than it is to make broad, condemnatory generalizations, but a check was made of the holdings reported in the OCLC bibliographic network, which admittedly is not a very good source of information about small and medium-sized public libraries. On the basis of that quick and dirty survey, it appears that of the two titles Schlafly thought should be in all libraries (one written by her and one about her), 425 libraries in twenty-five states and the District of Columbia held a copy of one title, and 559 libraries in forty-six states and the District of Columbia held a copy of the other. Several of the other titles made an even better showing; several did less well.

This doesn't prove much except that Schlafly rather overstated her case. What we cannot yet prove is that libraries do give just as much attention to the prejudices on Schlafly's side as they do to the prejudices on other sides. I like to think that a really thorough search of library holdings would show this to be true, because if it is not, librarians have some explaining to do.

The Balanced Collection

The key is balance, which does not necessarily mean an equal number of titles on every subject. But even a term like "balance" may not mean the same thing to different people. In his *Moral Majority Report* for March 1983, Jerry Falwell expands upon Phyllis Schlafly's suggested campaign to check libraries for conservative titles, to which he appends a much larger list of books that he thinks should be in the library. "If they don't put our books up," he says, "then take the liberal books down." In other words, balance to Falwell means a selected sample of titles from all other points of view as against the entire list of his recommendations.

But the librarian's responsibility is to identify interests and to make judgments with the entire collection and the entire community in mind, not just that part of it with the largest constituency or the loudest voices or the most intimidating threats. It sounds easier than it is, but that is true of all responsibilities. To make decisions, to make them for sound reasons, and to be able to defend them when they are questioned are characteristics of professional judgment that I like to think go with the librarian's territory.

The balanced collection, of course, will never completely satisfy the groups who want their own point of view more prominent. Against the more familiar complaints on the far Right—too much material on sex, too much material that is anti-religious, not enough material on the virtues of free enterprise and state's rights—there is the other extreme: not enough on sex, not enough material critical of the traditional religionist position, too much material "of interest to investors and business people."[2]

In other words, no subterfuge is going to avoid offending someone, and no amount of yielding to complaints is going to stop everyone. All we accomplish by giving in to such pressure is to shift the source of the complaints from those who want the material removed to those who want it retained and expanded. Which suggests that librarians may just have to take more responsibility for defining the nature of the collection, achieving balance as they see it, and be prepared for the denunciations. Have we known all along that any decision of any importance will offend someone, and have we then chosen to offend only those we think have the least-power to retaliate?

An Answer to the Censor

In 1774 Edmund Burke was speaking to a group of citizens prior to an election and reminded them, "Your representative owes you, not his industry only, but his judgment; and he betrays, instead of serving you, if he sacrifices it to your opinion."

Remember that in its eighteenth-century connotation, "your opinion" meant "your approbation." If we substitute the word librarian for representative, we find an answer to those who feel that as keeper of a publicly-supported institution, the librarian must defer to every complaint of pressure from a taxpayer: "Your librarians owe you, not their industry only, but their judgment; and they betray, instead of serving you, if they sacrifice it to curry your favor."

Librarians and users are in this together. We have a responsibility that goes with our title; they have a responsibility to try to see the total picture, not just their own segment of it. Both of us still have a lot to learn about the provision and dissemination of ideas, particularly when that entails, as it often does, not a clash between right and wrong, but among many rights. Seen in that light, ours is an important role that has implications far beyond any one item in the library or any one uncomfortable confrontation that we would prefer to avoid. Our responsibility is the defense of access to ideas, to information, to esthetic pleasure, to recreation in its literal sense of re-creation, and to knowledge or at least to the process that leads to knowledge.

So it really is not the one book or the one viewpoint that is at issue here, but the defense of ideas that is our concern. I still believe that the best solution to the problem of access is to add positively to the store of ideas, not negatively to reduce it.

Notes

1. Lester Asheim, "The Librarian's Responsibility: Not Censorship but Selection," in Frederic Mosher, ed., *Freedom of Book Selection* (Chicago: ALA, 1954), 95–96.
2. Sanford Berman, "Inside Censorship," *Wisconsin Library Bulletin* (Spring 1977), 2124.

Ethics in Academic Librarianship: The Need for Values

KENNETH G. PETERSON

In recent years, as increased emphasis has been placed upon personnel and management issues in academic libraries, two elements have become notably apparent. First, much attention has been focused upon the importance of planning to meet long-range goals and objectives. Second, the importance of setting policies and determining procedures to meet current needs has been stressed. While both elements are necessary, there is danger that concentrating efforts on long-range planning may result in questionable compromises stemming from an "end justifies the means" philosophy, or that strong commitment to carrying out policies and procedures will render current operations captive to legalistic restrictions. Thus, there is also an obvious need for value judgments to be made and ethical principles to be applied in the practice of academic librarianship.

Reprinted from *Journal of Academic Librarianship* 9(3) (July 1983): 132–137.

The Role of Ethics in Society

Ethics have played an important role in the lives of people and society throughout history. Stemming from the Greek word "ethos," ethics denotes the system of moral principles and the concepts that determine right and wrong conduct within a given society, nation, or religious group. In early societies, as people began to identify certain actions that led to conflict and those that resulted in a common good, standards of acceptable conduct evolved. In succeeding Roman, medieval, and modern societies, the philosophies of Western civilization reflected continued speculation about moral theories in an effort to establish principles of ethical behavior. In this process, human experience has shown serious consequences when moral concerns have been ignored.

In the article "Ethics in America," in *Leadership* magazine, three basic assumptions about ethics were pointed out. First, "all human beings have a set of values, no matter what their concept of the ultimate value may be." Second, "ethical behavior recognizes, and rests within, a shared interest." And third, "behavior becomes unethical when it favors a special interest out of proportion to, and without consideration for, the interests of society as a whole."[1] While these assumptions apply broadly in society, they are especially relevant for people in professional fields because a set of values, shared interest, and the good of society are at the core of professionalism. It has long been one of the recognizable signs of a professional group that it have a code of ethics or commonly held standards of professional behavior.[2] For people who are sincere in entering a profession and dedicated in its pursuit, value judgments are inescapable.

The Concern of Ethics in Librarianship

Librarianship, claiming status among the professions, has struggled over the years to clarify and arrive at a set of ethical principles. As a result of concerted efforts during the 30s, the Council of the American Library Association adopted a "Code of Ethics for Librarians" in 1938.[3] The Preamble, which sets the context for 25 principles of ethical behavior, states: "Those who enter the library profession assume an obligation to maintain ethical standards of behavior in relation to the governing authority under which they work, to the library constituency, to the library as an institution and to fellow workers on the staff, to other members of the library profession, and to society in general." While its intentions were lofty, the 1938 code, as one critic pointed out, was "not really an ethic at all . . . (but) rather a statement of the problems and insecurities that characterized the profession in the 1930's."[4] Samuel Rothstein wrote, "Librarians, like any other professional group, need some kind of statement which will indicate what they are and what they stand for. Indeed, we need such a statement more than most other professional groups, because we librarians have always had trouble in identifying ourselves to the general public—and even to ourselves."[5]

Some efforts to revise the code were made in the 50s and 60s. In the early 70s, upon the initiative of ALA's Library Administration Division, a committee was appointed which sought suggestions and consulted with interested people and groups. As a result, a Statement of Professional Ethics was put forth in 1975 and subsequently revised and published in 1979.[6] After undergoing further revisions, the Statement, including both a descriptive introduction and a six-part Code of Ethics, was presented to and adopted by the ALA Council at San Francisco in June 1981. After affirming that librarians have been guided by professional principles based upon a commitment to intellectual freedom and free access to information, the code affirms the need for highest level, fair and equitable service; resistance of censorship; protection of user's rights to privacy; adherence to principles of due process and equality of opportunity; distinction between personal philosophies and those of an institution or professional body; and avoidance of personal gain at the expense of users, colleagues, or the employing institution.[7]

Ethical Considerations in Academic Librarianship

In thinking about the future, we need to consider the importance of ethics in academic librarianship. It is already clear that the 80s will be marked by changes in librarianship and higher education stemming from shifting directions in the social and economic order. Accepting the fact that a single code of ethics cannot address all questions but that common moral principles are needed, let us consider three overriding areas where ethical values must influence academic librarianship as a profession—honesty, professional integrity, and respect for people.

Honesty

Foremost, the ethics of honesty need to be considered. This may sound simple and almost elementary, but being honest has implications that often become difficult to fulfill. Honesty may be described as being truthful, fair, and upright. It is the quality of character that is lacking in deceit or corruption. To say that a person is truly honest is to bestow one of life's greatest compliments.

People take vows and make verbal statements to signify acceptance of understandings that are held in common. While the importance of honesty is manifested in the laws of the government, the contracts of the business community, and unwritten agreements among people, honesty must be established first and foremost in the commitment of individuals to truthfulness as the basis for a personal ethic. Without this commitment on the part of people, efforts to preserve honesty in society are predestined to failure.

Consider several areas in which the ethics of honesty should guide our actions in academic librarianship.

Attitudes About Resources comes easily to mind. Higher education is emerging from several decades marked by unprecedented growth in numbers of students, expansion of programs and facilities, and increases in appropriations. Academic libraries and librarians benefitted greatly during those decades as collections rapidly multiplied in size, new buildings were erected, number of positions increased, and funds were provided for many new services and programs. The economy of the nation and of most states, however, has changed quite dramatically in recent years and the era of great abundance has passed. It is always more difficult to adjust to a declining than an expanding economy because the change requires a reassessment of our stewardship of the more limited resources available to us. In this process it becomes increasingly important to examine priorities honestly and realistically.

Collection Development is a field in which the ethics of honesty should influence the reassessing of priorities. Can acquisitions of little used materials in relatively esoteric fields be justified if they can fairly readily be borrowed from other libraries in the same state or region? While resource sharing is increasingly being discussed at professional meetings and in journal articles, an attitude still prevails that acquisitions policies and practices that have been followed for the past 20 or more years are sacrosanct. The prospect of more limited funds and continuing inflation in the 80s has already made clear that resource sharing will become necessary. While efforts are made to devise cooperative collection development guidelines and to establish more workable arrangements for exchanging materials, the willingness to give up as well as to acquire must be accepted. Librarians are often pressured by aggressive faculty colleagues to purchase materials in specialized areas knowing that these materials will be in little demand. Under such circumstances should not librarians honestly resist those pressures as they reassess collection development priorities, and facilitate greater reliance upon interlibrary borrowing? In the competition for acquisition funds, both subject fields and levels of collection development must constantly be evaluated so that the library's holdings most adequately and equitably support the institution's academic programs.

Space Needs   is a related field where the ethics of honesty apply. Over the past quarter century, seating space in academic libraries has been judged by the standard of accommodating 25 percent of undergraduates and 33 percent of graduate students. Yet, this standard may no longer be justified for librarians on many campuses across the nation as funds for capital improvements are not forthcoming and programs in other departments are being curtailed. Recognizing that crowding occurs mainly during the last few weeks of the semester, would it not be appropriate to arrange study space in classroom or student center buildings? Many students are primarily using their own textbooks and simply want a quiet place to study. Would it not be appropriate to work with student affairs personnel on campus to set up study areas in dormitories where quiet is maintained? Academic librarians need to work toward creative solutions to space problems as alternatives to the traditional proposals that buildings must be expanded or new buildings constructed.

Communication   is another area where honesty is crucial. Communication is indispensable to the functioning of any organization or agency. Communication may be direct, or indirect. Most people learn early that desired results can often be achieved by the way information is transmitted. Thus, one may be direct and forthright in asking questions, stating a position, or engaging in open dialogue where the intention is an honest desire to exchange information. Because communication is recognized as a powerful tool within organizational operations, there is sometimes a temptation to manipulate the facts to serve special interests. More subtly, there is a temptation to release information to some people while withholding it from others, or to give different interpretations of information to different people depending upon the circumstances. Absence of communication can be as dangerous as releasing false information because it creates a vacuum in which misunderstanding and unfounded speculation develop. In any case, the intentional misuse of communication or the intentional failure to communicate among colleagues and within the organizational structure raise serious questions about one's sense of honesty.

Consider an example of how communication is misused and may lead to confusion. A library administrator has released information by means of a memorandum to the staff or an announcement at a staff meeting. Because the issue being dealt with is one in which there are conflicting opinions, the statement has been carefully worded to be general and perhaps somewhat ambiguous. The administrator's intention is to avoid being explicit on the subject to allow time to assess staff reactions. Meanwhile, staff members are confused and become both frustrated and angry, feeling they are being used indirectly by the administrator in dealing with an issue rather than being given an opportunity directly to express their opinions and thus contribute openly in the decision-making process.

In another example, opportunity has been provided for staff members to express their opinions on a matter under consideration. While some people hold strong opinions and their positions vary from those of others, they are also reluctant to express their views openly when given the opportunity. Then, after the decision has been made they are dissatisfied and pursue a course of quiet noncompliance. These cases show how misuse and nonuse of communication may reflect compromises with honesty thereby resulting in misunderstanding and a breakdown of trust.

Evaluations   of staff members or colleagues and furnishing references is another area where the ethics of honesty should not be compromised. For example, a supervisor may be reluctant to inform a staff member about poor performance or to suggest how performance could be improved. Thus, the annual evaluation reports reflect favorable comments, and the individual is not helped to overcome certain limitations. Consequently, the staff member, believing that performance is satisfactory, becomes frustrated and confused because opportunities are not provided for professional advancement.

Consider the situation in which a librarian is being reviewed for promotion. Colleagues have been encouraging in face-to-face conversations with the candidate, but, in closed-door discussions where professional rivalries become more apparent, positive support is not forthcoming. In another case, a search committee, having reviewed the dossier of a candidate, decides to allow certain members to phone professional friends on the candidate's campus to obtain more personal comments about the candidate's qualifications. Yet, under such circumstances, measures are often not taken that will protect the candidate's right of privacy, or assure that the solicited comments will be reliable, objective, and free from personal bias. The ethics of honesty require that consideration be given to these important matters.

Professional Integrity

Professional integrity is a second area in which values need to be established and maintained. While integrity implies honesty and uprightness of character, in a broader sense it means soundness, wholeness, or a sense of being undiminished. When the textual critic refers to the integrity of a text, we understand this to mean that the text exists in a form that has not altered or compromised the author's creative work. When the integrity of a scholar or scientist or artist is referred to, it conjures up assurances of probity and correctness.

Commitment is a hallmark of professionalism. Although entering librarianship is not marked by formal rites or the taking of vows, it carries no less a commitment to professional integrity. Because the intellectual growth, spirit of inquiry, and right-to-know of children, young people, and adults fall within the provenance of librarianship, any compromise of professional integrity threatens the very foundations of human knowledge and learning. Thus, librarians must be commited to intellectual freedom while opposing censorship whenever forces in society would impose restrictions on free access to information or would hinder the search for truth.

There are a number of areas in which the roles and activities of librarians need to be considered to maintain professional values.

Status of Librarians   is still not clearly understood in the academic community. What is the appropriate role for librarians in colleges and universities? Does librarianship constitute a unique and distinctive profession within academe, or are librarians essentially faculty members who have areas of special responsibility? Over the course of several decades, this issue has been debated in the professional literature. The most concerted effort to resolve the issue and come to a consensus was the adoption of "Standards for Faculty Status for College and University Librarians," by the Association of College and Research Libraries in 1971.[8] This action has helped define the role and function of academic librarians, and gain recognition for librarians as faculty members at many institutions. Yet, a final resolution to the status issue has not been achieved as differences in status prevail from campus to campus.

While strong arguments have been made for full faculty standing, arguments also continue to support a status that more clearly reflects traditional performance roles and expectations. Under these circumstances, it is incumbent upon academic librarians to weigh the relative values of subject knowledge, creative intellectual activity, direct or indirect teaching, technical competence, and administrative expertise in considering professional status. Titles should be used to identify who librarians are and what they do rather than to gain acceptance by cooption with their classroom teaching colleagues or any other campus group. Although one may be proud in being identified as faculty, pride should also stem from identity as librarians, bibliographers and curators for which there is a long and respected professional heritage.

Research and Publishing by academic librarians are closely tied to the status issue. Over the years, librarians have devoted themselves to scholarly activities and have contributed valuable works in fields such as bibliography, textual and linguistic studies, literary criticism, and history. But the question remains: should librarians engage in research and publishing essentially because it has become a requirement for tenure and promotion? One would hope that research and publishing stem from scholarly interests, talent, and a desire to be creative and that the results make substantial contributions to knowledge. Within all professions, it is distressing to see the growing number of books and journal articles that lack quality and real scholarship. More time is required in reading professional literature to keep abreast of developments because the chaff is increasing at an exponential rate. Equally distressing are the number of compilations of previously published articles in which someone has used the work of others as a means to gain reputation or advancement. In this regard, librarians need to exercise greater professional integrity and critical judgment in the peer review process to uphold scholarly standards.

Use of Institutional Resources needs to be considered in support of research, publishing, and professional service activities. Where librarians are expected to engage in these activities to meet criteria for tenure and promotion, there should be some institutional commitment for postage, photocopying, and use of telephone. Under these circumstances, the degree to which institutional resources may be used should be clearly understood and the librarian should make clear the distinction between activities pursued to fulfill institutional expectations and activities undertaken for personal advancement or gain. If the library does not have clear policies on such matters, it should be incumbent upon an individual to indicate in advance both the reasons for and the amount of support needed, and to receive approval from the appropriate supervisor or administrator. For instance, a librarian may have accepted appointment as committee chairperson in a professional association where fulfilling the position's responsibilities will involve numerous long-distance calls, extensive photocopying, and a considerable amount of mailing. If the association has not provided a budget for these expenses, the librarian has an obligation to state needs and find out the amount of institutional support that can be committed. The question also arises about how much time during the regular work schedule may be spent on activities for professional organizations, especially if the librarian's performance of association business imposes added work upon colleagues within the department. Here, professional integrity calls for a sense of responsibility on the part of the librarian as well as the supervisor or administrator.

If a librarian has contracted for publication of a book from which compensation or royalties will be received, how much time and support should the institution be expected to provide, and how much should be provided by the individual? Obviously, the answers to this question will vary to a considerable degree based upon local circumstances. In terms of professional integrity, however, two facts become clear. First, librarians and their employing institutions should recognize a dual responsibility in the allocation of time and resources to support research, publishing, and professional service activities. While the institution should not expect the total obligation to be met by the individual, it is equally important to recognize that the individual's commitment carries with it also an expenditure of time and personal resources. Second, to avoid misunderstandings, the librarian should clarify with the appropriate supervisor or administrator the extent of commitment in terms of time and resources, and arrive at a clear understanding about the degree of institutional support prior to undertaking these activities.

Substantial Personal Gain   can also result from library activities, creating possible conflicts. Academic librarians have access to open collections that include many out-of-print and rare publications. Situations have been known in which librarians have been asked to furnish microform or photocopies of works not available on the market for individuals or other institutions. Is it ethical to allow these services to evolve into a profitable private business? Does an academic librarian have a right to accept payment for services or materials provided where the resources of the library have been the basis for the transaction? As online bibliographical search activities have become better known to library users, situations have arisen in which librarians have been asked to "moonlight" for outside interests to perform searches and provide information. If the expense of training the librarian has been borne by the institution, and if the resources or equipment of the institution are used to perform searches, is the librarian justified in accepting any remuneration or rewards (apart from actual reimbursement to the institution for online charges) in furnishing these services? Here again, if the institution does not have a policy governing such situations, it is incumbent upon the librarian to seek clarification about the extent to which searches for external groups may be provided and whether personal acceptance of any payments for services is permissible.

In instances in which a librarian has agreed to join with a group of professional colleagues in publishing a new journal or developing a database which will be marketed to libraries, how far can the librarian engage in these activities while still holding full-time employment at an institution, without incurring conflict of interest? To what extent should time from working hours or resources from the employing institution be used in support of these projects? Several other questions, however, also need to be considered. Is the librarian's position and institutional affiliation being used for personal gain? Are resources of the institution being used in lieu of personal investment by the sponsors of the project? Is the librarian's institution being viewed as a principal customer? Is the activity being pursued for personal gain rather than as a service to be offered in the normal course of fulfilling employment responsibilities?

In the area of professional integrity there are no easy answers. Each case or situation needs to be examined carefully and judged on the basis of its merits with due regard for the interests of both the librarian and the employing institution. In considering whether professional integrity is in danger of being compromised, it is necessary to consider whether the activities in question and the resulting effects have in any way marred an individual's or an institution's commitment to honesty, candor, and the highest standards of ethical behavior. Awareness of, and sensitivity to, these standards is the inimitable mark of professionalism.

Respect for People

In addition to honesty and a sense of professional integrity, respect for people is essential in academic librarianship. Respect denotes a sense of esteem for individuals, regard for their sense of worth, recognition of their intelligence, and trust in their judgments. Respect for people begins with respect for oneself. In this regard, there is need to cultivate self-understanding, to recognize personal strengths and limitations, to realize that one cannot be all things to all people, and that, amid the challenges of each day, it is not possible to serve others without first being true to oneself. Each individual possesses or acquires certain areas of interest which reflect degrees of intelligence, talent, and personal satisfaction. These areas may be perceived in terms of subject fields, or in terms of skills. While there are some people whose interests are so diverse and whose skills so broad that they are able to work successfully at many different activities, most people learn to identify personal areas of special interest and ability, and to direct their efforts accordingly. Within librarianship, for example, some people work best with special subject collections, or in cataloging, or in bibliographic instruction, or as administrators. Learning to respect oneself means accepting one's abilities to perform well in certain areas but not in others.

Respecting oneself also implies the ability to accept accomplishments with its rewarding satisfaction and also to accept failure with its painful disappointments. While failure is most frequently perceived in a negative sense, it is possible to derive positive reinforcement from failure if we are able to learn from its experience. A personal injustice is done when an individual sinks into despair because of failure, or denies that failure has occurred, or tries to shift the reasons for failure to someone else, or becomes defensive in the face of failure. The ethics involved in dealing with failure are based upon honesty and openness, upon accepting responsibility for one's mistakes for poor judgments, and upon a willingness to work with other people in a positive effort to remedy the situation.

Because people vary so greatly in terms of their rational and emotional make-up, working with them can be both immensely satisfying and completely exasperating. What librarian has not had to cope with a faculty member whose demands are unreasonable, or a student whose behavior is irascible, or an administrator who is lacking in understanding, or a colleague who is uncooperative? Under these circumstances, one's sense of professional calling and dedication is surely put to the test. The ethics involved in dealing with people remind us that librarianship is a service-oriented profession and that service must be rooted in a sincere effort to understand before reacting. When one responds to people in a manner that conveys respect and helpfulness, the first steps have been taken to change an exasperating situation into one of satisfaction.

Within the library, people, along with collections, are our most vital resources. Unlike the physical materials on our shelves, however, people think, have feelings, and can talk back. Library users or members of the staff cannot be categorized in the same way that books are fit into a classification system. Moreover, we need to recognize that people are capable of change. Thus, in academic librarianship it becomes important to consider how positive changes in people might be brought about to enhance professional contributions and services.

Opportunities for Professional and Personal Development can be provided as a means of encouraging positive changes among staff members. Professional associations have responded to the need for professional growth by sponsoring seminars, workshops, and special programs. While most institutions allow time to be taken for these opportunities, support for travel and related expenses is often very inadequate. The ethics involved in staff development are based upon substantial and consistent efforts by administrators and spokespeople within the library' governance structure to obtain adequate funds for these purposes. Development can also be fostered within the institution by providing pro grams and short-term courses aimed at dealing with a range of needs related to people's positions. Some libraries have been successful in sponsoring interest groups for staff members to discuss research activities, develop new skills, and become familiar with changes in the academic environment.

Recognizing Professional Accomplishments is important. Within the management framework of higher education, it is often assumed that the rewards system, denoted by salary increases and the granting of tenure and promotions, satisfies a need for recognizing accomplishment. While these rewards are important, they may be subject to guidelines or limitations over which library supervisors, administrators, and colleagues do not have final control. In a deeper sense, respect is based upon sensitivity and appreciation for people's intelligence, professional talents and skills, creative spirit, and dedication. A thoughtful expression or testimonial recognizing an individual's personal worth and positive contributions will provide valuable reinforcement for staff morale.

Making Promises and Keeping Commitments are also areas in which the ethics of respect for people are very important. Before promises are made, serious consideration needs to be given to the substance of what is being committed, and whether or not the person making the promise has the power or resources to keep it. In personnel administration and organizational management, promises are sometimes used to deal with situations hurriedly to placate someone. Such promises are unfortunate if they pledge future actions or resources without sufficient regard for the possibility that changes may occur during an interim period which could adversely affect keeping those promises. If a librarian, as colleague, supervisor, or administrator, makes a commitment, the ethics involved carry an obligation to fulfill the commitment within a reasonable period of time and in a manner that reinforces the dignity of all parties involved.

In his article entitled "The Myths and Mystiques of Personnel Administration," Herbert S. White makes a strong case for the need to respect people when he states, "Good library managers . . . are those who treat subordinates as individuals."[9] This statement may be expanded to include all librarians or professional people, not just managers. Treating colleagues as individuals involves understanding human values and committing oneself to an ethic rooted in respect for people. This ethic must be as integral to the practice of librarianship as it is to any of the other professions.

Conclusion

In a *Library Journal* editorial in 1968, Eric Moon wrote, "The profession [of librarianship] does have ethical questions to grapple with and should find a way to formulate a position on some of them."[10] It is clear that ethical principles and professional values are indispensable both in defining long-range goals and objectives on one hand, and in setting policies and determining procedures on the other. Thus, in concluding this discourse on ethics in academic librarianship, the thoughts of Sidney C. Sufrin are *apropos:* "The ethical system of our society is not an empty, formal, set of ideas that has no reality except in conversation; it is a set of values in action. The set may be for some systematized, or for others may consist of a set of discrete propositions. But it is operative. One may not like it, but there it is."[11]

Notes

1. "Ethics in America," *Leadership* 3 (September 1980): 11–12.
2. F.A.R. Bennion, *Professional Ethics: The Consultant Professions and Their Codes* (London: Charles Knight & Co., 1969), 27–34.
3. "Code of Ethics for Librarians," *ALA Bulletin* 33 (February 1939): 128–30.
4. Thomas M. Bogie, "Discussion in Dallas: Members of the Staff of the Dallas Public Library Speak Out on the Proposed Revisions of the Code of Ethics," *Library Journal* 92 (June 1, 1967): 2128.
5. Samuel Rothstein, "In Search of Ourselves," *Library Journal* 93 (January 15, 1968): 157.
6. "Statement on Professional Ethics, 1975," (revised 6/26/79), *American Libraries* 10 (December 1979): 666.
7. "Statement on Professional Ethics, 1981," *American Libraries* 12 (June 1981): 335.
8. "Standards for Faculty Status for College and University Librarians," *College & Research Libraries News* 33 (September 1972): 210–12.
9. Herbert S. White, "The Myths and Mystiques of Personnel Administration," *Information and Library Manager* 1 (September 1981): 45–46.
10. Eric Moon, "Ethical Bones," *Library Journal* 93 (January 15, 1968): 131.
11. Sydney C. Sufrin, *Management of Business Ethics* (Port Washington, NY: Kennikat Press, 1980): 111.

Ethics for Online Intermediaries

DONNA B. SHAVER
NANCY S. HEWISON
LESLIE W. WYKOFF

Since the development of computerized indexes and abstracts in the 1960s, the profession of online searcher has grown and matured, and the need for guidelines of appropriate conduct has deepened. As Trauth states in a 1982 article in *Computers & Society*, "In an increasingly technological and information-intensive society those who manipulate the tools and thereby manipulate the information must be held morally accountable for the power they possess."[1] At Online '83, Childress presented examples of ethical issues in online searching and noted that even under the umbrella of reference service, virtually no attention has been given to ethics in online searching.[2]

The American Library Association has long been concerned with the development of ethical standards for librarians and has written and adopted three formal statements of professional ethics since 1939, most recently in 1981. However, for several reasons this "Statement on Professional Ethics" is not adequate for the discipline of online searching. First, while traditionally most searchers were librarians, the increasing heterogeneity of backgrounds and work settings of the searcher population means that many searchers come from outside the library profession. They have not completed a library graduate program, do not work in libraries, and cannot be expected to subscribe to the mores of the library community.

Second, the ALA Statement includes a section on privacy which is in conflict with ethical practice in many organizations. Section III states: "Librarians must protect each user's right to privacy with respect to information sought or received, and material consulted, borrowed, or acquired."[3] Such conduct is indeed appropriate in many settings. However, in a special library where a company is paying the salaries of the

Reprinted from *Special Libraries* 76(4) (Fall 1985): 238–245.

searcher and the client in addition to the search costs, both client and searcher are accountable for proper use of online services. Search logs must therefore be open to management review. In addition, many companies consider it a function of the librarian to alert a client to the fact that someone else in the company is working on the same topic, thus saving the costs of duplicate searches and duplicate effort. While it is true that this situation exists in a corporate setting even in the absence of online services, the costs associated with searching make it particularly visible and more closely monitored.

At present, then, no existing set of guidelines or code of ethics is sufficient to cover the unique problems of information service through the new technologies.

Unique Characteristics of Online Searchers

Some would argue that the ethical conduct of online searchers does not differ from that of reference librarians, and it is true that the guidelines for ethical behavior proposed in this article would, with some substitutions or changes in terminology, make good guidelines for responsible reference service. In fact, there are distinct characteristics which set online searching apart from the provision of other reference services.

First, the online searcher is a gatekeeper—an intermediary between the information and the user of that information—to an extent not realized in the largely print-based profession of reference librarianship. While reference librarians serve in varying degrees as intermediaries for printed sources of information, clients who are unhappy with answers supplied by a reference librarian in a manual search generally have the opportunity to search the indexes themselves. When computerized sources are involved, the online searcher has the specialized knowledge, equipment, and access codes required to retrieve the information, while the client seldom has the means to bypass the searcher. The pool of information is hidden away in a distant computer and only that which is retrieved by the search strategy is available to the client. Thus the online searcher can be either a conduit or an obstacle.

Second, anyone can claim to be an online searcher. As Mintz notes in an article on information malpractice, unlike the situation in law and medicine, there are "no statutes prohibiting the unlicensed practice of information."[4] Neither the possession of a Master of Library Science degree, nor employment in a library or as an independent information broker, nor online training from a database vendor guarantee search quality.

The client is rarely in a position to judge the quality of a professional service and must rely upon "the standards of conduct maintained by the profession and by the reputation of individual practitioners."[5]

Third, in many online search settings, clients pay directly for all or some of the costs of a search. When people pay out-of-pocket for a service, their expectations for value are increased. To quote Mintz, "Clients are buying not only information but also, and most critically for the profession, they are buying the quality of know-how."[6] Although Mintz is referring to information brokers, the statement applies to online searchers in any situation in which clients are charged; clients who pay are more likely to hold the service provider accountable for the quality of the service.

Ethical Issues for Online Searchers

This article addresses the subject of ethical conduct for individual online searchers. Deliberately excluded are questions for which resolution is outside the province of the individual—issues which reflect institutionally-determined policies (charging for searches or the cancellation of subscriptions to printed indexes) or developments in the information industry (downloading, database quality control). Another development beyond the control of the individual searcher is that of end-user searching, the proliferation of which poses its own unique problems. End-user searching is only in its infancy. It will continue to grow, as will the population which either uses online searching infrequently or is unsophisticated in the use of information technologies and continues to rely on online searchers for assistance.

Searcher Competence

It is often difficult for the client of online services to accurately evaluate the level of service received, the results of a particular search (especially if the subject matter or the literature searched is outside the client's area of expertise), and the skills of the searcher. Clients who are very familiar with their subject matter and their disciplines can recognize incomplete or inaccurate search results. In general, though, the invisibility and lack of browsability of online information serves to shield the mediocre or incompetent searcher.

Another concern is that of competence in various databases and online systems. No online searcher can be highly competent in, or even familiar with, all systems and databases—just as no reference librarian can be conversant with all reference tools. In many cases, cost considerations or administrative decisions will limit a searcher's access to one or two online systems. Furthermore, most searchers do not have at their disposal all of the manuals, thesauri, and the like for all the databases to which they have access. Occasionally the use of an unfamiliar database is most appropriate for a given request. In such cases it is incumbent upon the searcher to apprise the client of the appropriate database and the searcher's level of expertise, if that may significantly affect the results of the search. Further, it is the responsibility of the searcher to spend additional time in search preparation, using the search aids available and consulting colleagues as necessary (with client permission).

While it may be said that the traditional reference librarian does not go into similar explanations at the reference desk, it is also the case that the client of manual reference services does not generally pay out-of-pocket for the results, as do many clients of online services. And, as noted earlier, the client of traditional reference services need not rely exclusively on the expertise of the reference librarian.

Searcher Bias

Most searchers have biases, that is, tendencies or inclinations toward or against certain databases, online systems, or search techniques. A searcher's bias against a particular online system may mean that the most appropriate database for a given search is not used. Biases in online search techniques are most likely to be habits that were developed because they were comfortable or because they were correct on a particular database or system at a particular time. Such search habits may, indeed, be efficient and effective. Some, however, may range from sloppy and inefficient to unproductive and misleading.

Whenever a client chooses to utilize an intermediary, the search request must be filtered through the mind of the online searcher. It is understood, of course, that the online searcher often must use skillful interviewing techniques to help the client express the need rather than to merely accept the request as the client initially states it. However, the searcher may feel a strong temptation, especially with an inarticulate or unsophisticated client, to "lead the witness," to deliver what the searcher thinks the client needs rather than what the client requests. There is an arrogance in this. The searcher needs to be acutely aware of the line which divides negotiation and problem clarification from information counseling. While information counseling may often be the highest professional service a searcher can provide, it must be done with searcher awareness and client consent.

Through excess enthusiasm for the capabilities of online searching, searchers may be biased toward its use even when the needed information may be more readily and cheaply available in other ways—a telephone call or an encyclopedia article. It is easy to oversell online searching, and it is difficult for most clients to make sound judgments about databases and systems other than on the recommendation of the searcher.

An important factor in dealing with searcher bias is the searcher's obligation to inform the client about appropriate databases and systems, their coverage and limitations, and relevant limitations in the searcher's expertise. Ideally, the client will receive adequate and accurate, but not excessive, information. Some publications on the search negotiation process, in detailing all the information which the searcher should convey to the client, suggest something more appropriate to a three-credit course than an online search interview. Just as the physician does not train the patient in medicine, so too does the searcher exercise professional judgment in his or her practice. However, both the good physician and the good searcher work on the principle of informed consent.

The Inaccurate Search

Even with the most careful preparation, the online searcher will occasionally deliver a flawed search, and the inaccuracy may only later become apparent to the searcher. It is sometimes difficult to deal with this "good faith" error. If, for example, the search was done to assist a student with a term paper and the term is over, locating the client and rectifying the error may be difficult. In general, however, the ethical response would be to inform the client and to perform a corrected search at no additional charge.

Misuse of Information

The online searcher, like the reference librarian, may be faced with a dilemma when he or she suspects that the information obtained from a search may be misunderstood or misused. This problem is exacerbated in the case of the online searcher, in that the searcher becomes a party to the abuse. An example would be an author and/or citation search requested for use in a hiring or promotion and tenure situation, in which candidates are evaluated partly on the basis of how much they have published or how many times their publications have been cited by other authors. In such a case, it becomes the duty of the searcher to explain to the client the fallacies inherent in such "evidence": many databases do not list all co-authors; coverage, in spite of the large number of databases, is not universal; the work of other authors with the same name may be retrieved. In the case of a citation search, the client should be made aware that papers are cited for many reasons, not all of which are to the credit of the cited author.

Other instances in which the searcher mistrusts the client's motives may be more difficult to deal with, raising the specter of searcher as censor. Librarians have frequently debated this issue (for example, dealing with requests for information on how to commit suicide or construct a bomb), and online searchers in their role as gatekeepers have a heightened responsibility in such situations. In a brief commentary on the ethics of reference librarianship, Murray warned:

> There is no way to define exactly when the professional who is making a decision as to the best available material to give the patron and elects one set of titles over another has crossed over into the ranks of censor. But if the use to which the material is going to be put or the opinion expressed by the user causes the librarian deliberately to withhold available information, some form of censorship is present.[7]

Another instance of misuse occurs when a client insists on an online search when a print source would be more appropriate. If any of the search costs are subsidized, it may be necessary to have a policy to cover this situation. Otherwise, the searcher's communication skills are called into play to deflect the client from a possibly inappropriate course of action.

Privacy and Confidentiality

In some settings, the client relinquishes the right to privacy by virtue of the manner in which both online charges and client salaries are paid. However, in public and academic libraries, and in the case of information brokers, the confidentiality of online search requests must be as inviolate as that of reference questions.

Problems may arise due to the paper trail that is inevitably created in online searching. While reference questions are logged in some institutions, the major part of the traditional reference interaction is verbal and information is delivered directly to the client by the librarian, or is sought by the client following guidance received. In online searching, however, the client or the searcher typically fills out a request form which will remain in the searcher's files, and the searcher logs the request so that it can be checked against the invoices from the online systems. In some search services, a copy of the search printout is kept on file. The recordkeeping requirements of the online searcher and the client's privacy can both be served if the searcher takes care not to leave the various parts of the paper trail in public view on desktops. Additionally, a records retention policy should be drawn up and adhered to, insuring that search-related records are kept only for the length of time that data may be needed for administrative purposes, and are then destroyed.

For some searches, the online searcher may need to consult colleagues more knowledgeable in the appropriate databases, or who have access to necessary search aids. As in manual reference work, the online client may be better served when the searcher seeks advice in this manner, and it is tempting to simply involve colleagues in formal or informal consultation without regard to the user. Like other professional groups, online searchers would be well advised to seek the client's permission before involving other information professionals, however innocently.

A Model for Ethical Decision Making

In this discussion of ethical issues for online searchers, it is apparent that awareness and searcher-client communication are keys to solving ethical problems. Many difficulties are readily resolved if the client and the searcher have the same understanding of the question, the means to answer it, and the powers and limitations of online searching. This shared understanding can be achieved during the search interview if the searcher is sensitive to what needs to be discussed and clarified. The Johari Window[8] is shown here in a version adapted for online searching, and can be used to help the searcher determine the ethical decision points in any given search negotiation. (Figure 1.)

Open.   The "open" area in the Johari Window is one of shared knowledge about the subject matter, the database(s), and the system(s). However, there is a clear danger of faulty assumptions by both searcher and client. The searcher may assume that the client understands the nature of searching, the content and coverage of particular databases, and/or the limitations inherent in online searching. The client may have requested online searches in the past and may feel that he or she "knows all about it," while having, in fact, developed a faulty idea of the universality of coverage or the reliability of information from a computer. The searcher needs to be aware of the danger of assumptions in the "open" area in order to give the client appropriate information.

	Known to searcher	Not known to searcher
Known to client	OPEN	BLIND
Not known to client	HIDDEN	UNKNOWN

FIGURE 1. Johari Window adapted for online searching

Blind. In many online search situations the client possesses relevant knowledge which the searcher, often a generalist rather than a specialist in a particular discipline, does not have. Such situations require in-depth search negotiation to enable the searcher to understand such things as terminology in the client's subject area. If the searcher is new to a field in which he or she will be doing a considerable amount of searching, it is incumbent upon the searcher to reduce the "blind" area by obtaining continuing education in the subject area.

Hidden. As was discussed earlier, the searcher must exercise professional judgment regarding the amount and level of information about online searching provided to clients to assist them in making intelligent decisions. This "hidden" information about databases, systems, search techniques, and the like, is vast. In each situation, the searcher should try to share appropriate information.

Unknown. The online searcher acts as an intermediary for the client in situations in which the structure and protocols of a collection of information are unknown to the client but, presumably, known to the searcher. However, online searchers must be sensitive to their own "unknown" area in order to act in an ethical manner. When the searcher's lack of knowledge or experience might affect the outcome of a search, he or she must make the client aware of these, as when the searcher is unfamiliar with the online system or database to be searched. In addition, the searcher has the obligation to make every effort to prepare adequately for a search, to reduce the extent of the "unknown" in the Johari Window by reading manuals, checking print equivalents, consulting with colleagues (with client approval), or requesting assistance from system and/or database help desks.

Suggested Guidelines for the Ethical Behavior of Online Searchers

A profession's ethical standards are distilled from the mores, tradition, and established practices of the profession. While online searching is a young profession, it has been guided by reference librarians, with departures from reference experience caused by the gatekeeper role of the online searcher and by the fact that many searchers are not librarians. The following is an attempt to define guidelines for the ethical conduct of online searchers.

- The online searcher has an obligation to his or her institution and to the user to maintain awareness of the range of information resources available in order to fairly and impartially advise the client.
- The online searcher must strive to maintain a reasonable skill level in the systems available for searching.
- The online searcher must eschew bias in the selection of appropriate databases and systems in order to meet the needs of the client.
- The online searcher must make the client aware of the searcher's level of expertise in searching a given database or system if that may affect the search results.
- The online searcher should be aware of the level of confidentiality required by both the setting and the request, and he or she should respect those boundaries.
- The online searcher must make clear the appropriateness of the online search in meeting the client's needs and the limitations of the search process for the client's intentions.
- The online searcher must guard against tendencies to fill the client's needs as the searcher sees them or as the client initially states them, but rather must utilize appropriate interview techniques to ascertain the client's needs.
- The online searcher must, if appropriate, apprise the client of major errors in previous searches, both in strategy formulation and database selection.
- The online searcher must resist attempts by the client to select inappropriate databases and/or systems.

Notes

1. Eileen M. Trauth, "The Professional Responsibility of the Techknowledgable." *Computers & Society* 13 (Winter 1982): 17–21.

2. Boyd Childress, "Ethics in Database Searching," *Online '83 Conference Proceedings,* (Weston, Conn: Online, Inc., 1983).
3. American Library Association, "Statement of Professional Ethics, 1981," *ALA Handbook on Organization, 1981/2, and Membership Directory* (Chicago, Il: American Library Association, 1981).
4. Anne P. Mintz, "Information Practice and Malpractice . . . Do We Need Malpractice Insurance?" *Online* 8(July 1984): 20–26.
5. Martha Boaz, "Does the Library Profession Really Have a Code of Ethics?" *Special Libraries* 59(May 1968): 353–26.
6. Mintz, "Information Practice and Malpractice . . ."
7. Kay Murray, "Advances in Reference Services," in *Advances in Librarianship* 11 (New York: Academic Press, 1981).
8. Joseph Luft, *Group Processes: An Introduction to Group Dynamics,* 2nd ed (Palo Alto, CA: Mayfield, 1970).

Acknowledgements: We would like to thank Nick Smith, Ph.D., Director, Research on Evaluation, Northwest Regional Educational Laboratory, Portland, Oregon, for suggesting the Johari Window model.

Information Malpractice: Some Thoughts on the Potential Liability of Information Professionals

MARTHA J. DRAGICH

For several years librarians and other information professionals have speculated about malpractice liability. Although many of us find it hard to believe that we will be faced with lawsuits filed by dissatisfied clients, the trend toward greatly increased malpractice litigation involving other professionals[1] gives us pause, especially as the commodity in which we deal—information—has taken on enormous value in our times.[2] To date

Reprinted from *Information Technology and Libraries* 8(3) (September 1989): 265—272.

we have only speculated about, and not actually faced, malpractice suits. This article examines the hypothetical cases of library malpractice posited in the literature. It then suggests other hypothetical situations in which information providers might face ethical dilemmas or charges of negligence. Finally, it discusses a few cases arising in other contexts that shed some light on how courts would react to malpractice suits against information professionals.

The classic hypothetical library malpractice case was put forth by Alan Angoff more than ten years ago. In Angoff's hypothetical, a public library patron sued the library for $250,000 for "injuries to his home and personal injuries to himself and his family as a result of . . . inaccurate information contained in a book recommended to him" by the reference librarian.[3] The patron had wanted to build a deck on his house and went to the library to find a how-to book. Although he followed the instructions in the book, the deck collapsed, injuring him and his two sons and damaging part of the house. The book recommended by the librarian was about ten years old, and the publisher was no longer in business. The patron claimed that the library was "grossly negligent" in circulating an antiquated book.

Law librarians have also speculated about malpractice liability.[4] Even law librarians who very carefully avoid giving legal advice wonder whether they could be charged with malpractice for recommending an outdated or inadequate law book. Typical examples include the patron who needs to find out the length of the statute of limitations that would apply to his legal problem, and the patron who wants to write his own will or do her own divorce.

Angoff's hypothetical was based on the traditional library setting where a brief, often anonymous transaction takes place and where the librarian's involvement in actually solving the client's problem is quite limited. The charge against the librarian rests on faulty information contained in the book itself. In order for the librarian to be found liable in such a case, the librarian's duty to the client would have to include verification of all the information in every book before recommending any book to the patron. Although it is a librarian's duty to build a good collection of sound materials, and to know the collection well, it is clearly impossible to undertake independent verification of the informational content of the collection.

Therefore, we should forego further speculation about malpractice liability in cases such as those posited thus far. No actual case on similar facts has been reported to date, and they are unlikely to arise in the future. We should turn our attention instead to the rather different situations in which we as "information providers" find ourselves and explore the possibilities for malpractice liability there.

Malpractice

One writer on the malpractice liability of librarians defines malpractice as "any professional misconduct or unreasonable lack of skill in the performance of professional duties through intentional carelessness or simple ignorance."[5] The legal requirements for a charge of professional negligence are that there be a duty owed by the professional to the client which was breached, causing actual damage to the client.[6] The scope of a professional's duty to her client does not extend so far as to guarantee a satisfactory result in the provision of every service.[7] Thus, each situation must be examined to see whether the professional had a duty to perform a particular action in a specified manner or to put it another way, to determine whether the professional's actions constituted breach of her duty. The balance of this article focuses on the elements of duty and breach of duty as they might apply to information professionals, particularly in light of the challenges we face in dealing with an ever-expanding universe of print and online resources. We will assume that the element of damage is satisfied.

Professional-Client Relationship

First, we must consider the concept of duty by examining the relationship between the information professional and the client. The duty of a professional to the client arises out of the relationship between the two parties.[8] The client entrusts his/her needs to the professional because the professional has knowledge or expertise the client lacks. This places the client in a vulnerable position and the professional in a corresponding position of power and responsibility. Although our transactions with library patrons were often anonymous, we are moving closer to the consultative model of other professionals.[9] Librarians traditionally provided access to sources of information in which patrons could find for themselves the information they needed. While in the past the librarian may have been the "organizer and dispenser of books and documents," the role of information providers today is more often to advise the client on information needs.[10]

Today, information professionals often provide either raw data or synthesized information to clients.[11] Anne Mintz, who writes on information malpractice, states that while in our earlier role it was improper for a librarian to interpret information for a patron, information professionals now are required to evaluate requests for information, determine the best databases for searching, translate the request into the appropriate search language, evaluate the results during and after the search, and decide whether the results are appropriate.[12] It is clear that a professional-client relationship does exist in the circumstances under which many independent information professionals currently practice.[13] This relationship results from the provision of more extensive services to clients and from the imposition of fees for services.

The "information profession" includes independent information brokers who specialize in conducting online research for clients in certain technical areas, operators of legal research services providing manual and online legal research for attorneys and law firms, and many other nontraditional roles. Clients retain information professionals to conduct research for them—not merely to direct them to sources of information in which they could do research themselves. The information provider is expected to find the information the client needs, not merely to recommend an item from a preexisting collection of materials. The information provider in these instances has taken on a more active role in solving the client's problem. The client likely has sought professional help precisely because the client's own skills do not enable her to undertake the kind of sophisticated research needed.

Other information professionals work as information consultants, whom law firms or businesses might hire to recommend and set up a litigation support system or business records management system to meet certain objectives. Here again, the professional possesses knowledge and expertise the client lacks and is expected to study the client's needs and come up with an appropriate solution for them. In all of these situations, the client pays for the services rendered. While this factor alone is not determinative, it goes a long way toward suggesting that a different relationship exists here than in the traditional library setting.

The client's increased reliance on our knowledge and judgment increases our duty to assume responsibility for the accuracy of the information we provide and for the manner in which it was obtained.[14] Even though we gather and use data originating with an author, database producer, publisher, or agency, we are called upon specifically to employ our knowledge and judgment to retrieve accurate and up-to-date information relevant to the client's information needs. We are not only the finders but also the evaluators and interpreters of the information— roles formerly performed by the client. Thus, it will be much easier for courts to find a duty sufficient to sustain liability in cases filed against us by disgruntled clients.

Having established that the relationship that exists between an information professional and the client is likely to give rise to a duty to act responsibly, we must define the scope of that duty in order to determine what would constitute its breach. One component of a professional's duty to the client is the need to act in an ethical manner. The second component of the professional's duty is the need to exercise reasonable care in the performance of professional services. Many professional codes of ethics include both provisions related to ethical behavior and provisions related to care, knowledge, and skill.[15] Library-based codes have focused almost exclusively on the former.

Ethical Issues

Several library associations have formulated codes of ethics by which to judge professional conduct.[16] Some of the more common provisions of these codes relate to the need to respect the privacy of the client and the need to be impartial in providing information. These codes, however, grew out of and still reflect the traditional library setting—that of the librarian dealing primarily with books and journals. Information practice today draws professionals from a wide variety of backgrounds who work not only in libraries or for corporations but also as solo or group practitioners.[17] They deal with information in diverse formats. Not all share a common educational preparation, and there is no single professional organization to which all belong. As Shaver noted, no license is required for the "practice of information."[18] Thus, the application of library-based codes of ethics to the "new breed" of information professional can be problematic.

For information professionals in the online environment, breaches of confidentiality and the misuse of information gained in the course of professional employment are the most likely ethical dilemmas. While traditional codes of ethics considered confidentiality mainly in the context of protecting circulation records, online searching has added a whole new dimension to the problem. For billing purposes, most search-intermediaries keep detailed records of the searches performed for clients, and the bills themselves often show the client's identification and the files searched, if not the actual content of the search. In addition, the use of online SDI services makes it possible to monitor and record a client's ongoing research. Ethical precepts designed to foster intellectual freedom and to protect the freedom to read do not adequately account for the competing concerns these situations present.

The following hypothetical case illustrates some of the ways nontraditional information providers run into problems with confidentiality issues. An independent information broker recently completed a project for Client A, for which A paid a fee. The broker kept extensive records and files of the search process and results. Today prospective Client B requested that the broker take on a substantially similar project for him. Clients A and B could be competing corporations, law firms representing opposing parties, or simply unrelated persons engaging in similar research. They happen to have consulted the same information broker.

Can the information broker accept the assignment, and if so, can the broker make any use of the information in A's files? The mere resale of information prepared for Client A to Client B would clearly be improper. As professionals, we have a duty to perform for B the services for which the client is paying. We also should recognize that even similar requests may require different search strategies to fulfill the client's particular needs, and by simply giving the previously compiled information to B we have failed to consider his needs fully.

The more difficult question is whether we can make any use of what we did for A—surely there is a profit-motivated desire to do so, and reference back to an earlier successful search may even improve our service to B. But any reference to A's request may raise questions about the breach of client confidentiality or even conflicts of interest. The Congressional Research Service of the Library of Congress has established a policy for this very situation. If two members of Congress make similar research requests, each request must be treated independently.[19] Breaches of confidentiality and conflicts of interest are matters typically governed by professional codes of ethics. We as a profession must ensure that our codes cover these issues, as they occur outside the traditional library setting.

A related problem is the misuse of information gained in the course of rendering professional services to one's client or employer. About two years ago, a former librarian at a New York law firm was charged by the SEC with violating the insider trading laws.[20] The librarian was responsible for files containing confidential information concerning the takeover plans of certain corporate clients of the law firm. According to the SEC, the librarian "routinely performed computer research on target companies and obtained documents and information for . . . attorneys working on proposed business combinations involving clients of the firm."[21] The SEC stated that the librarian's "position and assignments caused him to be entrusted with or enabled him to gain access to highly confidential information."[22] The suit alleges that the librarian leaked this confidential information to family members who used the information to make profits of over $400,000 trading in the stock of the companies concerned. This is a clear example of the increased economic value of information and the temptations that value might pose to information professionals.

These examples illustrate a few of the ethical dilemmas information professionals might face. Although code revisions might provide better guidance, ethical conduct ultimately must rest on the individual determination of the professional. This is especially true in an unlicensed profession whose codes of ethics typically have no enforcement mechanism.

Reasonable Care

That brings us to the second component of a professional's duty, the requirement for exercising reasonable care, skill, and diligence in the rendering of professional services. Problems related to the lack of reasonable skill are more difficult to define than ethical problems, in part because the concept of "reasonable skill" itself is hazy. The standard courts use to judge whether or not the professional breached a duty is what a member of the profession in good standing would have done under the same circumstances.[23] The members of any profession are expected "to possess a standard minimum of special knowledge and ability" not shared by the general public.[24]

Two additional hypotheticals further explicate the application of these concepts of breach of duty to information professionals. In the first, an information consultant was retained to advise a law firm on litigation support systems for a complex class action lawsuit it is handling, perhaps a case like the Agent Orange or Dalkon Shield litigation. The client's two main objectives were that information entered into the system be retrievable and that information about trial strategy and the like not be subject to discovery by the other side. As it happens, the system has not performed well in retrieving documents, and the entire database has been held discoverable.

In terms of retrieval ability, the consultant should have known the relative merits of the available systems, as well as any unique features of the data the client intended to include in the database that might have affected retrieval. The consultant should also have known that systems frequently have not performed to clients' satisfaction[25] and that fulltext-only systems, at least, have been shown by some studies to retrieve as little as 20 percent of the relevant documents in the database.[26]

As regards the discovery issue, the consultant should have been aware of rulings on the discoverability of information contained in various types of litigation support systems.[27] If the consultant recommended a fulltext-only system, for example, the consultant should have advised the client that the work-product exception to the discovery rules likely would not protect information in the database.

It's difficult to tell, of course, from these limited facts, whether the consultant failed to exercise reasonable knowledge and judgment in the selection of a system or merely failed to advise the client adequately about the expected performance of such systems in general. Either way, it is possible that the consultant could be found negligent if expert testimony by other information professionals convinces the court that his/her performance was not "reasonable."

In the second hypothetical, the information professional runs a legal research service for law firms. The researcher assigned to a particular project failed to locate a recently decided case that bears directly on the issue to be researched. Certainly this is a serious failure, but we cannot determine whether it was the result of negligence without knowing what steps the researcher took and where the information could have been found.

Let's consider a few possibilities. The case might have been available either online or in print, and the researcher simply missed it. Although this is the easiest case, it may still be difficult to prove that the researcher failed to exercise reasonable care in the search. Or, the case might have been available online but not yet in print. The researcher had access to the online systems but did not consult them. Was the researcher required to do so? Conversely, the researcher might have used only the online services, not realizing that some concepts are more easily or reliably located through controlled and coordinated indexes than by means of fulltext searching.[28] Or, the recent case might have been available on either Lexis or Westlaw but not both.[29] The researcher has access to both systems, but since they generally contain the same information, the researcher only searched one, in this case the one that didn't include the relevant case. Should the professional have searched both? Or, the case might have been available on both systems, but on one system the case contained a typographical error that prevented retrieval.[30] As it happens, this is the only system the researcher tried. Was the researcher negligent in failing to consult both systems?

The information profession has not articulated standards by which to judge this researcher's performance. We must define acceptable practice for information providers, not only in terms of ethical standards, but also by establishing procedural guidelines to ensure the quality of our services. That won't be easy, especially in the online environment. New databases appear almost daily, contents change, search logic and communications methods are improved. Clearly, we must stay on top of these changes by reading the literature, obtaining continuing education, and the like. But in the midst of such changes, who can say what a reasonable search might have been on a given day?

Court Cases

The traditional library malpractice hypotheticals failed because no professional-client relationship sufficient to give rise to a legal duty existed. But the problem they posed was, ultimately, whether the librarian could be held responsible for the information contained in the sources the professional recommended. Similar problems may face information professionals in many situations where there is a duty. We are all aware, for example, of inaccurate or "dirty" data online.[31] In fact, the problem of assuring the accuracy or validity of information provided to clients may be more acute in the online arena because our knowledge of and ability to access online information so far outstrips that of most clients. Our duty to the client requires that we exercise our professional knowledge and judgment. The question is whether we can be held responsible for retrieving information that is itself inaccurate.

There are no reported cases addressing this issue. Three cases arising in very different circumstances may nevertheless offer some guidance to information professionals. In *EWAP v. Osmond*, a defamation case, a video store was held not liable for disseminating libelous information contained in a video tape by showing that there was no reason for it to believe that the information was libelous.[32]

The court stated that "one who merely plays a secondary role in disseminating information published by another, as in the case of libraries, news vendors, or carriers," could not be held liable for defamation unless it knew or had reason to believe the information was libelous.[33] The court further stated that when the books of a "reputable author or publishing house" are offered for sale or free circulation, the vendor or lender is not required to examine them to determine whether they contain any defamatory information. But if a particular author or publisher "has frequently published notoriously sensational or scandalous books," a shop or library that offers them to the public may run the risk of liability to anyone defamed by them.

Although the law of defamation has many special rules, this holding suggests that information providers might not be found liable for malpractice in cases where the faulty information originated elsewhere. We cannot be held responsible for knowing and verifying the contents of all the sources we use, whether in print or online. We should heed carefully, however, the caution regarding the reputation of the authors or publishers of the information we provide. Information professionals are in a position in most cases to make some judgment about the general quality and reputation of the sources of information, and in our role as consultants on the information needs of our clients we should apprise them of the source and reputed quality of the information we provide.

In *Brocklesby v. Jeppesen*,[34] a $12,000,000 verdict was upheld against Jeppesen, a company that publishes aeronautical charts based entirely on data provided by the Federal Aviation Administration. The FAA data are originally published in tabular form: Jeppesen converts it into graphic form. In *Brocklesby*, a pilot used one of Jeppesen's charts to make a landing and crashed into a mountain, killing the entire crew and destroying the plane. The chart was followed correctly but provided erroneous instructions. It was stipulated that the inaccuracies were contained in the original FAA data, not created by Jeppesen.

Jeppesen is an information provider. It gathers data, repackages it, and sells it. If it merely passed on erroneous data provided by the government, how could it now be required to pay $12,000,000 to the survivors of the crew members? The court treated Jeppesen's chart as a product, thus allowing the case to be considered under the strict liability provisions of products liability law. This determination turned mainly on the fact that Jeppesen's charts are massproduced, not developed at the request of an individual client.[35] The court emphasized that Jeppesen had a duty to test its product and to warn users of its dangers.[36]

The *Osmond* and *Brocklesby* rulings pose an apparent conflict on our duty to test or verify the information contained in sources we use. The distinction turns. I think, on our role vis-à-vis the originator of the data. The video store in *Osmond* was merely a disseminator of information produced by someone else. Jeppesen, on the other hand, used information published by the FAA to produce a conceptually different package of information. Most of our practice falls somewhere between these two extremes. Taken together, these cases suggest that our potential for liability increases significantly as we become more active in providing raw data and especially in synthesizing the data into information useable by the client, rather than merely leading the client to sources of information.

In both *Osmond* and *Brocklesby*, the information was produced for the mass market. A third case, however, comes closer to approximating the situation of information professionals who provide information to specific clients. In *Dun & Bradstreet, Inc. v. Greenmoss Builders*,[37] the credit reporting agency erroneously reported to subscribers that Greenmoss had filed for bankruptcy. Dun & Bradstreet's employee had mistakenly attributed to Greenmoss a bankruptcy petition filed by one of its former employees. The jury awarded $50,000 in compensatory damages and $300,000 in punitive damages. Dun & Bradstreet moved for a new trial on the ground that punitive damages cannot be awarded absent proof of actual malice. The request for the new trial was granted but later reversed by the Vermont Supreme Court.

The United States Supreme Court agreed that a new trial was not required. The Court held that "permitting recovery of . . . punitive damages in defamation cases absent a showing of 'actual malice' does not violate the First Amendment when the defamatory statements do not involve matters of public concern."[38] The Court's focus on the law of defamation, along with the convoluted procedural history of the case, obscures the critical importance of this case to information professionals. Of the cases discussed in this paper, the facts of this case are most closely analogous to the practice of information professionals. Dun & Bradstreet's business is to research various records to find information on the financial status of companies. It is also a database producer that could face liability for erroneous information contained in its database and used by others. It should be of great interest and concern to us that a jury saw fit to award $300,000 in *punitive* damages for the provision of erroneous information, and the Supreme Court held that knowledge of or reckless disregard for the falsity of the information need not be proved to sustain the award.

Conclusion

The most fascinating and vexing aspect of the online environment is that the information universe with which we deal is invisible to us. This would make the independent verification of data exceedingly difficult. We cannot examine the source as a whole; we can only retrieve bits of it. The invisibility of the source also impedes judgments about the quality of our service. While it is relatively easy for doctors or lawyers to determine the state of medical or legal knowledge at a particular point in time so as to judge the performance of a peer in a particular case, information providers often cannot know what was in a database at a given time. The information in many databases is not "date-stamped," and even more importantly, changes in the data can be made without a trace.

Still, we as a profession can and should work towards a collective judgement about our standards of practice. Some of the questions we might consider are: What kinds of education and training do our present and future circumstances demand? What are the qualitative differences between print and online versions of the "same" source, and when should we use one format over the other? What role does cost play in that determination? How far should we go in analyzing, synthesizing, and repackaging, rather than merely gathering, information for clients?

To sum up, our concerns about malpractice may be speculative, but we do not engage in idle speculation. The incredible economic value of the information industry, the increase in malpractice suits against other professionals, and the suits against disseminators and producers of information in other contexts are ample evidence of the potential for liability on our part.

Notes

1. See "The Professionals' Liability Reform Act of 1988," remarks of Rep. Don Ritter, 134 *Congressional Record* E919 (3/31/88), 100th Congress 2d session, E.919.
2. As an example of the worth of the information industry, *Business Week* reported that Mead Data Central, the provider of Lexis and Nexis online services, had revenues of $154 million and before-tax profits of $20 million in 1986. "The Information Business," *Business Week*, (Aug. 25, 1986), 82. Dialog was sold in the summer of 1988 for $353 million. "The Media Business: Knight-Ridder to Buy Lockheed's Dialog Unit," *New York Times* (July 12, 1988).
3. Alan Angoff, "Library Malpractice Suit: Could it Happen to You?" *American Libraries* 7(Sept. 1976):489.
4. See, for example, Gerome Leone, "Malpractice Liability of a Law Librarian?" *Law Library Journal* 73(1980):44–65; and Robin Mills, "Reference Service vs. Legal Advice: Is It Possible to Draw the Line?" *Law Library Journal* 72(1979):179–93.
5. William Nasri, "Malpractice Liability: Myth or Reality?" *Journal of Library Administration* 1(1981):3.
6. *See Prosser and Keeton on the Law of Torts*, ed. W. Page Keeton (St. Paul, Minn.: West, 1984), 164–65.
7. Ibid., 186 (discussing physicians).
8. Ibid., 356.
9. See Durrance, "The Generic Librarian: Anonymity versus Accountability," *RQ* 22:278.
10. See, for example, Lancaster and Smith, "On-line Systems in the Communications Process: Projections," *Journal of the American Society for Information Science* 31(May 1980):194,199.
11. Kathleen Nichol, "Database Proliferation: Implications for Librarians," *Special Libraries* 74(April 1983):116.
12. Anne Mintz, "Information Practice and Malpractice," *Library Journal* 38(Sept. 15, 1985).
13. Ibid., 41.
14. Ibid., 38.
15. See, for example, the American Bar Association's Model Rules of Professional Conduct, adopted in 1983.
16. See, among others, the American Library Association Statement of Professional Ethics 1981, *American Libraries* 12(June 1981):335; and the American Association of Law Libraries Code of Ethics, *AALL Newsletter* 10(Jan. 1979):43.
17. See Donna Shaver, Nancy Hewison, and Leslie Wykoff, "Ethics for Online Intermediaries," *Special Libraries* 76(1985): 238,239; Lancaster and Smith, "Online Systems," 199.
18. Shaver, "Ethics Revisited: Are We Making Progress?" in *The Information Profession: Facing Future Challenges* (Washington, D.C.: Special Libraries Association, 1988) 103,106.
19. Telephone conversation with Roberta Shaffer, former special assistant to the Law Librarian of Congress, Oct. 4, 1988.
20. "Librarian Accused of Insider Trading," *Washington Post* (Dec. 25, 1986).
21. *BNA Daily Report for Executives* (January 6, 1987):A-6.
22. Ibid.
23. Prosser and Keeton, 175.
24. Ibid., 185.

25. See, for example, Rudolph Peritz, "Computer Data and Reliability: A Call for Authentication of Business Records under the Federal Rules of Evidence," *Northwestern Univ. Law Review* 80(1986):856,993–99 for an account of the problems several firms have encountered with computer systems.

26. David Blair and M. E. Marron, "An Evaluation of Retrieval Effectiveness for a Full-Text Document Retrieval System," *Communications of the A.C.M.* 28 (March 1985): 289,293.

27. See Edward Sherman and Stephen Kinnard, "The Development, Discovery, and Use of Computer Support Systems in Achieving Efficiency in Litigation," *Columbia Law Review* 79(1979):267 for a discussion of this issue.

28. See Mary Jensen, "Full Text Databases: When to Use Them and When Not to Use Them," *Law Office Economics & Management* 27(1986):77,81.

29. See Kelly Warnken, "A Study in Lexis and Westlaw Errors," *Legal Economics* 13(July/ Aug. 1987):39.

30. Ibid., 58.

31. See C. A. Cuadra, "Database Producers, Online Services, and Custom Information Services—Who Will Survive?" in *Information Policy for the 1980's: Proceedings of the Eusidic Conference, 5 October 1978* (Learned Information, 1979) 23,28.

32. Osmond v. EWAP, Inc., 153 Cal. App.3d 842, 200 Cal. Rptr. 674 (1984).

33. Ibid., 680.

34. Brocklesby v. Jeppesen, 767 F.2d 1288 (9th Cir. 1985), *cert. den.*, 474 U.S. 1101 (1986).

35. Ibid., 1295.

36. Ibid., 1297.

37. Dun & Bradstreet, Inc. v. Greenmoss Builders, 472 U.S. 749 (1984).

38. Ibid., 763.

Additional Readings for Chapter 8

BARNES, ROBERT F. "Some Thoughts on Professional Ethics Codes." *Bulletin of ASIS* 12(4) (April/May 1986): 19–20.

BARNES, ROBERT F. "The Making of an Ethics Code." *Bulletin of ASIS* 16(6) (August/September 1990): 24–25.

BENGE, RONALD C. "The Professional Idea." In *Libraries and Cultural Change.* London: Bingley, 1970.

BLAKE, FAY M. "Let My People Know: Access to Information in a Post-Industrial Society." *Wilson Library Bulletin* 52(5) (January 1978): 392–399.

CAPURRO, RAPHAEL. "Moral Issues in Information Science." *Journal of Information Science* 11(3) (1985): 113–123.

DURRANCE, JOAN C. "The Generic Librarian: Anonymity Versus Accountability." *RQ* 22(3) (Spring 1983): 278–283.

EVERETT, JOHN H. "Independent Information Professionals and the Question of Malpractice Liability." *Online* 13(3) (May 1989): 65–70.

FINKS, LEE W. "Values Without Shame." *American Libraries* 20(4) (April 1989): 352–356.

HARMON, GLYN. "Information Professionalism Within the Emerging Socio-

Economic Order." In *Proceedings of the ASIS Annual Meeting.* Minneapolis, MN (1979): 98–103.

LEE, JANIS M. "Confidentiality: From the Stacks to the Witness Stand." *American Libraries* 19(6) (June 1988): 444–453.

LANIER, DON and BOICE, DAN. "The Statement on Professional Ethics: Implications and Applications." *Serials Librarian* 8(2) (Winter 1983): 85–93.

MIKA, JOSEPH J. and SHUMAN, BRUCE A. "Legal Issues Affecting Libraries and Librarians, Lesson IV: Intellectual Freedom; Privacy and Confidentiality; Problem Patrons; Ethics." *American Libraries* 19(4) (April 1988): 314–317.

MINTZ, ANNE P. "Information Practice and Malpractice. . .Do We Need Malpractice Insurance?" *Online* 8(4) (July 1984): 20–26.

NASRI, WILLIAM Z. "Legal Responsibilities and Issues for Library Management." *Journal of Library Administration* 1(4) (Winter 1980): 3–7.

PRITCHARD, TERESA and QUIGLEY, MICHELLE. "The Information Specialist: A Malpractice Risk Analysis." *Online* 13(3) (May 1989): 57–62.

SNYDER, FRITZ. "Librarians and the Supreme Court: A Computer-Aided Look at High Court Cases Involving Librarians." *American Libraries* 17(3) (March 1986): 205–206.

Index